María Izquierdo & Frida Kahlo

María Izquierdo & Frida Kahlo

CHALLENGING VISIONS IN MODERN MEXICAN ART

Nancy Deffebach

UNIVERSITY OF TEXAS PRESS | AUSTIN

To my friends

Kim Grant, Daniel Nelson, Susan Webster,

Florencia Bazzano, and Ana Garduño

This book is a part of the Latin American and Caribbean Arts and Culture publication initiative, funded by a grant from the Andrew W. Mellon Foundation.

LATIN AMERICAN AND CARIBBEAN ARTS AND CULTURE

Printed in the United States of America
First paperback reprint, 2024

Requests for permission to reproduce material from this work should be sent to:
Permissions
University of Texas Press
P.O. Box 7819
Austin, TX 78713-7819
utpress.utexas.edu

The paper used in this book meets the minimum requirements of ANSI/NISO Z39.48-1992 (R1997) (Permanence of Paper).

Library of Congress Cataloging-in-Publication Data

Deffebach, Nancy, author.
María Izquierdo and Frida Kahlo : challenging visions in modern Mexican art / Nancy Deffebach. — First edition.
pages cm — (Latin American and Caribbean Arts and Culture publication initiative (Andrew W. Mellon Foundation))

Includes bibliographical references and index.
ISBN 978-0-292-77242-7 (cloth : alk. paper) — ISBN 978-1-4773-1281-0 (pbk.: alk. paper) — ISBN 978-1-4773-0049-7 (library e-book) — ISBN 978-1-4773-0050-3 (non-library e-book)
1. Izquierdo, María, 1902–1955—Criticism and interpretation. 2. Kahlo, Frida—Criticism and interpretation. 3. Women artists—Mexico. 4. Feminism and art. I. Title.
ND259.I97D46 2015
759.972—dc23 2014046327
doi:10.7560/772427

CONTENTS

ACKNOWLEDGMENTS

Many people helped me create this book. I especially wish to thank María Izquierdo's younger daughter, Aurora Posadas Izquierdo, and granddaughter, María Rosenda López Posadas. I first interviewed Aurora Posadas Izquierdo in 1995 and continued to interview and consult her for many years. I also want to thank Amparo Posadas de Carmona, Izquierdo's older daughter, whom I interviewed once in 2003 and who accompanied me on a daytrip to her mother's hometown, San Juan de los Lagos, the following day. These and other interviews have contributed enormously to my understanding of the art of María Izquierdo, Frida Kahlo, and modern Mexico. Some of my interviews preceded my graduate studies, some were conducted while I was researching my dissertation, and others were conducted specifically for this book. For interviews cited in this text, I thank Leonora Carrington, Jaime Cuadriello, Arturo Estrada, Fernando Gamboa, Arturo García Bustos, Alejandro Gómez Arias, Isolda Kahlo, Guillermo Monroy, Juan O'Gorman, Dolores Olmedo, Guadalupe Rivera Marín, Fernando Serrano Migallón, Rafael Vázquez, Héctor Xavier, Mariana Yampolsky, Alfredo Zalce, and Adelina Zendejas. In addition to the interviews that I cite here, I conducted many others that have also informed my understanding of Mexican art.

I am profoundly indebted to my friends Kim Grant, Daniel Nelson, and Susan Webster for reading drafts of chapters of the manuscript, giving me advice about writing, and making countless suggestions about how to express my ideas effectively. I am equally grateful to Ana Garduño for reading and commenting on the contents of the introduction and an early version of chapter 6. She also helped me in countless ways with research in Mexico. I thank Florencia Bazzano for many conversations about Latin American art. I dedicate the book to these friends.

Rosamaría Graziani translated to Spanish earlier versions of two chapters that were published in Latin America. She also helped with extensive correspondence in Spanish and other forms of research over many years. Unless otherwise noted, translations from Spanish to English in this book are mine, but corrected and revised by Rosamaría Graziani and other native speakers.

I have received help in various forms—letters, emails, permissions, information, insight, and other assistance—from the following people: Guadalupe Alonso Alanis, Tere Arcq, Marisol Argüelles, Virginia Armella de Aspe, Jacqueline Barnitz, Florencia Bazzano, Jo-Anne Berelowitz, Janice Bergman-Carton, Sheelagh Bevan, Andrés Blaisten, Laurel Bliss, Lucienne Bloch, Walther Boelsterly, Diana Briuolo, George Butler, Mario Campoamor, Deborah Caplow, Craig Carlson, Michael Coelho, Karen Cordero, Leigh Cotnoir, Charles Cramer, Jaime Cuadriello, Rafael Doniz, Eduardo Douglas, María Estela Duarte Sánchez, James Farmer, Barbara Fredrich, Amy Galpin, Ana Garduño, Marta Garsd, Jennifer Giancarlo, Catherine Gleason,

Danielle Goebel, Pablo Goebel, Pablo Gómez Ascencio, María de Jesus González, Martín González Figueroa, Kim Grant, Rosamaría Graziani, James W. Grebl, Cheryl Hartup, Linda Henderson, Gloria Hernández, Doris Heyden, Gerardo Hierro Molina, Javier Hinojosa, Daniela Kelly, Francisco Kochen, Peter Krieger, Ray Legans, Amna Malik, Carlos Martell, Mary-Anne Martin, Miguel Ángel Martínez Alfaro, Cuauhtémoc Medina, Pablo Méndez, Eliseo Mijangos, Paulina Millán Vargas, Debra Nagao, Hernán Navarrete, Daniel Nelson, Gabriela Núñez, James Oles, Blair Paltridge, Catha Paquette, Ramona Pérez, Santiago Pérez, Mariana Pérez Amor, Juan Antonio Pérez Simón, Cecilia Puerto, Alice Rahon, Fausto Ramírez, Lázaro Ramírez Victoria, Julio Revolledo Cárdenas, Alejandra Reygadas de Yturbe, Anitza Rodríguez, David Rohr, Judy Rohr, Claudia Salas Rodríguez, Osvaldo Sánchez, Linda Schele, Michael Schreffler, Pio Schurti, Vanina Scocchera, Erica Segres, Daniel J. Sherman, Jaime Soler, Juan Soriano, Elisa Téllez, Graciela Téllez Trevilla, Beatriz de la Torre, Hilda Trujillo, Beatriz Urías Horcasitas, Susan Vondrak, Jannelle Weakly, Barbara D. Webster, Grady L. Webster, Susan Verdi Webster, Marsha Weidner, and Allyson Williams.

At the University of Texas Press, I am enormously grateful to my editors, Theresa May, Kerry Webb, and Kathy Burford Lewis. Theresa May enthusiastically supported and encouraged this project from the initial proposal through the delivery of the final manuscript. Kerry Webb guided the project to completion, and Kathy Burford Lewis contributed careful copyediting; Maia Wright designed the book. The book also benefited from the help and expertise of John McLeod, Kaila Wyllys, Nancy Lavender Bryan, and Angelica Lopez. The two external reviewers provided astute suggestions for revising the text. Through the University of Texas Press, the book received a Latin American and Caribbean Arts and Culture grant from the Andrew W. Mellon Foundation.

I am grateful as well to Dr. Xavier Guzmán Urbiola, head of the Subdirección General del Patrimonio Artístico Inmueble, for allowing me to reproduce works by Frida Kahlo, María Izquierdo, Diego Rivera, José Clemente Orozco, and David Alfaro Siqueiros.

My research benefited from a Mellon Postdoctoral Fellowship at Rice University, a research grant from San Diego State University, a semester of sabbatical from San Diego State University in fall 2012, and travel funds from the San Diego State University Art Council.

For their affection, support, humor, and good company, I express my love and appreciation to my sister, brother-in-law, niece, nephew, and extended family on the central coast of California: Judy and David Rohr; Kacey, Brian, and Jase Burns; Danny, Tricia, Paxton, and Riley Rohr; Ray Legans and Rick Tulloss; and Fred Hindler.

I photographed the following images: figures 4, 5, 11, 15, 19, 20, 21, 24, 26, 27, 36, 37, 39, 61, 73, 80, 83, and 84 and plates 10, 12, 13, and 16.

María Izquierdo & Frida Kahlo

Introduction

You do not paint with your hands: the painting should be born in your soul, pass through your brain, and then your emotions must spill it onto a canvas, panel, or wall.

MARÍA IZQUIERDO, "MI PINTURA," 1950

The most important part of the body is the brain.

FRIDA KAHLO, IN AN INTERVIEW WITH OLGA CAMPOS, 1950

During the height of the Mexican muralist movement, María Izquierdo (1902–1955) and Frida Kahlo (1907–1954) established successful careers as easel painters and created bodies of work that have become integral to Mexican modernism (figs. 1 and 2). Izquierdo and Kahlo both began their artistic careers around 1929, nine years after the Mexican Revolution (1910 to ca. 1920) ended and seven years after the mural movement began.[1] The two women artists made small and medium-sized easel paintings. Most of their works represent women, and some address personal themes, even though the muralists advocated a radically different type of art.

Izquierdo and Kahlo emerged as artists when Mexican muralism was a dynamic young movement but already sufficiently established to dominate the Mexican art world and earn international acclaim. Both were profoundly affected by this context, but the two artists, who were affiliated with different groups within the Mexican art world, responded to this context differently. Neither was in total agreement with all the ideas of the muralists. How, where, and why they departed from the dominant discourse is central to this book. It examines the ways in which they participated in the national and artistic discourses of post-revolutionary Mexico by demonstrating how their work reveals intellectual engagement with the issues and ideas of their time, especially those regarding national identity and the role of women in society.

Artistic theory played a fundamental role in the rise of Mexican muralism and the so-called *escuela mexicana* (Mexican School), a term that I use to refer to the muralists and artists working in other media who shared their ideas about art. The goals of these artists were first expressed in the "Manifiesto del Sindicato de Obreros Técnicos, Pintores y Escultores" (Manifesto of the Technical Workers, Painters, and Sculptors Union). The manifesto was probably written by David

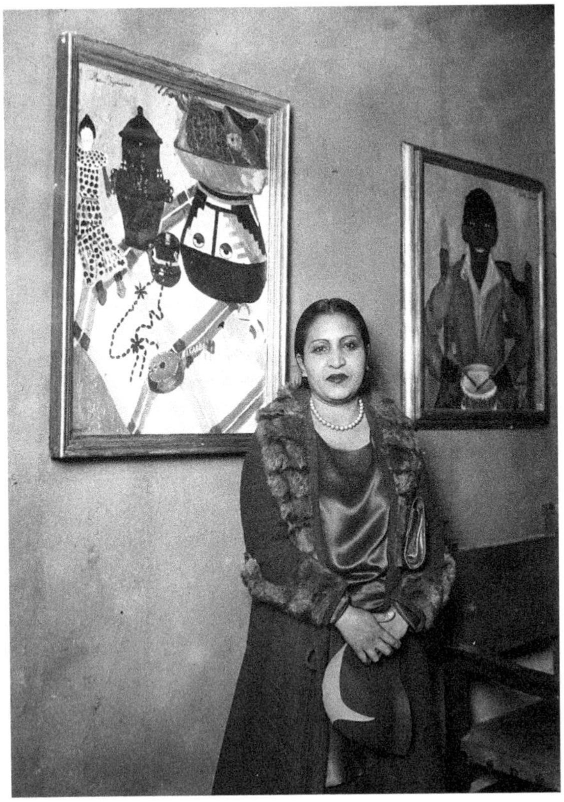

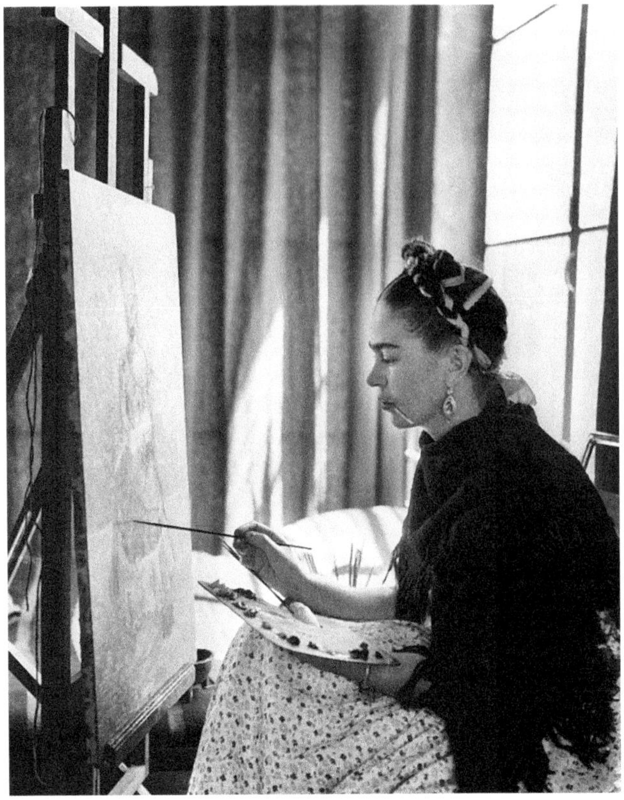

Fig. 1. Photograph of María Izquierdo at an exhibition of her paintings, ca. 1934. Photograph from the Casasola Archive of the Fototeca Nacional, Mexico. © 187798 CONACULTA.INAH. SINAFO.FN.MEXICO.

Fig. 2. Manuel Álvarez Bravo, photograph of Frida Kahlo painting, 1937. © Colette Urbajtel/ Archivo Manuel Álvarez Bravo, S.C.

Alfaro Siqueiros and was signed by Siqueiros, Diego Rivera, José Clemente Orozco, and five other artists in December 1923 and published in *El Machete* in June 1924. It valorized indigenous traditions, exalted monumental art, rejected easel painting, and advocated using art to overthrow bourgeois individualism. The manifesto argued that artists needed to maintain an ideological focus while society is in a transitional phase between the destruction of the old order and the establishment of a new order.[2]

Two decades later Siqueiros prescribed the goals of modern art at length in his book *No hay más ruta que la nuestra* (There Is No Other Route But Ours) of 1945, in which he advocated that art should be monumental, heroic, public, ideological, social, realistic, belligerent, and polemical. He dismissed easel painting as a decorative form suitable only for the homes of the elite oligarchy and repeatedly denigrated it with labels such as chic, snob, domestic, epicurean, decadent, metaphysical, poetic, and colonial.[3] While Siqueiros did not overtly address gender issues, his language reveals the extent to which gender structured his thinking about the goals of modern art. Throughout much of the twentieth century men were associated with culture and women with nature. These assumptions were not limited to Mexico but pervaded Western culture. In 1974 Sherry Ortner examined and refuted these views in her seminal article "Is Female to Male as Nature Is to Culture?"[4] But the association between men and culture and women and nature was widespread, widely accepted, and largely unexamined at the time when Siqueiros wrote *No hay más ruta que la nuestra*. When he used words like "heroic," "monumental," and "public," he implied that good art was masculine. Bad art, in contrast, was "chic" and "domestic," words that associated it with the feminine realm. Needless to say, the gendering of good art as male presented a major problem for women artists.

Cultural critic Jean Franco has noted that in the period following the Mexican Revolution national identity was essentially masculine identity. "The Revolution with its promise of social transformation encouraged a Messianic spirit that transformed mere human beings into supermen and constituted a discourse that associated virility with social transformation in a way that marginalized women at the very moment when they were, supposedly, liberated."[5] In the visual arts the construction of national identity as male was vigorously and effectively propagated by the muralists.

In an environment in which artistic and political discourse associated the nation with masculinity, Izquierdo and Kahlo negotiated female identity in their work in ways that involved significant dissent from prevailing views. Izquierdo and Kahlo supported the parts of artistic discourse that they agreed with; these were different for each artist, but they included an appreciation of Mexican popular culture and the valorization of indigenous traditions. They resisted other aspects of nationalist rhetoric, especially the glorification of male heroes. Both artists usually avoided politics in art, except in the sense that "the personal is political," though Kahlo created a few political images at the end of her life.[6] Because they explored gender issues and in varying degrees addressed personal themes in their paintings, their art has political aspects even when the politics are not overt. As Laura Mulvey and Peter Wollen write, "The phrase 'the personal is political' rejects the traditional exclusion and repression of the personal in male-dominated politics. It also asserts the political nature of women's private individualized oppression."[7] This book examines how Izquierdo and Kahlo negotiated female identity in a seemingly inhospitable context and succeeded in creating bodies of work that were accepted and appreciated during their lives—despite their considerable deviation from orthodoxy—and that still speak to wide and diverse audiences. Kahlo and Izquierdo were the two women who in different ways most directly challenged prevailing ideas about gender and what constituted important art. Paradoxically, they were also the two most successful Mexican women artists of their era.

Women Artists in Mexico

One of the peculiar characteristics of the Mexican postrevolutionary period (1920–1940) is that women artists emerged earlier than women writers as prominent figures who combined creativity with the struggle for women's rights. During Izquierdo's and Kahlo's lives, no Mexican women writers had a stature equal to theirs or prioritized gender to the same degree.

Izquierdo and Kahlo were not the only women artists active in Mexico from the late 1920s to the mid-1950s. Others included the photographers Tina Modotti and Lola Álvarez Bravo and the painters Rosario Cabrera, Cecilia Calderón, Olga Costa, Dolores Cueto, Nahui Olín, Aurora Reyes, Rosa Rolando, and Isabel Villaseñor. Between 1939 and 1943 the European surrealists Leonora Carrington, Kati Horna, Alice Rahon, and Remedios Varo fled war-torn Europe and settled in Mexico, where, without exception, they created their most important visual work. Carrington and Varo became major figures in the Mexican art world after the mid-fifties. Mariana Yampolsky came to Mexico to join the Taller de Gráfica Popular (TGP: People's Graphics Workshop) as a printmaker in 1945 and later became a photographer.

In Mexico women artists confronted substantial difficulties in addition to those faced by male artists. But it is important to note that, despite Mexico's reputation for machismo, women artists did not suffer from more discrimination in Mexico than in the United States. Writing in 1975, art historian Jacqueline Barnitz observed that in the preceding six decades "more Latin American than North American women have become well-known artists."[8] In fact, in the first half of the twentieth century, only Russia and Brazil seem to have provided more conducive environments for the development of women artists than Mexico.

Some of the problems that women artists faced in Mexico were specific to the country or took on a distinct character there. Foremost among these were the ways in which women were represented,[9] the degree to which national identity was constructed as masculine, and the strong resistance to women participating fully in the muralist movement during the years in which mural painting was considered the pinnacle of artistic achievement in Mexico.

The Relative Status of Izquierdo and Kahlo

In recent decades Frida Kahlo has become an internationally known artist whose fame—for better or for worse—extends into popular culture. Like Che Guevara's, her face is recognized by multitudes, many of whom have little or no knowledge of her work and ideas. At present María Izquierdo's reputation is limited to people knowledgeable about Mexican art. Nevertheless, during their lives the two artists had comparable reputations in Mexico. While many people may react to the preceding claim with skepticism or incredulity, overwhelming evidence exists to support it. Kahlo, as the wife of the *muy discutido* (much discussed) muralist Diego Rivera, always had a highly visible presence in the media and was much admired by the French surrealists. In innumerable instances, however, Izquierdo and Kahlo were included together in major exhibitions (with or without the inclusion of other women artists). They were invariably the only women artists chosen for the most important professional activities and honors.

In 1930 María Izquierdo and Isabel Villaseñor were the only women represented in the enormous *Mexican Arts* exhibition organized by René d'Harnoncourt for the Metropolitan Museum of Art in New York.[10] After this exhibition, until the late 1950s, important group exhibitions of Mexican art that included the big names—Diego Rivera, José Clemente Orozco, David Alfaro Siqueiros, and Rufino Tamayo—invariably also included Izquierdo and Kahlo. This was equally true for major exhibitions held in Mexico and in other countries. When other women artists were included, the selections varied. For example, *Twenty Centuries of Mexican Art* showed work by Izquierdo and Kahlo at the Museum of Modern Art in New York in 1940. The catalogue contains reproductions of Kahlo's *Las dos Fridas* (The Two Fridas) of 1939 and Izquierdo's *Mis sobrinas* (My Nieces) of 1940 and does not list pieces by other women. However, the exhibition was dramatically larger than the catalogue indicates, and Lola Álvarez Bravo, Rosa Rolando, and Isabel Villaseñor probably participated.[11] The 1943 exhibition *Mexican Art Today* at the Philadelphia Museum of Art included María Izquierdo, Frida Kahlo, Olga Costa, Isabel Villaseñor, Lola Álvarez Bravo, and Doris Heyden. In 1952 the exhibition *Art mexicain du Précolombien à nos jours* at the Musée National d'Art Moderne in Paris showed work by María Izquierdo, Frida Kahlo, Olga Costa, Dolores Cueto, and Andrea Gómez.

In 1942 the president of Mexico, Manuel Ávila Camacho, sent a request to Inés Amor, the director of the prestigious Galería de Arte Mexicano, asking to meet with a small group of painters at her gallery. The painters he wished to meet were Diego Rivera, José Clemente Orozco, Antonio Ruiz, Roberto Montenegro, Miguel Covarrubias, Juan O'Gorman, María Izquierdo, and Frida Kahlo. (Rufino Tamayo was in New York, while David Alfaro Siqueiros was in Chile.) Inés Amor hung one work by each artist in the gallery and set up mural-sized panels by Rivera in the patio. The tour of the exhibition began with some rather naïve questions from the president, who wanted to know if Orozco was a cubist. After viewing the work, the group gathered for drinks and hors d'oeuvres in another room. The president asked each artist for suggestions about how to promote Mexican art. Rivera, Orozco, and O'Gorman asked for mural commissions.[12] At the end of the meeting the president asked if he should know about any other group of artists. Kahlo replied: "Yes, Mr. President, there is another group headed by Carlos Ruano Llopis, but they are not worthwhile and you need not bother seeing them." After the president left, Kahlo turned to Amor and quipped: "What if the good ones turn out to be Ruano Llopis's group?"[13] No record survives of what Izquierdo said, but she must have made a positive impression. In 1942, at Ávila Camacho's suggestion, the Mexican government purchased *Mis sobrinas* for the collection of the Museo Nacional de México (National Museum of Mexico). The meeting between the president and these painters was a pivotal event. As art historian Ana Garduño observes, this was the first time that a Mexican president asked to meet with artists.[14] Years after the meeting, Inés Amor recalled that after this event "all the governments and all the presidents of Mexico have been interested in current art." For Amor, the interest of Mexican presidents in the country's contemporary art testifies to the importance that Mexican art has nationally and internationally "as an instrument of cultural prestige and presidential pride."[15]

In 1942 the painter Antonio Ruiz was appointed director of the Escuela de Pintura y Escultura (School of Painting and Sculpture), the art school popularly known as La Esmeralda because it was located in an alley of that name.[16] Ruiz's goal was to renovate art education, so he hired a prestigious faculty eager to employ innovative approaches to fostering creativity, including María Izquierdo, Frida Kahlo, Raúl Anguiano, José Chávez Morado, Jesús Guerrero Galván, Agustín Lazo, Carlos Orozco Romero, Diego Rivera, Manuel Rodríguez Lozano, Francisco Zúñiga, and others. Izquierdo taught watercolor, and Kahlo taught oil painting. For reasons related to her health, Kahlo soon moved the class meetings to her home.

Izquierdo and Kahlo each received major honors and awards. In 1946 Kahlo won a 5,000-peso prize for *Moisés* (Moses) of 1945 at the annual national exhibition at the Palacio de Bellas Artes (Palace of Fine Arts).[17] In 1944 Izquierdo was appointed ambassador of Mexican art by the minister of education, Jaime Torres Bodet; she was sent to Peru and Chile, where she held six solo exhibitions of her paintings.

Izquierdo and Kahlo appeared together in major group exhibitions countless times and participated equally in professional activities. Izquierdo's career can also be considered more professional than Kahlo's in other ways. Kahlo only had two solo exhibitions during her lifetime: the first at the Julien Levy Gallery in New York in 1938 and the second at Lola Álvarez Bravo's Galería Arte Contemporáneo (Contemporary Art Gallery) in Mexico City in 1953. In contrast, Izquierdo had at least twenty solo exhibitions during her life. Her second solo show was held at the Art Center in New York City in 1930, where she was touted as the first Mexican woman to exhibit her work in the United States.[18] In 1937 the French playwright and poet Antonin Artaud organized an exhibition of Izquierdo's work at the Galerie Van den Berg in Paris.[19] And in 1943 the Palacio de Bellas Artes in Mexico City hosted a major exhibition of Izquierdo's recent works, including sixty paintings created between 1939 and 1943.

Izquierdo's body of work is larger than Kahlo's, though the exact size of their oeuvres has not yet been established. The 1988 catalogue raisonné of Kahlo's work lists 176 paintings, 82 drawings (including 13 diary pages and several drawings made in the margins of letters), and 2 prints.[20] Since then, intense research about Kahlo has recovered additional works. But estimates of the size of Kahlo's oeuvre have become muddied with the introduction of a large body of forged objects that emerged during the first decade of the twenty-first century (discussed in greater detail below). There is no catalogue raisonné of Izquierdo's work. The catalogue to her 1988 retrospective at the Centro Cutural, Arte Contemporanéo provides visual documentation of 317 paintings, 12 drawings, and 2 prints.[21] After the retrospective, some additional works emerged. In the mid-1990s Luis-Martín Lozano estimated Izquierdo's oeuvre at around five hundred works,[22] which I consider a reasonable approximation. Izquierdo's last husband was the Chilean painter Raúl Uribe, whom she met in 1938 and married in 1944. Uribe was a mediocre painter but well connected with South American diplomats and used his connections with South American embassies to facilitate the sale of her paintings. Toward the end of her life, Izquierdo wrote that 80 percent of her art was in other countries.[23] The majority of Izquierdo's known works remain in Mexico, so a significant number of her paintings may have left Mexico without being documented.

In 1940, when Kahlo and Rivera remarried, one of her conditions was that she provide for herself financially. Although this was an admirable goal, their lifestyle and paying her high medical expenses depended on the relatively high prices that his work commanded. Izquierdo, in contrast, earned a living as a painter and teacher throughout most of her career.[24]

Philosophical Divisions in the Art World in Mexico

Izquierdo and Kahlo met by the late 1920s and both taught at the Escuela de Pintura y Escultura in the 1940s. The two artists were acquaintances rather than friends and usually maintained a certain distance, although at least once they took their students on a joint field trip to Teotihuacan.[25] In the early forties, when Rivera and Izquierdo became openly hostile to each other in the press, Kahlo and Izquierdo became even more distant. On at least three occasions Izquierdo made brief comments about Kahlo that were published in Mexico City newspapers: twice praising her work, and once vehemently criticizing her influence on students.[26]

Izquierdo and Kahlo held significantly different beliefs about art and were affiliated with different groups of artists that advocated opposing points of view about the role of art. For each artist the affiliation had an important personal element in addition to its philosophical and theoretical components. During Izquierdo's formative years as an artist, she was in a committed romantic relationship with the painter Rufino Tamayo. Izquierdo and Tamayo were among the visual artists allied with the Contemporáneos, an avant-garde literary group that believed in art for art's sake and took an international approach to art. Kahlo's marriage to Rivera in 1929 linked her socially to the muralists and other artists who thought that art should advance leftist political and social agendas and celebrate Mexican identity.

Kahlo, the Muralists, and the So-Called *Escuela Mexicana*

Frida Kahlo's art shares some iconographic and thematic elements with the work of her husband, Diego Rivera, and sharply diverges from it in other ways. The same is true about Kahlo's painting in relation to the *escuela mexicana* in general. The term *escuela mexicana* (Mexican School) is usually used to designate the muralists and artists working in other media who shared the muralists' conviction that art should advance leftist political and social agendas and celebrate Mexican identity. This is how I use the term throughout the book, although the term has two drawbacks. First, no absolute consensus exists as to what the Mexican School includes and excludes. Some people use it to designate virtually all art created in modern Mexico. The U.S. art historian MacKinley Helm, for example, who promoted Mexican art in the United States in the 1940s and 1950s, used it for all modern Mexican art.[27] The second problem is that the term has become dated. Since the 1980s Mexican art historians have increasingly rejected narrow definitions of Mexican art and critiqued nationalist rhetoric. To younger and/or more theoretical art historians, the phrase *escuela mexicana* implies an overly restricted vision of what constitutes Mexican art. Ana Garduño sometimes refers to the "so-called *escuela mexicana*" or employs a phrase such as "what was then known as the Mexican School of painting" as a way of problematizing the term.[28] In this introduction (and occasionally elsewhere) I use *escuela mexicana* in order to distinguish the work of the muralists and like-minded artists from artists associated with the Contemporáneos and have therefore adopted Garduño's strategy to acknowledge the problems with the designation. In the rare instances in which I forego the qualifying phrases, I continue to use the words to signify a group of artists with shared values in a specific historical period, not as a prescription for what Mexican art should be.

Kahlo's themes, iconography, and media often adhere to widely accepted ideas of the dominant Mexican art movement, but she also departed from them in significant ways. One of the goals of this book is to look carefully at which aspects of the theory and practice of the so-called Mexican School she embraced and which she ignored, resisted, or contested. Central to this study is the issue of how Kahlo promoted her own beliefs in ways that sometimes affirmed and sometimes resisted the dominant discourse.

The short manifesto (approximately 900 words) issued by the Sindicato de Obreros Técnicos, Pintores y Escultores is the single most influential document in the history of modern Mexican art. The manifesto, which was probably written by Siqueiros, advocated social and political art that supported the goals of the Mexican Revolution. It called for art to be collective, monumental, popular, and national. It praised the Mexican people, especially "our natives," and recognized "the physical and spiritual existence of our race as an ethnic force." The manifesto proclaimed: "*The art of the people of Mexico is the greatest, healthiest spiritual expression in the whole world, and its indigenous tradition is simply the best of them all.*"[29]

By the time the manifesto was signed in December 1923, the majority of signatories had already painted murals at the Escuela Nacional Preparatoria (National Preparatory School). The word "mural" was not used in the manifesto, but the document called for an art that was collective, monumental, ideological, and for the people. The artists who signed the manifesto would no doubt have agreed that these goals could best be addressed in large-scale works in public places. The manifesto was written while postrevolutionary Mexican art was in a nascent phase. It did not describe work that had already been created; rather, it voiced the artists' goals for the future.[30] After the manifesto was written, Rivera, Siquieros, and Orozco began painting images that were more national, political, and revolutionary than their first murals.

The manifesto stated that indigenous traditions are at the heart of Mexican art. Representations of indigenous people and Precolumbian cultures of Mexico, which were already important subjects in nineteenth-century academic painting, became a salient feature of modern Mexican art.[31] But Rivera's, Siqueiros's, and Orozco's representations of native peoples and ancient civilizations developed in divergent ways. These differences are substantial, but beyond the scope of this book. Because of Rivera's relationship with Kahlo, his treatments of these themes are the most relevant for this particular study. He is the artist who most frequently portrayed modern indigenous people and ancient cultures of Mexico. His paintings protest the abuse of indigenous workers, document native artisan traditions, praise traditional clothing, and celebrate regional customs. Rivera conducted extensive research before depicting the ancient cultures of Mexico in murals, where he promoted an idealized view of the Precolumbian past.[32]

A related concern of the manifesto was *lo popular* (the popular, in the sense of being of the common people), especially as it was linked to art. The manifesto asserted that popular painting, literature, and music could combat bourgeois influence and that popular indigenous taste had "a purifying effect in intellectual circles."[33] It promised to fight the decline of the popular indigenous aesthetic, which, according to the manifesto, only survived among the lower classes. In Spanish the words *arte popular* signify what would usually be translated into English as "folk art," "artisan objects," or "craft." While the manifesto did not use the phrase *arte popular*, it repeatedly used the word *popular* in statements about taste, aesthetics, and painting, thus implying support for the artisan traditions of Mexico. The manifesto was not the origin of the rising appreciation for artisan objects, which had long been despised by the majority of middle- and upper-class Mexicans and greatly admired by artists, but it affirmed the valorization of popular culture.[34] Many modern Mexican painters incorporated elements of *arte popular* into their work as a way of expressing admiration for indigenous aesthetics and declaring allegiance to campesinos (peasants) and indigenous people.[35] This is one of the principal ways in which Mexican artists expressed *mexicanidad* (Mexicanness).

The manifesto rejected easel painting and bourgeois taste. In order to reach a proletarian audience, mural painting became the preferred form of art. Murals in public venues satisfied the criteria of being monumental, collective, public, and accessible to everyone.[36] Rivera, Orozco, and Siqueiros considered murals the pinnacle of artistic achievement and based their reputations on their murals. Nevertheless, easel painting did not disappear. Even the most successful muralists went through long periods when they could not obtain mural commissions, and many artists who wished to paint murals had limited or no opportunity to do so. Prints were an effective alternative for reaching a wide popular audience and avoiding the pitfall of bourgeois tastes, so printmaking, which already had a strong tradition in Mexico, still flourished. Nonetheless, despite the artistic hegemony of muralism and the more easily accessible alternative of printmaking, easel painting continued to thrive. Ironically, most members of the so-called *escuela mexicana* pursued the goals of the manifesto by using the taboo form of easel painting. Even Orozco, Rivera, and Siqueiros produced quantities of easel paintings, which provided an important source of income.

The muralist movement was supported by the Mexican government, served didactic purposes, and promoted nationalism. The audience that the muralists wished to reach included peasants and workers, who had a high rate of illiteracy. To communicate with this audience, the muralists narrated Mexican history in visual form through panoramic images on the walls of government buildings. Many of the murals created in the 1920s bear witness to the recent Mexican Revolution, while others communicate the epic of Mexican history from the Precolumbian era to the present. By the 1930s the leading muralists began to place their social, political, and historical subjects in global contexts.

Monumental images of heroes dominate many Mexican murals and fill innumerable canvases. The muralists chose heroes who fought for liberty, represented Marxist ideology, or brought culture to their people. Rivera's heroes were Emiliano Zapata, Quetzalcoatl, Vladimir Lenin, and the common man. He created numerous images of Zapata, the agrarian leader of the Mexican Revolution, as a romantic horseman, revolutionary martyr, and secular saint. He depicted Lenin in the ill-fated mural at Radio City, New York, and endured the destruction of his mural rather than kowtow to his patron's pressure to remove the likeness of the Communist leader. Rivera presented Quetzalcoatl—a Mesoamerican deity, Toltec ruler, and cultural hero—three times in his mural *México prehispánico* (known in English as *The Aztec World*) of 1929 at the Palacio Nacional (National Palace). Rivera also represented heroes who were not members of the elite. For example, he created a narrative sequence about a brave unnamed peasant wearing blue overalls and a red shirt in the panels about social revolution on the left wall of the former chapel at the Universidad Autónoma de Chapingo (Autonomous University of Chapingo). At the end of his life, Rivera proclaimed that one of the greatest contributions of Mexican art was that artists made the common man the hero of monumental art for the first time in the history of art.[37]

Orozco portrayed Quetzalcoatl, Prometheus, and Miguel Hidalgo. For him, Quetzalcoatl symbolized the achievements of a lost golden age. Orozco repeatedly portrayed the Greek god Prometheus, whom he considered a benefactor of humankind, rising boldly from conflagrations. Orozco also represented a dynamic Miguel Hidalgo—the priest who proclaimed Mexican independence from Spain in 1810—emerging from a fiery background and looming large above writhing masses of people (fig. 3).

Siqueiros's favorite heroes were Cuauhtemoc, Zapata, and himself. He eulogized Cuauhtemoc, the last Aztec ruler, who defended the nation's integrity against foreign invaders. Siqueiros presented himself as the *coronelazo* (big hard-hitting colonel), whose clenched fist thrusts aggressively toward the viewer.

The hero in Mexican art of the 1920s and 1930s can be a common man, a general, a ruler, or a god, but he is always male. The muralists utilized the image of the dynamic male hero to dramatize history, construct national identity as masculine, and associate virility with social transformation.

During the postrevolutionary period (1920–1940) and beyond, women were depicted in murals and other media in ways that were distinct from the representations of men. In art and in the ideology of the postrevolutionary state, motherhood was women's most valued contribution. After the devastating loss of life in the Mexican Revolution, the Mexican government promoted population growth and the maternal role of women. Art historian Mary K. Coffey observes that motherhood was "the only acknowledged form

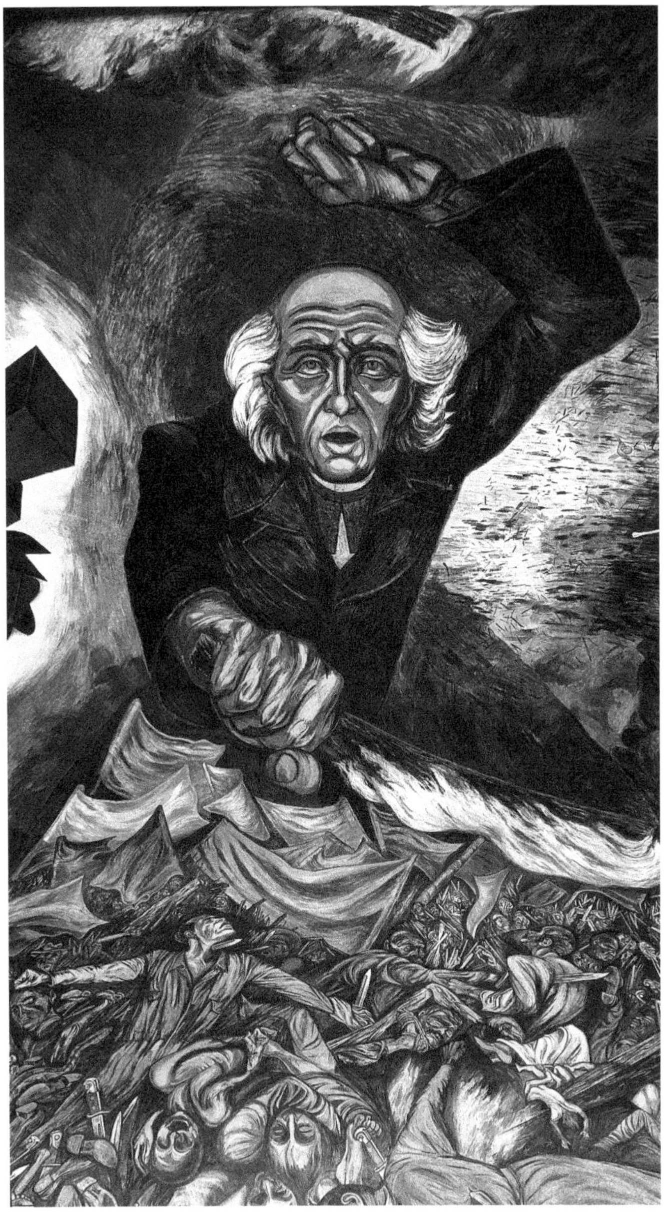

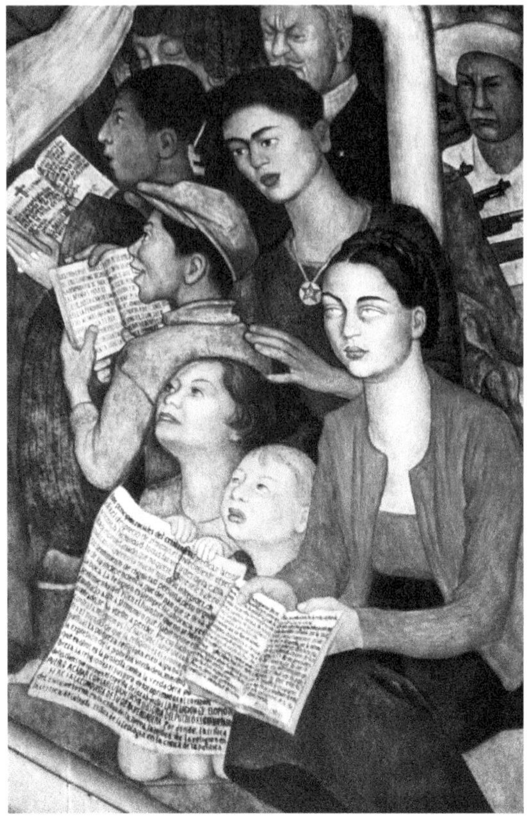

Fig. 3. José Clemente Orozco, *Hidalgo*, 1937, fresco, Palacio del Gobernador (Governor's Palace), Guadalajara, Mexico. Photograph by Rafael Doniz. © 2014 Artists Rights Society (ARS), New York/SOMAAP, Mexico City. Reproduction authorized by the Instituto Nacional de Bellas Artes y Literatura, 2015.

Fig. 4. Diego Rivera, detail of *El mundo de hoy y de mañana* (known in English as *Mexico Today and Tomorrow*), 1935, fresco, Palacio Nacional (National Palace). © 2014 Banco de México Diego Rivera Frida Kahlo Museums Trust, Mexico, D.F./Artists Rights Society (ARS), New York. Reproduction authorized by the Instituto Nacional de Bellas Artes y Literatura, 2015.

of female citizenship."[38] Women could not yet vote, but their ability to nurture future (male) citizens was valued.[39] Orozco's *Maternidad* (Maternity) of 1923 and Siquieros's *Madre campesina* (Peasant Mother) of ca. 1931 pay homage to the theme of motherhood. Artists also frequently portrayed women as teachers, Tehuanas (women from Tehuantepec), *indias bonitas* (pretty Indians), flower vendors, *soldaderas* (women who followed their men to war) trailing behind the troops,[40] and embodiments of the fecundity of nature. Men were envisioned as leaders who fought, governed, and changed the world; women were cast in supporting roles as wives, mothers, teachers, and helpers.

Rivera, like other muralists, almost always represented women in secondary roles in his frescos. In *El mundo de hoy y de mañana* (known in English as *Mexico Today and Tomorrow*) of 1935 at the Palacio Nacional, he depicted his sister-in-law, Cristina Kahlo, with her two children holding up political documents, while Kahlo herself teaches a dark-skinned working-class boy to read (fig. 4). In *En el arsenal* (known in English as *Distribu-*

tion of the Arms) of 1928 at the Secretaría de Educación Pública, he portrayed Kahlo as a young Communist (she wears a red star on a red shirt) handing out rifles to soldiers. Jean Franco observes that Rivera's images of women show that they have entered new social spaces, where they are teachers and comrades, yet "they are still represented as 'helpers' in the epic narrative."[41]

In addition to portraying women in auxiliary roles, the muralists occasionally featured allegorical female figures. In *Nueva democracia* (New Democracy) of 1944–1945, Siqueiros personified Liberty as a woman (following Eugène Delacroix's *Liberty Leading the People*). Orozco, in contrast, deeply mistrusted traditional academic allegories, a distrust that probably contributed to his invention of the garish green-skinned whore who lies on her back with her legs spread on the left side of *Katharsis* (Catharsis) of 1934, an unforgettable sign of social disorder and corruption.[42] Usually, however, the muralists merely relegated women to minor roles in the great drama of Mexican history.[43]

The ways in which Kahlo's representations of women diverged from the norm is a major theme in this book. Yet she also embraced aspects of the so-called *escuela mexicana*. Like many other artists associated with the dominant trends in Mexican art, she greatly admired Mexican popular culture and artisan objects, which she used in her daily life and cited in her art. She incorporated Mexican popular arts into her work by adopting the medium (oil on tin), format, and small size of *retablos* or ex-voto paintings, for paintings such as *Hospital Henry Ford* (Henry Ford Hospital) of 1932 and *Mi nana y yo* (My Nurse and I) of 1937. As an affirmation of *mexicanidad* she wore traditional Mexican clothing: *rebozos* (shawls), *huipiles* (sleeveless blouses or shifts), long skirts, and especially the regional clothing of Tehuantepec.

Kahlo's citations of Precolumbian art and culture are one of the major issues of this book. Chapter 2 includes a discussion of her use of Precolumbian iconography. Chapter 3 analyzes her representations of ancient figures from West Mexico in paintings, and chapter 4 focuses on an understudied painting that Kahlo created in 1942 and exhibited two years later under the title *La niña, la luna y el sol* (The Girl, the Moon, and the Sun).

While Kahlo concurred with the so-called *escuela mexicana* with regard to the valorization of popular art, indigenous people, and ancient Mexican civilizations, she also differed from the dominant school of art in fundamental ways. At a time and place when art was supposed to be monumental, political, public, and collective, she created small easel paintings about intimate and sometimes intensely personal subjects. She is best known for self-portraits, which are highly individualistic, even though the manifesto linked easel paintings and individualism with the bourgeoisie. The discrepancies between Kahlo's work and the dogma of the *escuela mexicana* are usually related to gender issues.

Kahlo held the work of her husband in the highest esteem and presumably admired the work of some of the other artists in the so-called *escuela mexicana*. When she took issue with parts of their rhetoric, she expressed her own ideas in the imagery of her paintings but appears not to have verbalized her differences. The one exception is the issue of the hero. In 1945 she was commissioned to paint *Moisés* (Moses), her only image of a hero and the only work in which she presents a panoramic vision of history (fig. 5). Although the painting is modest in size (20 × 37 inches), the composition resembles that of a mural. Unlike the muralists' presentation of bold heroes, however, Kahlo portrays Moses as an infant floating helplessly in a basket on the Nile. Rather than glorifying a human hero, she exalts the fertile and procreative elements of nature—sun, rain, womb, fetus, cells, sperm,

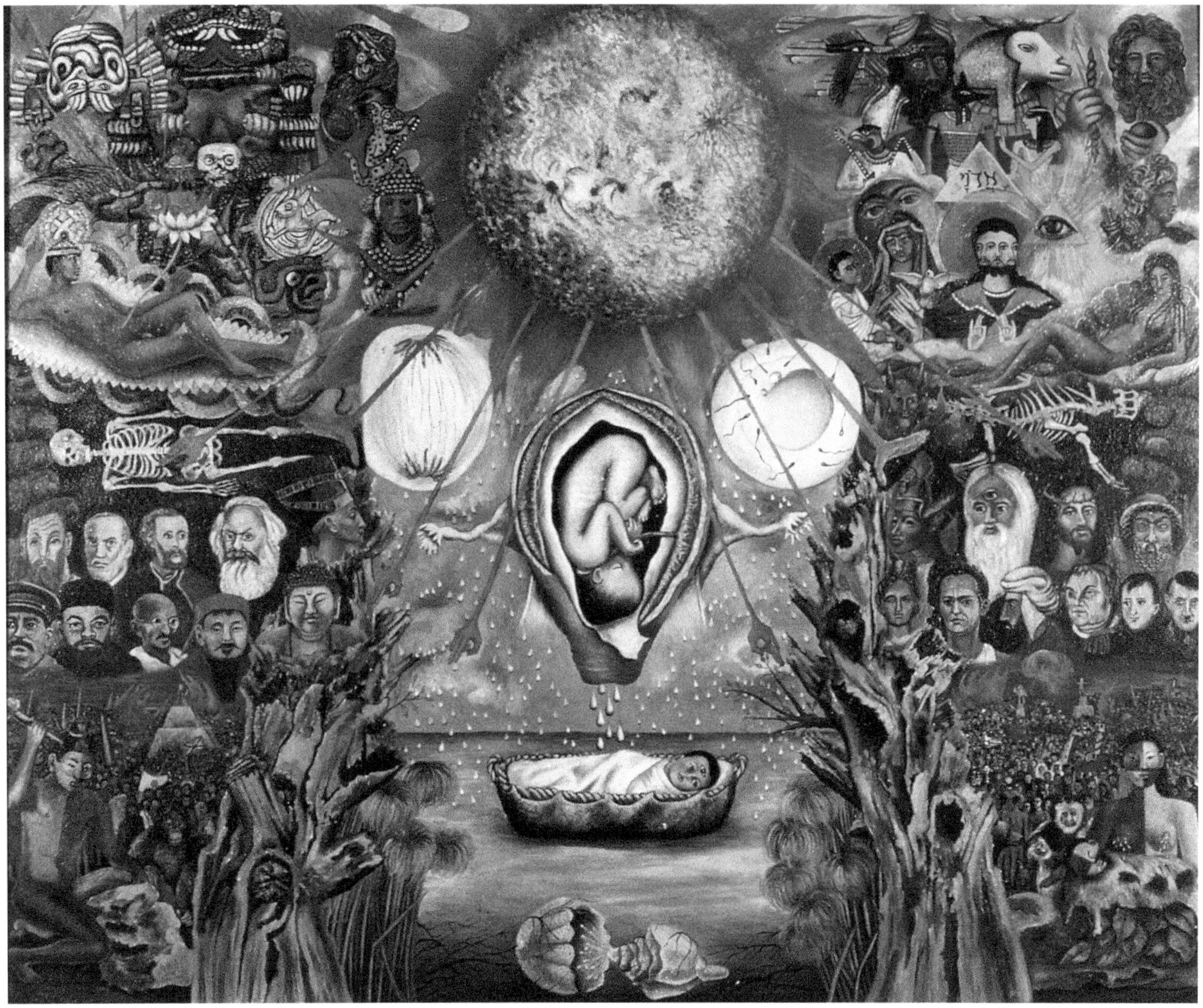

and ovaries—to which she gives pride of place at the center of the composition. At the unveiling of the painting, she said: "What I wished to express most intensely and *clearly* was that the reason that people need to invent or imagine *heroes* and *gods* is unmitigated FEAR. Fear of life and fear of *death.*" She added: "Like Moses, there have been and there will be a great number of 'higher ups,' transformers of religions and of human societies. It may be said that they are a type of *messengers* between the people whom they manage and the 'gods' invented by [the managers] in order to manage [the people]."[44] Clearly, Kahlo did not consider the glorification of heroes to be in the best interest of most people.[45]

Fig. 5. Frida Kahlo, *Moisés* (Moses), also known as *Núcleo solar* (Solar Nucleus), 1945, oil on Masonite, 20 × 37 inches (61 × 75.6 cm), private collection, Houston, Texas. © 2014 Banco de México Diego Rivera Frida Kahlo Museums Trust, Mexico, D.F./Artists Rights Society (ARS), New York. Reproduction authorized by the Instituto Nacional de Bellas Artes y Literatura, 2015.

Outside of Mexico, Kahlo is often considered a surrealist, but this designation is highly problematic. Evidence indicates that Kahlo had some knowledge of surrealism by the early 1930s and her first solo exhibition (in 1938) was held at a New York gallery with strong ties to surrealism.[46] After 1938 Kahlo frequently expressed disapproval of the surrealists, whom she considered decadent, especially the poet André Breton, who wrote the two manifestos of surrealism (1924, 1930). In 1938 Breton invited Kahlo to hold a solo exhibition in Paris. But when she arrived in January 1939, she discovered that he had failed to make preparations of any kind for the show. Marcel Duchamp quickly got her paintings out of customs and arranged an exhibition of Mexican art that included her work at the Renou & Colle gallery.[47] In a letter written in English in mid-February she described

Duchamp as a "marvelous painter" and observed that he was "the only one who has his feet on the earth, among all this bunch of coocoo lunatic sons of bitches of the surrealists."[48] Kahlo utilized surrealist ideas and visual strategies in her work when they suited her purposes, but she was not a member of the group, did not adhere to surrealist theory, and after her trip to Paris vehemently rejected being labeled a surrealist. As art historian Mari Carmen Ramírez observes, "in Latin America the marvelous is not outside the real, but an integral part of it; it exists within the real as a faith that carries the potential for a transformation of perception and thereby consciousness."[49] Kahlo used fantasy and fantastic imagery to communicate her version of reality with an intensity that surpassed a literal recounting of facts. But she also believed that the reason she did not have a solo show in Mexico until 1953 was because she had been called a surrealist—a member of a European art group, which was a serious liability in a country eager to assert the native origins of all its art movements. "They thought I was a surrealist," she protested, "but I wasn't. I never painted dreams, I painted my own reality."[50]

While Kahlo's ties to surrealism have been exaggerated, the intellectual impact of another international connection has gone largely unrecognized until now. Significant changes took place in Kahlo's art in 1937. Before 1937 Kahlo had created some seminal paintings—two oil on metal paintings about her miscarriage in 1932 and her indictment of violence against women, *Unos cuantos piquetitos* (A Few Small Nips) in 1935—but the quantity of paintings she produced was small indeed. In 1937 she began to work more consistently; the paintings she produced in the next fifteen years constitute her most important achievements. Kahlo's greater dedication to her work during this time may have been due at least in part to the artistic freedom advocated by Leon Trotsky, who entered her life when Rivera sought and obtained political asylum for Trotsky from the president of Mexico, Lázaro Cárdenas. Trotsky and his wife Natalia lived in the *casa azul*, Kahlo's blue house in Coyoacán, from January 1937 to April 1939; the Riveras moved to their studios in nearby San Ángel.[51] In 1938 "Manifesto: Towards a Free Revolutionary Art," which was signed by Rivera and Breton, was published in *Partisan Review*.[52] Although the essay was signed by the Mexican muralist and the French poet, it was actually written by Trotsky, who could not sign it because he had been granted political asylum in Mexico under the condition that he abstain from all political activity. Although Trotsky may have been the sole writer, he wrote the manifesto after numerous conversations with Rivera and Breton, who eagerly sought him out when he came to Mexico in April 1938.[53]

In "Manifesto: Towards a Free Revolutionary Art," Trotsky quoted the following statement from Karl Marx: "The writer naturally must make money in order to live and write, but he should not under any circumstances live and write in order to make money. . . . The first condition of the freedom of the press is that it is not a business activity."[54] Trotsky believed that Marx's words should be used to refute "those who would regiment intellectual activity in the direction of ends foreign to itself, and prescribe, in the guise of so-called reasons of state, the themes of art."[55] He asserted that the artist has an inalienable right to the free choice of themes and the absence of all restrictions. The manifesto unequivocally advocated complete freedom in art and concluded with the words: "The independence of art—for the revolution. The revolution—for the complete liberation of art!"[56]

The ideas expressed in "Manifesto: Towards a Free Revolutionary Art" in 1938 contradict those advocated by the "Manifesto del Sindicato de Obreros Técnicos, Pintores y Escultores" in the early 1920s. The earlier Mexican manifesto rejected easel painting, criticized bourgeois individualism, and insisted that art should have an ideological focus. The 1938 manifesto contained no proscriptions against easel painting, implicitly encouraged individualism, and explicitly warned against governments determining artistic content. The 1938 manifesto must have been profoundly liberating for Kahlo, whose own artistic inclinations and abilities did not conform to all the rules of the earlier manifesto. Her greater dedication to her career beginning in 1937 was facilitated by Trotsky's support for artistic freedom first in conversations at the *casa azul* and then in the manifesto. For Kahlo, who was a Marxist, it mattered a great deal that she had unconditional support for her highly individualistic work from her husband and from Trotsky, a leading figure in the Russian Revolution of 1917 and a prolific writer of Communist theory and history.

Izquierdo and the Contemporáneos

During her formative years as an artist, Izquierdo was closely associated with the painter Rufino Tamayo (1899–1991), who was her lover from 1929 to 1933. During these years, they shared a studio on the *azotea* (rooftop) of a building located at Soledad 9, immediately to the east of the Palacio Nacional in the very heart of the historic center of Mexico City.[57]

Tamayo and Izquierdo were linked to the Contemporáneos, a group of talented young avant-garde writers who formed the loyal opposition to the politically driven goals of the most famous muralists and published the literary and art journal *Contemporáneos* from 1928 to 1931. Because the writers were united by a shared philosophy of art rather than by adherence to any one style, the Contemporáneos have been referred to as a *grupo sin grupo* (group without a group). They worked in a variety of literary genres but are best known for poetry and criticism. They situated Mexican literature and cultural identity within Western culture, objected to an overly determined nationalism, and prioritized creative freedom over political ideology. The magazine published literature from Mexico, Europe, the United States, and South America. Every issue contained reproductions of visual art, and many also included essays about art.

The principal contributors to *Contemporáneos* were Bernardo Ortiz de Montellano, Jaime Torres Bodet, José Gorostiza, Xavier Villaurrutia, Salvador Novo, Enrique González Rojo, Jorge Cuesta, and Gilberto Owen. Other writers linked with the group socially, philosophically, and through their contributions to the journal include Carlos Pellicer (considered by some to be a full member), Celestino Gorostiza (brother of José Gorostiza), Elías Nandino (a physician), Rubén Salazar Mallén, and Ermilo Abreu Gómez. While the group takes its name from the journal, the contributors published other journals before and after *Contemporáneos*, and their influence extends far beyond its publication dates. Most of the members were born between 1899 and 1905, so they were quite young during the years when *Contemporáneos* was published. They became leading writers of their generation in Mexico. Xavier Villaurrutia, Salvador Novo, Carlos Pellicer, José Gorostiza, Jorge Cuesta, Gilberto Owen, and Jaime Torres Bodet are the preeminent poets of the period.

From the journal's inception, contentious debates raged between the muralists and the Contemporáneos. The first issue of *Contemporáneos* featured a controversial article by the Spanish-born painter Gabriel García Maroto about Rivera's murals at the Secretaria de Educación Pública (Ministry of Public Education) and the Universidad Autónoma de Chapingo. García Maroto, whose own work was influenced by synthetic cubism, praised Rivera's use of form and color but criticized his choice of subjects. He observed that

Rivera's murals "led the spectator outside the proper bounds of aesthetic values, and in so doing he turned art into a mechanized and unrefined political-social instrument."[58] Rivera retaliated in a public lecture in which he hurled various insults at the Contemporáneos and allegedly called them *maricas*, a derogatory slang term for homosexuals.[59] This incident set the tone and established the issues in the debate between the muralists and the Contemporáneos.

Several members of the Contemporáneos were in fact homosexual, including Novo, Villaurrutia, and Pellicer. Hence the sexual orientation of some members and the literary and artistic preferences of all of them stood in stark contrast to the priorities of the muralists, who promoted an aggressively masculine national identity and ideological art.

The Contemporáneos advocated "art for art's sake" (*arte puro*) and the exploration of formal issues. They wanted to insert Mexican creative writing into international discourses on literature and to provide their readers with access to a wide variety of trends in literature. They made available in translation writings by Guillaume Apollinaire, William Blake, Jean Cocteau, T. S. Eliot, Paul Éluard, André Gide, Langston Hughes, D. H. Lawrence, Paul Valéry, Thornton Wilder, and others. They also published reviews of writings by André Breton and Federico García Lorca and paid homage to Marcel Proust on the sixth anniversary of his death. In addition, the South American vanguard was represented with poetry by Jorge Luis Borges, Vicente Huidobro, Juana de Ibarbourou, and Pablo Neruda. While the Contemporáneos had an international perspective, they nonetheless vigorously supported Mexican literature and art. The subtitle of the journal was *Revista Mexicana de Cultura* (Mexican Magazine of Culture), and the principal contributors were Mexican.[60] In addition to publishing their own poetry, reviews, essays, and stories, they published numerous other Mexican authors, including Mariano Azuela, Sor Juana Inés de la Cruz, Andrés Henestrosa, Samuel Ramos, and Alfonso Reyes.[61]

Art historian Karen Cordero observes that the Contemporáneos group proposed "a modern Mexican art based on formal and cosmopolitan values rather than on historical or folkloric themes."[62] Instead of promoting a *mexicanidad* that was based on a nationalist valorization of the indigenous heritage, they sought to express Mexican identity through a dialogue with Western culture. In 1928 Tamayo expressed his preference for an international approach to art: "The problem in our painting lies in its unresolved Mexicanism. Until now, Mexicanism has been interpreted only folklorically or archaeologically, having more to do with anecdote than essence. My work is oriented toward pure plastic expression."[63] The visual artists who associated with the Contemporáneos, as well as the writers in the group, were interested in expressing Mexican identity; but they did not want to interpret it narrowly or to position it outside of and separate from the international sphere. They believed that creative freedom trumped nationalistic and political agendas and that artists and writers had the right to express themselves as individuals.

The Contemporáneos published visual art from Europe and the United States but especially promoted their own generation of Mexican artists. The magazine reproduced work by Agustín Lazo, Manuel Rodríguez Lozano, Julio Castellanos, Carlos Orozco Romero, Abraham Ángel, Manuel Álvarez Bravo, Rufino Tamayo, and María Izquierdo. They also published art by Jean Charlot, Carlos Mérida, and Tina Modotti, who were born in other countries but worked in Mexico and were accepted as part of the Mexican art world. While the Contemporáneos were not generally in favor of muralism, they admired the art and ideas of José Clemente Orozco and reproduced his work in three issues.

Scholarly literature about the Contemporáneos identifies the members exclusively as writers. Even Agustín Lazo, who in addition to being a painter was a playwright and Villaurrutia's partner, is usually ignored. The first exception to this exclusion is Salvador Oropesa's *The Contemporáneos Group: Rewriting Mexico in the Thirties and Forties* (2003), which devotes a chapter to Lazo's plays and collaborations with Villaurrutia. Oropesa also notes that Villaurrutia considered Tamayo a member of the Contemporáneos.[64] In a 2012 essay about the philosophical and aesthetic differences between the Contemporáneos and the muralists, Robin Greeley incorporates the art of Tamayo into her analysis of the debates.[65] A study that provides an in-depth holistic view of the contributions of all the visual artists linked to the journal has yet to be done.[66]

Izquierdo was affiliated with the Contemporáneos rather than being a true member, but this tie was crucial for her career. In 1929 four of her paintings were reproduced in *Contemporáneos*: a nude, a portrait, a landscape, and a still life.[67] Members of the group attended her openings, occasionally gave talks about her work at galleries, wrote reviews of her exhibitions, penned newspaper articles about her work, and contributed essays to her exhibition catalogues.[68] This support was especially strong at the beginning of her career but continued long after the magazine ceased publication and after Izquierdo and Tamayo had separated. The Contemporáneos and other writers linked to the group who wrote about her art included Jorge Cuesta, José Gorostiza, Celestino Gorostiza, Carlos Pellicer, Xavier Villaurrutia, Ermilo Abreu Gómez, Elías Nandino, and Rubén Salazar Mallén. As minister of public education, Jaime Torres Bodet appointed her ambassador of Mexican art and sent her to South America. Izquierdo illustrated a children's book titled *Pirrimplin en la luna* (Pirrimplin on the Moon) written by Ermilo Abreu Gómez. José Gorostiza and Elías Nandino owned paintings by her, and she painted a portrait of Nandino, who was also her physician.

Izquierdo's apartment became a gathering place for artists and writers.[69] The people who congregated in her home included the Contemporáneos Xavier Villaurrutia, Salvador Novo, and Jorge Cuesta; Izquierdo's closest women friends Lola Álvarez Bravo, Guadalupe Marín, and Margarita Michelena; the artists Rufino Tamayo (until 1934), Juan Soriano, Manuel Álvarez Bravo, and Roberto Montenegro; the singer-songwriter Concha Michel; and the writers Luis Cardoza y Aragón, Alí Chumacero, Andrés Henestrosa, and Rodolfo Usigli.[70]

Throughout her life, Izquierdo maintained her belief in *arte puro* and her affiliation with the Contemporáneos group. She did, however, make some changes in her art around 1939 that include a shift in subject matter, which brought some of her paintings in line with mainstream ideas about *mexicanidad*. Between 1930 and 1938 Izquierdo used a low-key palette dominated by red but otherwise earthy and fairly neutral (fig. 6). She painted in a loose, painterly style, usually working in watercolor, which she applied so thickly that it has often been mistaken for gouache. She painted circus scenes, still lifes, nudes, allegorical figures, portraits, self-portraits, and landscapes. While the subjects of some of her early paintings are recognizably Mexican, most of them are not. During this period her choice of subjects fits the Contemporáneos' idea that Mexican identity need not be bound by strict adherence to "Mexican" subjects. But in 1939 Izquierdo began to make significant stylistic and thematic changes to her work. By 1940 she consistently used lighter, brighter colors, rendered figures in a more defined and less painterly way, and more frequently employed the medium of oil on canvas (fig. 7). She continued to paint most of the subjects

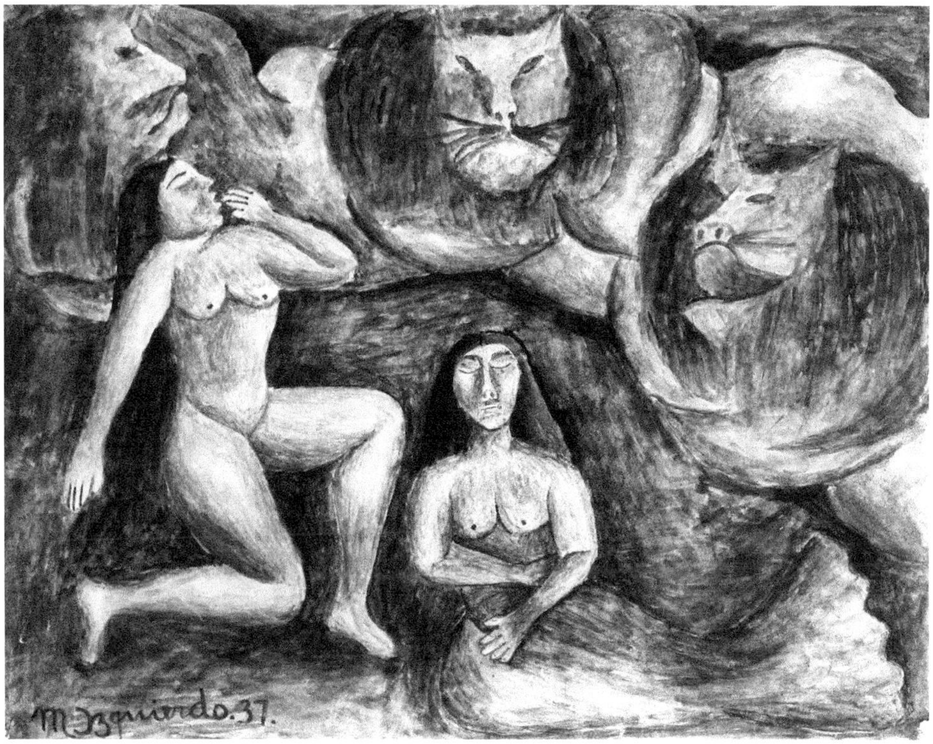

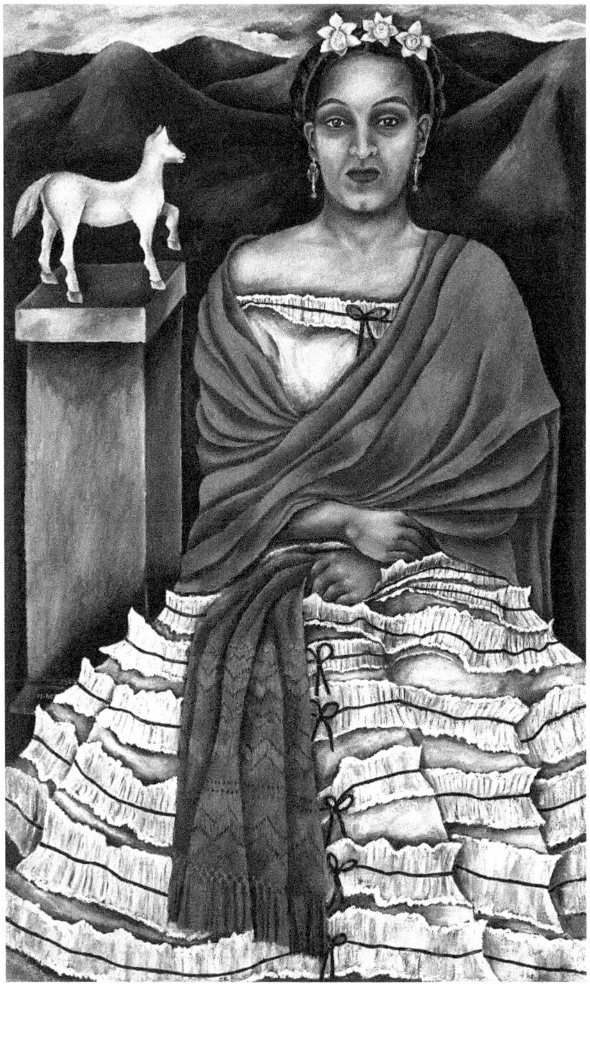

Fig. 6. María Izquierdo, *Sirena y leones* (Siren and Lions), 1937, watercolor, 7 ⅞ × 10 ¼ inches (20 × 26 cm), Estate of Robert Brady, Cuernavaca, Morelos, Mexico. Photograph by Francisco Kochen. Reproduced with the permission of María Rosenda López Posadas, legal representative of the intellectual property of María Izquierdo. Reproduction authorized by the Instituto Nacional de Bellas Artes y Literatura, 2015.

Fig. 7. María Izquierdo, *Autorretrato* (Self-Portrait), 1940, oil on canvas, 55 ⅛ × 34 ¼ inches (140 × 87 cm), collection of Andres Blaisten. Reproduced with the permission of María Rosenda López Posadas, legal representative of the intellectual property of María Izquierdo.

that she had always painted,[71] but she endowed more of these subjects with recognizably Mexican features. For example, around 1942 she began a series of landscape paintings that include granaries. The paintings represent rural gardens in the state of Morelos, so their location would have been identifiable to a Mexican audience in the forties. In 1943 she initiated another series representing home altars for the Virgin of Sorrows. The images of altars fit within the genre of still-life painting, a genre that she had employed since she had begun painting, but they also document a form of folk Catholicism practiced in some regions of Mexico.[72] These new subjects coincide with the so-called Mexican School's ideas about *mexicanidad.*

Despite these changes, Izquierdo seems never to have altered her core beliefs. In 1947 she wrote an artistic credo in which she declared, "I flee from anecdotal, folkloric, and political subjects because these subjects do not have aesthetic or poetic force."[73] Three years later she wrote about her art:

> I desire to achieve in [my painting] personality, pictorial quality, Mexicanism (without falling into Mexican curios), technical perfection (without descending into cold, precise virtuosity), unity between line and color, between the drawing and the coloristic material. I also attempt to express in simple and deeply felt themes the human and mysterious poetry of my country. I long to find the light and shadow, the mystery of "lo mexicano" in the exact tone found by Silvestre Revueltas in music; López Velarde in poetry; Guadalupe Posada in prints; the painters of Bonampak in their frescoes; the Maya, Aztec, and Totonac architects and sculptors in their imponderable works; and, in conclusion, to look long and fully at the red *tezontle* of Mexican stone, to discover its chromatic mysteries, to listen to its message, to squeeze its color, and, finally, to hope that the miracle is produced so that something of its essence and of its red juice impregnates my brushes and remains like kisses in my paintings.[74]

Izquierdo's desire to create Mexican art without depicting "folkloric" subjects or "falling into Mexican curios" distances her from an overly determined concept of what constitutes being Mexican. Her strategy of being "Mexican" through her use of color is similar to the approach of Tamayo, who believed his work was Mexican in his use of color and proportion.[75] When Izquierdo stated her goal of achieving "lo mexicano" in her work in a way similar to Revueltas, López Velarde, Posada, and the painters of Bonampak, she cited a musician, a writer, and artists who were so widely respected that they transcended divisions in the Mexican art world. Her statements of 1947 and 1950 testified to her continuing belief in the poetry of visual art, in *arte puro.*

Several art historians, including Olivier Debroise and Adriana Zavala, have expressed a strong preference for Izquierdo's work from the 1930s. Zavala makes a distinction between Izquierdo's early work, which employs a dark palette and "offers evidence of Izquierdo's early commitment to avant-garde aesthetic sensibilities and subjects," and her post-1939 paintings, which use brighter colors and "suggest a commercially motivated picturesque folkloric impulse."[76] While I appreciate the attraction to Izquierdo's dark, mysterious, and soulful early work, she also created compelling images in the forties. My own focus is less on aesthetics than on her strategies for representing women in ways that insert them as equal partners into the artistic and nationalistic discourses of Mexico. By 1932 Izquierdo had begun to represent women as active, strong, and brave in her paintings of female circus performers. While she continued to depict images of intrepid female circus artists for many years, by the early 1940s she had also developed other strategies for addressing gender issues in art. Her new visual strategies included the series of granaries (discussed in chapter 5) and the altars to the Virgin of Sorrows (discussed in chapter 8).

For the generations of artists who were active in the decades immediately following the Mexican Revolution, loyalty to either *arte puro* as advocated by the Contemporáneos or social and political art as promulgated by the muralists and like-minded artists ran deep. Even in 1981, when the Museo Rufino Tamayo (Rufino Tamayo Museum) opened, for many people these conflicting views about the role of art were still controversial. The museum, which provides a home for the 300 works of twentieth-century art that Tamayo gave to the people of Mexico in 1981, is located in Chapultepec Park in Mexico City. The collection that Tamayo donated is international in scope. Its strength is European modernism (Salvador Dalí, Max Ernst, Fernand Léger, René Magritte, Joan Miró, Pablo Picasso, and others), but it also includes modern and contemporary art from the United States, South America, and Mexico.[77] For some, it was problematic that the museum was built on government-owned land. For others, Tamayo's making foreign art available in Mexico was inherently heretical.[78] The Rufino Tamayo Museum was the first museum in Mexico regularly to exhibit modern and contemporary art from other countries. At the opening ceremony, Tamayo said: "I hope that the people of Mexico can enter this door unburdened by the prejudice that artistic creation should be oriented in a single direction." To make it clear that he was referring to the long-standing feud between the artists who advocated *arte puro* and those who promoted political art, he added: "You know that famous phrase of Siqueiros: 'Ours is the only path.' Can you believe that, to say that ours is the only path when the fundamental thing in art is freedom!"[79]

Despite the considerable hostilities between the two groups, which were especially strong in the decade following the inauguration of *Contemporáneos*, the interchanges between the groups ebbed and flowed; intergroup relationships varied with individual artists and over time. The Contemporáneos admired Orozco, who abhorred the idea that Mexican identity should be represented by "the ridiculous *charro* [horseman] and the insipid *china poblana*" and shared the Contemporáneos' aversion to facile political ideologies.[80] Orozco, who caricatured the Contemporáneos as fey dandies, seems not to have reciprocated their admiration. Salvador Novo helped organized Siqueiros's first solo exhibition in 1932 in his role as undersecretary of education, and for a brief period Siqueiros soft-peddled his usual rhetoric.[81]

On a social level the groups were not impermeable. Some artists and writers managed to maintain friendships with everyone regardless of the polemics of the art world. Explaining his social fluidity, the painter Juan Soriano gleefully confessed: "I was very hypocritical, I belonged to all the groups then. Sometimes I couldn't sleep from remorse. How horrible! What a hypocrite I am, because I would say one thing to María Izquierdo and another to Frida Kahlo."[82] Pellicer, who was affiliated with the Contemporáneos and wrote two essays about Izquierdo, was also a longtime close friend of Kahlo. Pellicer wrote three sonnets about Kahlo and directed the transformation of the *casa azul* into the Museo Frida Kahlo (Frida Kahlo Museum) after her death. Lola Álvarez Bravo was close to both Izquierdo and Kahlo. She lived with Izquierdo and her children for several years after her separation from Manuel Álvarez Bravo in 1934, participated in the frequent social gatherings of artists and writers in Izquierdo's home, and included her work in at least three group shows in her gallery in the early 1950s.[83] Lola Álvarez Bravo also created an extensive series of photographs of Kahlo and organized her only individual exhibition in Mexico during her life.

Art institutions in Mexico incorporated both the so-called Mexican School and the Contemporáneos. Government-supported museums exhibited work by artists of both groups. The inclusion of visual artists associated with the Contemporáneos was in part because several Contemporáneos and other writers closely associated with the group intermittently held important government positions in the fine arts.[84] When they were in positions of cultural power they made sure that the artists whose work they admired received support for their projects.[85] The art school popularly known as La Esmeralda primarily employed teachers associated with the dominant artistic movement, but the Contemporáneos' point of view was well represented by Izquierdo, Lazo, and Rodríguez Lozano. In the private sector, Inés Amor, the astute director of the Galería de Arte Mexicano, represented the best artists working in Mexico regardless of their affiliation.[86]

Because this book focuses on Izquierdo, who was loosely affiliated with the Contemporaneous, and Kahlo, who was associated socially with the muralists and other artists who advocated politically committed art, I have focused on the philosophical positions of these two groups. But these groups were not the only tendencies in art in postrevolutionary Mexico. In 1921, two years before Izquierdo arrived in Mexico City, when both she and Kahlo were still teenagers, Manuel Maples Arce wrote the manifesto of *estridentismo* (stridentism), which called for artists to seek inspiration in technology. During World War II, a number of European surrealists immigrated to Mexico and flourished in their new environment, albeit as a tightly knit group that had limited interactions with other artists. Subgroups and trajectories within the Mexican art world also included LEAR (Liga de Escritores y Artistas Revolucionarios/League of Revolutionary Writers and Artists) from 1933 to ca. 1937 and Taller de Gráfica Popular, a group of dissident printmakers who broke away from LEAR in 1937.[87] In 1942 Rivera wrote an article in which he declared that Kahlo was the nucleus of a small group of brilliant young painters whose other members were Juan O'Gorman, Antonio Ruiz, and Fernando Castillo.[88] This claim seems to be primarily a strategy for positioning Kahlo as a leader among talented artists, rather than a description of any actual group.

Methodology

In this study I combine a variety of methodologies, principally iconography (signs and symbol) and gender studies. The book examines equally the work of Izquierdo and Kahlo, but the methodology responds to problems in the scholarship on Kahlo. To date the literature on Kahlo is overwhelmingly biographical: her paintings are seen as merely or primarily responses to the events of her personal life. Some of what has been written about her is feminist in rather superficial ways, and other texts condescendingly attempt to explain her work through psychoanalytic theory. Most of these interpretations ultimately lead to reductive explanations of her art.

Kahlo and Izquierdo were intelligent, analytical people who created images of women that often diverged sharply from the usual representations of women in postrevolutionary Mexico. Their imagery questions gender roles, critiques the status quo, or presents a more empowering alternative for women. Through the iconographic analysis of individual paintings and related groups of paintings, I focus on each artist's strategies for negotiating female identity and affirming parts of artistic and nationalistic discourses while rejecting others. Izquierdo and Kahlo did this in different ways, and each employed more than one tactic to deconstruct the dominant discourses. This book places Izquierdo's and Kahlo's work in its cultural context and examines the ways in which they selectively affirmed and resisted the national and artistic discourses of postrevolutionary Mexico. I demonstrate how their work reveals intellectual engagement with the issues and ideas of their time, especially national identity and the role of women in society. In short, I map the paths that they used to claim interpretive power.

Brief Review of the Literature

Frida Kahlo is one of the most studied women artists in the history of art; consequently, the following brief discussion of the scholarly literature on her work makes no attempt to be complete. Rather, it examines the strengths and weaknesses of pivotal publications that contribute to our knowledge and understanding of Kahlo's art and life, predispose us to certain methodologies, or significantly affect my own thinking about Kahlo's work and what constitutes useful art history. Because of the sheer quantity of catalogues to exhibitions of Kahlo's paintings, I do not refer to them individually in this overview, although they have contributed greatly to the rise of her reputation and popular awareness of her work. While my summary of the literature about María Izquierdo is equally brief, I do discuss select exhibition catalogues, because most of the essential publications about her have been produced in conjunction with exhibitions. In the chapters of this book in which I analyze paintings by Izquierdo or Kahlo, I address other texts that directly pertain to these works.

Frida Kahlo's posthumous fame is vastly greater than her reputation during her lifetime. During her life she was known as the handsome, exotically dressed, invalid wife of Diego Rivera, who was also a painter in her own right. By the late 1930s she had established herself as a serious painter. In the years immediately following her death, she became a largely forgotten artist. Few people other than connoisseurs of Mexican art would have recognized her name. In the 1960s information about her in English was found almost exclusively in books about Rivera. That situation started to change in the mid-1970s, when feminist art historians in the United States discovered Kahlo and began to resurrect her as a prime example of a female artist whose work merited greater recognition. In Mexico Teresa del Conde published a brief book titled *Vida de Frida Kahlo* (Life of Frida Kahlo) in 1976. The following year Raquel Tibol, who interviewed Kahlo in 1953, published *Frida Kahlo: Crónica, testimonios y aproximaciones* (Frida Kahlo: Chronicles, Testimonies, and Approximations). Numerous articles about Kahlo were published in the United States and Mexico, and major retrospectives of her work were held in both countries. By the end of the seventies she had become a counterculture heroine whose reputation was growing exponentially.

The single most influential publication for Kahlo scholarship and her diffusion in popular culture is Hayden Herrera's *Frida: A Biography of Frida Kahlo*. The publication of Herrera's biography in 1983 marked a quantum leap in the amount of information available about Kahlo and a seismic shift in the level of public awareness of her. Within a few years Kahlo went from being a little-known artist to being a major figure in the art world. Herrera's biography is based on her doctoral dissertation in art history.[89] She interviewed dozens of Kahlo's relatives, friends, students, and colleagues and conducted extensive archival research in Mexico and the United States. The strengths of Herrera's book include the detailed information about Kahlo's life, the numerous citations of her words and letters, and the substantial bibliography, which contains quantities of articles published about Kahlo during her life. Herrera writes at length about Kahlo's paintings, especially the self-portraits, and interprets them according to the artist's personal life. The problem with this biography is that it frequently offers a rather simplistic cause and effect interpretation of Kahlo's life and art, in which the paintings are seen as unmediated responses to events in her life.

Most subsequent writers have repeated and extended Herrera's biographical methodology to such an extent that it has become almost monolithic. Interpretations of Kahlo's work are filtered through what is known, conjectured, or fantasized about her personal life and mental states.

Joan Borsa's insightful article "Frida Kahlo: Marginalization and the Critical Female Subject" (1990) critiques the reception of Kahlo's work and the literature in English about her. Borsa notes that most authors who write about Kahlo's exploration of subjectivity and personal history have "all too frequently denied or de-emphasized the politics involved in examining one's own location, inheritance and social condition."[90] She observes that even though the motto "the personal is political" has been widely accepted by feminists since the 1960s or 1970s, most writings about Kahlo's work give cursory attention to her complex reworking of the personal while disregarding or downplaying her interrogation of cultural identity, gender, sexuality, marginality, politics, and power. Borsa acknowledges the comprehensive nature of Herrera's biography but objects to the repeated explanation of Kahlo's imagery in relationship to her love affairs, tumultuous marriage, and medical problems. She argues that Herrera's 500-page biography establishes that "Frida Kahlo's life revolved around love, marriage, and pain; in short a rather traditional feminine sphere has been presented." She asserts that it is not that Kahlo did not experience marriage, love, and pain but that reading her work as a "fixed text" that confirms traditional spaces assigned to women is highly problematic: "What is missing is a more *critical* reading of the *gaps* between the author and the text."[91]

In her 1993 article "Like an Artist," art historian Janice Bergman-Carton voices similar concerns about simplistic and depoliticized interpretations of Kahlo's art. Bergman-Carton observes that Herrera's biography "brought Kahlo to her current prominence" and notes, with considerable irony, that it "gave scholarly respectability to the impulse to read Kahlo's art through the torment of her life."[92] After discussing Kahlo's appropriation of religious imagery and refashioning of social codes in sometimes painful canvases such as *La columna rota* (The Broken Column) of 1944, Bergman-Carton insists that, despite the pain that such images evince, "these paintings are not the agonizing cries of a victimized female; they are the transfiguring and intellectualized resurrections of a life that is devoted to the mind as much as the body." Bergman-Carton notes that Herrera's "distillation of a very complex artist into a single essential 'Frida' facilitated the transformation of Kahlo into a cult figure whose physical features have . . . become etched onto our collective visual memory."[93] In the years since "Frida" entered popular culture, the media industry has neutralized the criticism inherent in her manipulation of gender codes and resistance to fixed identity boundaries. While journalists recognize Kahlo's defiance and "otherness," they do so less as a challenge to social norms than as a way of noting her marketability. "In the same breath that her difference is acknowledged, it is often reinserted into the narrative of artistic fashion in a way that defuses its cultural critique."[94]

Margaret Lindauer's *Devouring Frida: The Art History and Popular Celebrity of Frida Kahlo* (1999) is the first book about Kahlo to break away from the biographical model. Lindauer employs a semiotic, feminist analysis to examine the construction of the "Frida myth." Of particular interest is the chapter "Fetishizing Frida," in which she critiques the artist equals art paradigm that banishes visual art to an ahistorical and apolitical realm.[95] Lindauer cites Griselda Pollock, who, in an essay titled "Artists, Mythologies and Media," argues that artists and art have been "'evacuated from history . . . [and] history from art history' through 'psychobiographical interpretations.'"[96] As Lindauer notes, "at the same time that a product (painting) becomes synonymous with the producer (painter), the artist is reduced to personal, psychological, and biological histories constructed parallel to, but separate from, social histories."[97]

The tendency to interpret art by women as unmediated responses to their personal lives rather than as intentional statements commenting on broader issues is not limited to Kahlo. Artist Judy Chicago notes "an unfortunate tendency . . . to strip women artists of their aesthetic agency. In Kahlo's case, by viewing her paintings in relation to Rivera's behavior, her works are demeaned, turning them into *reactive* rather than *active* creations." As Chicago sardonically observes, "Imagine a biography that examined the career of Jackson Pollock (1912–1956) in relation to the ups and downs of his marriage with fellow artist Lee Krasner (1908–1984)—inconceivable, yet usually unquestioned with Kahlo and O'Keeffe."[98]

During the same years when art historians began critiquing these biographical and psychological methodologies, other scholars were making key primary sources available. The publication in Spanish of Kahlo's diary, *Frida Kahlo: Diario* (1994), provides small photographs of every page of the diary with a transcription of the text directly below the photograph. In 1995 Harry N. Abrams and the Mexican publisher of the diary jointly released a handsome facsimile edition and English translation, with an introduction by Carlos Fuentes and commentary by Sarah Lowe.[99] In 2001 the collected writings of Kahlo, selected and annotated by Raquel Tibol, were published in *Escrituras: Frida Kahlo. Escrituras* includes Kahlo's letters, telegrams, and notes to friends, family, and collectors as well as an original ballad that she composed for the owners of her self-portrait *El venadito* (The Little Deer) of 1946. At the end of Rivera's life, when he set up a trust fund to support and manage the Museo Frida Kahlo and Anahuacalli, the museum that houses his vast collection of ancient Mexican artifacts, he asked his close friend Dolores Olmedo to keep the archives and not make them public until fifteen years after his death. Olmedo, the long-time director of the museums, never made them available. After her death in 2002, the committee that manages the two museums opened the archives, catalogued them, and began to make the information available to the public.[100] In 2004 an armoire containing clothing, letters, and photographs was found in a sealed-up section of the Museo Frida Kahlo. Photographs of the clothing were published in *Self Portrait in a Velvet Dress: Frida's Wardrobe* in 2008. Less sensational but more important is the publication of *Frida Kahlo: Sus fotos* (*Frida Kahlo: Her Photos*) in 2010 with reproductions of over five hundred photographs from Kahlo's vast collection, including four previously unknown photographs created by Kahlo in 1929 and 1930.[101] Photographer Pablo Ortiz Monasterio, who edited the book, observes that Kahlo "surely took many more pictures"; but even when we cannot be sure that she took a photograph, we can be certain "that many of these images relate to her paintings."[102]

Just when Kahlo scholarship showed signs of becoming more insightful, relevant, and diverse, a new problem emerged with the publication of an enormous cache of forged art and objects attributed to Kahlo by its present owners, Carlos Noyola and his wife, Leticia Fernández, antique dealers from San Miguel de Allende. *Finding Frida Kahlo* (2009) claims to present "an astonishing lost archive" of paintings, drawings, letters, poetry, recipes, keepsakes, clothing, and objects "full of ardent desire, seething fury, and outrageous humor" that had been "hidden from view for over half a century."[103] The Noyolas acquired approximately 1,200 objects between 2004 and 2007 from a lawyer, who purchased them from a woodcarver (now deceased), who claimed to have received them from Kahlo. The contents of the collection have been universally denounced as forgeries by art historians who have written extensively about Kahlo, respected art dealers specializing in Latin American art, the director of the Museo Frida Kahlo, and the Instituto Nacional de Bellas Artes (National Institute of Fine Arts) of Mexico.[104] The reasons for the consensus among specialists are easy to understand. The paintings and drawings are clumsy pastiches of Kahlo's known works, and the letters and poetry are poorly written. The New York–based art dealer Mary-Anne Martin says: "In my view the publishers have been the victim of a gigantic hoax . . . The perpetrators have constructed all these letters, poems, drawings and recipes, using Frida's biography and her published letters as a roadmap." Martin notes that "the drawings are badly done, the writing infantile, the content crude. . . . The provenance provided is unverifiable and meaningless."[105] Raquel Tibol, who compiled Kahlo's writings, observes that the letters in the Noyolas collection are not in the artist's handwriting and "are written in a bawdy, vulgar, coarse language, which is not to be confused with Frida's popular, naughty language, a language of wit and propriety."[106]

What is particularly pernicious about *Finding Frida Kahlo* is that it has a convincing veneer of respectability that can fool people who are not visually discerning and have limited knowledge of Kahlo's work. The Princeton Architectural Press is a commercial press not connected with Princeton University; as James Oles observes, it failed to use minimum standards of academic vetting for this project.[107] To the degree that this book is accepted as a reliable source, Kahlo's reputation is severely damaged. Given the existing tendency to see Kahlo as an artist who created paintings in response to emotional issues in her life, rather than as an intellectual who critiqued the construction of gender, *Finding Frida Kahlo* is harmful indeed.

Although the literature about María Izquierdo is significantly less extensive, it is substantial. Izquierdo's active exhibition record and compelling personality led to a steady flow of modest exhibition catalogues and countless essays, articles, and reviews during her life. In addition to articles written by the Contemporáneos, other major writers such as Antonin Artaud, Luis Cardoza y Aragón, Justino Fernández, Andrés Henestrosa, Pablo Neruda, and Elena Poniatowska contributed to the literature on Izquierdo while she was alive.

Nevertheless, the first major studies of Izquierdo's work were published in Mexico in the late 1980s. Major Mexican corporations frequently publish lavishly illustrated books that are given to their important clients. In 1986 the Casa de Bolsa Cremi, an investment firm, produced a book about María Izquierdo with a new essay by Carlos Monsiváis, reprints of twenty-seven earlier essays by major writers, and reprints of Izquierdo's published writings, which are primarily reviews of other artists' work and articles about her travels in South America. In Mexico republished essays are referred to as *refritos* (refried ones), an obviously derogatory label; however, the custom has some advantages. In this case the book made available a corpus of primary sources. Books published by Mexican corporations are given exclusively to their most valued clients, are not sold in bookstores, and seldom enter library collections but are potentially, as in this case, valuable to scholars if they can obtain copies.[108]

More influential is the exhibition catalogue produced in conjunction with a major retrospective of Izquierdo's work held at the Centro Cultural, Arte Contemporáneo in Mexico City from November 1988 to February 1989. The catalogue contains essays by five scholars, the most thorough visual record of her work compiled to date, a chronology of her life, and a remarkably complete bibliography that is indispensable for anyone interested in consulting primary sources.[109] The exhibition generated excitement about Izquierdo's art; renewed interest in her work can be dated to this show.

In the mid-1990s two retrospectives of Izquierdo's work were presented by arts organizations in the United States. The bilingual catalogues that accompanied the exhibitions provided information not previously available in English. The first exhibition, *María Izquierdo,* 1902–1955, was held at the Mexican Fine Arts Center Museum in Chicago in 1996 and traveled to the Museo de Arte Moderno in Mexico City in 1997. The catalogue features an essay by curator Luis-Martín Lozano. The second exhibition, *The True Poetry: The Art of María Izquierdo*, was curated by Elizabeth Ferrer for the Americas Society Art Gallery in New York in 1997.[110]

In her 2000 article "Painting Mexican Identities: Nationalism and Gender in the Work of María Izquierdo," Robin Greeley provides the first serious study of gender issues in Izquierdo's oeuvre. Greeley examines the reception of Izquierdo's work from the 1930s to the 1988 retrospective at the Centro Cultural, Arte Contemporáneo and concludes that Izquierdo's supporters see her imagery as an expression of nationalism that challenges the Marxist focus on workers of the most famous muralists. As Greeley observes, "The historical circumstances of Izquierdo's peculiar inclusion into a Mexican nationalist discourse suggest ways of bringing together several sets of discourses too often kept separate: those of Latin America, of feminism, of modernism, and of nationalism." Greeley asserts that Izquierdo's paintings deconstruct "'heroic' Mexican nationalism."[111]

Luis-Martín Lozano's lavishly illustrated book *María Izquierdo: Una verdadera pasión por el color* (María Izquierdo: A True Passion for Color) was published in 2002 to celebrate the centennial of the artist's birth.[112] When Izquierdo was fourteen years old, her family married her to an older man she did not know.[113] It has always been assumed that the man she married as a girl in northern Mexico was Cándido Posadas, the man she lived with and called her husband in Mexico City in the late 1920s. Lozano asserts that Cándido Posadas was not her husband from the arranged marriage. Rather, her first husband was a military man.[114] "For reasons never confessed but easy to understand, María Izquierdo escaped from that relation in order to establish sentimental ties with a journalist, Cándido Posadas."[115] This is an important point. Despite my strong objections to the overuse and misuse of biography in the interpretation of Kahlo's art, there is an incredible lack of the most basic information about Izquierdo's life from the time she left San Juan de los Lagos when she was about six years old until she enrolled in the art academy in Mexico City approximately twenty years later.

Among the most innovative studies of Izquierdo's art are the texts written by art historian Adriana Zavala. Zavala contributed a section about Izquierdo to *The Eagle and the Virgin* (2006) that focuses on the artist's affiliation with the Contemporáneos group and the series of female nudes that she began in 1929. According to Zavala, Izquierdo's untitled nude published in *Contemporáneos* in 1929 "subverts the accepted, ostensibly unthreatening relationship normally established in classically rendered images of the female body." Zavala observes that Izquierdo's series of over forty paintings of "nude and naked women in primordial landscapes . . . represent one of the earliest focused engagements with the female nude in Mexican art."[116] Zavala's book *Becoming Modern, Becoming Tradition: Women, Gender, and Representation in Mexican Art* (2010) employs the methodologies of social history and gender studies to analyze the changing representations of women from the nineteenth century to the 1950s.[117] In addition to expanding on the ideas published in *The Eagle and the Virgin*, Zavala provides extensive historical context that monographs about individual artists tend to lack.

The scholarship about Izquierdo does not suffer to the same degree as the scholarship on Kahlo from the tendency to interpret every painting according to the events of her personal life, even though Debroise, Ferrer, and Tibol have interpreted the allegorical female nudes that Izquierdo began painting in the early thirties as sorrowful reactions to her separation from Tamayo.[118] But the literature about Izquierdo has other recurring problems. Until recently a high percentage of authors writing about Izquierdo labeled her work naïve or commented on her indigenous appearance, as if her ancestry automatically conferred authenticity on her art. (Izquierdo was mestiza, with pronounced indigenous features.) Sometimes these assumptions are linked to the belief that she was making art without making decisions about what she was doing. Early examples of the stereotypes imposed on Izquierdo and her art include the essays by the French playwright and poet Antonin Artaud, who believed that she painted by "reaching into the well of her racial unconsciousness."[119] In 1936 he wrote: "Undoubtedly, María Izquierdo is in communication with the true force of the Indian soul. Its drama, which she carries within her, is unaware of its sources." He insisted, "The spirit of the Indian race speaks so strongly in her that, even unconsciously, she repeats its voice."[120] Artaud came to Mexico in search of a "primitive" culture with a magical spirit, so for him this was high praise indeed; however, as art historian Gina Tarver notes, he portrayed Izquierdo "as a passive vessel, an artist who is entirely unaware of her sources of inspiration."[121]

Artaud was one of many critics who failed to perceive Izquierdo's agency in the creative process. In 1938 the Mexican poet Rafael Solana wrote: "This thing of Maria Izquierdo is not painting as a conscious action ruled by will and the intellect; this is to secrete painting, in a natural incontinent way, like crying or bleeding. . . . María's is not painting born of the mind but of flesh."[122] U.S. art historian MacKinley Helm admired Izquierdo's art, which he considered "naïve and primitive"; his estimation of her work, albeit misguided, fit comfortably into his belief that true Mexican art exhibited "primitive," naïve, and indigenous qualities.[123] In a 1988 interview the poet Octavio Paz described Izquierdo's work as "accomplished more by instinct than by intellect." He recalled that she "looked like a pre-Hispanic goddess. A face of sun-dried mud perfumed with copal incense. Highly made up, with . . . lips like red-hot coals, cannibal teeth, wide nostrils to breath in the delicious smoke of supplications and sacrifice."[124] These writers all seem unaware that Izquierdo was a thinking person who made decisions about the style and content of her art.

In addition to art historical texts about the work of Izquierdo and Kahlo, the present study is indebted to the field of gender studies, especially Jean Franco's seminal book *Plotting Women: Gender and Representation in Mexico* (1989). Franco explores Mexican women's struggle for interpretive power in relation to church and state from the colonial era to the postmodern period. Particularly pertinent to this book is her analysis of the construction of national identity as masculine during the postrevolutionary period, women intellectuals' resistance to this construction, and their strategies for asserting their own voices. Most of the women that Franco discusses were writers (the exception is Kahlo), but her analysis of women's struggle for interpretive power clearly transcends vocational labels and disciplinary boundaries. Manuel Castells's *The Power of Identity* influenced my conclusion in chapter 9. Castells insists on the variety of feminism*s* and argues that their essence is the rejection of patriarchal definitions of female identity and the (re)definition of women's identity by women.[125] Although I have only cited Castells in chapter 9, his ideas are relevant to the entire book. Izquierdo and Kahlo employed diverse strategies, including some that implied essentialized views of women and others that did not. Regardless of their tactics, the two artists consistently created their own identities.

The "Self-Taught" Label

Several authors, including ones who are otherwise insightful, have referred to Kahlo and Izquierdo as self-taught artists. Because Kahlo never attended art school, the "self-taught" label is technically correct but misleading. Kahlo was the daughter of a highly accomplished photographer and the wife of the most famous painter in Mexico. As a teenager she briefly took classes in printmaking from Fernando Fernández, and her father taught her to use a large-format camera, develop prints, and retouch photographs.[126] She was a student at the prestigious Escuela Nacional Preparatoria during the years when the first Mexican murals were painted there, so she personally witnessed the birth of Mexican muralism.[127]

Many versions exist of the story of how Kahlo and Rivera met a few years later. Herrera remarks that "there seem to be as many different versions as there are tellers, and Frida herself remembered the meeting in different ways at different times."[128] Although the couple probably actually met at a party at Tina Modotti's home,[129] the official story begins with Kahlo bringing a few of her first paintings to the Secretaría de Educación Pública, where Rivera was painting frescoes and demanding that he come down from the scaffolding to talk to her. Kahlo later recalled that she said: "Look, I have not come to flirt or anything even if you are a woman-chaser. I have come to show you my painting. If you are interested in it, tell me so, if not, likewise, so that I will go to work at something else to help my parents."[130] He replied that he was indeed interested, "above all in this portrait of you, which is the most original. The other three seem to be influenced by what you have seen. Go home, paint a painting, and next Sunday I will come and see it and tell you what I think."[131]

In 1953 Kahlo told Raquel Tibol a different story: "I felt a tremendous desire to paint in fresco. I showed Diego the works I had done and he said to me: 'Your will has to lead you to your own expression.' Then I began to paint things that he liked. From then on he admires me, he loves me."[132]

In his autobiography, Rivera recalled that before Kahlo showed him her work she said: "I have not come to you looking for compliments. I want the criticism of a serious man. I am neither an art lover nor an amateur. I'm simply a girl who must work for her living." She then asked if he believed that she should continue to paint or find some other work. After looking at her paintings, he said, "In my opinion, no matter how difficult it is for you, you must continue to paint."[133] Kahlo's and Rivera's many accounts of their first meeting testify to the degree to which the couple built their relationship around making art.

Hayden Herrera notes that Rivera became Kahlo's mentor, rather than her teacher in the usual sense; he fostered her unique talents as she watched, listened, and learned from him.[134] In 1950 Kahlo told a journalist: "Diego showed me the revolutionary sense of life and the true sense of color."[135] The following year she told another journalist: "Diego is the only one who has taught me about painting without ever placing ideas in my head or telling me what I should or should not do."[136] This statement, while largely true, excludes Rivera's lack of support for her early fascination with fresco. Except for discouraging her from pursuing fresco, he encouraged Kahlo as an artist throughout her life and was responsible for the creation of the Museo Frida Kahlo after her death.

The Riveras knew all of the most interesting artists and intellectuals in Mexico as well as many of the most innovative and influential artists and writers in Europe and the United States. Social gatherings in the *casa azul*, house guests at their homes, visits to museums and galleries, and travels to San Francisco, Detroit, New York, and Paris contributed to Kahlo's unconventional yet relevant and current art education.

The "self-taught" label is even less appropriate for Izquierdo, who became a student at the preeminent art academy in Mexico, the Escuela Nacional de Bellas Artes (National School of Fine Arts) in January 1928. In April 1929 Rivera became director of the art school. He intended to convert the prestigious but old-fashioned academy into a modern, experimental art school for worker-artists. When he reviewed an exhibition of student work, he declared the three canvases signed by M. Izquierdo to be the only interesting student work being done at the academy. Rivera did not know who painted these works, presumed that M. Izquierdo was male, and expressed surprise when he learned that the artist was female.

Rivera's admiration of Izquierdo's paintings led to her first solo exhibition in November 1929, at the Galería de Arte Moderno (Gallery of Modern Art) in the Teatro Nacional (National Theater), the building later renamed Palacio de Bellas Artes. For this exhibition he wrote an essay appropriate for a talented emerging artist.[137] It also led to an abrupt end to Izquierdo's studies at the art academy. Her fellow students did not understand why she had been singled out as the only student with talent and were bitterly envious. As Izquierdo later told the story, Rivera promised to give a series of lectures explaining modern art and the merits of her work. He devoted the first lecture to explaining the differences between academic art and modern art; in the second lecture he spoke about the three paintings by Izquierdo. After the second lecture, a gang of students threw things at her and dumped buckets of cold water on her. She abruptly ended her studies at the academy in June 1929.[138] Rivera was forced to resign as director of the art school in May 1930.[139]

Before leaving art school, Izquierdo had formed a close relationship with Rufino Tamayo, with whom she shared a studio from 1929 to 1933. Tamayo was only three years older than Izquierdo but had begun studying at the art academy at the age of fifteen, had lived in New York from 1926 to 1928, and was already teaching drawing at the Escuela Nacional de Bellas Artes when they met. During this period, their work is remarkably similar in style and themes. Some of their still-life paintings employ the same props and may have been painted at the same time from different viewpoints. Conventional wisdom argues that Tamayo, the more established artist, influenced her. Fernando Gamboa, who at various times in his life was a painter, curator, museum director, and promoter of art and who knew Tamayo and Izquierdo when they were a couple, concurs with this view:

> I believe the advice that Tamayo would have given her . . . was very fruitful for María Izquierdo's art. The relation of teacher–student for four years of disciplined work . . . had a very positive result. There are those who say that it was the reverse, that María taught and influenced Tamayo, which is absurd, because by then Tamayo was already a real painter.[140]

Gallery director Inés Amor argued that in fact Izquierdo influenced Tamayo in ways that were decisive and enduring. According to Amor, Izquierdo taught Tamayo how to use the type of color for which he became famous:

> María Izquierdo, absolutely indigenous, with the innate sense of color of her race . . . began to teach Tamayo a different language and a different way of painting. The drawing was simple, the composition the simplest possible, the color taken at random from the ocher and sienna earths of the Mexican landscape, with the festive greens and blues of the small village houses. The texture: what can be said of the texture! María painted with her Indian blood in the tip of the brush and it was from there that Tamayo emerged, surpassing all his colleagues and making every step of his painting the glory of good art.[141]

This quotation is another example of someone linking Izquierdo's artistic abilities to her ethnicity, but it is also an extraordinarily strong statement about Izquierdo's influence on Tamayo. It comes from the most powerful and discerning gallery director in Mexico, who represented the work of both artists in her gallery and was not a close friend of Izquierdo. In fact, Izquierdo had been publicly critical of Amor on numerous occasions, and Amor was aware of the criticism.[142]

Although no one can know exactly what happened in Tamayo and Izquierdo's shared studio, it seems highly probable that a lively interchange about formal issues and the process of making art benefited both artists. Tamayo surely contributed to Izquierdo's knowledge about art and literature in several ways. Because he had lived in New York from 1926 to 1928, he could have provided her with extensive up-to-date information about current U.S. and European art movements. It was also probably through him that she became friends with the writers associated with the journal *Contemporáneos*. In 1930 she traveled with Tamayo to New York, and he undoubtedly helped her arrange her solo exhibition at the Art Center in New York, where he had previously exhibited.[143]

Many years later Izquierdo traveled on her own as an ambassador of Mexican art to Peru and Chile, where she held a series of exhibitions of her paintings. In Chile she reunited with and married her last husband, the Chilean-born painter Raúl Uribe, in 1944.

From the nineteenth century through the postrevolutionary period, the vast majority of leading Mexican artists were trained at the prestigious art academy in Mexico City. The academy, which was officially founded in 1781, changed names many times. It was best known as the Academia de San Carlos (Academy of San Carlos) but had been renamed the Escuela Nacional de Bellas Artes before Izquierdo studied there. At the academy students usually underwent a rigorous twelve-year program. Studies there were frequently followed by extensive travel and study in Europe, often supported by a government stipend.

Neither Kahlo nor Izquierdo had all the advantages that the most talented male painters received: Kahlo never went to art school, Izquierdo never traveled to Europe. Nevertheless, calling them "self-taught" is misleading for both artists. The term implies an outsider relegated to the periphery who creates naïve or "primitive" art and may know little about art history and less about contemporary art. Izquierdo and Kahlo were smart, urban, cosmopolitan people, who traveled widely, participated in the stimulating artistic and intellectual circles of Mexico, and were informed about international art movements. This is a crucial point: at the heart of this book is the assertion that Izquierdo and Kahlo intentionally made choices about the representation of themselves and other women that responded to the artistic and nationalist discourses of modern Mexico and that they employed their art to establish a more powerful role for women. The following chapters examine how they achieved this goal.

The Representation of Gender and National Identity in the Work of Izquierdo and Kahlo

This book examines the strategies that Izquierdo and Kahlo used to affirm the parts of artistic and nationalistic discourses that they supported and to contest those that they opposed. Both artists employed a variety of tactics to create work that empowered women in general and themselves in particular. This study is organized around five core issues presented in five parts. The five sections address (1) how Izquierdo and Kahlo counterbalanced the prevalence of male heroes in Mexican art with images representing strong women, (2) the use of older, indigenous traditions to legitimate female power, (3) Izquierdo's failed attempt to paint a mural in a prestigious government building, (4) selected themes that Izquierdo and Kahlo developed within the seemingly innocent genre of still-life painting, and (5) what is known and not known about Kahlo's and Izquierdo's views about women's rights. Each part of the book contains from one to three chapters. Each chapter except for the last is devoted to either an individual painting or a corpus of closely related images created by one of the artists.

Part one (The Problem of the Hero) examines how Izquierdo and Kahlo responded to the pervasive images of male heroes in Mexican art, especially in the work of the muralists. Both women eschewed representing male heroes, repeatedly created images of female protagonists, and found ways to empower their images of women. Chapter 1, "Women on the Wire," discusses Izquierdo's extensive series of circus scenes. Most of these works represent female performers who walk tightropes, fly from one trapeze to another, or balance *en pointe* atop galloping horses. These acts call attention to the women's daring, bravery, skill, and balance. Chapter 2, "Saints and Goddesses," shows how Kahlo responded to the hero problem by creating self-portraits that draw on Catholic and Precolumbian symbolism to endow her own image with the spiritual power of a goddess or a saint. The chapter also demonstrates how she turned traditional religious symbols into a secular, personal language.

Part two (Legitimating Traditions) contains three chapters that explore the ways in which Izquierdo and Kahlo contested the construction of national identity as masculine by invoking older Mexican traditions that were not gendered as male, were less gendered, or were potentially gendered as female. Chapter 3, "Revitalizing the Past," discusses Kahlo's representations of ancient West Mexican artifacts in six paintings: four self-portraits, one still life, and a recently recovered work that does not fit within traditional genre categories. In each case Kahlo retained some of the artifact's ancient meaning, while using it in a way that relates to her life and personal philosophy or, in the case of the newly recovered painting, to national politics.

Chapter 4, "Beyond the Personal," analyzes one painting, Kahlo's *La niña, la luna y el sol* of 1942. In this work Kahlo portrays a twentieth-century adolescent indigenous girl in front of the Pyramids of the Sun and Moon at Teotihuacan. The girl, who holds a model airplane in her hands, is seated at the crossroads of Mexico's past and future. This chapter traces the subtle references in the painting to the Aztec creation myth of the Fifth Sun (our era) and discusses Kahlo's positioning of a female, indigenous, and poor adolescent as the heir to the future.

In the early 1940s Izquierdo created ten paintings that represent a *coscomate*, an indigenous granary for storing corn. Chapter 5, "Mother of the Maize," explores how she used images of granaries to link women, abundance, land, and Mexico, thus overriding the twentieth-century construction of Mexico as *patria* in favor of more ancient views of the earth's gender.

Part three (The Wall of Resistance) contains one chapter about Izquierdo's attempt to paint a mural in a prestigious government building on the Zócalo, the central plaza at the heart of Mexico City. From the inception of the muralist movement in 1922 until at least the late 1950s, muralism was unflaggingly proclaimed as the pinnacle of artistic achievement and was dominated by three male artists. Women were largely excluded from the movement. While a few women managed to paint murals individually or as part of a group in relatively low-status locations, no woman was able to obtain and complete a major mural commission in an important public building in the capital during the years when muralism reigned. In 1945 Izquierdo signed a contract to paint frescos about "The History and Development of Mexico City" in the building of the Departamento del Distrito Federal (Department of the Federal District) located on the Zócalo. Although she had a legal contract, Rivera and Siqueiros prevented her from executing the murals. When she fought to keep the commission, a major scandal erupted. Chapter 6, "What Sex Is the City?," analyzes the complex issues surrounding her loss of the commission and how the controversy was affected by the power inherent in the location, artistic rivalry, and Izquierdo's plan to depict women as the dominant figures.

Part four (Still-Life Paintings) examines the strategies that Kahlo and Izquierdo used to transform the seemingly innocuous genre of still-life painting into a viable space for expressing their thoughts on everything from eroticism to national identity. Both artists dedicated significant portions of their oeuvres to still-life painting at a time and place in which the genre possessed a rich and distinct national heritage, but its status was at its nadir. The muralists had effectively reasserted the hierarchies of the Renaissance, in which history painting reigned and still-life painting lacked status. Chapter 7, "*Picantes pero sabrosas*" (Hot But Full of Flavor), shows how Kahlo took what seemed like a ladylike art form and stood it on its head.

Chapter 8, "Grain of Memory," examines how Izquierdo's images of home altars to the Virgin of Sorrows mix gender issues and *mexicanidad.* In the 1940s Izquierdo created a series of paintings that represent ephemeral domestic altars to the Dolorosa. This type of altar is traditionally made on Viernes de Dolores, the sixth Friday of Lent. While the altars are a prelude to Holy Week, they are also tied to the agricultural cycle of central Mexico.

Part five (Women's Rights in Modern Mexico) consists solely of chapter 9, "Beyond the Canvas." It documents what Kahlo and Izquierdo said, wrote, or did beyond their work as artists in relation to women's rights. Some people consider Kahlo a feminist heroine; however, other than the images she painted, scant evidence survives to indicate that she participated in the movement for female emancipation in Mexico. Izquierdo avoided being labeled a feminist, but she spoke and wrote in favor of greater rights for women over a period of almost twenty years. Some of what she said is uncomfortably timid and obliging by the standards of feminism in the twentieth-first century; on numerous other occasions she wrote clearly and assertively about the problems facing women, especially women artists. While I (and presumably many other feminists) would have preferred that she had claimed the feminist label and been consistently firm in expressing her convictions, what she wrote is more revealing about the real situation that women faced in Mexico from 1930 to the mid-1950s. Her writings expose the difficulties of trying to be persuasive in a context where even women's right to work was considered controversial by many.

PART ONE

The Problem of the Hero

In terms of women's emancipation, the Mexican Revolution and the years that followed were "a study in contradictions."[1] In the closing years of the Mexican Revolution and the beginning of the postrevolutionary period, women made modest political gains. President Venustiano Carranza's Law of Family Relations of 1917 granted married women the right to draw up contracts, participate in legal suits, and act as guardians. These rights were implemented in the Federal District (roughly equivalent to Mexico City) in 1927, when single women were also permitted to leave their parental home at the same age as men. Married women still needed their husband's permission to work outside the home. Mexican women did not obtain the right to vote in presidential elections until 1953.

After the revolution, women were urged to resume or continue their traditional roles within the home. As Adriana Zavala notes, "while Mexican society undoubtedly changed as a result of the decade-long revolution, what emerged as the gendered and raced social and symbolic order was in some ways a new version of the nineteenth-century dominant order, dressed up, so to speak, in revolutionary and *indigenista* clothing."[2] In *Plotting Women*, Jean Franco asserts that the revolution's promise of social transformation promoted a fervent belief in the transformation of mere mortals into supermen, encouraged a discourse that associated virility with social transformation, and marginalized women at just the time when they were supposed to be liberated.[3] Franco is discussing national discourse in general, not writing specifically about visual art, but the canonical images of Mexican muralism bear witness to her assertions. The image of the male hero is one of the principal tropes of modern Mexican art, especially in muralism.

Mexican muralism is history painting on a grand scale. The muralists made history palpable, personal, and pertinent through dynamic portrayals of heroes: Quetzalcoatl, the Feathered Serpent, patron of learning, the arts, and the priesthood, whose identity was often conflated with that of a tenth-century king of Tula; Cuauhtemoc, the last and bravest Aztec emperor, who stoically resisted the torture of the Spanish conquistadors; Miguel Hidalgo, the parish priest who instigated Mexican Independence with his *grito de independencia* (cry of independence), which exhorted his disenfranchised parishioners to rise against the Spanish; and Emiliano Zapata, the dashing leader of the Mexican Revolution who fought for the peasants' right to own land. The hero could be a god, a king, a general, or a common man who fought for a noble cause. The muralists also represented international leaders and, occasionally, ancient deities of other cultures: Rivera portrayed the Communist revolutionary Lenin in *Man at the Crossroads*, while Orozco extolled the Greek god Prometheus in his mural at Pomona College. Considerable variety existed in the social origins of heroes, but those chosen for apotheosis were virtually always male.

While it is possible to find an occasional image of a historical female hero in Mexican muralism, such images are extremely rare; in order to find an example, it is necessary to look beyond the work created by Orozco, Rivera, and Siqueiros in Mexico City during the postrevolutionary period as it is strictly defined (1920–1940).

In general, postrevolutionary Mexican art communicates clearly prescribed gender roles: men fought, governed, and changed the world, while women supported them as mothers, wives, teachers, and helpers. In murals, easel paintings, and prints, women are repeatedly assigned secondary roles.

Intelligent women artists could not have failed to notice the relentless messages about gender imbedded in Mexican art and visual culture. Izquierdo and Kahlo negotiated female identity in relation to national and artistic discourses, affirming some aspects and disputing others in their imagery. While both artists occasionally portrayed men, they primarily represented women in ways that reinvent and resignify female identity. The visual rhetoric of male heroes is a major point of contention for both artists. Chapters 1 and 2 examine trajectories in the oeuvres of Izquierdo and Kahlo that directly address the problem of the rampant idealization of male heroes and the need, from the perspective of these two artists, to endow women with active, starring roles. Izquierdo created over fifty paintings of the circus in which women demonstrate their courage, skill, and strength; chapter 1 discusses these works. Kahlo appropriated religious iconography in ways that empower her own self-portraits while at the same time ironically undermining the authority of religion; chapter 2 examines how she achieved this.

1

Women on the Wire

Izquierdo's Images of Circus Performers

María Izquierdo's depictions of female circus performers bear witness to the women's daring, bravery, physical skill, and strength. Women dressed as ballerinas stand on one leg atop galloping horses, intrepid tightrope walkers traverse high wires, trapeze artists fly through the air, and animal trainers command lions and elephants. In *Amazona malabarista* (Juggling Horsewoman) of 1939, a woman juggles three balls while standing on a horse that is leaping over a log, thereby emphasizing her skill and control of the animal. In *Zenaida, la domadora de leones* (Zenaida, the Lion Tamer) of 1945 the female animal trainer subdues a ferocious lion by showing him his reflection in a mirror.

Izquierdo's images of female circus performers testify to the women's extraordinary balance, their power to tame wild beasts, their courage, and their ability to command the attention of the audience. These assets do not match conventional ideas of the time about the qualities of Mexican womanhood, whose virtues were stereotypically thought to include their self-sacrificing, submissive, maternal, modest, and pure nature. In fact, daring, bravery, skill, and strength were qualities typically ascribed to male leaders. These are precisely the qualities emphasized in innumerable representations of male heroes in Mexican murals: José Clemente Orozco's tributes to Prometheus and Quetzalcoatl, Diego Rivera's homages to Emiliano Zapata and Vladimir Lenin, and David Alfaro Siqueiros's visions of Cuauhtemoc and himself as the coronelazo. The paintings of the muralists with their countless images of male heroes promoted a virile image of the nation. As critic Jean Franco notes, national identity was essentially masculine identity in postrevolutionary Mexico.[1] Izquierdo's images of female circus performers insist that women can be strong, brave, and skillful, too. Her portrayals of women gracefully performing dangerous and physically challenging acts provide a counterpart to the muralists' innumerable depictions of male heroes; thus her images can be understood as an attempt to negotiate a more central, assertive role for women in the artistic discourse of Mexico.

Izquierdo's images of circuses are customarily watercolor or gouache, small (the horizontal works, for example, range from under eleven inches to twenty-four inches in width), and usually represent a performance taking place within a tent, although the tent is seldom depicted.[2] The earliest paintings typically represent one or two figures or a single figure with an animal. Characteristic of this period are *L'écuyère* (Horsewoman) of 1934 (fig. 8), presenting a woman in a tutu commanding a chestnut horse, and *Bailarina ecuestre* (Horseback Dancer) of 1932 (plate 1), showing the back of a female rider balancing on one leg atop a white horse. In 1939 she began to portray small groups: two standing riders jumping a hurdle in tandem (fig. 9), three jugglers performing, four trapeze artists flying through the air, or a lion tamer coaxing four lions onto a platform. She also changed her use of color and brushstrokes at about this time. Prior to 1939 she used a low-key palette dominated by red but otherwise earthy and fairly neutral. By 1940 she employed lighter, brighter colors. Her earlier paintings are looser and more painterly than her later work. These shifts in her treatment of color, value, and brushwork are true for all her work.

Izquierdo's depictions of individual performers are usually female; scenes that portray more than one performer almost always include at least one woman and are often dominated by women. Several paintings feature female ropewalkers. *En el circo* (At the

Fig. 8. María Izquierdo, *L'écuyère* (Horsewoman), 1934, gouache and watercolor on paper, 11 × 8 ½ inches (28 × 21.5 cm.), private collection, photograph by Francisco Kochen. Reproduced with the permission of María Rosenda López Posadas, legal representative of the intellectual property of María Izquierdo. Reproduction authorized by the Instituto Nacional de Bellas Artes y Literatura, 2015.

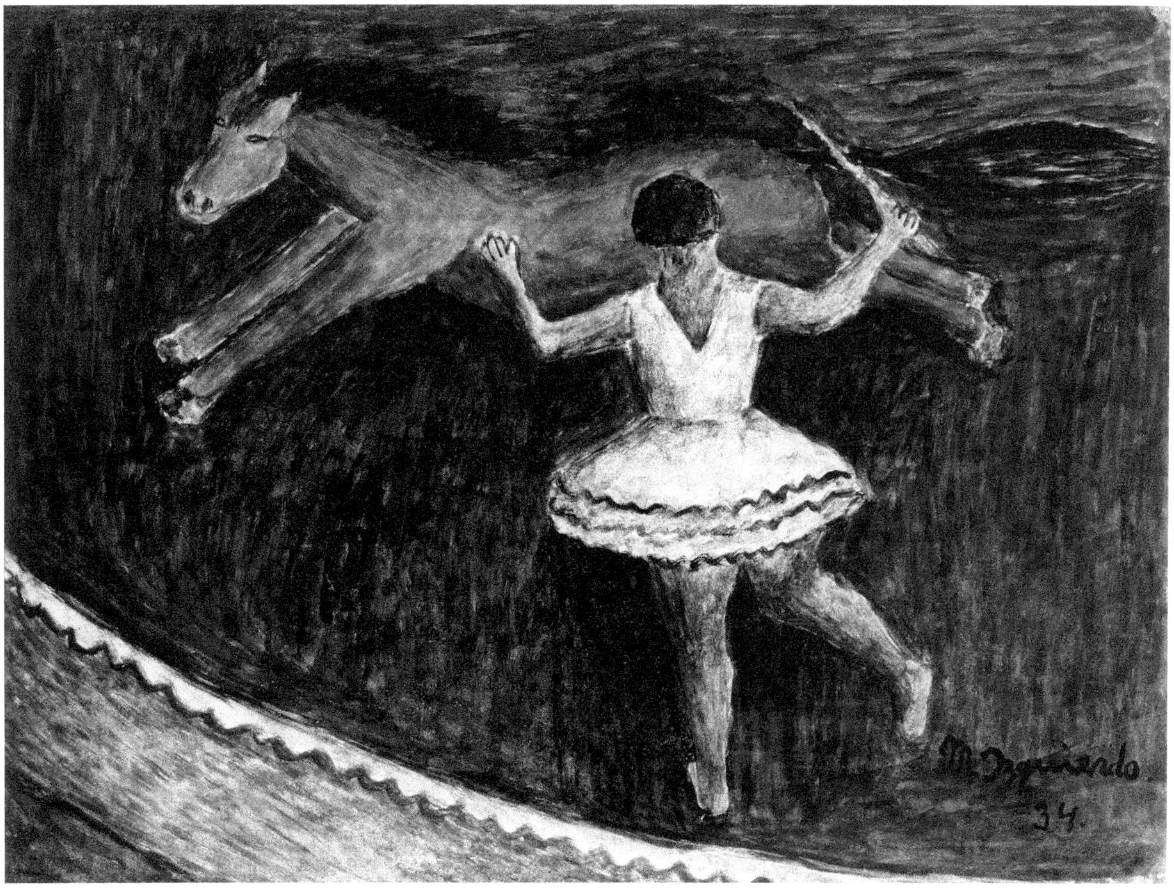

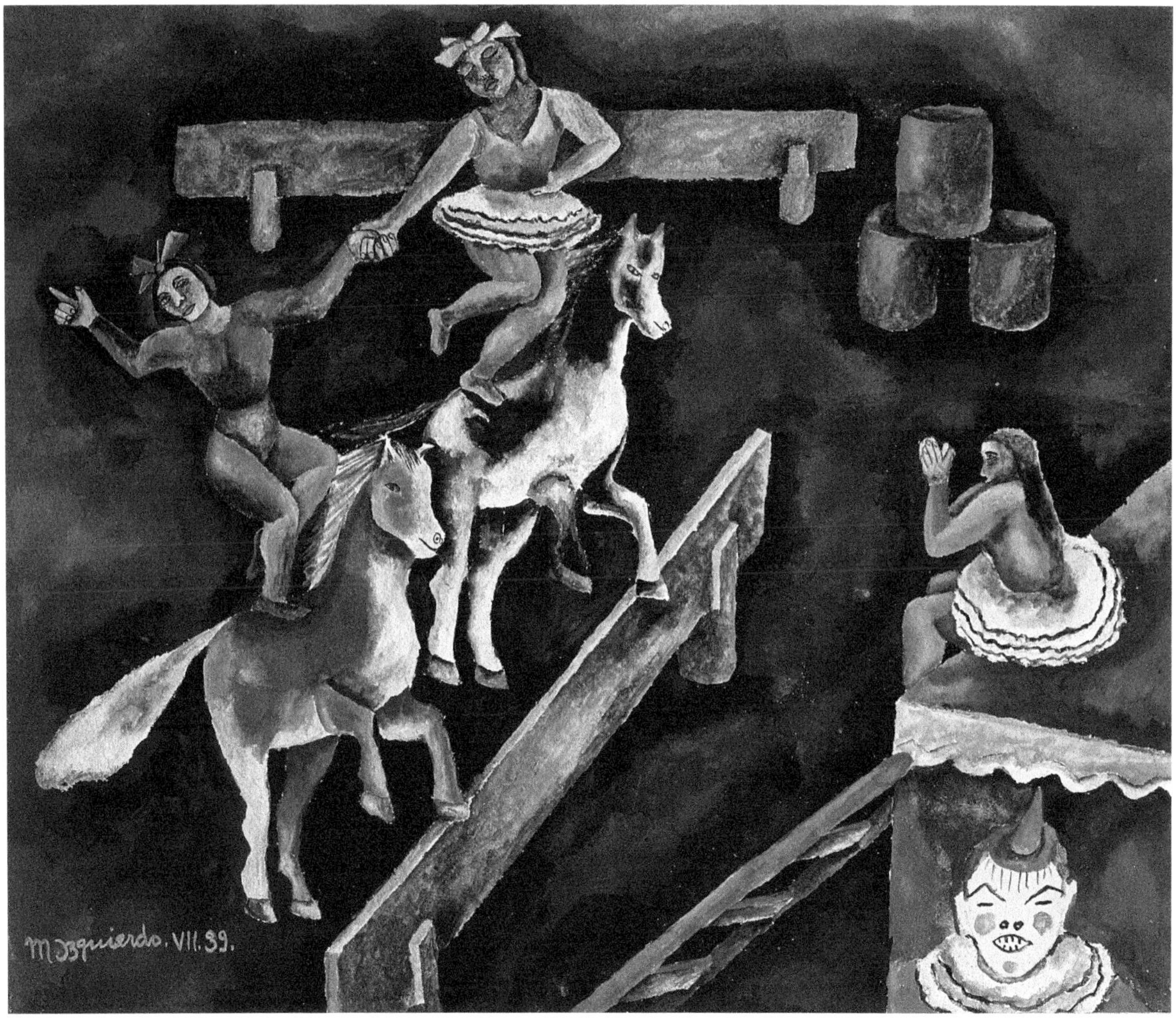

Fig. 9. María Izquierdo, *Les écuyères* (The Equestriennes), 1939, gouache on paper, 16 ⅛ × 24 inches (41 × 61 cm), collection of Mariana Pérez Amor. Photograph by Francisco Kochen. Reproduced with the permission of María Rosenda López Posadas, legal representative of the intellectual property of María Izquierdo.

Circus) of 1939 represents part of the audience as well as the performers, an unusual feature in her work (fig. 10). In the foreground, at the edge of a circus ring, a small group of spectators with their backs to the viewer enthusiastically applauds a high-wire act. The shallow space of the painting creates the illusion that the act is taking place almost directly above the spectators. The two rope walkers are small in proportion to the people in the audience and seem isolated in the empty space at the top of the tent. The rope is slack, its curve echoes that of the circus ring, and its lack of tautness signals increased danger for the performers.[3] The female performer to the left, in a pink leotard and a white tutu, stretches out both arms for balance as she steps gingerly along the wire. The sex of the second performer, who wears a lavender leotard and tights and yellow shorts, is less certain. She (or he) holds up a rose umbrella for balance while kneeling on one knee to take a bow at the center of the sagging rope. The majority of the performers in Izquierdo's paintings are clearly either female or male; however, the sex of several figures is unclear because the body type and costume are ambiguous or because the performer's body is partially hidden by other elements of the composition.[4] Regardless of the sex of the performers, Izquierdo represents their bodies as strong and healthy but without exaggerated musculature: they do not resemble the frail harlequins of Picasso's Rose Period or the Michelangeloesque physiques of Siqueiros's heroes.

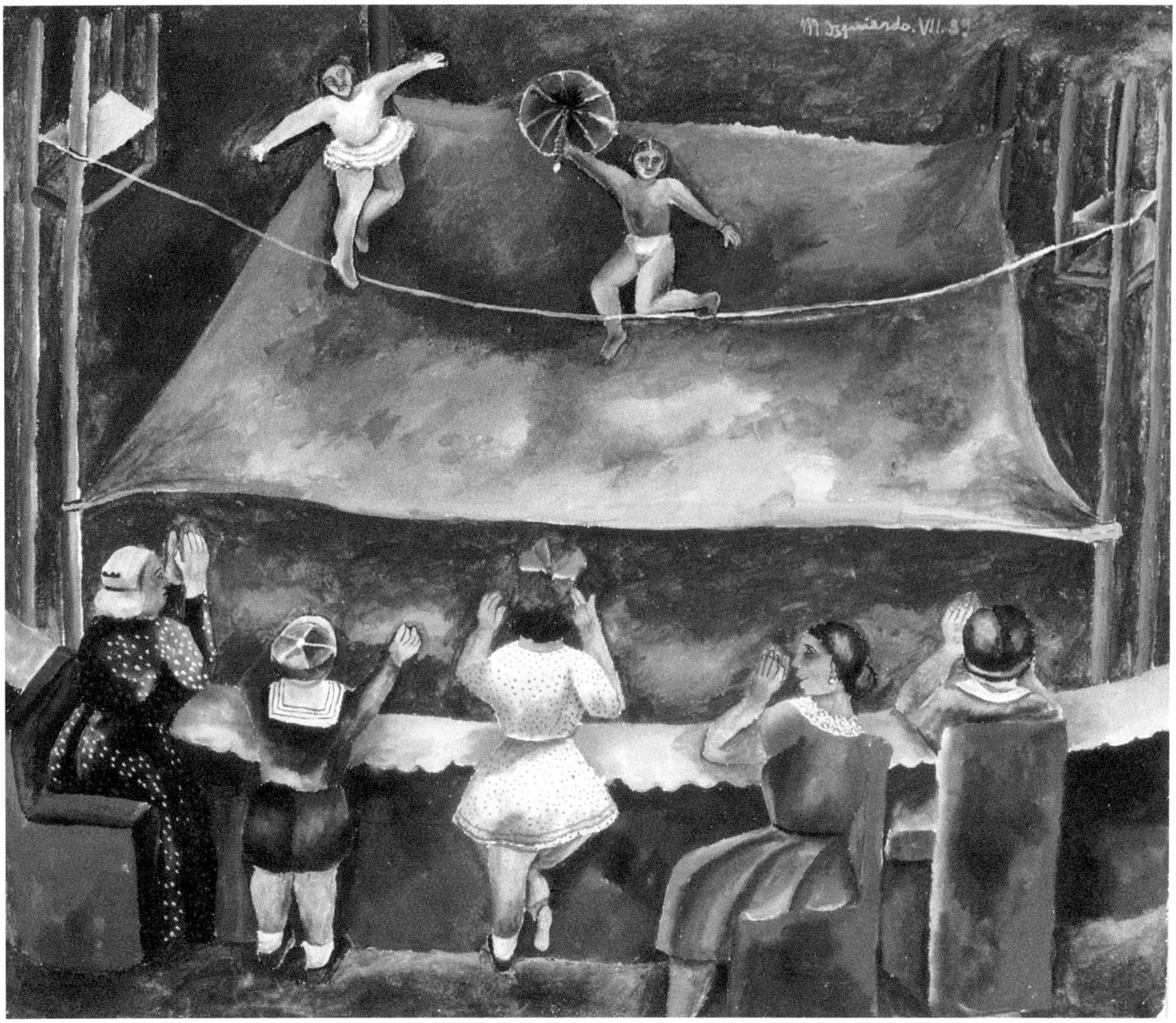

Fig. 10. María Izquierdo, *En el circo* (At the Circus), 1939, watercolor and tempera on paper, 16 ⅛ × 19 ¹⁄₁₆ inches (41.5 × 50 cm), private collection, USA. Photograph courtesy of Mary-Anne Martin Fine Art, New York. Reproduced with the permission of María Rosenda López Posadas, legal representative of the intellectual property of María Izquierdo. Reproduction authorized by the Instituto Nacional de Bellas Artes y Literatura, 2015.

In addition to depicting circus artists performing, Izquierdo occasionally represented the members of the circus troupe behind the scenes: women preparing for the show in a dressing room and acrobats rehearsing by a circus wagon.[5] Circus animals—horses, lions, elephants, zebras, bears, and dogs—play major roles in the paintings. The most important is the horse, which appears in numerous circus paintings and other works by Izquierdo.

Review of the Literature

In his 1988 essay "María Izquierdo," Olivier Debroise provided an overview of the artist's life and work, in which he linked her love of the circus to happy memories of her childhood and the annual fair in her hometown, San Juan de los Lagos, Jalisco. As an adult she frequented the small circuses on the outskirts of the Mexico City. Debroise argued that these paintings are not exclusively Mexican, although many people would like to see Mexican elements in her circus images. Rather, they are the opposite of the nostalgic rediscovery of peasant culture that marks Mexico's official nationalism.[6]

In 2006 Adriana Zavala wrote a short essay about a 1932 painting of a female bareback rider in the collection of the Blanton Museum at the University of Texas at Austin in which she links Izquierdo's depictions of the circus to religious beliefs related to San

Juan de los Lagos. Izquierdo's hometown was (and still is) a pilgrimage destination for devotees of the Virgin of San Juan de los Lagos, a small, corn-paste statue enshrined in the basilica. Zavala explains that the first miracle attributed to the statue involved circus performers: "According to legend, in 1623 the image of the Virgin resuscitated the young daughter of a knife-thrower, mortally wounded during a performance."[7] Zavala observes that Izquierdo would have been familiar with the legend.

In a chapter in *The Many Worlds of the Circus* (2007), María de Jesus González and Lucelley Gallegos establish a link between gender issues and the central role of women in Izquierdo's circus paintings. They argue that in order to understand these paintings it is necessary to consider the status of women in Mexico during her life:

> The proscribed role of women at this time dictated that she be submissive, abnegated, completely dedicated to her family, and dependent on her husband. A female circus performer did not fit the mold of the traditional woman. Female circus performers were working women who made their living by their talents. . . . Izquierdo found a kindred spirit with these women and could relate her own life to that of a female circus performer.[8]

González and Gallegos contend that "Izquierdo's representation of female circus performers reveals, and parallels, the notion of the 'modernized' woman in the circus as well as in society in general." They conclude that Izquierdo, as a woman in a male-dominated society and art world, "took it upon herself to present scenes of independent women like herself creating an art that was an alternative to the masculine, political art of her day."[9]

González and Gallegos's assertion that these representations must be considered within their social context and in relation to the traditional role of women in postrevolutionary Mexico is fundamental. Especially important is their observation that she presented images of women that provided an alternative to the virile political art of the time."[10]

The goals of this chapter include amplifying the discussion of the relationship of Izquierdo's circus paintings to the traditions of San Juan de los Lagos and delving deeper into the ways in which the images construct alternate views of gender. I add to the documentation about Izquierdo's personal knowledge of the circus, explore the multiple sources of the theme of the circus, document the exhibition history of these works, and establish that she used the theme in ways that are unique to her. The principal assertion of this chapter is that Izquierdo created scenes in which female circus artists demonstrate their strength, bravery, daring, and skill and that these images question and counterbalance the pervasive presence of male heroes in postrevolutionary Mexican art.

Izquierdo's Personal Connections to the Circus

Izquierdo's family and friends testify to her keen interest in the circus. Her younger daughter, Aurora Posadas Izquierdo, remembered that her mother sometimes went to see the performers in the morning when they were rehearsing: "She made friends with the dancers, with the clowns, with the jugglers, with the acrobats who performed tricks too, she made friends with everyone."[11] Izquierdo's close friend the photographer Lola Álvarez Bravo recalled:

> She liked everything of the people, what was truly Mexican: the [music halls in] tents, the songs, the fairs, the trees, the fruits, the bars, the [forgotten] corners of the towns, the circuses that make up her paintings, that are very naïve, and she was nurtured by themes of the earth.

> . . . The pleasure that María got from the people was not that of the spectator; rather she almost seemed to be inside, like one more popular element: she didn't just like the itinerant music halls, but had lots of friends who were performers and touring singers.[12]

Art historians have affirmed that Izquierdo's personal involvement in the circus distinguishes her work from that of the most famous European artists who have depicted the circus. Olivier Debroise noted that Izquierdo had close friendships with circus performers and comics from the theater. Debroise insisted that the presence of circus performers in Izquierdo's work "is not casual or folkloric, as in the cases of Seurat or Degas, who visited circuses or dance studios for the sole purpose of painting them. María Izquierdo painted things and beings that were close to her."[13] Debroise also observed that Izquierdo made certain forms of déclassé entertainment—such as the circus and the Bar Leda—fashionable among her intellectual friends. According to Debroise, she frequented the small circuses at the edge of the city, the *carpas* (music halls in tents) in the working-class neighborhood of Guerrero and the old barrio of Tepito, and seedy cabarets like the Bar Leda.[14]

Izquierdo's unpublished memoirs imply, as Debroise and González have convincingly argued, that her images of circuses draw on her childhood memories of provincial circuses and horse fairs in San Juan de los Lagos, where she was born and spent her early childhood.[15] According to María Izquierdo, her first memory was being kidnapped at the age of two by a group of itinerant circus performers, who had set up their tent in San Juan de los Lagos. She recalled that for twenty-four hours she lived "the bohemian and magic world of the circus people in their most intimate aspect."[16] Several accounts of the kidnapping exist. Izquierdo's younger daughter stated that her mother disappeared for three days and was found by her grandfather, who spotted his granddaughter's legs dangling out of a circus wagon that was on the point of departing.[17] Artist Joseph Raskob told a more fanciful story: "When María was only two and half years old, she was stolen by the gypsies and forced to wander with them throughout the country. During her six months stay with them, she was trained as a dancer in the gypsy circus. She excelled in the Spanish Jota. The trained animals became her friends."[18]

Some—and perhaps all—versions of the story may be apocryphal, which in no way diminishes its significance. Many artists have told tales of their early childhood that may not be literally true but nonetheless express their deepest values and communicate how they wish to be perceived. For example, according to Diego Rivera, when he was two he was thin and had rickets. To improve his health his parents sent him to live with his indigenous nurse Antonia in the mountains of the Sierra. Antonia allowed him to roam freely in the woods in the company of a female goat who provided him with fresh milk.[19] In another famous example of an artist's legendary beginnings, Michelangelo claimed to have been suckled by a wet nurse who was the wife of a stonecutter, implying that he somehow imbibed the essence of stone through his nurse's milk.[20] The artists' accounts of their earliest years all promote myths of authenticity that are linked to their creative production and artistic values.

In addition to Izquierdo's early memories and imaginative stories about the circus, another crucial element links San Juan de los Lagos and her circus paintings. San Juan de los Lagos is a pilgrimage site, a sacred destination for believers who come to pray to the reportedly miraculous Virgin of San Juan de los Lagos. Her first recorded miracle occurred in 1623, when the young daughter of an itinerant circus family—a girl who was perhaps nine or ten years old—slipped while rehearsing somersaults above a carpet of daggers, fell on the blades, and died instantly. She was placed in a chapel prior to burial. An indigenous woman named Anna Lucía, the wife of the sacristan, came to the chapel along with other mourners. Seeing the parents' grief, she went to the sacristy, brought back a small old statue of the Virgin that was stored there, and placed it on the girl's chest. After a while the girl stirred and began to move. When the mourners cut open her shroud, the girl miraculously arose.[21]

Two anonymous untitled paintings in the chapel of the Pocito del Primer Milagro (Little Well of the First Miracle) at San Juan de los Lagos record this event. The undated paintings are from the eighteenth century according to local tradition but were probably created later, perhaps during the late nineteenth century.[22] One painting depicts the accident, while the other shows Anna Lucía placing the statue on the girl's chest as the mourners look on. The first painting depicts a young girl in a blue dress flying through the air (fig. 11). The bar of the trapeze is behind her, rather than in front of her where she could grasp it.[23] Directly below her is a plank spiked with erect knives. On the left, the girl's mother clasps her hands in prayer; another girl, presumably an older sister, throws her arms around the mother's waist. On the right the girl's father, who wears an Elizabethan-style costume, stretches out his right hand in horror, while a small boy clings to his right leg. In the background two other performers and several villagers watch the accident unfold. A plaque below the painting states: "In 1623 a family of circus performers stopped in this place to work, with such bad luck that the little girl fell on the daggers and died instantly."[24]

The chapel of the Pocito del Primer Milagro, which houses the paintings, and the adjacent Capilla del Primer Milagro (Chapel of the First Miracle) are located two blocks from the place where Izquierdo lived as a small child.[25] The proximity to the Izquierdo home and the religious practices of her grandmother and aunt guarantee that Izquierdo was intimately familiar with these paintings. The images of the first miracle would have been among the few paintings that she would have seen in the first years of her life. Their

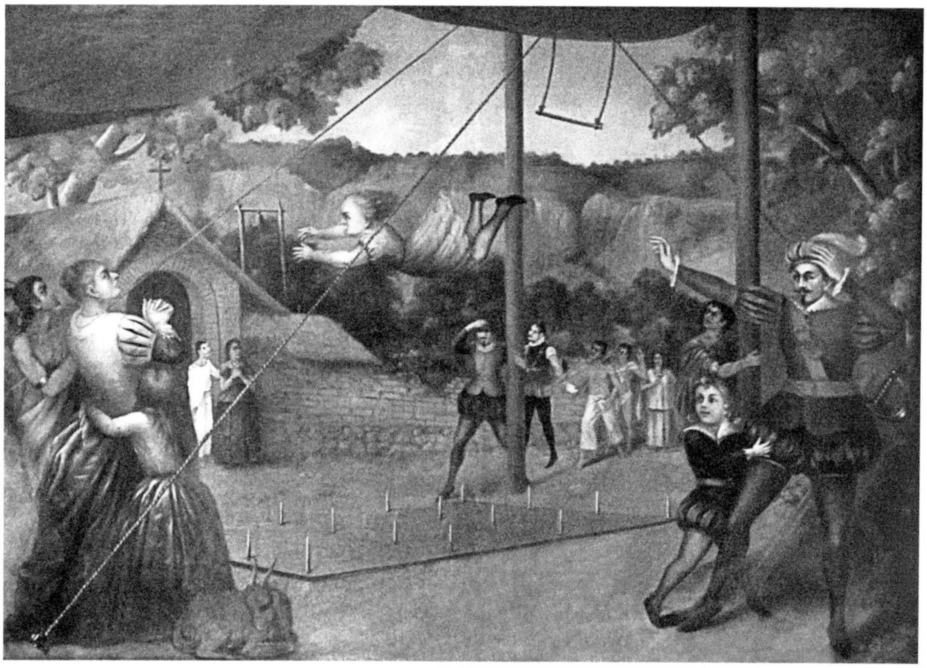

Fig. 11. Anonymous, untitled painting representing the accident that led to the first miracle of the Virgin of San Juan de los Lagos. The painting is located in the chapel of the Pocito del Primer Milagro (Little Well of the First Miracle), San Juan de los Lagos, Jalisco, Mexico. Image in the public domain.

subjects were sure to impress a child who was attracted to art and spectacle. Izquierdo moved away from San Juan de los Lagos when she was approximately six years old. But either consciously or subconsciously she must have remembered the painting of the flying girl in the chapel of the Pocito del Primer Milagro, for this painting is the prototype of Izquierdo's numerous depictions of circus performers.[26]

In Izquierdo's work, images of impending circus accidents are rare. In *Equilibrista* (Rope Walker) of 1932—which is one of Izquierdo's earliest surviving images of the circus—a female performer wearing a white tutu and holding a red and blue umbrella totters atop a slack rope (fig. 12). A man in the foreground, with his back to the viewer, raises his hands in dismay. Clearly the ropewalker will fall, but the relative positioning of the two figures reveals that the wire is not high and implies that the accident will not have tragic consequences. Another painting, *Caballos engalanados* (Decorated Horses) of 1940, known only from a poor-quality newspaper reproduction, also represents an accident about to happen, in this case a fall from a horse.[27] Like *Equilibrista,* the scene suggests a minor accident.

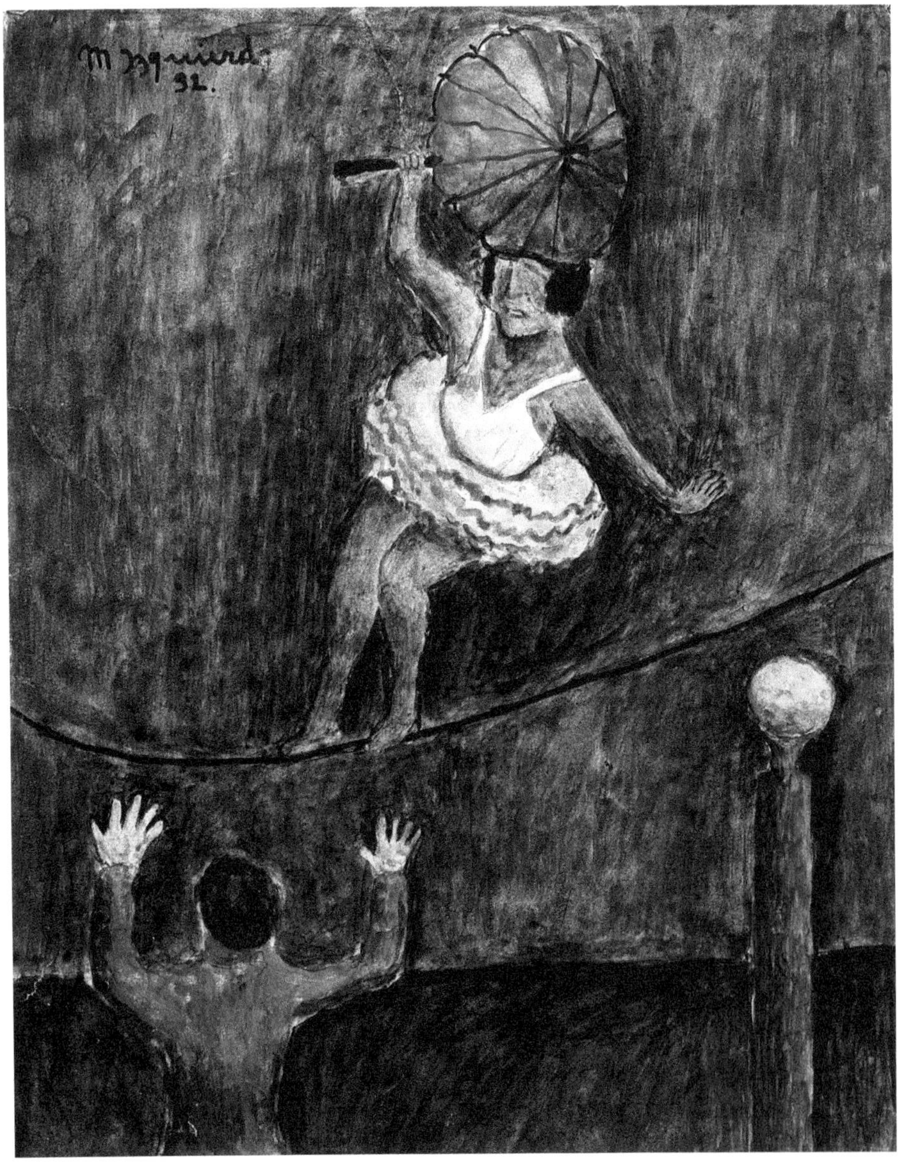

Fig. 12. María Izquierdo, *Equilibrista* (Rope Walker), 1932, watercolor on paper, 10 ⅝ × 8 ¼ inches (27 × 21 cm), collection of the Museo de Arte Moderno de Gómez Palacio, Durango, Mexico, and the Instituto Nacional de Bellas Artes. Photograph by Francisco Kochen. Reproduced with the permission of María Rosenda López Posadas, legal representative of the intellectual property of María Izquierdo. Reproduction authorized by the Instituto Nacional de Bellas Artes y Literatura, 2015.

In Izquierdo's other images of circuses, the circus artists execute their performances with consummate skill. Women wearing tutus stand on one leg atop galloping horses, agile rope walkers cross high wires, trapeze artists fly through the air, and animal trainers command dogs, lions, and elephants to perform tricks. The impending accidents in *Equilibrista* and *Caballos engalanados* and the latent danger in all of the circus paintings emphasize the bravery and prowess of female circus artists.

Izquierdo's Circus Paintings in Context

The art of Europe and Mexico contains countless precedents of circus imagery, but art historians and critics have often exclusively linked Izquierdo's images of the circus with the work of two artists: Rufino Tamayo and Pablo Picasso. At the time when Izquierdo began creating images of circuses, she shared a studio with Rufino Tamayo, who was her lover between 1929 and 1933. When they met, Tamayo was a professor at the Escuela Nacional de Bellas Artes, where she studied. Although they were close in age, he was the more professionally established artist. Mexican curator and museologist Fernando Gamboa noted that Izquierdo absorbed Tamayo's sensibilities and adopted some of his subjects, claiming: "The circus, for example, is a completely Tamayo-like motif."[28] This is a bizarre assertion given that the circus is a minor theme in Tamayo's oeuvre and the dominant theme in Izquierdo's.[29] While no catalogue raisonné of Tamayo's complete oeuvre exists, the catalogue raisonné of his graphic works shows that only 4 of his 357 prints clearly represent circus subjects.[30]

Octavio Paz, who was friends with Izquierdo from 1938 until he left Mexico in 1943, saw European echoes in her work. "Her paintings with a circus motif come from European painting. . . . Picasso had a decisive influence on many [Mexican] painters of that period. . . . In María the influences of modern European painting were filtered through Tamayo's example." Later in the same interview Paz provided a less simplistic account of Izquierdo's sources:

> Circuses . . . are a universal motif, which, in modern art, harks back to Picasso as a precedent and, in poetry, to Apollinaire and Rilke. But the circus is engraved on popular memory; it appears once again in López Velarde—there is an unforgettable line in *Memorias del Circo*: "the widower swinging on the trapeze"—and, of course, in many of Posada's woodcuts. María saw, read, and lived all of that.[31]

Izquierdo would have agreed with Paz that Picasso had a major impact on Mexican art. In 1953 she told the writer Elena Poniatowska: "Yes, I believe there is foreign influence in Mexican painting. I myself very much like painters like Rousseau, Van Gogh, Picasso, and Dalí."[32] Yet Izquierdo consciously avoided closely modeling her work on Picasso's. In 1942 a journalist asked her if she agreed with Diego Rivera's categorization of her as one of the painters who "still suffer from acute 'Picassitis' and 'Miroquiricosia'?" She retorted, "I don't even look at Miró because I don't like his work. Picassitis! . . . Now that you've seen my work, did you run into any skinny harlequins?"[33]

Izquierdo's sources for circus imagery are substantially more diverse than Gamboa and Paz implied. Mexican precedents include not only the prints of José Guadalupe Posada (1852–1913) (fig. 13), but also the work of the earlier printmaker Manuel Manilla (ca. 1830–ca. 1893).[34] In 1924 Edward Weston and Tina Modotti, who were visiting Mexico,

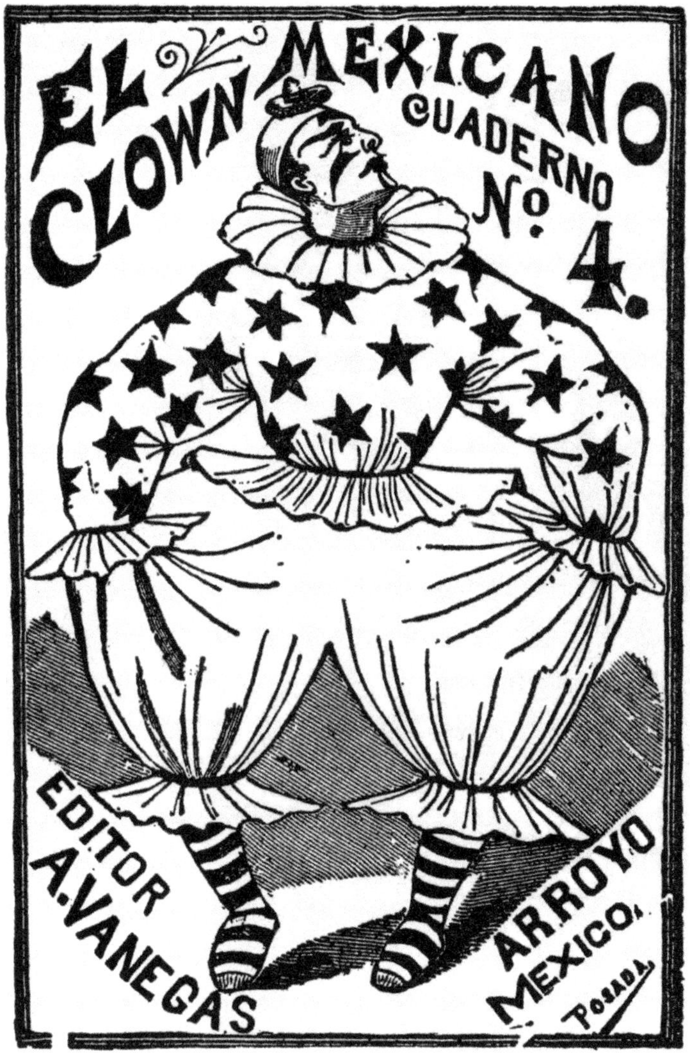

Fig. 13. José Guadalupe Posada, cover of *El Clown Mexicano* (The Mexican Clown), late nineteenth century. Image in the public domain.

photographed interiors of circus tents in ways that emphasized their striking geometric forms. In 1929 Carlos Orozco Romero painted *El acróbata* (The Acrobat), which features a contortionist performing on a mat with a crowd encircling him. That same year the vanguard group ¡30–30! (which criticized academic art and promoted popular urban culture) held a large exhibition of prints depicting diverse subjects in the tent of the Amaro circus. The thirty members of ¡30–30! included three of Izquierdo's classmates from the Escuela Nacional de Bellas Artes.[35]

In the fall of 1930 Izquierdo and Tamayo traveled together to New York to exhibit their work. Both artists showed paintings in the enormous *Mexican Arts* exhibition organized by René d'Harnoncourt for the Metropolitan Museum of Art.[36] The exhibition, which included 1,200 objects from the sixteenth century to 1930, was at the Metropolitan Museum of Art from October 13 to November 9 and then traveled to seven other venues in the United States. Izquierdo also had a solo show at the Art Center in New York City from November 17 to 29, 1930, where she exhibited fourteen paintings and was promoted as the first Mexican woman to show her work in the United States. The paintings that she showed at the Art Center were images of people (including nudes but not circus scenes), landscapes, architecture, fruit, flowers, and other still lifes.[37]

A partial account of Izquierdo's trip to New York survives in her unpublished memoirs, which she recounted to a secretary at the end of her life and were written in the third person singular. Oddly, the memoirs provide more information about what Izquierdo saw at Coney Island than about the art that she viewed in the museums and galleries of New York:

> During the month and a few days that she stayed in New York, she spent all her time visiting museums, art galleries, concert halls, theaters, skyscrapers, the black neighborhood of Harlem, the parks, zoos, New Jersey, the aquarium and the circus, Coney Island with its monumental fair, roller coasters, games, and the famous human freaks, such as the worm-woman, the smallest, biggest, skinniest, fattest, tallest men, etc. . . . In the world's largest city, her activity was intense.[38]

Izquierdo returned to Mexico with "her eyes and soul overflowing with new visual elements and human knowledge."[39]

Although Izquierdo did not recount which art exhibitions she saw, it is important to note that the circus appeared with extraordinary frequency while she was in New York as the subject of art exhibited in museums and galleries and reproduced in magazines and books. The exact dates of her trip do not survive, but her stay in New York presumably included the month of November—while *Mexican Arts* was still at the Metropolitan Museum and her solo exhibition was at the Art Center—along with a couple of days in late October or early December. During November museums and galleries exhibited images of the circus by Honoré Daumier, Eugène Atget, Georges Rouault, Reginald Marsh, and Walt Kuhn.[40] Maud Dale's lavishly illustrated new book on Picasso, which contained many reproductions of his images of circus performers, was reviewed in the *New York Times*.[41] Art magazines from mid-October to early December included numerous reproductions and mentions of art with circus themes by Pierre-Auguste Renoir, Edgar Degas, Pablo Picasso, Thomas Hart Benton, Gifford Beal, and Esther Bruton as well as by the artists who were currently showing in New York.[42] The theme of the circus, which had been used by major artists in the nineteenth and early twentieth century, appears to have peaked in New York in 1930. While it is not possible to state with absolute certainty that Izquierdo saw specific individual works, she could not have failed to notice that the circus was a major theme that had been employed by modern masters and was currently being used by successful contemporary artists.

According to a list of Izquierdo's individual exhibitions published in *María Izquierdo: Monografía* (María Izquierdo: Monograph) in 1985, she showed work depicting circus subjects in February 1931.[43] If this information is accurate, then she would have shown her first collection of circus images only three months after returning from New York, where the circus had been a prevalent theme in numerous exhibitions. However, I have not been able to locate any primary source to substantiate that she had an exhibition dedicated to the circus in 1931.[44] Nor is there a record of Izquierdo's paintings of circuses from 1931 or earlier.[45] But abundant documentation provides evidence that Izquierdo created at least nine images of the circus in 1932 and held a solo show that presented her circus paintings in February 1933. The exhibition *17 acuarelas de María Izquierdo* took place from February 1 to 15 in the studio of Frances Toor, the director of *Mexican Folkways* magazine, at Madero 27 in the historic center of Mexico City. At least seven of the watercolors represented circus performers or circus animals. A daring female rider is featured in three paintings: *Amazona azul* (Blue Horsewoman), *Amazona blanca* (White Horsewoman), and *Amazona roja* (Red Horsewoman). The Spanish titles of these paintings use the word *amazona*, which in addition to meaning a female rider also alludes to the mythological race of female warriors; unfortunately, the full connotations of the titles are lost in translation.[46] *Amazona blanca*, the only work to be reproduced in the exhibition catalogue, represents a woman wearing a short white costume standing on one leg atop a tiny white pony (fig. 14). This work now belongs to the Blanton Museum of Art, where it is known as *Caballista del circo* (Circus Bareback Rider) of 1932.[47] Other titles in Izquierdo's 1933 exhibition include *Payaso* (Clown), *Domadora* (Female Animal Tamer), *Leones* (Lions), *Equilibristas* (Acrobats), *Bailarinas* (Female Dancers), and *Mujeres y caballos* (Women and Horses).

Izquierdo received strong support for the *17 acuarelas* exhibition from poets and critics associated with the Contemporáneos. Celestino Gorostiza and Jorge Cuesta wrote essays for the catalogue, José Gorostiza spoke about Izquierdo's work at the opening, and Celestino Gorostiza gave a lecture the evening the exhibition closed.[48] In his catalogue essay Celestino Gorostiza observed that "María Izquierdo's principal concern seems to be finding the perfect point of balance between the tragic and the comic, which is born from a biting, but veiled and subtle irony that constitutes the salient characteristic of the Mexican personality."[49] He attributed the artist's choice of subject matter to the tragedy and comedy inherent in the circus. The opening was attended by a mix of people that included the Contemporáneos writers Salvador Novo and Bernardo Ortiz de Montellano and the visual artists Rufino Tamayo, Carlos Mérida, Francisco Díaz de León, and Paul Strand.[50]

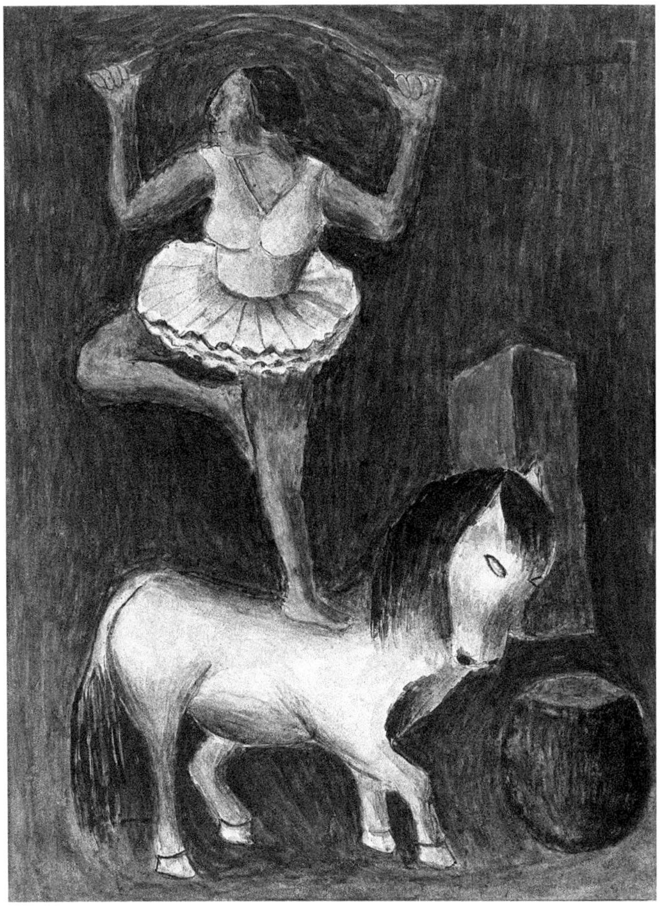

Fig. 14. María Izquierdo, *Amazona blanca* (White Horsewoman), also known as *Caballista del circo* (Circus Bareback Rider), 1932, watercolor and gouache on paper, 11 × 8 ½ inches (27.9 × 21.6 cm), Blanton Museum of Art, University of Texas at Austin, gift of Thomas Cranfill, 1980. Photograph by Rick Hall. Reproduced with the permission of María Rosenda López Posadas, legal representative of the intellectual property of María Izquierdo. Reproduction authorized by the Instituto Nacional de Bellas Artes y Literatura, 2015.

Izquierdo shared with Picasso and other artists a strong identification with circus performers, but she established her link in ways that are stylistically distinct and express ideas unique to her. In 1933 she painted a self-portrait whose circus setting is implied by the curved wall of the ring behind her and a leaping white horse.[51] The white horse, which is depicted in a dramatically smaller scale than the self-portrait, soars toward her; its nose seems to touch the top of her head.[52] The odd tangential relationship, simultaneously awkward and engaging, suggests a strong connection between horse and artist.[53] Unlike Izquierdo's other early circus paintings, the medium of the self-portrait is oil on canvas.[54] The current location of this work is unknown.

The concepts underlying Izquierdo's and Picasso's identifications with circus performers are also significantly different. According to art historian Theodore Reff, the harlequins, saltimbanques, and clowns of Picasso's Rose Period were "the first fully realized alter egos" in his art.[55] Reff observes that Picasso utilized these characters to express themes of alienation, fraternity, jealousy, and love. During the Rose Period, Picasso often portrayed circus performers as sickly and exhausted, emphasizing the emaciation of their bodies and the extreme pallor of their skin. Ronald Johnson traces the tradition of artists identifying with circus performers to the commedia dell'arte of the early eighteenth century. He asserts that the role of Pierrot and the tradition of saltimbanques were both associated with tragedy and rejection from society. Johnson places Picasso's images of harlequins and saltimbanques within this tradition and sees them as a "new type of tragic-heroic figure: their outsider status speaks of freedom from society and the heroism of loneliness."[56]

Images of the circus are informed not only by the personal philosophy of each artist who creates them but also by the culture in which the artist lives and works. In Mexico, as elsewhere, circus performers' lives are separate from mainstream society, but in Mexico visual artists are not marginalized in the same way that they often are in the United States and Europe. Art historian Karen Cordero writes that between 1910 and 1930 "Mexican criticism took up the idea of the artist as a worker at the service of society, rather than as a marginalized visionary creator."[57] As artist-activist Guillermo Gómez-Peña observes, "In Latin America the artist has multiple roles. He/she is not just an image-maker or a marginal genius, but a social thinker/educator/counterjournalist/civilian diplomat/human-rights observer. His/her activities take place in the center of society and not in specialized corners."[58] Izquierdo was less political than the majority of her Mexican colleagues, but she embodied the concept of the artist as a socially responsible person at the center of society by teaching art at the Escuela de Pintura y Escultura, writing reviews of art exhibitions and essays about women's rights, speaking on the radio, and traveling to South America on a cultural mission sponsored by the minister of education in 1944.[59] While Izquierdo would not have felt marginalized as a Mexican artist, however, she did feel marginalized as a woman artist. Recalling the beginning of her career, Izquierdo stated that it was "a *crime to be born a woman*, and if the woman had artistic abilities, it was much worse."[60]

In 1943 Izquierdo formed a five-member group called Pentágono (Pentagon) with three other artists and a writer who shared her interest in the circus. The other members were the Chilean painter Raúl Uribe (Izquierdo's husband from 1944 to 1953), the Spanish painter Lucio López Rey (who had been an acrobat in his youth), the Spanish painter Luis Marín Bosqued, and the Mexican poet Roberto Guzmán Araujo. The group's second exhibition, titled *El circo* (The Circus), took place at the Biblioteca Benjamin Franklin (Benjamin Franklin Library) from June 26 to July 13, 1945.

The opening of *El circo* was conceived as a circus event. The one-page catalogue was designed as a circus program and printed on bright paper; a different ringmaster introduced the work of each painter. Roberto Guzmán Araujo recited his poem "Circo de Nubes" (Circus of Clouds),[61] whose title was probably inspired by Apollinaire's poem "Un fantôme de nuées" (Cloud Phantom) of 1913 about a small group of acrobats and strong men.[62] The small gallery of the Biblioteca Benjamin Franklin was filled beyond capacity, with the crowd spilling onto the streets.

The ringmaster who introduced Izquierdo's paintings was the writer and radio personality Álvaro Gálvez y Fuentes, who presented a "Saeta a María Izquierdo" (Paean to María Izquierdo) in her honor. A *saeta* is a passionate religious poem sung during Holy Week to images of the suffering Virgin and Christ. While Gálvez y Fuentes's *saeta* is secular, the following excerpt shows that his *saeta* to Izquierdo—or perhaps more properly to her images—combines the concepts of suffering and transformation to glory that is characteristic of the poetic form: "María Izquierdo now takes a subject that is also painful and, surprisingly, resolves it with the sweet eyes of a girl. Thus, the atmosphere of poverty, sadness, sordidness, and dust that trembles in the circus that adults see does not exist in these paintings filled with childlike and diaphanous happiness."[63]

Izquierdo exhibited twelve paintings in *El Circo.* Ten of the titles include the name of the performer and briefly identify the act; for example, *Las encantadoras caballistas, Lolita y Juanita* (The Enchanting Horsewomen, Lolita and Juanita) of 1945 and *Zenaida, la domadora de leones* (Zenaida, the Lion Tamer) of 1945. Some of the titles contain adjectives that give a sense of the fanfare of the circus: *La famosa caballista Adelita Villa* (The Famous Horsewoman Adelita Villa) of 1945 and *La temeraria alambrista Bárbara Rodríguez* (The Daring Tightrope Walker Bárbara Rodríguez) of 1945. Izquierdo's paintings in this exhibition depict the performers facing the viewer, which emphasizes their individual identities. The combination of titles, subjects, and viewpoints suggests that the images and titles were developed together and, like the catalogue to the show, were inspired by circus programs.

Izquierdo's inclusion of several full names of circus performers in the titles of her 1945 paintings implies that she portrayed members of a real circus troupe. In contrast to earlier images of the circus, many of the featured performers are represented in relatively stationary positions, suggesting that the paintings are true portraits. However, the performers she depicted are personages that she invented, rather than identifiable circus artists. Mexican circus historian Julio Revolledo Cárdenas notes that the names in Izquierdo's titles cannot be linked to circus performers of the period.[64]

At the exhibition Izquierdo told a journalist from the magazine *Don Timorato* that *La temeraria alambrista Bárbara Rodríguez* was a self-portrait, but she also provided an odd story about the woman whose name appears in the title that seems to contradict this claim. According to Izquierdo, "what set this rope walker apart was that, instead of balancing on any telephone wire, she started to walk on the electric energy cables to save on trolley fare. Engaging in such risky behavior, one day she was burnt to a crisp."[65] According to Aurora Posadas Izquierdo, *La temeraria alambrista Bárbara Rodríguez* is not a self-portrait of her mother.[66]

In addition to substantial coverage of *El circo* in *Don Timorato*, the exhibition elicited numerous articles in the press that took the form of reviews of the show, descriptions of the opening, and name-dropping in society columns. Considered as a group, the articles devoted roughly equal attention to the work of Izquierdo, López Rey, and Marín Bosqued. Uribe was less frequently mentioned, but two of his paintings were reproduced in Horacio Quiñones's article "Mexicanos y españoles" (Mexicans and Spaniards), in which the author complained bitterly that art criticism in Mexico was dominated by Spaniards, thereby implying that the two Spanish artists in the show, López Rey and Marín Bosqued, had received unwarranted amounts of attention in the press.[67] Although the reviews did not say so, the paintings by the members of Pentágono reproduced in newspapers and magazines revealed that Izquierdo's work was significantly more dynamic and innovative in style and subject than that of the other members of the group.

The last year in which Izquierdo is known to have created more than one image of the circus is 1945. The catalogue to her 1988 retrospective at the Centro Cultural, Arte Contemporáneo, which contains the most complete inventory of her work published to date, includes only one post-1945 painting of the circus: *Escena de circo* (Circus Scene) of 1954. *Escena de circo* depicts a daring female horsewoman standing on one leg atop a red horse galloping toward the front edge of the composition. Horse and rider are flanked on the left by a multicolored drum, and on the right by a woman brandishing a whip. The scene, which takes place within a circus ring, is depicted in an extremely shallow space. While Izquierdo's late work includes some compelling paintings, her post-1948 work is uneven. She suffered major strokes in 1948, 1950, and 1952. After each stroke she resumed painting through force of will, but with extreme difficulty. Her struggle to continue painting at the end of her life left visible traces in *Escena de circo*, where the paint is applied in an oddly mottled way that diminishes the aesthetic quality of the work but testifies to her fierce determination to make art.

Conclusion

María Izquierdo's paintings of the circus embody her personal memories and draw on her substantial knowledge of the history of the representation of the circus in modern art. Her memories included the story of the first miracle of the Virgin of San Juan de los Lagos, the itinerant circuses that visited her hometown, the *carpas* and circuses that she saw in Mexico City, her friendships with performers, and her visits to rehearsals. Her knowledge of the theme of the circus in art began with the little-known anonymous nineteenth-century painting in the chapel near her childhood home and embraced famous images by José Guadalupe Posada, Pablo Picasso, Rufino Tamayo, Henri de Toulouse-Lautrec, Georges Seurat, Honoré Daumier, Georges Rouault, Eugène Atget, and Carlos Orozco Romero. She probably also saw some of the circus images by Manuel Manilla, Tina Modotti, Edward Weston, Reginald Marsh, Gifford Beal, and Walt Kuhn. She read the poetry of Roberto Guzmán Araujo and Ramón López Velarde and may have known some of Guillaume Apollinaire's poetry. Her images of the circus are part of the vast, diverse corpus of art dedicated to this theme. They are also as unique as those of any artist who has ever employed it. Izquierdo's paintings of female circus performers represent women who are brave, strong, daring, and skillful; they also voice the challenges and dangers facing women and hint at their outsider status in postrevolutionary Mexico. This imagery—which she extended over two decades—projects a powerful statement about the abilities of women that defied the gender stereotypes of her era. She created a commanding body of images that provides a counterpart to the innumerable representations of male heroes depicted by Rivera, Orozco, Siqueiros, and others. National identity was constructed as masculine identity in postrevolutionary Mexico, but this rhetoric was not uncontested. The oeuvre of María Izquierdo contributed to the dynamic discourse about the roles of women and art in Mexico; her representations of female circus artists are her most compelling assertion that women can be as courageous, strong, and powerful as any male hero. With these paintings that now form an integral part of Mexican modernism she lobbied for an equal role for women in the artistic discourse of her country.

2

Saints and Goddesses

Kahlo's Appropriations of Religious Iconography in Her Self-Portraits

For Frida Kahlo and other women artists of the postrevolutionary period, the construction of national identity as masculine, the ubiquitous images of male heroes, and the representation of women in secondary roles presented a formidable problem. How could an artist portray women who were simultaneously Mexican, traditional, modern, feminine, and powerful? To a large degree Kahlo's art is a response to this challenge. She met the challenge by repeatedly using her own image to create a strong female protagonist, and she appropriated and transformed religious symbols as a way to legitimate and empower her self-portraits. Through an astute combination of religious iconography, *mexicanidad*, vanguard style, masquerade, and irony she invented herself as a subject who transcended the paradox of being traditional and modern and projected a commanding female presence.

In essence, Kahlo appropriated religious imagery as a means of communicating power at a time and place where women had limited political and economic rights[1] but were stereotypically believed to be especially religious and therefore endowed with power in spiritual matters. Kahlo surely did not buy into essentializing views about women's innate religiosity, but she manipulated these assumptions in ways that simultaneous co-opted the efficacy and authority of religious visual languages and critiqued selected aspects of religion. This chapter examines how she appropriated Christian and Precolumbian religious imagery to construct her own mythology. Because Kahlo's art embodies her ideas, I begin by documenting her thoughts on religion.

Kahlo and Religion

Kahlo's mother, Matilde Calderón de Kahlo, was a devout Catholic, and her father, Guillermo Kahlo, was an atheist. When he was nineteen, her father emigrated from Germany to Mexico, where he became a photographer. Until recently it was believed that he was a Jew. However, in an essay titled "Die Legenden um Fridas Abstammung" (The Legends of Frida's Ancestry) of 2005, Helga Prignitz-Poda establishes that Guillermo Kahlo's mother and father were both Protestant.[2] Frida Kahlo's father was born on October 26, 1871, in the town of Pforzheim in Baden and baptized Wilhelm Karl Kahlo in the local Protestant church on January 1, 1872.[3] Frida Kahlo or Diego Rivera probably invented the idea that her father was Jewish as an effective way of distancing him, herself, and her paternal ancestry from Adolf Hitler and Nazism, which she abhorred.[4] In 1952 she painted a portrait of her father with his large-format camera. On a scroll at the bottom of the composition she noted that he was part Hungarian and emphasized that he was anti-Hitler: "I painted my father, Wilhelm Kahlo of Hungarian-German origin, artist-photographer by profession, in character generous, intelligent and fine, valiant because he suffered for sixty years with epilepsy, but he never stopped working and he fought against Hitler, with adoration. His daughter Frida Kahlo."[5]

In addition to being a highly accomplished photographer specializing in architectural photography, Guillermo Kahlo read about science, history, and geography. His small, carefully selected library included books by Friedrich Schiller, Johann Wolfgang von Goethe, and other European writers. Ironically, although Guillermo Kahlo was an atheist, he is best known for his exquisite photographs of Mexican colonial churches, which were published in Dr. Atl's luxurious, large-format, multivolume *Iglesias de México* (Churches of Mexico) between 1924 and 1927.

Under her mother's guidance, Frida received a traditional Catholic education, which included attending mass and going on retreats before Easter. In her early teens she began to move away from religion toward leftist politics. She later confided to Raquel Tibol that her mother had been an enormous friend, but they had never agreed on religious issues. According to Kahlo, her mother "became hysterical about religion." At thirteen Kahlo joined a leftist student organization. "For me the basis for this determination was the clear and precise emotion that I retained of the Mexican Revolution. Around 1914 in the market of Coyoacán I had heard the propaganda in favor of Zapata."[6] Kahlo's claim that the Mexican Revolution was the basis for her rejection of religion reflects the conflict between the Catholic church and the leaders of the Mexican Revolution. When she was seventeen, she joined the Communist Youth, an affiliation that further polarized the realms of religion and politics in her life.

At the age of forty Kahlo began to write about her personal philosophy in her diary. Her journal testifies to beliefs that were part Marxist and part personal invention. In an undated entry made between August and November of 1947, she wrote in a stream-of-consciousness style about revolution and life:

> *Revolution* is the *harmony* of *form and color* and everything exists, and moves, under only one *law* = life = Nobody is separate from anybody else—Nobody fights for himself. Everything is *all* and *one*. Anguish and pain—*pleasure* and death are no more than a *process* for *existence*—the revolutionary struggle—in this process is a doorway open to intelligence.[7]

In another undated diary entry, probably written in 1950, Kahlo again expressed her thoughts about the meaning of life, this time combining Marxist dialectical materialism, reincarnation, and a belief in the interrelationship of all things: "No one is more than a function—or part of a *total* function. Life goes by, and sets paths, which are not traveled in vain. But no one can stop 'freely' *to play* by the wayside, because he will delay or upset the general atomic journey."[8] As she explained, "We are no more than *vectors direction* construction and destruction."[9] As living beings we feel the anguish of waiting for the next moment and floating in the complex current, "not knowing that we are headed toward *ourselves*, through millions of stone beings—of bird beings—of star beings—of microbe beings—of fountain beings toward ourselves."[10] She also referred to "the *sum* (sometimes called *God*—sometimes *freedom* sometimes *love*)." She concluded that "we are hatred—love—mother—child—plant—earth—light—ray—as usual—world bringer of worlds—universes and cell universes—Enough!"[11]

In a page that was tipped into the diary, probably toward the end of her life, Kahlo asserted her disagreement with "the whole gamut of bourgeois *tricks*," which include counterrevolution, imperialism, fascism, capitalism, and religion.[12] She expressed a desire to cooperate with the revolution to transform the world into a classless society.

Kahlo's diary testifies to her harshly critical attitude toward religion. Her views about religion, dialectical materialism, and the need for a classless society were obviously inspired by Marx and other Communist theoreticians. Yet her diary also shows that her political convictions were mixed with ideas and attitudes from other sources. She implied a belief in reincarnation with her avowal (cited above) that we are headed toward ourselves through millions of stone beings, bird beings, and star beings. She allied herself with the ancient Mesoamerican worldview in which all forms of life are interconnected when she affirmed that "we are hatred—love—mother—child—plant—earth—light—ray." Kahlo was Marxist, but she was not an orthodox Marxist. She incorporated ancient ideas from Asia and Mesoamerica into her Marxism and so created a philosophy that defies labels.

Kahlo did not usually speak or write about religion in relation to her paintings. The exception is an informal lecture that she gave about *Moisés* (Moses) of 1945, a painting commissioned by José Domingo Lavin. He lent Kahlo a copy of Sigmund Freud's *Moses and Monotheism*; after she told him that she found the book fascinating, he asked her to create a painting based on it.[13] In *Moses and Monotheism* Freud expounded the theory that Moses was not a Jew but an Egyptian follower of the pharaoh Akhenaton, who practiced and promoted monotheistic worship of the sun god, Aton (also Aten).[14] At the top center of *Moisés* Kahlo painted the sun with long, thin rays ending in hands, which is the ancient Egyptian symbol for the sun disk of Aton. In the lecture she gave at Lavin's home Kahlo stated that she "painted the sun, as the center of all religion, as FIRST GOD and as creator and reproducer of LIFE." She explained that the many smaller gods on either side of the sun were "those who have direct relation with the sun."[15] To the right of the sun she depicted ancient deities of the Near East and Mediterranean: "the Assyrian winged-bull, Amun, Zeus, Osiris, Horus, Jehovah, Apollo, the Moon, the Virgin Mary, Divine Providence, the Holy Trinity, Venus and . . . the devil."[16] To the left of the sun she portrayed several Mesoamerican gods and a few Asian gods.[17] In her lecture she identified the ancient Mexican deities in the painting as "Lightning, the Strike of Lightning, and the Wake of Lightning, that is to say Hurakán, Kukulkán and Gukamatz, Tlaloc, the magnificent Coatlicue, mother of all the gods, Quetzalcoatl, Tezcatlipoca, [and] Centeotl."[18] The gods

Hurakán, Kukulkán, and Gukamatz are Maya lords who participated in the Maya creation story as recounted in the *Popol Vuh*. The other deities she named are Aztec: Tlaloc the rain god, Coatlicue the earth goddess, Quetzalcoatl the Feathered Serpent, Tezcatlipoca the Smoking Mirror, and Centeotl the corn god. While Kahlo used Aztec names for these gods, they are all major deities with equivalents in other Mesoamerican cultures.[19]

Despite Kahlo's affection for the Precolumbian cultures of Mexico, in her lecture about *Moisés* she argued that gods were invented by the rulers to control the masses: "Like Moses, there have been and there will be a great number of 'higher ups,' transformers of religions and of human societies. It may be said that they are a type of *messengers* between the people whom they manage and the '*gods*' invented by [the managers] in order to manage [the people]."[20] For Kahlo, all gods—whether Greek, Christian, Hindu, or Aztec—were tools of the ruling classes. Despite her great esteem for Mesoamerican culture, she ultimately assigned Mesoamerican deities to the same category as other gods: symbols manipulated by rulers to control the common people.

Although Kahlo rejected religion, she celebrated most of the popular religious holidays, gave lavish *posadas* for the entire neighborhood at Christmas,[21] and accepted the responsibility of being the godmother of a local vegetable vendor's baby. Her stepdaughter, Guadalupe Rivera Marín, recalls that Kahlo celebrated Christmas in the traditional fashion but notes that Kahlo was motivated by solidarity with the local holiday spirit rather than by religious belief. Her secular approach to the holidays did not go unnoticed by her neighbors: when she showed up for midnight mass on Christmas eve, the rest of the congregation gossiped about "'that godless Communist Frida Kahlo' who sat listening to the priest just as calm as she could be."[22]

Kahlo, Religion, and Visual Language

Kahlo's art is notable for its religious references, for the ways these references are incorporated, and for what is missing. With the exception of *Moisés*, her oeuvre lacks direct, unmitigated representations of deities or worship.[23] Although Kahlo fiercely objected to religion, she consistently addressed spiritual issues in her work. Her paintings speak of birth, life, death, and renewal; her favorite themes include the life cycle and dualism (in the Mesoamerican sense of the term).[24] She resolved her objections to religion and her fascination with spiritual issues by co-opting Christian iconography for secular purposes and subtly evoking the ancient cultures of Mexico with symbolic elements from Precolumbian art.

Kahlo's Appropriation of Christian Iconography

Hayden Herrera identifies several instances in which Kahlo portrays herself as Christ or as a male saint. Referring to the crown of thorns that encircles Kahlo's wounded neck in *Autorretrato* (Self-Portrait) of 1940 (private collection, USA), Herrera notes the disturbing contrast between the beautiful opalescent tones and the graphic rendering of her bleeding neck. "One is reminded of the lacerated Christ figures in Mexican churches, where gruesome wounds are surrounded by pretty flowers, luxurious laces, velvets, and gold."[25] In *La columna rota* (The Broken Column) of 1944, Kahlo depicted her nude torso rent apart: a crumbling Doric column occupies the space where her spinal column should be, her torso is held together with the thick straps of a medical corset, her flesh is studded with nails, and her hips are enveloped in a white cloth that is reminiscent of Christ's winding sheet (fig. 15). As Herrera observes, "Frida displays her wounds like a Christian martyr; a Mexican Saint Sebastian, she uses physical pain, nakedness, and sexuality to bring home the message of her spiritual suffering."[26]

Less obvious, but equally important, are Kahlo's allusions to the Virgin Mary. In *Fulang-Chang y yo* (Fulang-Chang and I) of 1937, she portrays herself in a head-and-shoulders length portrait with her pet monkey Fulang-Chang in front of her (fig. 16). She has rendered her hair and the monkey's fur in a way that emphasizes similarities in texture and color, and the monkey looks directly at the viewer, mimicking her gaze. Fulang-Chang is in the position that a child would occupy in a mother and child portrait. The size and placement of the monkey and the physical relationship between the artist and her pet evoke traditional European and viceregal paintings of the Madonna and Child (fig. 17). Kahlo's subsequent self-portraits with monkeys also subtly hint at a mother-child relationship.

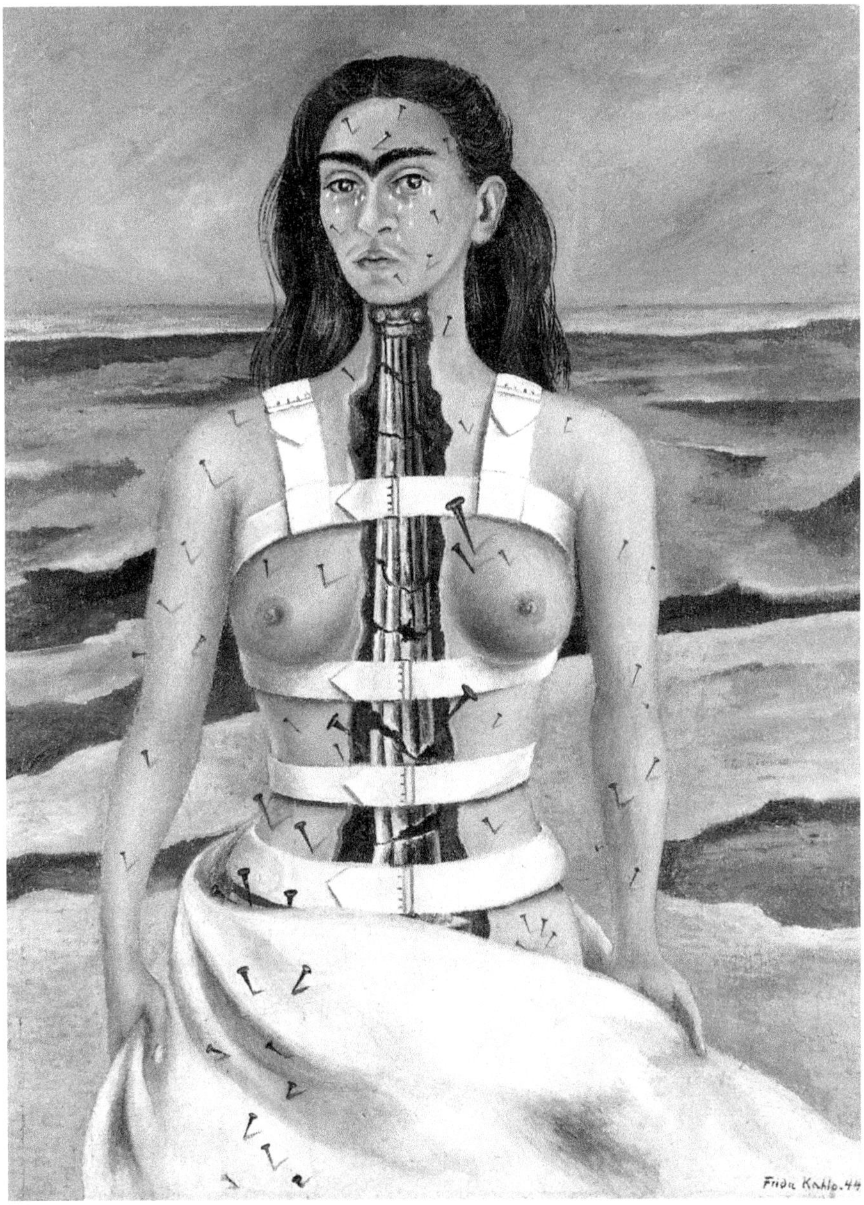

Fig. 15. Frida Kahlo, *La columna rota* (The Broken Column), 1943, oil on canvas, 15 ¾ × 12 ⅛ inches (40 × 30.7 cm), Museo Dolores Olmedo. © 2014 Banco de México Diego Rivera Frida Kahlo Museums Trust, Mexico, D.F./Artists Rights Society (ARS), New York. Reproduction authorized by the Instituto Nacional de Bellas Artes y Literatura, 2015.

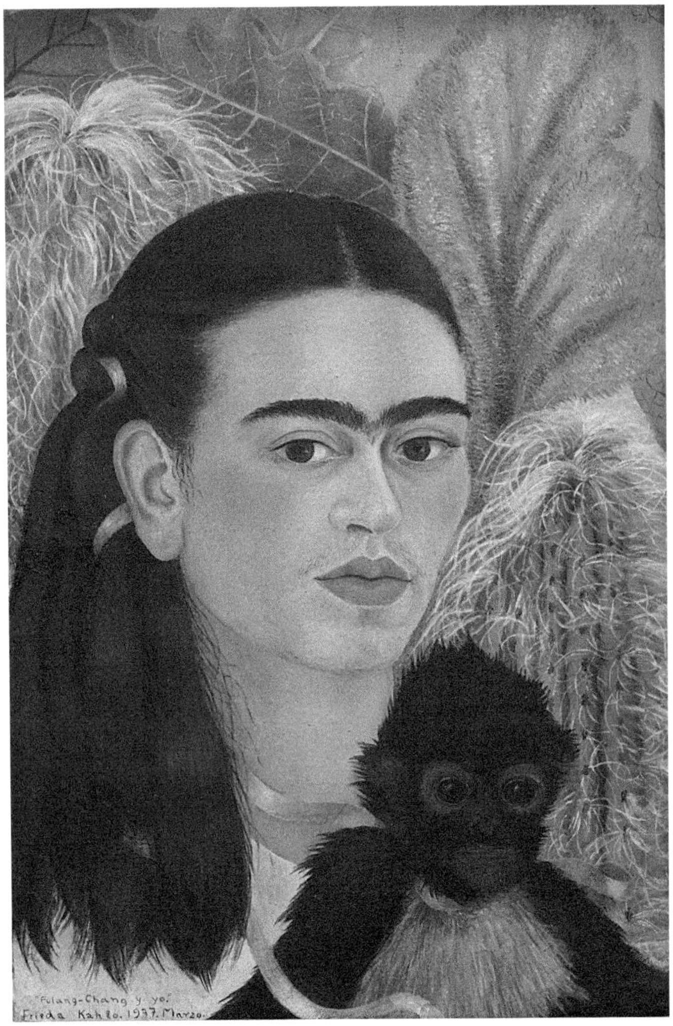

Fig. 16. Frida Kahlo, *Fulang-Chang y yo* (Fulang-Chang and I), 1937, oil on Masonite, 15 ¾ × 11 inches (40 × 28 cm), Museum of Modern Art, New York. © 2014 Banco de México Diego Rivera Frida Kahlo Museums Trust, Mexico, D.F./Artists Rights Society (ARS), New York. Reproduction authorized by the Instituto Nacional de Bellas Artes y Literatura, 2015.

Fig. 17. Detail of anonymous, *La Virgen con el niño rodeada de ángeles* (Virgin and Child Surrounded by Angels), no date, oil on wood, Museo Nacional de San Carlos. Photograph by Francisco Kochen.

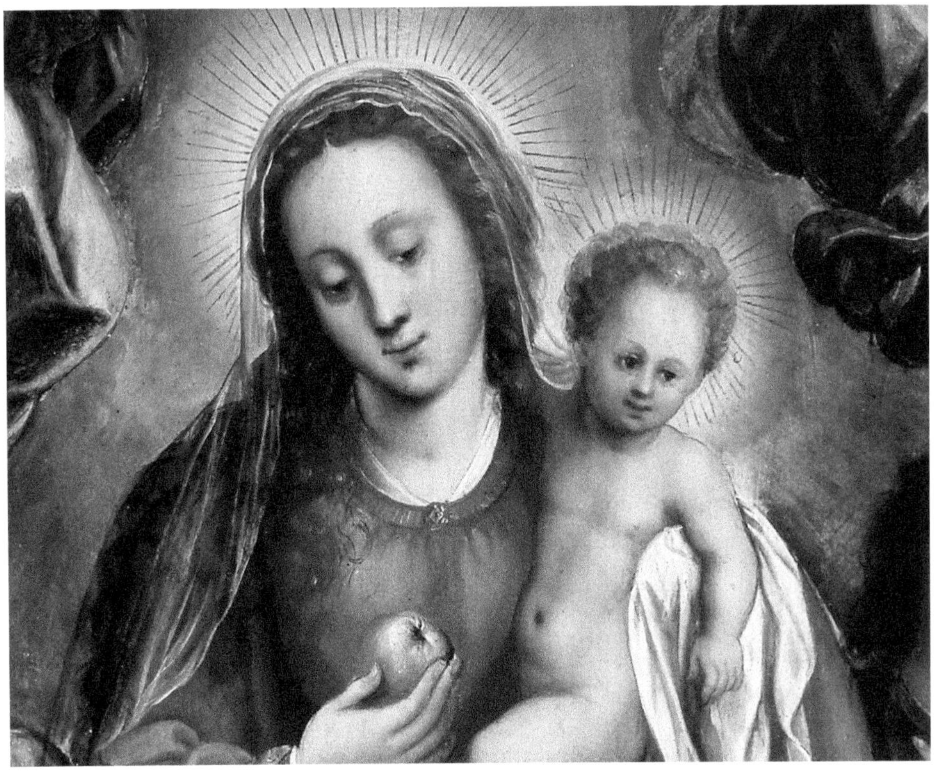

Fulang-Chang y yo is one of Kahlo's happiest and most contented self-portraits, but other self-portraits are less upbeat. In several works Kahlo identifies herself with the Virgin of Sorrows, who has lost her son.[27] Images of the Virgin of Sorrows (Mater Dolorosa) represent her weeping, with a sword or swords piercing her breast (fig. 18). Kahlo represents herself crying in several paintings.[28] She first portrayed herself in this way in two works that record her miscarriage in Detroit in 1932: *Henry Ford Hospital* and *Frida y el aborto*. That same year she painted *Mi nacimiento* (My Birth), also known as *Nacimiento* (Childbirth), in which she graphically depicted her mother giving birth to her (fig. 19). In this painting Kahlo's head emerges from her mother's vagina. Her mother's upper body and face are covered with a sheet, indicating that she is dead, while the sheet below the newborn's head is stained with blood.[29] On the wall behind the bed hangs a painting of a weeping Virgin of Sorrows, whose breast is pierced with two daggers. Like traditional ex-votos, *Mi nacimiento* is painted in oil on metal and is quite small (12 ½ × 14 inches). At the bottom of the composition a beige scroll stretches along the base. A traditional ex-voto would contain a written message in the lower part of the painting that gives thanks to the Virgin or saint who intervened, states the name of the person who had received the miracle, describes the miracle, and records the date and place it occurred. In *Mi nacimiento* the scroll is blank, presumably because the Virgin failed to deliver. Despite (or because of) the lack of miracles in her life in 1932, Kahlo testifies to her identification with the Dolorosa by placing the Virgin of Sorrow's image above the bed where she was born.

An image of the Virgin of Sorrows also appears prominently in an ex-voto that Kahlo or one of her students found and altered in 1943.[30] It represents a traffic accident that resembles to a remarkable degree the one that destroyed Kahlo's health when she was eighteen. The ex-voto depicts a red bus crashing into a yellow trolley; the sole victim, a girl with cropped hair, lies on the trolley tracks, her legs extended precariously under the vehicles at the point of impact. In the upper left corner the Virgin of Sorrows, shown with a red heart pierced by a gold dagger, witnesses the accident and weeps. The following

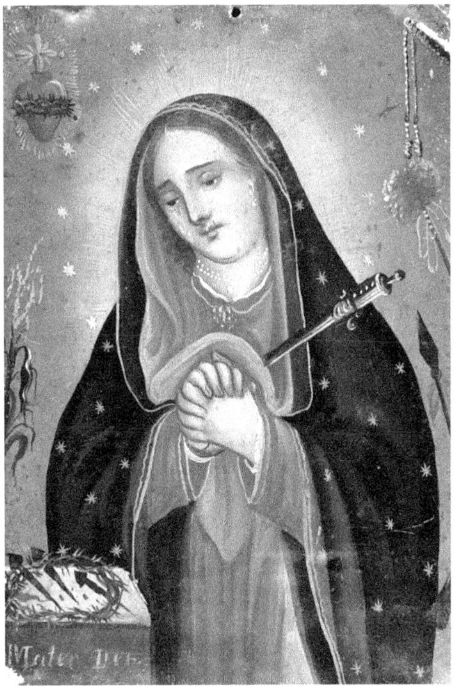

Fig. 18. Virgin of Sorrows (also known as Mater Dolorosa), undated, 4 ¾ × 6 ¾ inches (12 × 17 cm), Mexico. Photograph by Helga Teiwes-French, from the collection of Arizona State Museum, University of Arizona.

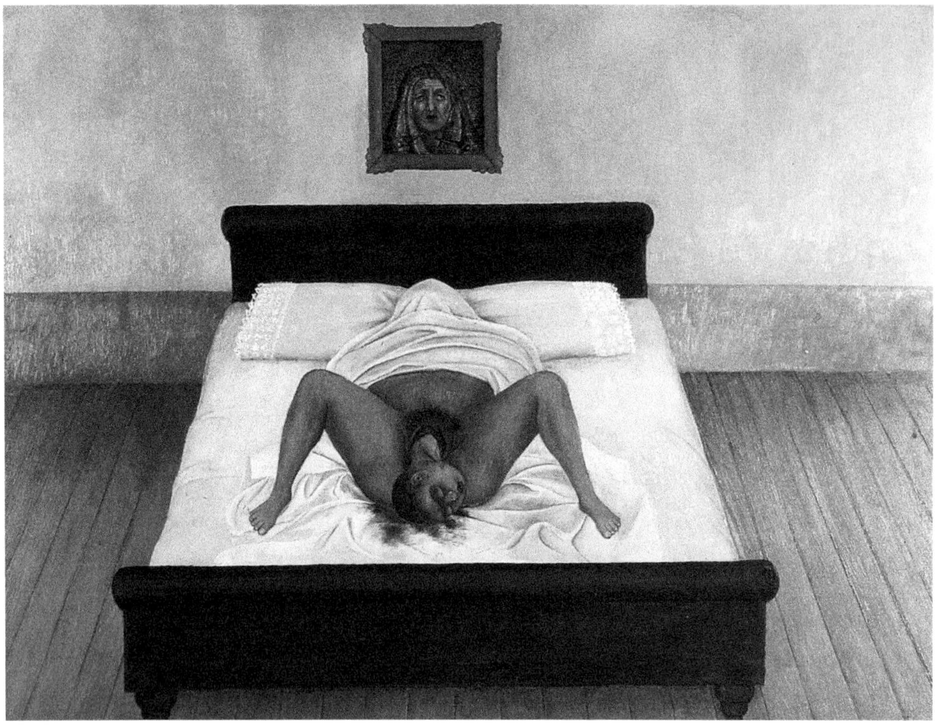

Fig. 19. Frida Kahlo, *Mi nacimiento* (My Birth), also known as *Nacimiento* (Childbirth), 1932, oil on metal, 12 ½ × 14 inches (31.8 × 35.6 cm), private collection. © 2014 Banco de México Diego Rivera Frida Kahlo Museums Trust, Mexico, D.F./Artists Rights Society (ARS), New York. Reproduction authorized by the Instituto Nacional de Bellas Artes y Literatura, 2015.

message was added to the bottom of the composition: "The spouses Guillermo Kahlo and Matilde C. de Kahlo give thanks to the Virgin of Sorrows for having saved their girl Frida from the accident that occurred in 1925 at the corner of Cuahutemozín and Calzada de Tlalpan."[31] In addition to the inscription, Kahlo made at least two changes to the image so that it recounts her story and no one else's. She wrote the name of her hometown, Coyoacán, on the side of the bus and joined the girl's eyebrows to form her signature unibrow. The degree to which the original ex-voto depicted an accident nearly identical to the one that Kahlo suffered prompted the appropriation of the object. The Virgin of Sorrows presides over the scene, which probably contributed to its resonance for her.

The Structure of the Images

Although Kahlo believed gods were something "man invented in his delirium,"[32] she appropriated the visual languages of religion because they communicated effectively. Christian symbols provided (and continue to provide) a rich, accessible vehicle for communication because the iconography has been honed over centuries to communicate with everyone, from kings to peasants, from the birthplace of Christianity in the Near East to Europe and the European colonies. The efficacy of Catholic symbols is particularly relevant in Mexico: beginning in the sixteenth century, priests used pictures for didactic purposes to convert and sustain the indigenous population in the Catholic faith. Because the population remained largely illiterate until after the Mexican Revolution, images took precedence over the written word.

In her self-portraits Kahlo presents herself as a goddess, a madonna, or a saint. Her images of herself are frontal, immobile, hieratic, and laden with symbolic elements that are associated with her. One characteristic of visual representations of deities, whether Mesoamerican, Egyptian, Hindu, or Greek, is that they can be identified by their attributes. For example, the Aztec earth goddess Coatlicue, whose name means She of the Serpent Skirt, always wears a skirt of entwined snakes. When the Hindu goddess Kali appears in her positive aspect, she holds a golden ladle and the vessel of abundance; when she assumes her terrible aspect as the all-annihilating principle of Time, she holds a noose, iron hook, rosary, and prayer book.[33] Demeter, the Greek goddess of the harvest, often holds stalks of wheat or barley. Visually, Catholic saints and advocations of the Virgin function in the same way. The Virgin of Guadalupe is instantly recognizable to all Mexicans by her olive complexion, star-studded turquoise mantle, and spiky full-body halo. Catholic saints can be identified by the symbols of their martyrdom: Saint Lucy, for example, holds a plate with her extracted eyes.

Kahlo created images of herself that are structurally equivalent to goddesses, madonnas, and saints. Her consistent features are her conjoined eyebrows, her hair braided with colored yarn, and her traditional Mexican clothing, especially the *huipiles* (upper body garments used by indigenous women), long skirts, and lace headdresses from Tehuantepec. She also endowed herself with supplementary symbols that include monkeys, *xoloitzcuintle* dogs, birds, jade necklaces, Precolumbian sculptures, wounds, thorns, the sun and the moon, and a wide variety of Mexican plants. The plants, animals, and objects function as secondary attributes with which she communicates her current aspect and the theme of the painting.

In the 1960s Irene Nicholson wrote about Mesoamerican mythology in a way that evokes Kahlo's approach, although that was not her intention. "The myths of Mexico and Central America create a world compact of jewels and flowers and birds, bright as a kaleidoscope and as ever changing. No single event can be trapped by logic because the myths belong to another world." Nicholson explains: "Each god can be his twin and corollary. Each story can be interpreted in several different ways according to the context and the reader's understanding. The symbols are few and concentrated, manipulated with such economy that each is made to serve a wide range of philosophical and religious ideas." Particularly relevant is Nicholson's observation: "The images used as symbols are limited and may even seem monotonous until we begin to search for their deeper meanings."[34] Flowers, jade, shells, birds, hearts, arrows, maize, and cactus thorns keep recurring. These elements are skillfully handled to express all the concepts needed for a complete philosophy and cosmology. The images that Nicholson lists as having symbolic meaning in ancient Mexico—flowers, jade, shells, birds, hearts, arrows, maize, and thorns—are precisely those that Kahlo chose for herself. When these elements appear in Kahlo's art, they retain traces of their ancient symbolism, which she transformed and adapted to narrate her life and express her personal philosophy. By drawing on Precolumbian connotations she imbued her work and her own image with a sense of myth.

Kahlo and Precolumbian Art

Kahlo's use of symbolic Precolumbian elements is less obvious than her appropriation of Christian iconography. When the architect and artist Juan O'Gorman, who was Kahlo's close friend, was asked about the influence of Precolumbian art on her work, he replied:

> This is a matter of sensitivity. I cannot say how, and I cannot put my finger on it, because it is a feeling. She did not copy Prehispanic art, she just had the feeling of what Prehispanic art *means*. . . . When you see her paintings, you get a similar feeling sometimes [as you do from]

> Prehispanic art. Therefore, there is an influence that speaks to the unconscious, not to the conscious, because you cannot point it out.[35]

While I believe that it is possible to identify Precolumbian elements in Kahlo's work, I am in absolute agreement with O'Gorman that Kahlo's evocations of ancient Mexican culture prioritize meaning over superficial appearance.

Kahlo's method of evoking Precolumbian art and culture was dramatically different from that of Rivera, who depicted the cultures of ancient Mexico in a literal and idealized way, as well as from that of Rufino Tamayo, who employed the colors and proportions of Mesoamerican art in semiabstract figurative compositions that prioritized formal qualities over meaning. Fernando Gamboa, a friend of Kahlo and long-time museum director, distinguished the differing approaches of Rivera and Tamayo. According to Gamboa, Rivera was the most historical in his approach, while Tamayo "returned to his roots through a sense of color and aesthetics of the ancient Mexicans, but superficially." Tamayo's colors are "the colors of Mexican nature which were used in antiquity and formed a taste for color."[36]

Kahlo took a radically different approach to incorporating Precolumbian art and culture into her work. Before 1937 she had occasionally included Precolombian elements within paintings, but her commitment to exploring mythic thought and employing Precolumbian symbolism began in earnest when she painted *Mi nana y yo* (My Nurse and I) in 1937 (fig. 20).[37] In this narrative self-portrait she depicted herself as an infant suckled by a robust earth-brown indigenous woman, who cradles her in strong arms. Kahlo represented herself with the body of a baby and the head of an adult. The wet nurse's face is concealed by a Precolumbian mask from Teotihuacan, suggesting that she is not an individual but a symbolic being. Although the indigenous woman's face is not visible

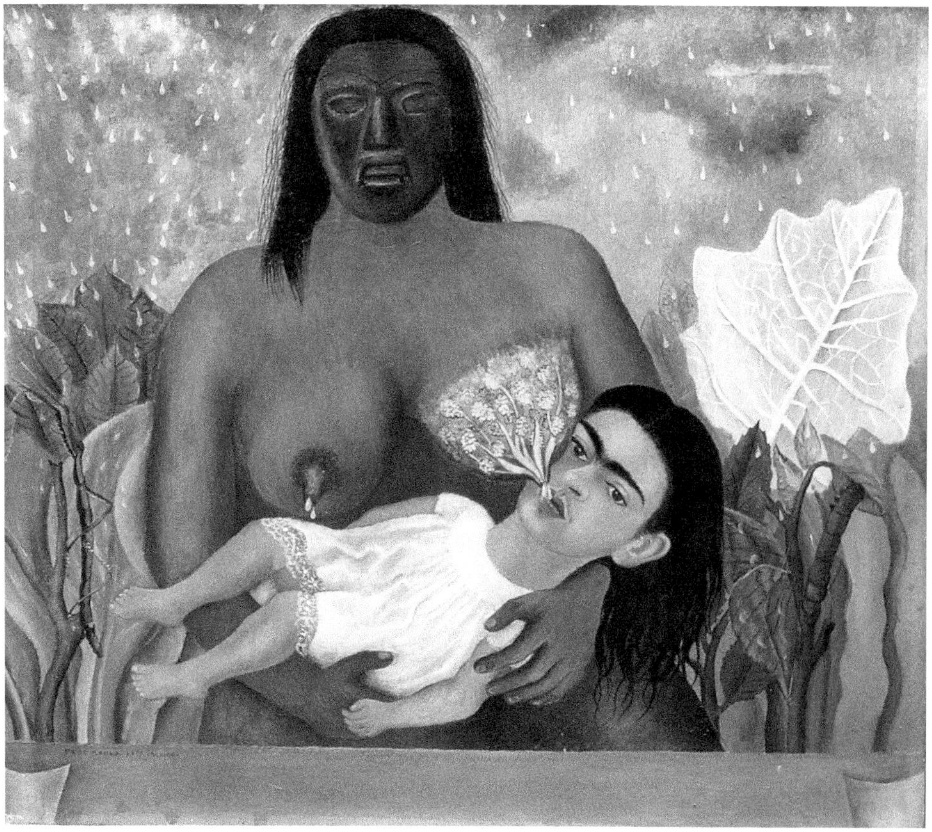

Fig. 20. Frida Kahlo, *Mi nana y yo* (My Nurse and I), 1937, oil on metal, 12 ⅛ × 14 ⅝ inches (30.5 × 37 cm), Museo Dolores Olmedo. © 2014 Banco de México Diego Rivera Frida Kahlo Museums Trust, Mexico, D.F./Artists Rights Society (ARS), New York. Reproduction authorized by the Instituto Nacional de Bellas Artes y Literatura, 2015.

and the child's skin is noticeably lighter, a sense of kinship unites the two figures. Both have almost straight, black, shoulder-length hair, and the eyebrows of the Precolumbian mask join in the middle just the way that Kahlo's do. Tiny white flowers/glands cover the nana's left breast; their stems/ducts form the nipple from which the milk flows into Kahlo's mouth. Large drops of rain or milk fall from the sky as a dense wall of vegetation rises behind Kahlo and her wet nurse. A light cocoa-colored scroll occupies the very bottom of the composition, which is blank except for Kahlo's minuscule signature, the date of the painting, and the place where it was created (Mexico); this information is written in red on the far left of the scroll.

Like most of Kahlo's self-portraits, *Mi nana y yo* is loosely based on biographical fact and intimately related to her personal beliefs. Kahlo actually had an indigenous wet nurse when she was a baby. However, the significance of *Mi nana y yo* is not that she was breastfed by a woman other than her mother but that she was nourished culturally by the indigenous heritage of Mexico. The bouquet of flowers on the nurse's breast is an allusion to ancient Mexican culture. The Aztecs associated the days of their calendar with parts of the human body. One of the twenty days in the Aztec calendar is *xochitl* (flower), which they associated with the nipple or breast.[38] In the late 1930s Kahlo sometimes used Xochitl as a nickname,[39] so a constellation of symbolic elements in this painting connects Kahlo, flowers, Precolumbian art, breasts, nourishment, and nurturing.

Kahlo's former student Arturo Estrada recalls that she called Precolumbian art "the root of our modern art."[40] *Mi nana y yo* embodies the idea that the ancient cultures of Mexico continue to provide sustenance. Of all her paintings, this one was Kahlo's favorite, perhaps because it vividly expresses her conviction that the Mesoamerican heritage continues to nurture modern Mexican artists and because it was a pivotal work in her career. After painting *Mi nana y yo*, she regularly incorporated Precolumbian symbolism into her work for the rest of her life.

The same year that Kahlo created *Mi nana y yo* she began a series of self-portraits in which a monkey appears as her companion. Between 1937 and 1945 she painted at least eight self-portraits in which she is accompanied by one or more monkeys. The monkeys were pets that lived in the garden of the blue house in Coyoacán and in the Riveras' studios in San Ángel, but they were also beings laden with symbolic meanings in ancient Mexico. In Mesoamerica monkeys were associated with the arts and the deities of fertility and dance. Archaeologist Alfonso Caso wrote that for ancient Mexicans the monkey was "a happy and playful animal, companion and sometimes symbol of the gods of Dance, Flowers, Sports, and Love."[41] *Ozomatli* (monkey) was a day sign in the Aztec calendar. It implied cleverness, craftsmanship, and instability. The day was associated with Xochipilli, the god of flowers, dance, song, and games, and was considered an auspicious time for marriage.[42] Those born on the day of the monkey were reputed to be skilled in all the arts and regarded as expert artists, dancers, and singers. Women born on the day *ozomatli* were credited with cheerful dispositions but were not considered very respectable.[43] Among the Maya the monkey's strongest association was with the visual arts.[44]

For Kahlo the monkey was a Precolumbian symbol that she could employ in a flexible and fluid manner. The monkey was simultaneously an emblem of the artist, an expression of desire for fertility and freedom of movement, and a celebration of sexuality and joy. The meanings of the monkeys in Kahlo's self-portraits shift slightly with each painting and are communicated by other elements in the compositions that establish context. For

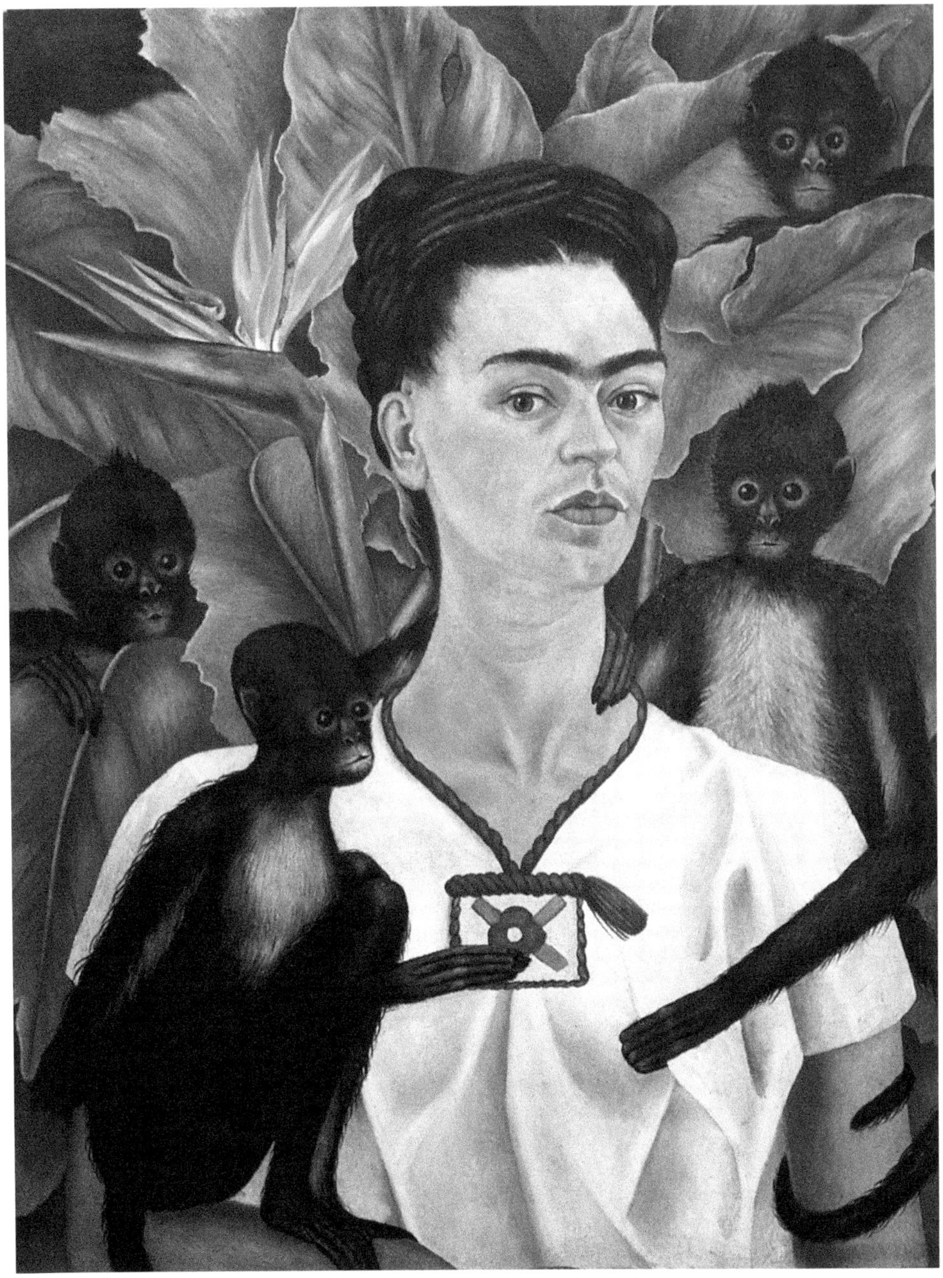

Fig. 21. Frida Kahlo, *Autorretrato con monos* (Self-Portrait with Monkeys), 1943, oil on canvas, 32 × 25 inches (81.5 × 63 cm), Jacques and Natasha Gelman collection. © 2014 Banco de México Diego Rivera Frida Kahlo Museums Trust, Mexico, D.F./Artists Rights Society (ARS), New York. Reproduction authorized by the Instituto Nacional de Bellas Artes y Literatura, 2015.

Fig. 22. Aztec glyph *ollin*, signifying earthquake, movement, or motion (after Sahagún, *Florentine Codex*, Paso y Troncoso facsimile, book 4, plate 35).

example, in *Autorretrato con monos* (Self-Portrait with Monkeys) of 1943, she surrounds herself with four pet spider monkeys; two of them embrace her, while two others peer from behind the lush foliage of a bird-of-paradise plant that fills the background à la Henri Rousseau and is graced with one spectacular orange and blue flower (fig. 21). The monkey perched on Kahlo's arm places one paw on a red and orange design embroidered or appliquéd within a rectangle at the neckline of her *huipil*. The monkey standing behind her reaches his dark arm around her body and tugs gently at the fabric of her *huipil* near the design at the neckline, a gesture that draws attention to this area of the composition. The design within the rectangle is the Aztec glyph *ollin* (also *olin*), which means earthquake, movement, or motion (fig. 22). The four monkeys in *Autorretrato con monos* thus express the idea of motion.

Kahlo owned a *huipil* similar to the one that she depicted in *Autorretrato con monos*, but it did not have a glyph. Kahlo's niece, Isolda Kahlo, recalled that the glyph was an element that her aunt added to the painting.[45] The addition of the glyph and the rectangle makes the garment resemble the clothing worn by Aztec women before the Conquest. Illustrations of Aztec matrons in the *Florentine Codex* repeatedly show them in white *huipiles* with a rectangle at the neckline, which often contains a simple design (fig. 23). The *Florentine Codex*, written in the sixteenth century by the Franciscan friar Bernardino de Sahagún and illustrated by indigenous artists, contains extensive ethnographic research obtained from native informants. Because Sahagún had a reputation for being pro-Indian, his writings were scrutinized by the Inquisition, confiscated, and not published until the nineteenth century. Rivera frequently consulted the *Florentine Codex* when conducting research about ancient Mexico for his murals, and Kahlo's work also contains numerous references to this important source. The archives of the Museo Frida Kahlo contain copies of the *Florentine Codex* and other Precolumbian and sixteenth-century codices. The version of the *ollin* glyph that Kahlo cites in *Autorretrato con monos* comes from the *Florentine Codex*.[46]

Three years earlier Kahlo had depicted herself wearing a similar sixteenth-century style white cotton *huipil* in *Autorretrato* (Self-Portrait) of 1940 (fig. 24). The self-portrait was part of a commission from the U.S. engineer Sigmund Firestone, who had requested two life-size self-portraits, one by Kahlo and one by Rivera. Firestone asked that the paintings be the same size because he intended to hang them together in memory of the warm hospitality that the Riveras extended to him and his daughters in Mexico. Ironically, the paintings were completed after the Riveras were divorced in late 1939. In the self-portrait for Firestone, Kahlo portrays herself with a neutral expression and erect posture that draws attention to her elegant long neck. In the upper right corner is a trompe l'oeil note with a message in Spanish: "Mexico, Coyoacán.—I painted this self-portrait for Sr. Sigmund Firestone and his daughters Alberta and Natalia with all affection, in February 1940.—Frida Kahlo."[47] Although Kahlo exhibits no obvious indication of pain, several details speak of her somber mood after the divorce. She wears her hair braided with purple yarn and covered with a black Spanish mantilla; in Mexico purple and black are associated with mourning. From her Precolumbian jade necklace hang four seashells that

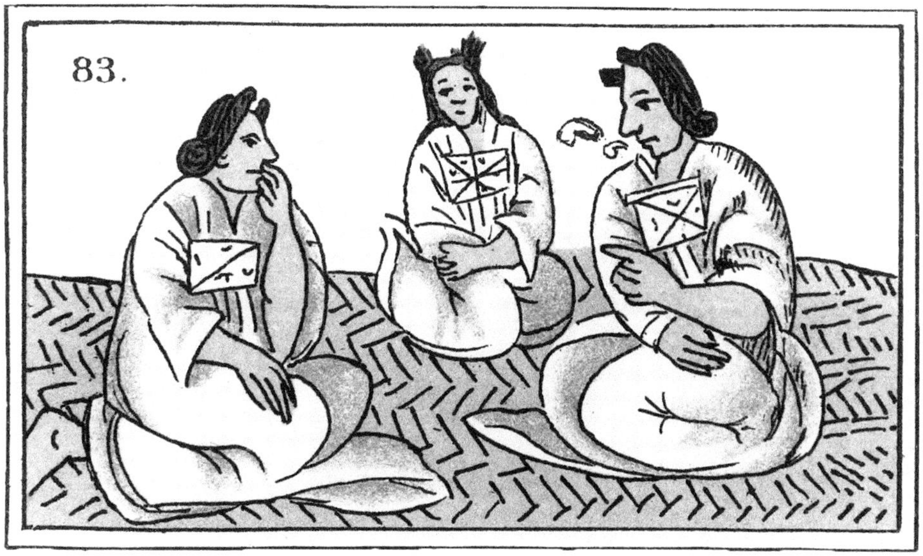

Fig. 23. Aztec women wearing *huipiles* with a rectangular design at the neck (after Sahagún, *Florentine Codex*, Paso y Troncoso's facsimile edition, book 10, plate 69, figure 83).

have been tossed by the sea for so long that they are pitted with holes. The background of the painting is chartreuse, a color that she associated with madness and mystery.[48] Embroidered in lilac thread at the neckline is a rectangle that contains an Aztec glyph.

The Aztec glyph on Kahlo's *huipil* comes from Bernardino de Sahagún's *Codices matritenses*, in which the glyph is identified as Nahui Quiahuitl (Four Rain) (fig. 25).[49] Rain is one of the twenty day signs in the Aztec calendar. The Aztecs and other Mesoamerican cultures had more than one calendar. The oldest and most sacred was the 260-day calendar, which was common to all Mesoamerican cultures and so important that its use defines the limits of high civilization in Mesoamerica.[50] In this calendar a repeating cycle of twenty day names is combined with thirteen numbers to produce a count of 260 days. Each day has both a name and number. In the Aztec version of the calendar, for example, the days would be named the Nahuatl (Aztec language) equivalents of one caiman, two wind, three house, four lizard, and so forth. The 260-day calendar is not related to

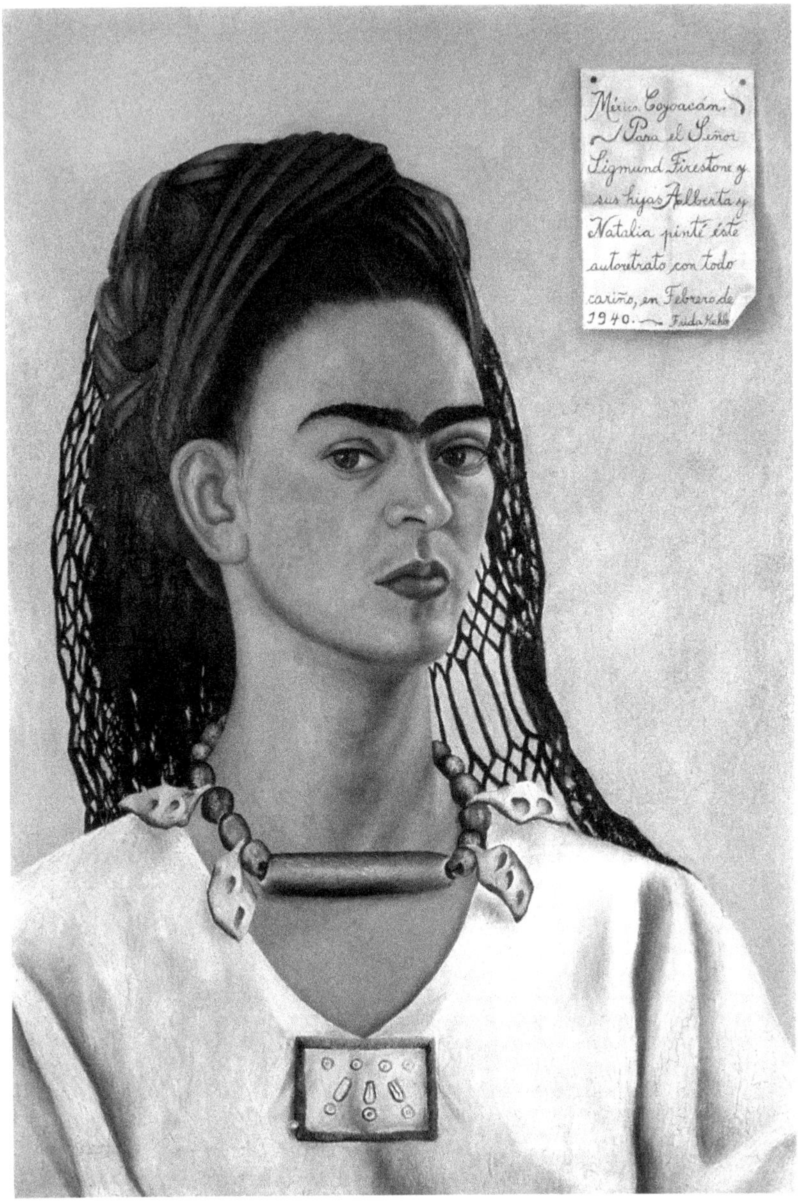

Fig. 24. Frida Kahlo, *Autorretrato* (Self-Portrait), 1940, dedicated to Sigmund Firestone and his daughters Alberta and Natalia, oil on Masonite, 24 × 16 ⅞ inches (61 × 43 cm), private collection, New York. © 2014 Banco de México Diego Rivera Frida Kahlo Museums Trust, Mexico, D.F./Artists Rights Society (ARS), New York. Reproduction authorized by the Instituto Nacional de Bellas Artes y Literatura, 2015.

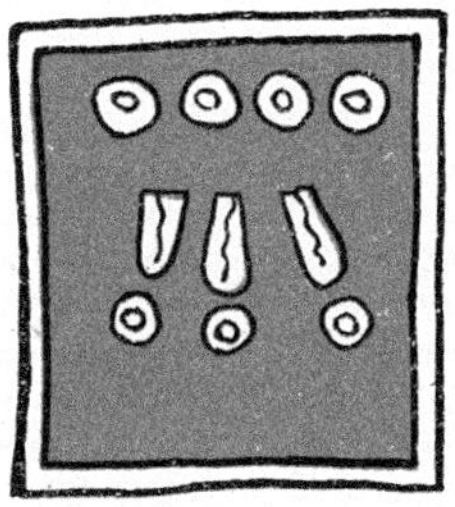

Fig. 25. Aztec glyph Nahui Quiahuitl (Four Rain) (after Sahagún, *Historia general de las cosas de Nueva España, Códices Matritenses*, Paso y Troncoso facsimile edition, vol. 6, p. 77).

astronomical or agricultural phenomena. Mesoamerican scholars Mary Miller and Karl Taube assert that "it was probably devised by midwives to calculate birthdates, working from first missed menstrual period to birth, approximating the nine-month human gestation period."[51] The 260-day calendar is often referred to as an "almanac" and was used for divination. In many parts of Mesoamerica, a child was named for the date on which he or she was born, and the date determined his or her gifts and shortcomings.[52] The Aztecs called this calendar the *tonalpohualli.* The book in which they recorded the 260-day cycle was named the *tonalamatl*, which was "the fundamental guide to the future."[53] Each day augured a fate that was good, bad, or indifferent.

The glyph on Kahlo's *huipil* in the self-portrait for Sigmund Firestone is not auspicious. Rain was one of seven signs considered evil for those born under it. According to the sixteenth-century Dominican friar Diego Durán, all those born under the sign *quiahuitl* (rain or rainstorm) "were augured very bad luck."[54] I do not mean to suggest that Kahlo's day sign was Four Rain according to the *tonalamatl.*[55] The day Four Rain has a more transcendent meaning. According to Aztec cosmology we live in the era of the Fifth Sun. Four previous suns or worlds have been created and destroyed. Our world, too, is destined for destruction. Each of the five suns is named after the day on which it will end, and each sun is identified with the deity that presided over its creation. Accounts vary as to the order of the four previous suns. The Third Sun, called Nahui Quiahuitl (Four Rain), was created by the rain god Tlaloc. It was destroyed by fiery rain, which may allude to a volcanic eruption.[56] The people who lived during the era of Nahui Quiahuitl perished or were turned into birds. Nahui Quiahuitl was destroyed on the day Four Rain.[57] When Kahlo painted the glyph Four Rain on her *huipil* in the self-portrait for Firestone shortly after her divorce, she marked the end of an era and inserted her personal narrative into Aztec cosmology.

Our present era is the Fifth Sun. The era is named Nahui Ollin (Four Motion). The Fifth Sun was created at Teotihuacan through acts of sacrifice by the gods. Like the four previous worlds, it will eventually end. It is destined to be destroyed by earthquake on the day Nahui Ollin. The Aztecs and other Mesoamerican people believed in multiple creations. They had a cyclical view of time in which creation, destruction, life, and death were inextricably linked.

Returning to *Autorretrato con monos*, the *ollin* glyph that Kahlo displays on her *huipil* together with the number four (the four monkeys) suggests that in 1943, three years after remarrying Rivera, she saw herself in a new era, the Fifth Sun, known as Nahui Ollin. The lush green foliage and the bright bird of paradise flower indicate a propitious environment. According to Isolda Kahlo, the bird of paradise was the flower that her aunt liked best and associated with love.[58] The iconography of the paintings implies that the Fifth Sun was a better world for Kahlo, at least for a while.

Autorretrato of 1940 and *Autorretrato con monos* are closely connected paintings. Although they are different sizes, they are more of a pair than the self-portraits that Kahlo and Rivera created in identical formats for Firestone. The two self-portraits by Kahlo are eloquent examples of Janice Bergman-Carton's assertion: despite the pain that some of Kahlo's paintings evince, they "are not the agonizing cries of a victimized female; they are the transfiguring and intellectualized resurrections of a life that is devoted to the mind as much as the body."[59] When the meanings of the glyphs in *Autorretrato* of 1940 and *Autorretrato con monos* are understood, it becomes clear that Kahlo performed acts of transformation, intellectualization, and renewal in her art. In these self-portraits she inserts her own joys and sorrows into Mesoamerican cosmology, thereby becoming part of a universe in which multiple acts of creation are possible: creation and destruction are part of the same process.

Conclusion

Kahlo was not religious in the usual sense, but she employed Christian and Precolumbian religious imagery throughout her work. She used Christian iconography because it was a long established visual language that communicated effectively. This is true throughout Western civilization, but it is especially true in Mexico, where Catholicism is the dominant religion and Catholic pictures had been used for didactic purposes since the sixteenth century. When Kahlo represented herself as if she were Christ, the Virgin, or a Christian martyr, she endowed her own image with spiritual power and at the same time undermined Western religion through irony.

Kahlo's use of Precolumbian symbolism is different. In most of the paintings discussed in this chapter, the Precolumbian symbolism is as subtle as the Christian references are overt. It is not employed ironically. Kahlo utilized Precolumbian elements to incorporate her own story into Mesoamerican cosmology and to assert the importance of Precolumbian roots for modern Mexico. She appropriated Precolumbian symbolism to inscribe herself into the panorama of Mexico's history and culture. Her appropriation of Precolumbian visual language was not, however, entirely pragmatic and nationalistic. Despite her Marxist rejection of religion, certain aspects of the Mesoamerican worldview appealed to her on a deep level. While she was skeptical of deities, she believed in the interrelatedness of all life forms and held a cyclical view of life. Birth, sex, life, death, and renewal are recurring themes in her art. These are spiritual as well as biological issues and are central to Kahlo's message.

Kahlo's ability to turn stereotypes about women's alleged religiosity upside down and transform religious symbols into signs of personal power allowed her to project an image that synthesized tradition and modernity, femininity and power. The way she did this has had lasting consequences, although the long-term effects were slow to take hold. In the decade immediately after Kahlo's death, she became an artist who was only known to true connoisseurs of Mexican art. Since the early 1980s she has become an internationally famous artist and entered popular culture. She has become a modern myth. The Mexican critic Carlos Monsiváis wrote in an essay about Kahlo: "No myth is invented without its own consent."[60] I believe that the gridwork for the Frida myth is embedded in Kahlo's imagery, in the way she presented herself as a goddess, a madonna, or a saint.

PART TWO

Legitimating Traditions

Part two consists of three chapters that examine Kahlo's citations of Precolumbian art and architecture and Izquierdo's portrayal of indigenous vernacular structures. In some ways Kahlo and Izquierdo employed their references to indigenous art forms quite differently. Kahlo rendered Precolumbian ceramic figures in six paintings (discussed in chapter 3) and created one painting of an indigenous girl in a deserted plane with two Mesoamerican pyramids in the distance (chapter 4). In these works Kahlo's references to ancient Mexican art and architecture are overt. In contrast, Izquierdo created an extended series of paintings representing rural gardens with traditional granaries (chapter 5). Izquierdo's depictions of granaries are as much about native form and tradition as the works by Kahlo discussed in chapters 3 and 4, but the allusions are less obvious and less ancient. Izquierdo preferred to cite living traditions, especially vanishing ones that evoke nostalgia for a recent past.

After the Mexican Revolution, artists and intellectuals sought to revalue indigenous people and culture and to promote *mestizaje* as an ideal, but they did so in ways that usually left existing hierarchies of race and gender intact or reasserted them.

In *Becoming Modern, Becoming Tradition*, Adriana Zavala contends that indigenous cultures were feminized in order to reaffirm racial hierarchies and patriarchal privilege. Zavala convincingly argues that Mexican women were expected to perform their allegiance to the nation during the postrevolutionary period by adopting traditional (indigenous) clothing and mores and rejecting styles and conduct associated with international modernity. Thus, during Izquierdo's and Kahlo's lives, being a modern woman paradoxically meant performing tradition.[1]

The paintings discussed in this part of the book all link women and indigenous traditions and profess allegiance to Mexico. However, Kahlo and Izquierdo did not merely conform to assigned spaces and accepted behavior in these paintings. Rather, they worked within the arena of expectations to create narratives that transcend the then current expectations about the roles of women. Kahlo and Izquierdo turned the usual discourse upside down by using ancient and indigenous traditions as a way to legitimate female power.

These three chapters examine how Izquierdo and Kahlo employed indigenous traditions—ancient, recent, and living—to construct narratives that empowered themselves and other Mexican women and thereby challenged perceptions of the gender of the nation. This is one of several strategies that they assiduously utilized to insert their voices into Mexican modernism and enrich it with views that challenged and brought diversity to the dominant nationalist discourse.

3

Revitalizing the Past

Precolumbian Figures from West Mexico in Kahlo's Paintings

Una es más auténtica cuanto más se parezca a lo que se ha soñado de sí misma.

The closer you are to what you dreamed for yourself, the more authentic you will be.

THE CHARACTER OF AGRADO IN PEDRO ALMODÓVAR'S
Todo sobre mi madre (All About My Mother), 1991

Frida Kahlo appropriated the Precolumbian art of West Mexico to create a narrative in which she positions herself within the history of Mexican art. Kahlo represented at least one Precolumbian artifact in eight paintings, and in six of them she depicted a ceramic figure from West Mexico. These paintings comprise four self-portraits, one still life, and one painting of an artifact in a landscape. She created these works between 1932 and 1951, so they span nearly two decades, testifying to the enduring significance of this theme for the artist.[1] In each of the paintings the figure from West Mexico is based on a real artifact and fulfills a significant function in the painting. Kahlo employed these figures to build a narrative or develop the theme of the painting; the ceramic figures may embody emotional states or project intellectual ideas or both. This chapter explores why she had a special interest in the art of West Mexico, identifies which Precolumbian artifacts she depicted, and analyzes the role of the ceramic figure in each painting. The figures from West Mexico testify to Kahlo's profound appreciation of the art of ancient Mexico and her belief in the importance of Precolumbian art. At the same time, in most of these paintings she appropriated the West Mexican figures to position herself within the history of indigenous Mexican art and to proclaim her authenticity. Authenticity, of course, is a highly problematic term.[2] In Pedro Almodovar's film *Todo sobre mi madre*, the character of Agrado, a transsexual who has invested heavily in plastic surgery to create the face and body she wants, tells an audience: "It takes a lot to be authentic, ma'am. And here you cannot be stingy. Because the closer you are to what you dreamed for yourself, the more authentic you will be."[3] Kahlo utilized the figures from West Mexico to construct the image of herself that she wanted to project.

This chapter examines the role of the Precolumbian figures from West Mexico in the six paintings. I interpret the four self-portraits in ways that refer to events in Kahlo's life. Nevertheless, I believe strongly that the role of biography and psychoanalysis has been misused in the interpretation of Kahlo's work. Too often Kahlo's paintings have been read as purely emotional reactions to painful events in her personal life rather than as intentional constructions of her persona, critiques of society, or contributions to the artistic discourse in Mexico. One of my goals in this chapter is to explore how Kahlo used the figures from West Mexico in the four self-portraits to create narratives about her life and to position her work within the broader context of Mexican art. In the process I examine how she fluidly moved between personal concerns and intellectual ideas. Kahlo's work is not about the body versus the mind or the personal versus the political; it is about the union of all these elements.

Kahlo, Rivera, and the Art of West Mexico

Although Kahlo left virtually no record, outside of the paintings themselves, of why she had a special interest in the art of West Mexico, some aspects of her preference can be surmised. Kahlo's husband's avid interest in Precolumbian art, especially the art of West Mexico, preceded hers and is more widely known. While relatively little information survives about why Rivera also held the art of West Mexico in high esteem, considerable documentation exists for his collection of Precolumbian art and promotion of the cultures of ancient Mexico.

According to Rivera, he first encountered Precolumbian art as a small boy in his childhood home in Guanajuato, where the head of a "Tarascan dog" was embedded in the fountain. "There, in that place, my interest in archaeology awoke; because of this since I was six years old I dedicated myself to collecting little faces and figures that the indigenous people from time to time brought to my city to sell."[4] During Rivera's life the cultures of West Mexico were believed to be Tarascan, so this story directly links Rivera's nascent interest in Precolumbian art to the cultures of West Mexico. Rivera's daughter Guadalupe Rivera Marín places the beginning of her father's serious interest in collecting the art of West Mexico at a later date. According to her, when her parents first traveled to Guadalajara to meet her mother's family, her mother's brothers Federico and Francisco Marín "were very informed about all the culture of West Mexico. At my grandmother's house there were already very beautiful pieces from the West, and my father saw them and that sparked his interest in traveling to the states in West Mexico."[5] Diego Rivera and Guadalupe Marín were married in Guadalajara in June 1922, so this statement places Rivera's interest in Precolumbian artifacts from West Mexico several years earlier than U.S. scholars writing about Rivera's collection have suggested.[6]

In 1941 selected works from Rivera's collection were published in *Art in Ancient Mexico: Selected and Photographed from the Collection of Diego Rivera*.[7] While the book includes a smattering of Olmec, Zapotec, Toltec, Mixtec, and Aztec artifacts, approximately 60 percent of the objects were from Nayarit and Colima, thus manifesting Rivera's predilection for the art of West Mexico.[8] Three of the Precolumbian sculptures that Kahlo represented in her paintings are reproduced in this book; two are from West Mexico.

In 1946 the first major exhibition devoted exclusively to the art of West Mexico was held at the Palacio de Bellas Artes in Mexico City.[9] Rivera's collection formed the nucleus of the exhibition, and other artists were among the collectors who lent objects.[10] Salvador Toscano, Paul Kirchhoff, and Daniel F. Rubín de la Borbolla wrote essays for the catalogue, which reproduces three of the West Mexican ceramic sculptures that Kahlo represented in her paintings.[11]

Over the years Rivera amassed a gargantuan collection of Precolumbian art. Around 1943 he began building a home for his collection, which he called Anahuacalli (House of the Valley of Mexico, in the Nahuatl language), in the Pedregal of San Pedro Tepetlapa. According to Rivera he designed the building in "a composite of Aztec, Mayan, and 'Rivera Traditional' styles" (fig. 26).[12] The building is constructed from monumental slabs of volcanic stone extracted from the site. Rivera was the architect of Anahuacalli, which was built by a small crew of men who worked intermittently over the next fifteen years when Rivera could afford to pay them. In his autobiography Rivera recalled passing many happy hours arranging the artifacts in the rooms of Anahuacalli. According to him, the anthropologist Alfonso Caso and his colleagues "were enthusiastic about my collection, declaring that while my dating of some pieces might be in error, I had shown an uncanny instinct for what was authentic and important." Rivera proudly declared that Caso rated his collection "among the best in the world."[13]

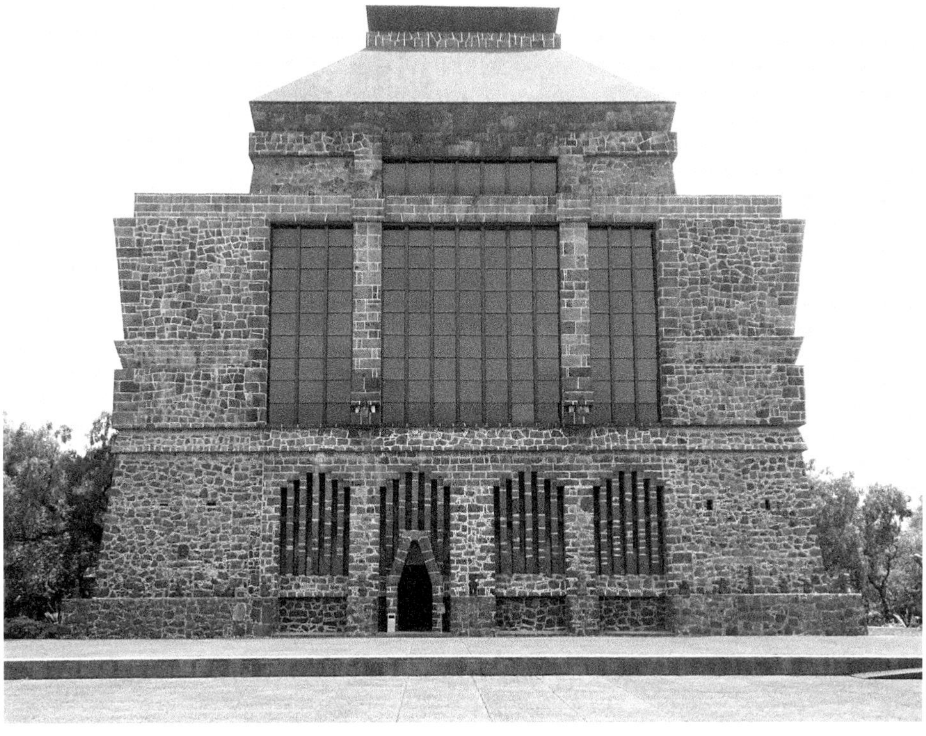

Fig. 26. Anahuacalli, designed by Diego Rivera. Construction was begun around 1943 and completed after Rivera's death. The museum opened to the public in 1964.

When Rivera died in 1957, he left a collection of 59,400 Precolumbian artifacts and the building to house them to the people of Mexico.[14] This vast collection of ancient Mexican art is the largest ever created by a private collector in Mexico.[15] Archaeologist Felipe Solís Olguín, who was the director of the Museo Nacional de Antropología (National Museum of Anthropology) from 2000 until his death in 2009, pointed out that Rivera's collection is almost half the size of the entire national collection of the Museo Nacional de Antropología.[16]

Although Rivera claimed that Alfonso Caso credited him with choosing authentic and important works, it is likely that not everything in the collection is genuine. In a 2008 essay about Rivera's archaeological collection, Solís observed that rumors have long circulated that a significant percentage of the pieces at Anahuacalli are not Precolumbian artifacts but objects created by modern artisans to pass as ancient art. He commented that the only way to put these rumors to rest would be to apply current technology such as thermoluminescence to date the clay objects. Solís wondered why Rivera, who had notable archaeologists as advisors, did not apply strict selection criteria to his acquisitions; he concluded that the artist's trust in his own personal taste and his insatiable appetite for collecting were determining factors.[17]

Two years before his death, Rivera set up a trust fund through Banco de México to provide for the administration of his collection and Anahuacalli. The construction of Anahuacalli, which was not finished at the time of Rivera's death, was completed under the direction of architects Juan O'Gorman and Ruth Rivera (Rivera's younger daughter from his marriage to Guadalupe Marín). Anahuacalli opened to the public on September 18, 1964. While only a small percentage of the collection is on view, the artifacts on display reveal similar collecting preferences to those that Rivera demonstrated in *Art in Ancient Mexico* in 1941.[18] The collection includes artifacts from all the cultures of Mesoamerica, but it does not represent them equally. Few Maya artifacts are exhibited, while displays of ceramic sculpture from Colima, Nayarit, and Jalisco fill several rooms.

Several scholars have linked Rivera's preference for the Precolumbian art of West Mexico to his political convictions and the recurring themes of his art. Barbara Braun asserts that he cherished the "frank expression of death and sex" in the ancient art of West Mexico and observes that his collection as a whole eschews large monuments and sumptuary items in favor of objects related to the art and life of common people.[19] She argues that the emphasis of his collection is undoubtedly an indictment of capitalist values as embodied in U.S. collections of Precolumbian art, such as those of Nelson Rockefeller and Robert Woods Bliss, which focus on rare, precious, and monumental objects.[20] Peter Furst relates Rivera's enthusiasm for West Mexican ceramics to his Marxist ideology, noting that Rivera and many of his contemporaries believed that West Mexican artifacts were "completely secular and unfettered by religious precepts." Furst, however, who has written extensively about shamanism, insists that the artifacts are not secular.[21] Despite Rivera's enormous collection of objects from West Mexico, Judy Sund observes that he seldom quotes them in his murals. She argues that Rivera's tendency to idealize the Precolumbian past and the nationalistic agenda of his murals led him to emphasize the more advanced Maya and Aztec civilizations.[22]

While these observations offer a range of interpretations and insights into the reasons behind Rivera's affection for the art of West Mexico, very little survives that can be attributed directly to the artist. His published statements about the ceramics of West Mexico are "few and vague."[23] He called them *ídolos* (idols) and "found them 'extraordinary,' 'marvelous,' and 'amazing,'" but did not provide specifics.[24]

Kahlo's former student Arturo Estrada, who worked as an assistant for Rivera in the creation of the first mosaics at Anahuacalli, affirms that Rivera admired the art of West Mexico for "the beauty of movement."[25] Another of Kahlo's students and Rivera's assistants, Guillermo Monroy, explains: "Diego Rivera, collector, was like a child amazed by the beauty of the forms of West Mexican sculptures." Monroy recalls that Rivera used the phrases "content of the form" and "the form in movement" to describe why these works were important.[26]

Fernando Gamboa explained Kahlo's interest in the art of West Mexico in a similar way. "She really liked the figures from West Mexico for their liberty of form." As Gamboa observed, "The art of West Mexico is probably the freest of all the expressions of diverse cultures. It encompasses a very long panorama of many centuries. It is a funerary art, it is not an art of deities. It is an art that represents people, sometimes healthy people, sometimes athletic, sometimes sick, sometimes grotesque, but it is a domestic art. There is not a single god there."[27]

The perceived lack of deities in the art of West Mexico is undoubtedly a major factor in Kahlo's appreciation of these images. Kahlo was a Marxist and eschewed religion. While her work often addresses spiritual issues and draws on religious iconography (both Christian and Mesoamerican), with the exception of *Moisés* of 1945, which was a commission and distinct from the rest of her work in several ways, Kahlo's oeuvre lacks direct, unmitigated representations of deities. Kahlo believed that gods were something that humans invented in their delirium.[28] Her representations of ceramic figures from West Mexico allowed her to extol Precolumbian art, while abstaining from portraying deities.

By the late twentieth century scholarship about West Mexico recognized more religiosity and social hierarchy in the artifacts of these cultures than was usually perceived during Kahlo's life. Some of the ceramic male figures with horned headdresses have been identified as shamans by Peter Furst and rulers by Mark Miller Graham.[29]

Kahlo and Rivera were knowledgeable about the European discourse on primitivism and utilized it in various ways. Art historian Karen Cordero notes that Mexican intellectuals in the early twentieth century took up "the Romantic idea that popular culture embodies a national essence and is related to values of the genuine, as well as purity, spontaneity, primitivism and community."[30] Nevertheless, Mexican artists did not think about "primitivism" in quite the same way as European and U.S. artists did. In an essay about Mexican popular art, Mexican art historian Ana Garduño posits that folk art and muralism were two cultural myths invented during the early 1920s. She asserts: "Autogenesis was the generally accepted requirement for both mural painting and folk art."[31] According to Garduño, Mexican artists tended to disavow any relationship between their work and early twentieth-century French primitivism or European murals, perceiving their own work as arising entirely from the local aesthetic traditions. While Garduño is discussing folk art and muralism, a similar pattern emerges with the valorization and appropriation of Precolumbian art. Both Kahlo and Rivera emphasized the national origins of their art. In the case of Kahlo, the desire to be perceived as a Mexican artist with native roots is at the heart of her fierce post-1938 disavowal of the surrealist label.[32]

Kahlo's Paintings and West Mexican Figures

The first work in which Kahlo represented Precolumbian artifacts, including one figure from West Mexico, was *Autorretrato en la frontera entre México y los Estados Unidos* of 1932, which she painted while living in the United States (fig. 27). Kahlo depicts herself standing near the center of the composition. She is flanked on the right by the Detroit skyline and on the left by a Precolumbian archaeological site. Instead of her Tehuana dress, she wears a long pink evening gown and long white lace gloves. Although she is appropriately dressed for Detroit's high society—which she found excruciatingly dull—she smokes a cigarette, wears a Precolumbian necklace, and holds a tiny red, white, and green flag, details that hint at her true preferences.

Poised between conflicting cultures, Kahlo reflects on their differences. To her the United States epitomizes modernity. She represents this by skyscrapers, the Ford factory whose smokestacks belch smoke, a U.S. flag whose colors are diminished by air pollution, anthropomorphic machines, and electrical appliances whose wires descend into the earth. Kahlo portrays Mexico as ancient and eternal. A Precolumbian pyramid in ruins dominates the horizon. The sun and moon appear simultaneously in the sky above the

Fig. 27. Frida Kahlo, *Autorretrato en la frontera entre México y los Estados Unidos* (Self-Portrait on the Border between Mexico and the United States), 1932, oil on metal, 12 ½ × 13 ¾ inches (31.8 × 34.9 cm), collection of María Rodríguez de Reyero, New York.

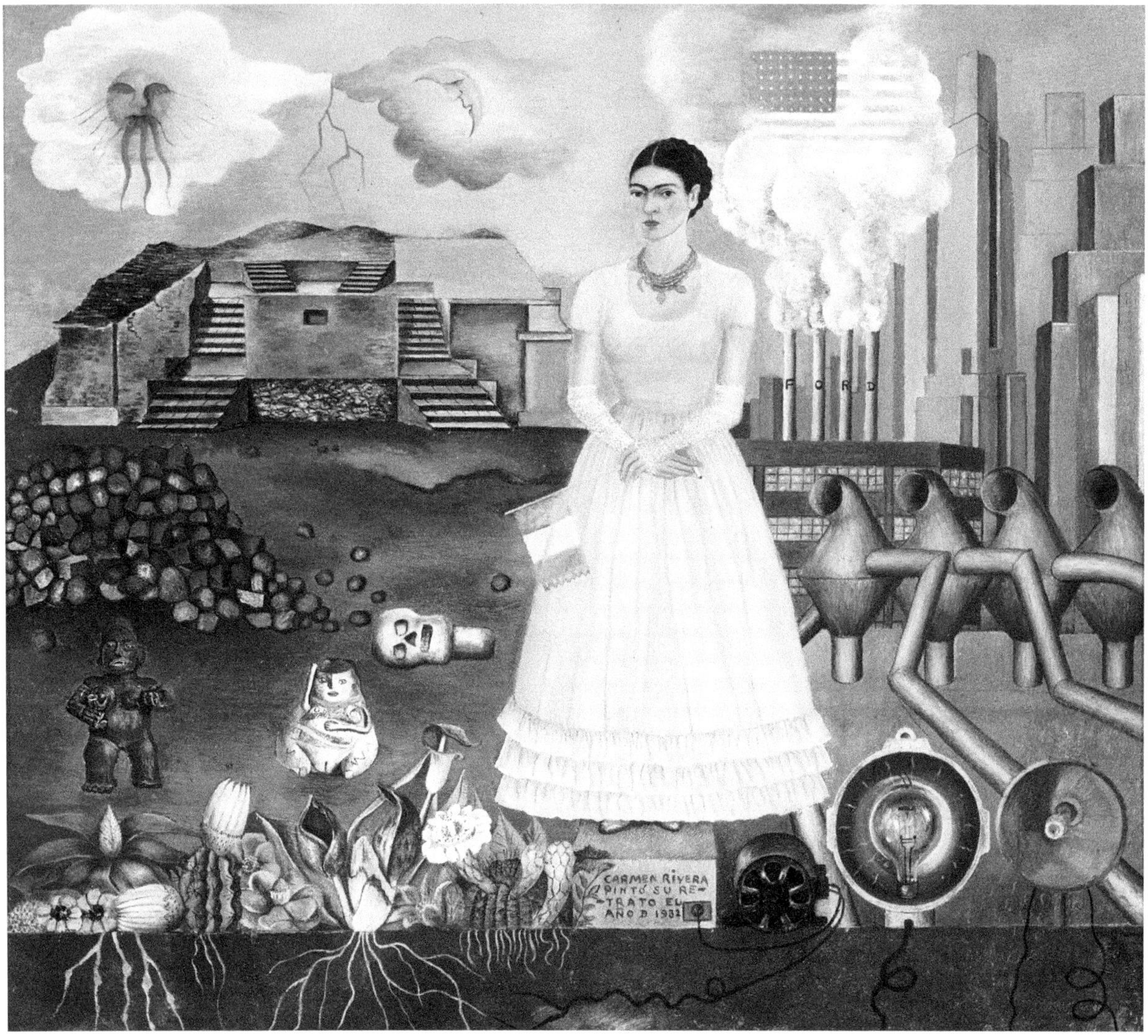

pyramid. A crumbling stone wall, three Precolumbian artifacts, and a row of tropical flowers with visible roots are below the pyramid. Although Kahlo represents Mexico in ruins, her image of her homeland exudes vitality in a way that the machines and skyscrapers of the United States do not.

Kahlo's contrast of U.S. machinery with Mesoamerican art was probably a reaction to Rivera's comparison of these elements. Hayden Herrera notes that "Diego was forever comparing the beauty of American machines and skyscrapers with the splendor of pre-Columbian artifacts."[33] In his mural program at the Detroit Institute of Arts, he covertly alluded to the Aztec earth goddess Coatlicue in the blocky form of the largest machine in the assembly line scene on the south wall.[34] Several years later he produced an overt version of this concept in *Pan American Union* (1940), where he created a figure that was half Coatlicue and half industrial stamping press. While Kahlo adopted the analogy between U.S. machinery and Precolumbian art from Rivera, it is clear from her rendering of machines in *Autorretrato en la frontera entre México y los Estados Unidos* that she did not share his admiration for them. For her, Mexico's ancient culture, though in ruins, trumps the machines and modernity of the United States.

The Mesoamerican pyramid in *Autorretrato en la frontera entre México y los Estados Unidos* has been identified by Jacinto Quirarte as the Aztec temple at Malinalco.[35] However, while the pyramid in Kahlo's painting strongly resembles the structure at Malinalco, it is not identical. In fact the excavation of Malinalco was not begun until 1936, so the similarity either is based on information about the site prior to its excavation or is coincidental.[36]

On the other hand, Kahlo rendered two of the Precolumbian artifacts in *Autorretrato en la frontera entre México y los Estados Unidos* with such accuracy that their original sources can be identified (the third artifact is a skull that is too generic to identify).[37] The female figure on the far left of the painting is a nude woman holding up a bowl of food in her left hand and carrying a suckling infant in her right arm. The figure is an exact copy of one from Jalisco in the collection of Museo Nacional de Antropología in Mexico City (fig. 28). The figure in the collection of the museum is damaged: the infant's head has been broken off, a defect that Kahlo meticulously recorded and that probably alludes to her recent miscarriage.[38]

The other identifiable artifact in *Autorretrato en la frontera entre México y los Estados Unidos* is an anthropomorphic vessel from Casas Grandes. Although it is not from West Mexico, it is important to mention because it clearly demonstrates the intentionality with which Kahlo chose the artifacts. The anthropomorphic vessel, which belonged to Rivera and was later reproduced in *Art in Ancient Mexico*, represents a woman and is decorated with bold geometric patterns (fig. 29).[39] Casas Grandes is located in northwestern Mexico, approximately 100 miles south of the border between Mexico and the United States. The site was active from about 1150 to 1400 CE and functioned as a trading center between Mesoamerica and the American Southwest.[40] Kahlo's choice of an object from a site that has always straddled two cultures contributes to the painting's focus on international borders and cultural differences. Both the original artifact and Kahlo's rendition of it emphasize the woman's genitalia in a pronounced way, suggesting the importance of sexuality and fertility for both the Casas Grandes culture and Kahlo. Thus the artifact's subject matter and provenance contribute to the themes of *Autorretrato en la frontera entre México y los Estados Unidos.*

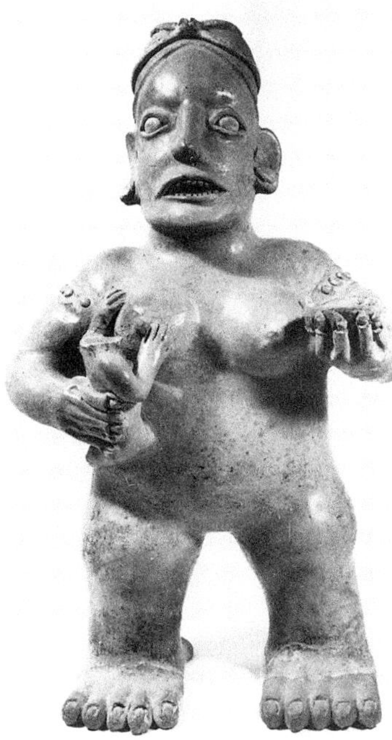

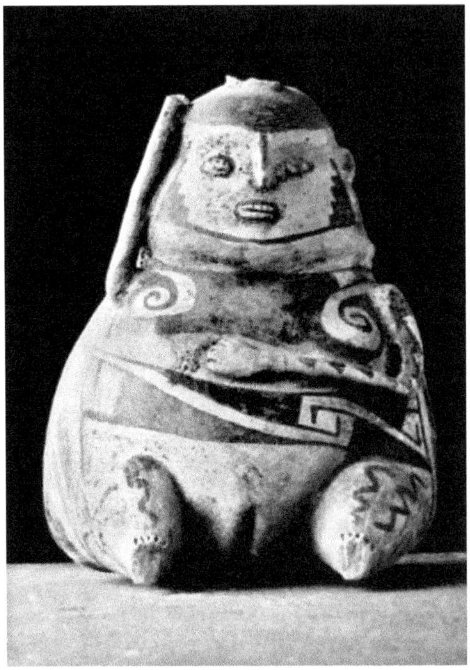

Fig. 28. Precolumbian female figure with infant from Jalisco, collection of the Museo Nacional de Antropología, Mexico City. Photograph courtesy of the Museo Nacional de Antropologia.

Fig. 29. Anthropomorphic vessel from Casas Grandes. This artifact is from northwestern Mexico rather than West Mexico. Casas Grandes was a trading center between Mesoamerica and the American Southwest active from about 1150 to 1400 CE. The inclusion of this artifact in Kahlo's *Autorretrato en la frontera entre México y los Estados Unidos* is due in part to the way Casas Grandes straddled two cultures (after Médioni and Pinto, *Art in Ancient Mexico*, fig. 208).

Lucienne Bloch, who worked as Rivera's assistant from 1932 to 1933 and lived with the Riveras in Detroit, recalls that Kahlo painted the Precolumbian artifacts "from photos and books Diego had brought from Mexico." Bloch comments that it was "just like Diego Rivera" to bring books and pictures of Precolumbian art with him to the United States. In regard to Kahlo's uses of these visual reference materials, Bloch observes that "she believed in being *exact*."[41]

In 1938 Kahlo created two paintings that represent different ceramic figures from West Mexico. One of the paintings is a tiny work in oil on tin, whose impact greatly exceeds its size (6 ½ × 4 ¾ inches). *El superviviente* (The Survivor) features a squat terra-cotta-colored male figure from West Mexico in the foreground of a barren ocher landscape (fig. 30). In the distance a mysterious rectangular portal stands at the crest of the horizon before a stormy sky. The ceramic figure appears to be moving rapidly toward the viewer, an illusion created by the active, asymmetrical position of his arms and legs, which seem to be pumping to propel his stocky body toward the viewer. Kahlo depicted the figure from a high angle that emphasizes his head and shoulders and added a panache of long, pale feathers to the headdress that flows to the left and contributes to the animate quality of the figure. Kahlo framed *El superviviente* in a decorative handmade tin frame from Oaxaca that is bigger than the painting.

Kahlo based the male figure in *El superviviente* on an artifact in Rivera's collection, which he identified as a warrior ballplayer from Colima.[42] In this context the term "ballplayer" refers to the ritual ballgame played throughout Precolumbian Mesoamerica. The ballgame was probably invented about thirty-five hundred years ago by the Olmecs, the first great culture of Mesoamerica, who lived in the tropical rubber country along the Gulf Coast.[43] The ballgame was played by two teams with a solid latex rubber ball in an I-shaped stone court with parallel masonry walls. The game had secular aspects but also had profound religious significance and frequently involved the sacrifice of players, whose blood was offered to the gods.[44] According to archaeologist Jane Stevenson Day,

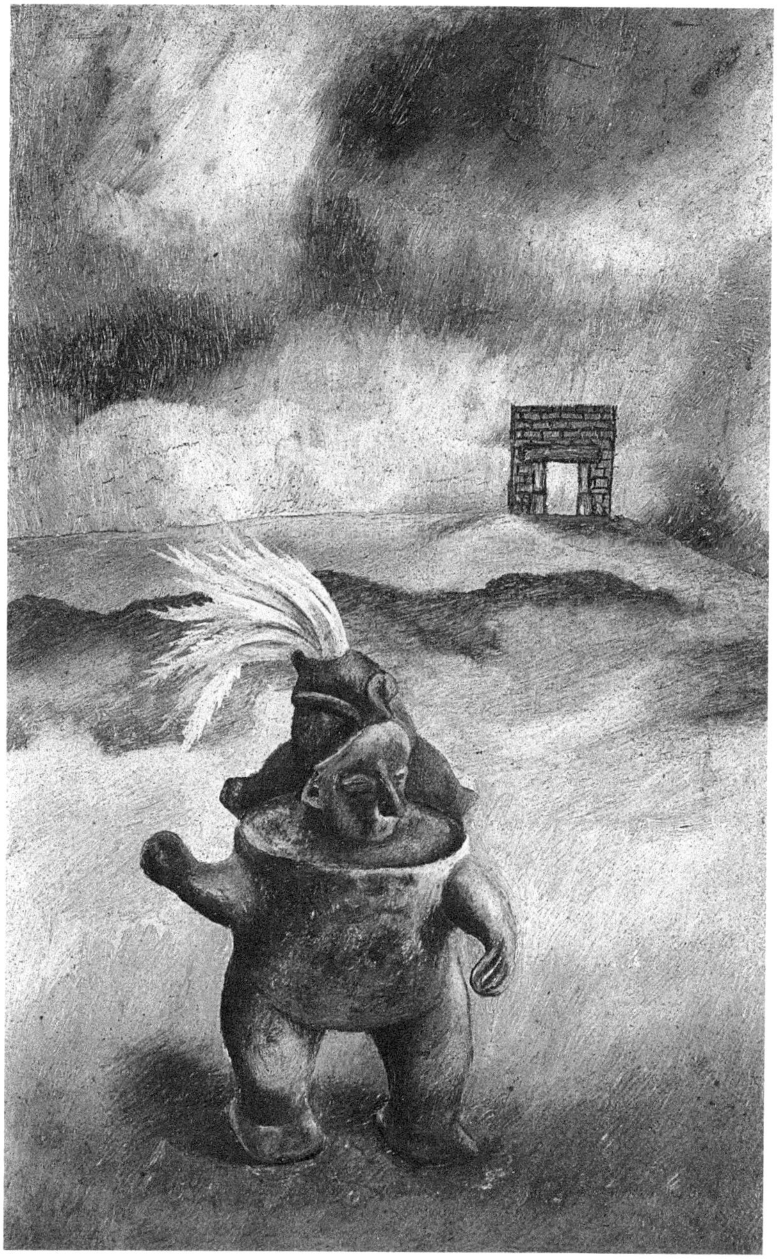

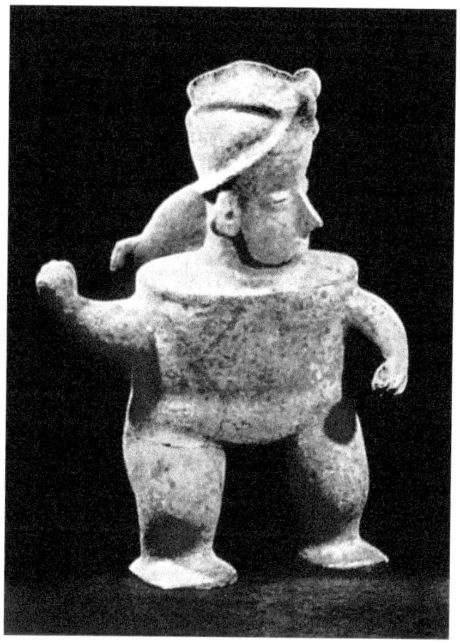

Fig. 30. Frida Kahlo, *El superviviente* (The Survivor), 1938, oil on tin, 6 ½ × 4 ¾ inches (16.5 × 12 cm), Pérez Simón collection, Mexico City. Photograph courtesy of Christie's Images Limited 2010. © 2014 Banco de México Diego Rivera Frida Kahlo Museums Trust, Mexico, D.F./Artists Rights Society (ARS), New York. Reproduction authorized by the Instituto Nacional de Bellas Artes y Literatura, 2015.

Fig. 31. Precolumbian figure from Colima in the collection of Diego Rivera, who identified the figure as a warrior ballplayer (after *Arte precolombino del Occidente de México*, fig. 62).

the movement of the ball in the court represents the movement of heavenly bodies in the sky. "The opposition of day and night, light and dark, and life and death were symbolically enacted on the ballcourt."[45] Art historian Mary Ellen Miller notes that in the Maya book of creation called the *Popol Vuh* "the confrontation of life and death is couched in terms of a ballgame."[46]

The ceramic figure from Colima that Rivera identified as a warrior ballplayer and Kahlo portrayed in *El superviviente* is reproduced in the catalogue to the 1946 exhibition of West Mexican art at the Palacio de Bellas Artes (fig. 31).[47] Representations of warriors and ballplayers occur frequently in the art of West Mexico. Although Rivera identified the male figure from Colima as a warrior ballplayer, the figures are usually identified as either warriors or ballplayers, not both. The warriors often hold a spear or a stick in both hands, and the figure that Kahlo rendered in *El superviviente* may have once held a weapon in his outstretched arms. Male figures from West Mexico are sometimes represented wearing an odd tubular costume or with a geometric tubular torso similar to the cylindrical body of the stocky figure in *El superviviente*.[48] This may be protective attire worn by ballplayers or warriors. If it is ballplayers' gear, then it is a regional substitution for or variation of the yoke that is worn around the waist by Mesoamerican ballplayers. Of all the Precolumbian artifacts that Kahlo represented, the figure in *El superviviente* is the one that best embodies the vivid sense of movement that prompted Rivera to praise "the beauty of movement" and "the form in movement" of West Mexican art (as noted above).

Kahlo exhibited *El superviviente* in her solo show at the Julien Levy Gallery in New York in November 1938. In an article titled "Ribbon around Bomb" in the *New Yorker*, an unidentified journalist wrote that the painting "consists of a Mexican idol looking lonely on a large field. This symbolizes the survival of Mexico in a shaky world."[49] The anonymous author did not attribute the words to Kahlo. He spoke to her at the opening, however, and she was almost certainly the source of the assertion that *El superviviente* symbolizes Mexico's survival in an unstable world. It was 1938, a perilous year. Europe was on the brink of World War II, and the Spanish Republican government was falling to Francisco Franco's army. On March 18, 1938, Mexican president Lázaro Cárdenas nationalized the oil companies, which had long been owned by foreigners. American, British, and other foreign oil companies waged an effective commercial boycott against Mexico and paid writers to promote a negative image of Mexico as a country that "stole whatever it could get its hands on."[50] The Mexican government severed diplomatic relations with Britain, and tensions between Mexico and the U.S. government remained high until the United States entered World War II on December 7, 1941. Although it is not visually apparent, *El superviviente* expresses the dangers confronting the Mexican Republic in 1938: the painting is political.

El superviviente was the first work to sell at Kahlo's solo exhibition at the Julien Levy Gallery, where the art critic and curator Walter Pach purchased it for $100. Pach, who had been one of Rivera's strongest supporters during the 1933 controversy over Rivera's mural at Radio City, also wrote a brief positive review of Kahlo's exhibition for *Art News*.[51] After the exhibition ended, *El superviviente* disappeared from public view for the next seventy-two years. In 2010 it was auctioned by Christie's for $1,178,000, presumably on the strength of the provenance (it had stayed in Pach's family) and the beauty of the painting, even though the tiny work was only known to a handful of people prior to 2010 and had no visual record prior to its publication in the auction catalogue.

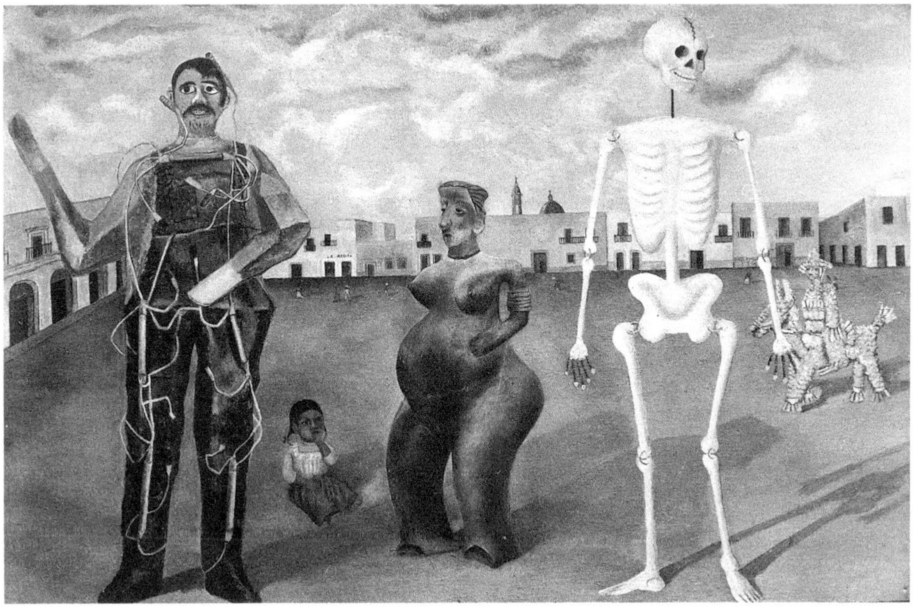

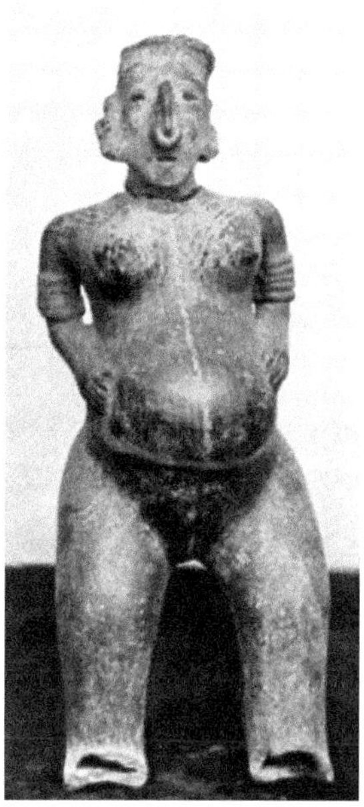

Fig. 32. Frida Kahlo, *The Square Is Theirs*, also known as *Cuatro habitantes de la Ciudad de México* (Four Inhabitants of Mexico City), 1938, oil on metal, 12 ¾ × 18 ¾ inches (32.4 × 47.6 cm), private collection, California, USA. © 2014 Banco de México Diego Rivera Frida Kahlo Museums Trust, Mexico, D.F./Artists Rights Society (ARS), New York. Reproduction authorized by the Instituto Nacional de Bellas Artes y Literatura, 2015.

Fig. 33. Precolumbian figure of pregnant woman from Nayarit, collection of Diego Rivera (after Médioni and Pinto, *Art in Ancient Mexico*, fig. 60).

The second painting that Kahlo created in 1938 that includes a ceramic figure from West Mexico is *The Square Is Theirs* (fig. 32). Although the work was first exhibited as *The Square Is Theirs* at the Julien Levy Gallery, it is now often called *Cuatro habitantes de la Ciudad de México* (Four Inhabitants of Mexico City). The painting depicts five figures in an otherwise deserted plaza. The smallest is a little girl about three years old who looks up in awe at the four larger inhabitants of the plaza: a Precolumbian figure of a pregnant woman from West Mexico, a grinning skeleton, a toy horse and rider woven from *petatillo* (tule reed), and a papier-mâché figure of a man in overalls. The last is a *judas*, an effigy figure wired with firecrackers and exploded on the Saturday before Easter.

When Kahlo discussed the imagery of this painting with Parker Lesley in 1939, she told him that the little girl represented herself. She described the grinning skeleton as "death, very gay, a joke" and said that she included the toy horseman "because he is weak, and at the same time has such elegance and because he is so easy to destroy."[52] She did not explain the *judas*, but the Riveras collected the figures. A similar *judas* of a man in blue overalls stands at the entrance to the Museo Frida Kahlo.

The figure of the pregnant woman from Nayarit is located at the exact center of the composition. The little girl (Frida) raises her eyes in wonder at this figure, her hand instinctively clasped to her mouth in awe. The statue is a reddish-brown clay figure of a naked woman in her ninth month of pregnancy, her breasts enlarged and her abdomen swollen with life. Kahlo based the image of the pregnant woman on a figure from Nayarit in her husband's collection, reproduced in *Art in Ancient Mexico*. The reproduction reveals that Kahlo rendered the original with painstaking fidelity, even copying its broken feet and cracked neck (fig. 33).[53] Kahlo's choice of a damaged figure may suggest a personal identification (a reference to her health problems), yet this object has broader significance. Kahlo told her students that Precolumbian art is the "root of our modern art."[54] The pregnant figure from Nayarit personifies Kahlo's belief that the Precolumbian past is still a fertile source for Mexican artists.

Two years later Kahlo again portrayed herself among a similar cast of characters. In *La mesa herida* of 1940 she presents herself seated behind a table in a stagelike setting framed by thick theatrical curtains (fig. 34). Kahlo is joined at the table by a Precolumbian figure from Nayarit, a papier-mâché skeleton, a *judas* figure of a workman wearing overalls, two children (her niece Isolda and her nephew Antonio), and her pet deer Granizo. While three of the guests at the table are Kahlo's old comrades from *The Square Is Theirs*, the mood of the painting has changed dramatically. In the two years between the creation of *The Square Is Theirs* and *La mesa herida*, the Riveras had separated and divorced. Kahlo began painting *La mesa herida* just as the divorce became final. Although she portrays herself surrounded by people and objects that she loved, the canvas exudes pain. Blood seeps from the knots in the wood of the table top, and the table's legs are human legs that have been flayed to reveal tendons and muscles.

The most distressing aspect of the painting is the bizarre relationship between Kahlo and the figure from Nayarit seated next to her. For no apparent reason Kahlo's right arm ends in a stub above her elbow. A pipelike prosthesis attached to the stub extends down, where it bends and rests on the table then continues up to offer a bowl to the figure from Nayarit.

The figure from Nayarit depicted in *La mesa herida* is part of a larger sculpture that belonged to Rivera. The complete piece, which is illustrated in *Art in Ancient Mexico*, is actually two united figures: a man and a pregnant woman, who holds up a cup of food or drink to her mate (fig. 35). The same sculpture is reproduced in the exhibition catalogue *Arte precolombino del Occidente de México*, where it is identified as a "couple in loving attitude" from Ixtlán, Nayarit, in the collection of Diego Rivera.[55] It is now on display at Anahuacalli.

In *La mesa herida* Kahlo has depicted the male figure and eliminated the woman. Thus in this painting the male figure from Nayarit can be interpreted as a proxy for Diego Rivera. The disturbing connection between her self-portrait and the figure from Nayarit may be an expression of the painful disruption of their union.

While the clay couple from Nayarit that Kahlo quotes in *La mesa herida* is on display at Anahuacalli, an almost identical object is in the collection of the Museo Frida Kahlo.

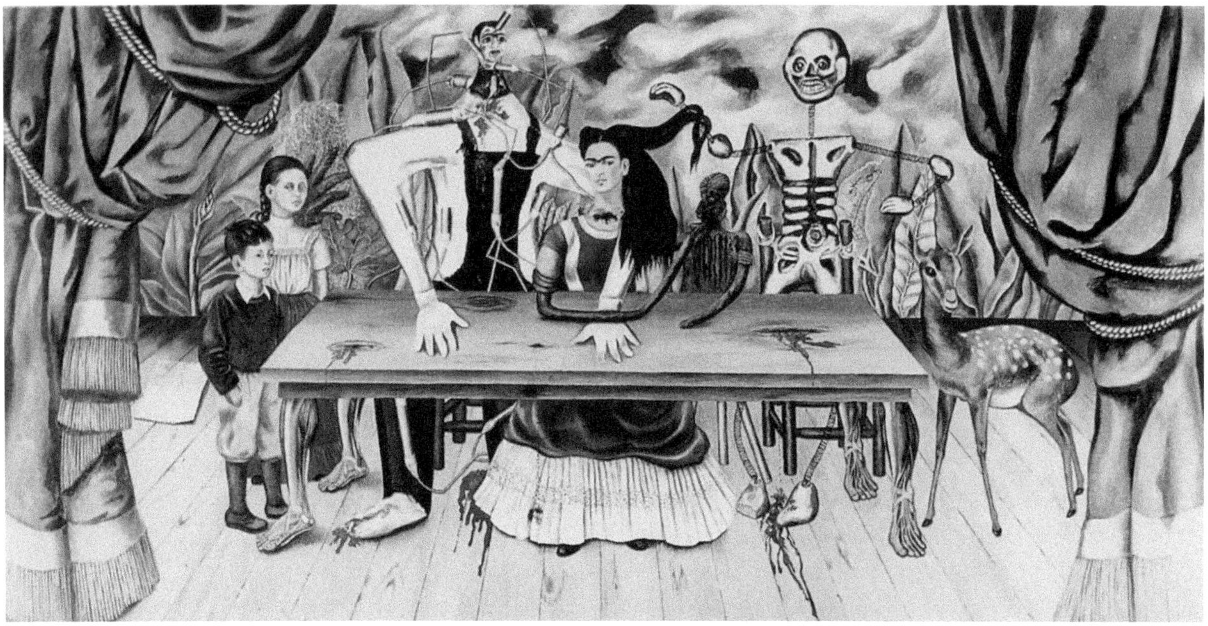

Fig. 34. Frida Kahlo, *La mesa herida* (The Wounded Table), 1940, location unknown. © 2014 Banco de México Diego Rivera Frida Kahlo Museums Trust, Mexico, D.F./Artists Rights Society (ARS), New York. Reproduction authorized by the Instituto Nacional de Bellas Artes y Literatura, 2015.

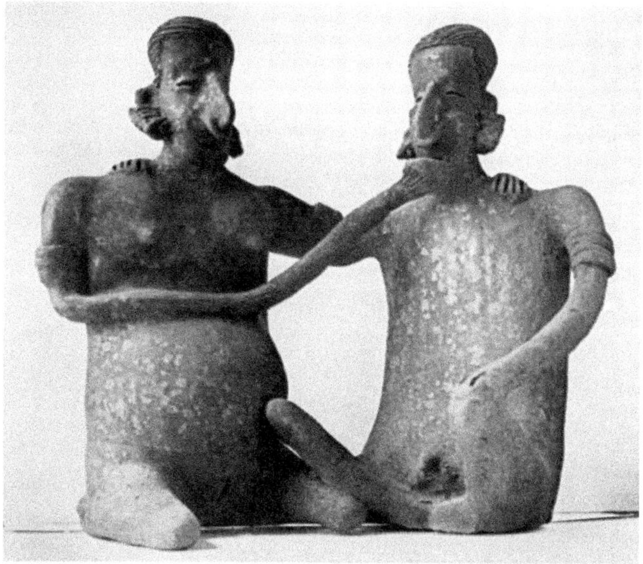

Fig. 35. Precolumbian marriage pair from Nayarit, collection of Diego Rivera (after Médioni and Pinto, *Art in Ancient Mexico*, fig. 52).

The piece in the Museo Frida Kahlo is a mirror image of the marriage pair at Anahuacalli (the female is on the right, the male on the left). From 1958, when the Museo Frida Kahlo opened, until the late 1980s or early 1990s, this marriage pair was prominently displayed in a room dedicated exclusively to Kahlo's collection of Precolumbian art from Mexico. Most of the artifacts in the room were exhibited in glass cabinets along the walls, but the couple from Nayarit, which is approximately twenty inches tall, was given pride of place on top of a display stand at the center of the room.[56] The museum was originally arranged by Kahlo's close friend Carlos Pellicer, who presumably knew that the couple from Nayarit held special meaning for her. In the early 1990s, when the Museo Frida Kahlo was modified to accommodate the dramatic rise in the number of visitors, the sculpture at the center of the room was removed to facilitate the flow of traffic.[57] The marriage pair now sits on the top of a tall bookcase in Kahlo's studio, unprotected from possible earthquake damage. The couple from Nayarit also appears in the background of several photographs of Kahlo in her studio in the early 1940s, testifying to its daily presence in her life.[58]

Five years after Kahlo painted *La mesa herida*, she once again depicted a Precolumbian artifact in a self-portrait. In *Autorretrato con changuito* (Self-Portrait with Small Monkey) of 1945, she portrayed herself accompanied by her pet monkey, a ceramic figure from West Mexico, and her dog (fig. 36). Kahlo, the monkey, and the dog are immobile and gaze directly at the viewer. A yellow ribbon descends from the top left of the canvas, loops around a trompe l'oeil nail, individually encircles the necks of the monkey, artist, Precolumbian figure, and dog, then lassoes the signature and date in the upper right corner. The connecting device of the yellow ribbon asserts that Kahlo, her pets, and the figure from West Mexico are united in a loose but irrefutable bond.

The sculpture Kahlo portrayed in *Autorretrato con changuito* represents a squatting man with one knee raised, with his head and one arm propped on his raised knee. He seems to be lost in thought. Kahlo rendered the pensive figure from an artifact from Nayarit in Rivera's collection, which was published in *Arte precolombino del Occidente de México*, although the reproduction shows it from a viewpoint so different from the one that Kahlo used that it is virtually unrecognizable.[59] The actual figure is on display at Anahuacalli (fig. 37).

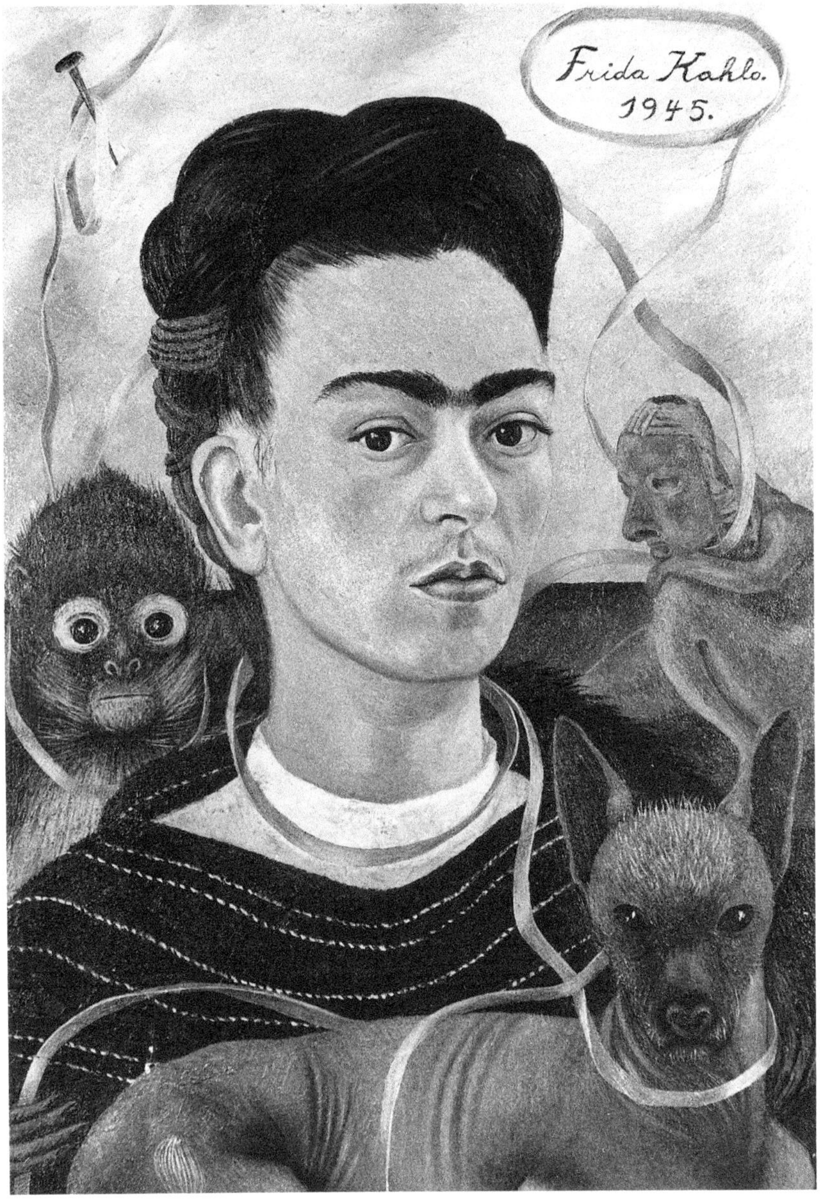

Fig. 36. Frida Kahlo, *Autorretrato con changuito* (Self-Portrait with Small Monkey), 1945, oil on Masonite, 22 1/16 × 16 3/8 inches (56 × 41.5 cm), collection of the Museo Dolores Olmedo, Xochimilco, Mexico, D.F.

Kahlo's depiction of the Precolumbian figure in *Autorretrato con changuito* captures the remarkable plastic fluidity of the art of West Mexico and convincingly communicates a person deep in thought. Kahlo must have realized that the position of the figure from Nayarit bears a striking resemblance to that of Auguste Rodin's *The Thinker* (ca. 1880) and rendered it from a viewpoint that makes this similarity apparent (fig. 38). Kahlo became intimately acquainted with Rodin's *The Thinker* when Rivera painted frescoes at the Detroit Institute of Arts in 1932. At the time, the institute's 1904 version of the sculpture was on display in the Great Hall, located between the main entrance to the museum and the courtyard where Rivera was painting. Kahlo would have seen *The Thinker* every time she went to the museum to visit her husband while he worked, which she did frequently. She probably also saw *The Gates of Hell*, 1880–1917 (where the pensive man is the central figure), and an early version of *The Thinker* at the Musée Rodin when she visited Paris in early 1939.

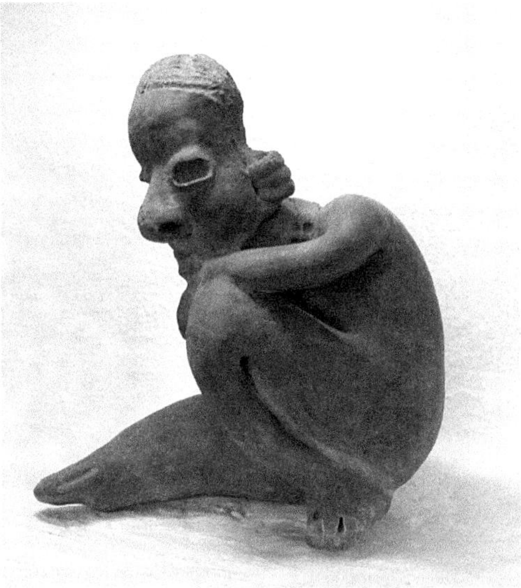

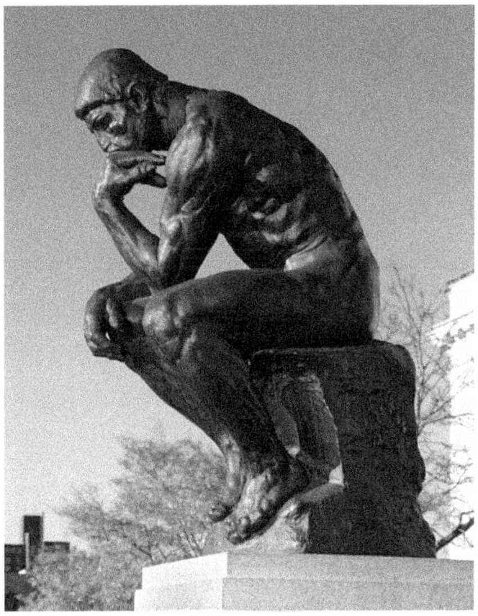

Fig. 37. Precolumbian figure from Nayarit, collection of Diego Rivera, on display at Anahuacalli.

Fig. 38. Auguste Rodin, *The Thinker*, 1904, Detroit Institute of Arts, gift of Horace H. Rackham, Bridgeman Art Library.

The gray dog in the foreground of *Autorretrato con changuito* was one of Kahlo's favorite pets, a *xoloitzcuintle* dog named Señor Xolotl. Kahlo and Rivera owned several *xoloitzcuintle* dogs, a native Mexican breed. In ancient Mexico dogs were valued for their companionship and warmth. (The hairless *xoloitzcuintle* has a high body temperature, so people who suffered from arthritis and other ailments slept with their dog for the warmth it provided.) Dogs were buried with their owners, because it was believed that the dog would act as a guide in the afterlife, helping the deceased in their arduous four-year journey through the underworld and safely guiding them across the river to Mictlan.[60]

Kahlo named her dog Señor Xolotl after the Aztec god Xolotl. Xolotl, who was often represented with a dog's head, was the twin of Quetzalcoatl and associated with dual phenomena, Venus as the evening star, twins, monsters, sorcery, and the underworld. Raquel Tibol recalls that Kahlo's favorite dog once urinated on several watercolors that Rivera had just painted. "Furious, Rivera ran though the house pursuing the dog with a big machete, determined to kill him." But when Rivera caught him, the dog wagged his tail and looked up at him with such a wry, remorseful expression that Rivera picked him up, petted his smoky gray skin, and said, "Señor Xolotl, emperor of Xibalba, lord of darkness, you are the best art critic."[61] This story illustrates the affection and tolerance that the Riveras felt toward their pets and testifies to the way they linked their pets to the roles that animals played in Mesoamerican mythology.

Kahlo has not just depicted herself with her favorite pets and a figure from West Mexico in *Autorretrato con changuito*. She has surrounded herself with two animals and an object that held symbolic meaning in the Precolumbian era, drawing on these meanings and transforming them for her own purposes. She stands like a goddess or saint encircled by her attributes: the monkey, which the Aztecs associated with fertility, dance, and the arts; the dog, symbolizing death and the underworld; and the pensive West Mexican sculpture, which she employs to suggest meditation about life and death.

In the Precolumbian era life and death were not viewed as opposites but as parts of the same cycle that includes birth, life, death, and renewal. In 1943 Kahlo painted a self-portrait titled *Pensando en la muerte* (Thinking about Death), a concept that she expressed by painting a skull and cross bones on her forehead at the third eye point. Two years later, in

Autorretrato con changuito, she invented a way to communicate thought about the entire life cycle by connecting herself to animals that were associated with fertility and the arts and death and the underworld in the Precolumbian era. In this painting the effigy from West Mexico appears to be Kahlo's proxy, expressing her meditation on the life cycle.[62]

In 1951 Kahlo painted *Naturaleza muerta* (Still Life) for her dentist, Samuel Fastlicht (fig. 39). At the center of the composition stands a small gray-brown ceramic figure of a dog from Colima, which is surrounded by a rainbow of fruits and vegetables. A lemon perches on the spout that rises from its head. A small pink flag on a wooden stick planted in a honeydew melon proclaims, "I belong to Samuel Fastlicht. I was painted with utmost love by Frida Kahlo, in 1951. ~ Coyoacán~."[63] Another small flag on a stick sports the three colors of the Mexican flag. The ceramic dog from Colima belonged to Kahlo (fig. 40) and is in the collection of the Museo Frida Kahlo; when I last visited the museum it sat inconspicuously on the bottom shelf of the bookcase in her studio.

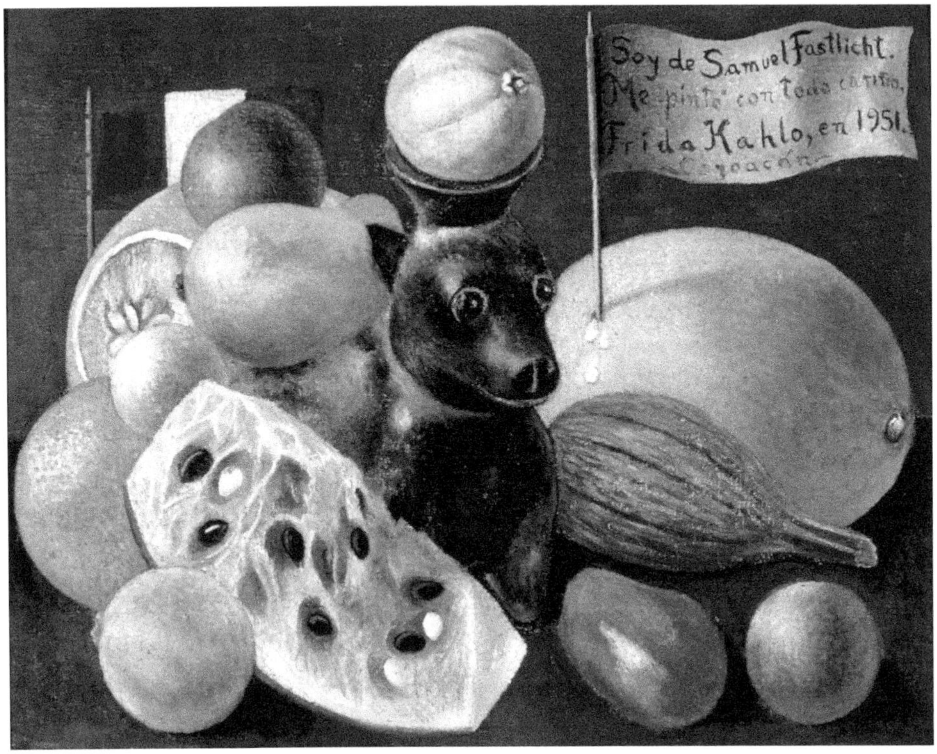

Fig. 39. Frida Kahlo, *Naturaleza muerta* (Still Life), 1951, oil on canvas, 11 ⅛ × 14 ¼ inches (28.2 × 36 cm), private collection. © 2014 Banco de México Diego Rivera Frida Kahlo Museums Trust, Mexico, D.F./ Artists Rights Society (ARS), New York. Reproduction authorized by the Instituto Nacional de Bellas Artes y Literatura, 2015.

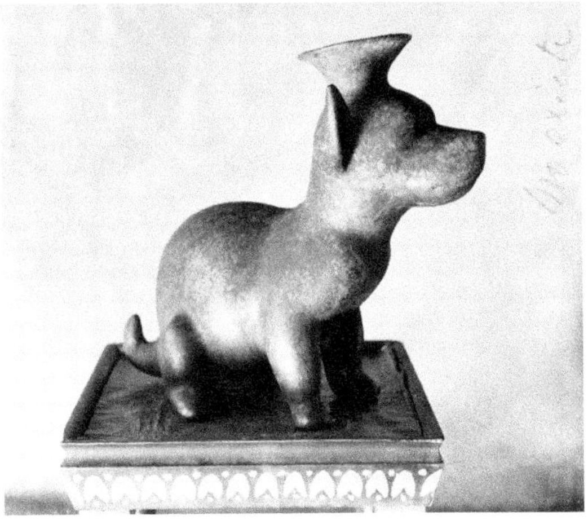

Fig. 40. Photograph of Precolumbian ceramic figure of a dog from Colima. The photograph was among the documents found in an armoire in a sealed-up section of the Museo Frida Kahlo in 2004. © Diego Rivera and Frida Kahlo Archive, Banco de México, Fiduciary of the Trust related to the Diego Rivera and Frida Kahlo Museums.

Because dogs were guides to the underworld in ancient Mexico, the dog from Colima reminds us of the transience of life. *Naturaleza muerta* is not, however, a true *vanitas* painting. As a Marxist who thought that people invented or imagined gods out of fear, Kahlo would never have produced a painting whose principal goal was to meditate upon the transitory nature of worldly pleasures and the need to prioritize the salvation of the soul. Kahlo does not admonish us to save our souls; rather, she urges us to gobble up life's pleasures while we can.

Conclusion

When the six paintings in which Kahlo depicted figures from West Mexico are considered together, a number of patterns emerge. Kahlo's predilection for the art of West Mexico was based on the aesthetic quality of the figures, the esteem for these artifacts that she shared with her husband, the domestic subject matter, and the perception that this work was secular. Although she selected artifacts that do not represent deities, all the paintings in which the ceramic figures appear have a spiritual component: each painting includes references to life and death.[64] The artifacts in *Autorretrato en la frontera entre México y los Estados Unidos* are a nursing mother with a headless infant from Jalisco, a fertility figure from Casas Grandes, and a skull of unknown origin. *The Square Is Theirs* depicts a pregnant figure from Nayarit and a skeleton. *La mesa herida* brings together children and a skeleton. *Autorretrato con changuito* portrays Kahlo with animals that the Aztecs associated with sex and death, while the burial effigy of the dog in *Naturaleza muerta* of 1951 is surrounded by fresh fruit and vegetables in vibrant colors. Even *El superviviente*, which is something of an anomaly, refers to the survival of Mexico in a time of crisis; the main figure, whether a warrior or a ballplayer or both, confronts mortal danger. Kahlo's persistent association of figures from West Mexico with the life cycle coincides with Rivera's interest in the "frank expression of death and sex" in these objects that Barbara Braun noted.

The ceramic sculptures from West Mexico that Kahlo represented are well-known types: the ancient art of West Mexico includes countless examples of nursing mothers, pregnant women, marriage pairs, warriors, ballplayers, pensive figures, and dogs. While Kahlo chose familiar types of West Mexican art, she represented specific artifacts. The exact artifacts that she used can be identified, and the majority are from Rivera's collection. Kahlo selected each West Mexican figure for its subject matter (and sometimes its condition) and how it could contribute to the narrative or theme of her painting. Her choices of a figure of a nursing mother with an infant whose head had broken off and a pregnant woman with broken feet are not coincidences but references to problems in her life. Yet the selection of the work is not limited to the personal. The pensive Precolumbian figure in *Autorretrato con changuito* embodies the concept of meditating on the life cycle, and the pregnant figure from Nayarit that appears in *The Square Is Theirs* personifies her conviction that the art of ancient Mexico continues to be a fertile source for the modern art of Mexico. *El superviviente* addresses the political challenges that Mexico faced in 1938. It may also allude to the survival and enduring value of Precolumbian art.[65]

Kahlo appropriated the Precolumbian figures from West Mexico to recount her personal story and project her intellectual and political ideas. The stories that she tells in the four self-portraits inextricably weave her life into the history of Mexican art in a way that positions her work among the art she most admired: the Precolumbian and popular arts of

Mexico. In a 1942 article Rivera wrote that Kahlo was the nucleus of a small group of brilliant young painters that included Antonio Ruiz, Juan O'Gorman, and Fernando Castillo. According to Rivera, these painters "can definitively be called Mexicans, because they are embedded magnificently in the tradition that comes from the remote and extraordinary Tarascans of Colima and Nayarit."[66] Rivera made this statement after Kahlo had already created four paintings in which she incorporated a figure from West Mexico into the composition, so his statement was surely prompted by the content of her paintings. Like the character of Agrado in *Todo sobre mi madre*, Kahlo constructed an image of herself that resembled her ideal self. It was inextricably bound to the indigenous traditions of Mexico, whose origins could be traced to the ancient cultures of West Mexico.

4

Beyond the Personal

Kahlo's *La niña, la luna y el sol* of 1942

In 1942 Kahlo created a painting that depicts an indigenous girl seated on a rock at the center of a vast, deserted plain. She is wearing a thick sweater with a striking pattern of black and white triangles and holds a model airplane with an odd abstract green and ocher curvilinear design painted on it. In the background, on the edge of the horizon, stand two Precolumbian pyramids, positioned on either side of the girl; the pyramid on the right is significantly larger than the one on the left. The sun and the moon appear in the sky simultaneously, and their disparate potencies cause a division in the color of the sky: the solar side is a pale blue-violet, while the lunar side is a deep nocturnal blue. The contrast in value is mitigated by wispy white clouds that lace the entire sky. The light-dark division is repeated in the lower half of the painting, where the earth is ocher on the right and sepia on the left.

The following year Kahlo's husband wrote an essay titled "Frida Kahlo y el arte mexicano" (Frida Kahlo and Mexican Art) in which he referred to this painting. In the first three-fourths of the article Rivera provided a Marxist interpretation of the hybrid nature of Mexico's Spanish and indigenous heritage from the Conquest to the beginning of the postrevolutionary period. One of his principal concerns was the suppression of indigenous culture by the church and state and the survival of indigenous imagery despite this repression. When Rivera finally discussed Kahlo, he concentrated on her work and only added a trace of biography, not mentioning that she was his wife. In the pages devoted to her work he wrote in an almost stream-of-consciousness style in which his words evoke images that she had painted. Although he never cited a single title, his phrases conjure specific paintings. "The nourishing nana . . . [with] the Indian mask of hard stone" summons *Mi nana y yo*. "Frida, alone in the industrial space, stretched out on a cot, from where she sees through her tears that the fetal-life is machine-flower, slow snail, manikin, and skeletal armature" calls up *Henry Ford Hospital.* The following passage alludes to the painting of 1942:

> Beyond the wide open door of the sky there was only relentless and marvelous space, in which the sun and the moon co-exist above the pyramids, portending grandeur in their microscopic size in relation to the star and planet, and immense in their systems of proportions, which are those of the entire universe. The little girl seated in the center of the world possessed a toy airplane whose velocity is much greater than the speed of light, and equals that of imagination-reason.[1]

In 1944 Kahlo exhibited the painting for the first time, under the title *La niña, la luna y el sol* (The Girl, the Moon, and the Sun) in an exhibition called *El niño en la plástica mexicana* (The Child in Mexican Art) at the Biblioteca Benjamin Franklin (Benjamin Franklin Library) in Mexico City (fig. 41). The painting has been exhibited and published with other titles since then, but I believe that the title that Kahlo chose when she first exhibited it is the best.

When Kahlo had her first solo exhibition in Mexico in 1953 at Lola Álvarez Bravo's Galería Arte Contemporáneo, the painting appeared as *Mujer de sarape,* a title that could be translated as *Woman in a Sarape* or *Woman Wearing a Sarape.*[2] It is a surprising title, because the person represented is a girl in a sweater, not a woman in a sarape, although the geometric pattern of the sweater resembles the designs of some sarapes.

In 1987 Mexican author Martha Zamora published the painting under the title *La tehuacana Lucha María* (The Tehuacana Lucha María) in her first book about Kahlo. Zamora noted that the painting had been exhibited on various occasions under the title *El sol y la luna* (The Sun and Moon) but that the words "La tehuacana Lucha María" were written on the back of the painting in Kahlo's own handwriting.[3] Based on her conviction that the inscription is in Kahlo's handwriting, Zamora believes that *La tehuacana Lucha María* is the best title for the painting. Other writers have followed her example, usually publishing the painting with two titles: *La tehuacana Lucha María* or *El sol y la luna.* However, it is not fully established that Kahlo wrote the inscription.[4]

Regardless of whether Kahlo wrote the words on the back of the painting, problems exist with the uncritical use of *La tehuacana Lucha María* as a title. This title was never used in an exhibition or publication during Kahlo's lifetime. The word *tehuacana* refers to a girl or woman from Tehuacán, a town located approximately 120 miles to the southeast of Mexico City. Tehuacán is famous for its mineral springs, and a popular brand of sparkling mineral water is named Tehuacán.[5] The girl depicted in the painting was named Lucha María, but she was probably not from Tehuacán. The site depicted in the painting is most definitely not Tehuacán.

The girl portrayed in the painting looks directly at the viewer. Her dark complexion and two long black braids indicate that she is indigenous. Her bare feet imply that she is poor. According to one of Kahlo's former students, the girl is Lucha María, the daughter of one of Kahlo's domestic employees.[6] According to Kahlo's stepdaughter Guadalupe Rivera Marín, the girl is named Luz María and her grandparents, Tomás and Rosa Teutli, lived on the outskirts of the archaeological zone of Teotihuacan. Rivera Marín considers the Teutli family to be "direct descendants of the builders of Teotihuacan."[7]

The painting is not a portrait in the sense of being a detailed rendering of the girl's features or a psychological study. In Kahlo's portraits the subject's face usually fills up a significant portion of the canvas, and she faithfully records any irregularities in the sitter's features. In *Retrato de Natasha Gelman* (Portrait of Natasha Gelman) of 1943 and *Retrato de Ing. Marte R. Gómez* (Portrait of Engineer Marte R. Gómez) of 1944, only the subjects' faces and shoulders are depicted, while the backgrounds are restricted to a single flat color. When Kahlo invented a more involved background, the elements that she added reveal something about the person portrayed. For example, in *Retrato de Guillermo Kahlo* (Portrait of Guillermo Kahlo) of 1952, she included her father's large view camera and a scroll with a message testifying that he had been her first artistic role model.

In *La niña, la luna y el sol* Kahlo deviated from her usual format for portraits. The girl does not fill up the composition but rather becomes part of the setting. In this respect the work resembles certain of Kahlo's self-portraits in which she imagined a scene or invented a fantastic situation that communicates concepts that facial expressions alone could not convey. Such works include *Mi nacimiento* of 1932, *Mi nana y yo* of 1937, and *El venadito* of 1946. Unlike these imaginary settings, however, the locale of *La niña, la luna y el sol* is a recognizable site: the archaeological zone of Teotihuacan.

Teotihuacan

Teotihuacan is located approximately thirty miles northeast of Mexico City. The site was first settled in the Late Formative era and rose to power around 100 CE. The city was designed on a grid with its most famous structures, the Pyramid of the Moon (by 100 CE) (fig. 42) and the Pyramid of the Sun (by 225 CE) (fig. 43), positioned to the north and east of the ritual road called the Way of the Dead. At its height the city had a population now estimated at approximately 200,000 people, making it one of the largest cities in the world at the time. Sometime between 550 and 650 CE the city was invaded and burned; the majority of its inhabitants went into exile or fled.[8] The site has been extensively excavated, but profound questions remain, including the ethnicity of Teotihuacan's population. The Aztecs, who migrated to the region several centuries later, thought that the two gigantic pyramids and other large structures of Teotihuacan had been built by gods or giants who inhabited the earth before humans arrived. *Teotihuacan* means "place of the gods" or "place where the gods created man."[9] In spite of the disappearance of the civilization of Teotihuacan, the site continued to be considered sacred. The Aztecs believed that it was the birthplace of the present sun, which they considered the Fifth Sun. The first four suns had already been created and destroyed, just as our own will eventually end in cataclysm.

Kahlo brought groups of students to Teotihuacan on at least three occasions. These were festive field trips; Rivera attended one of these outings, and María Izquierdo came along on two others. The painter Héctor Xavier, who was Izquierdo's student, also went to Teotihuacan with the group. He believed that these trips were motivated by Kahlo's desire to show her students "what the indigenous people had achieved in this beautiful architecture impelled . . . by the gods or *for* the gods. Frida insisted on this: the great religious force of the indigenous people in order to achieve works of the magnitude of the two pyramids."[10]

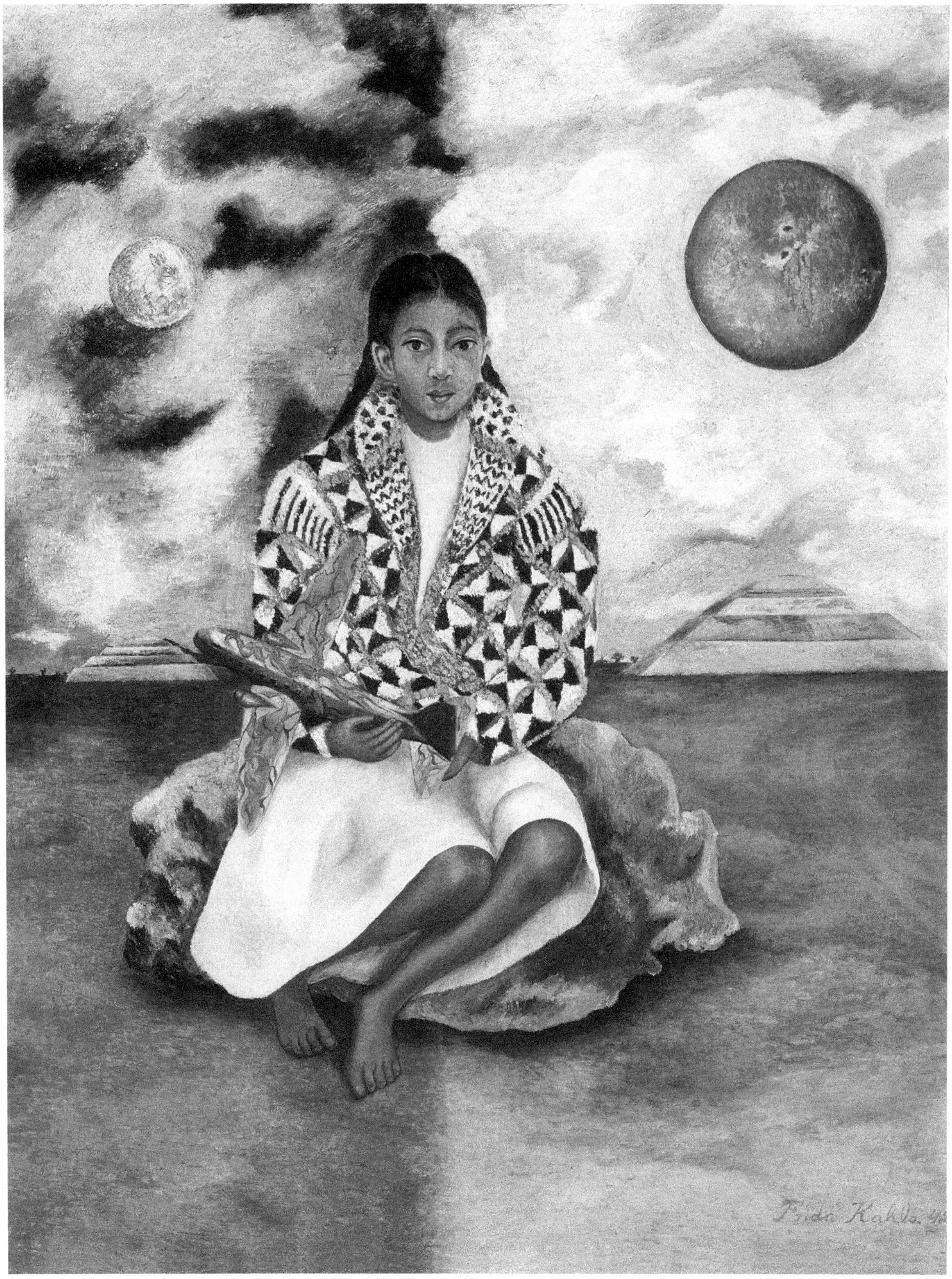
Frida Kahlo 42

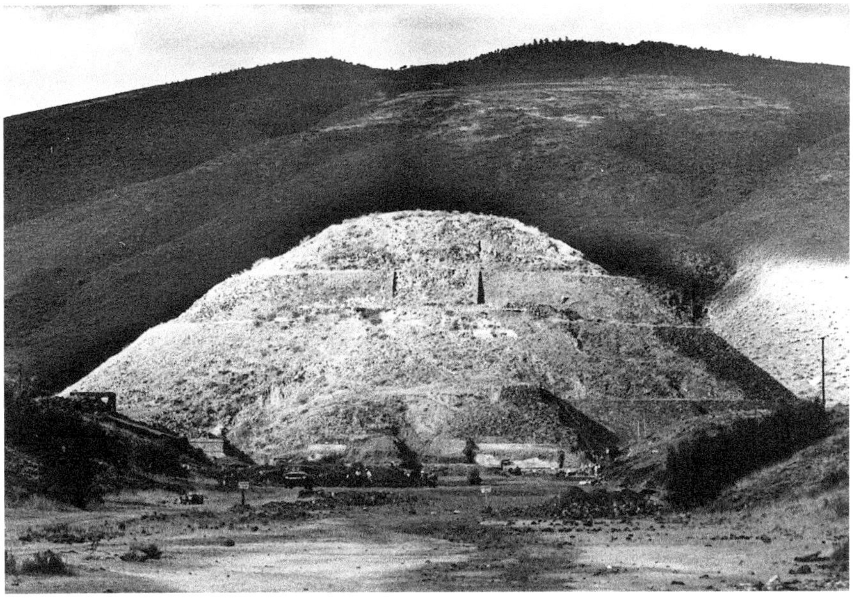

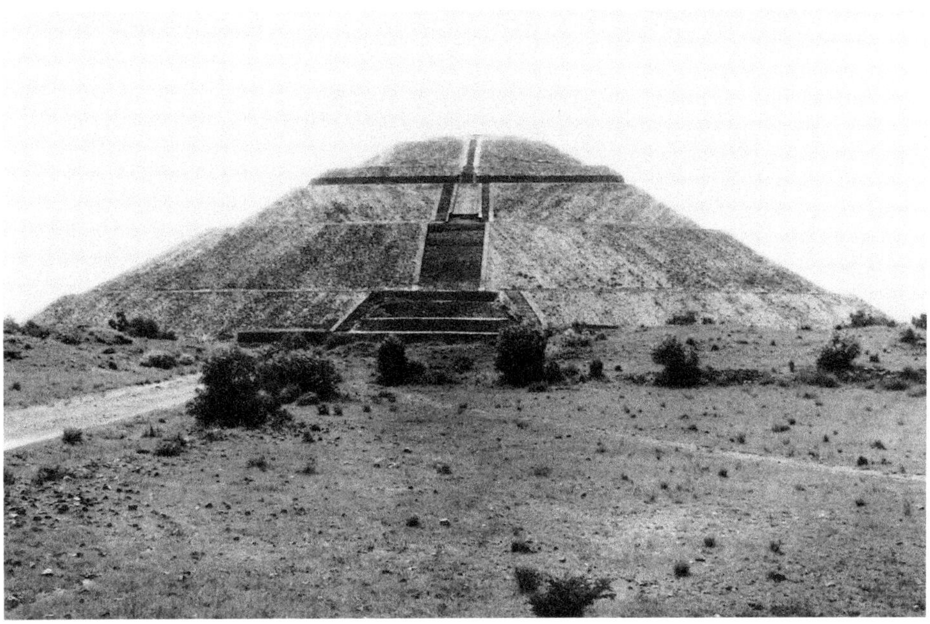

Fig. 41. (*facing page*) Frida Kahlo first exhibited this painting under the title *La niña, la luna y el sol* (The Girl, the Moon, and the Sun), 1942, at the Biblioteca Benjamin Franklin (Benjamin Franklin Library) in Mexico City in 1944. Since 1987 the painting has been known as *La tehuacana Lucha María* (The Tehuacana Lucha María) or *El sol y la luna* (The Sun and the Moon). Oil on Masonite, 21 ½ × 17 inches (54.6 × 43.1 cm), Pérez Simon collection, Mexico City. © 2014 Banco de México Diego Rivera Frida Kahlo Museums Trust, Mexico, D.F./Artists Rights Society (ARS), New York. Reproduction authorized by the Instituto Nacional de Bellas Artes y Literatura, 2015.

Fig. 42. (*top*) Pyramid of the Moon, Teotihuacan, by 100 CE. Photograph ca. 1950, courtesy of Benson Latin American Library, University of Texas at Austin.

Fig. 43. (*bottom*) Pyramid of the Sun, Teotihuacan, by 225 CE. Postcard, 1930s to 1950s, courtesy of the Benson Latin American Library, University of Texas at Austin.

Various elements within *La niña, la luna y el sol* testify to Kahlo's familiarity with the myth of the creation of the Fifth Sun at Teotihuacan, even though the girl's sweater and toy airplane insist that the painting takes place in the twentieth century. The work is neither a historical scene nor a depiction of a myth, but rather a representation of a modern girl in front of the pyramids of Teotihuacan in 1942. The elements in the painting that refer to the myth pertain to Kahlo's choice of setting and the way she rendered it. The myth that she subtly alluded to is widely known in Mexico, and fully understanding the painting depends on knowing it. The myth has numerous versions; the following one was recorded in the sixteenth century by the Franciscan friar Bernardino de Sahagún in the *Florentine Codex*.[11]

The Creation of the Fifth Sun at Teotihuacan

Before the Fifth Sun was created, all was in darkness. The gods gathered at Teotihuacan in order to bring light to the world. Because the sun could only be created if a deity cast himself into a sacrificial fire, the gods asked who would dare to do this. The proud Tecuciztecatl promptly volunteered. A second god was also needed, but the other gods were afraid and drew back. Finally the gods drafted a humble, scab-covered god who stood quietly at the edge of the group. The scabby one, Nanahuatzin, accepted willingly.

The gods built two hills where Tecuciztecatl and Nanahuatzin performed penance for four days. After four days the gods assembled at midnight on either side of the great pyre to witness Tecuciztecatl's heroic sacrifice. Tecuciztecatl prepared to throw himself into the fire and rushed toward it, but when he reached the pyre, terror overcame him, and he stopped short. Four times he tried to cast himself into the flames, but each time he failed. Discouraged, the other gods turned to the scabby one, who hardened his heart, shut his eyes, and leapt into the flames, where his body crackled and sizzled. When Tecuciztecatl saw Nanahuatzin had succeeded, he too leapt into the fire.

The gods waited, and after a while the sky grew light and the sun rose in the east from Nanahuatzin's sacrifice. Later the moon rose in the east from Tecuciztecatl's sacrifice, and it burned as bright as the sun. When the gods saw that the sun and the moon shone equally, they became worried and discussed whether this was right. Suddenly one of the gods flung a rabbit at the moon, darkening its surface and diminishing its power to emit light. Afterward the ancient Mexicans saw a rabbit in the dark patches of the moon, rather than the man in the moon of Western tradition.

When the sun and moon were first created they hung in the sky together, still and motionless. In order to set them in motion, the gods agreed to be sacrificed and chose Ehecatl, the wind god, as their executioner. Although Ehecatl carried out the sacrifice, the sun and moon remained inert, until he blew fiercely and violently at the sun, setting it on its path across the sky. When the sun set, Ehecatl turned to the moon and blew it into motion, too. And so the legend goes.

The Painting, the Site, and the Myth

We can see the subtle but definite ways in which Kahlo's painting is linked to the creation myth of the Fifth Sun. Kahlo used the site that was believed to be the birthplace of the Fifth Sun. The two pyramids on the horizon are the two "hills" where Tecuciztecatl and Nanahuatzin performed their self-sacrifices. The larger structure is the Pyramid of the Sun; the smaller one is the Pyramid of the Moon. Kahlo has positioned the sun directly over the Pyramid of the Sun and placed the moon squarely above the Pyramid of the Moon.[12] The two celestial bodies appear in the sky together just as they did at the time of creation.

Close inspection of the moon reveals a slightly darker crescent on the left and a faint impression of a rabbit at the center (fig. 44). The image of the rabbit has dimmed the moon's light and caused the lunar half of the sky to darken so that the moon no longer rivals the sun. While the moment that Kahlo depicted comes after the rabbit was flung at the moon, it was before the sun's and moon's movement. The wind god Ehecatl, who is an aspect of Quetzalcoatl (the Feathered Serpent), has not yet blown them across the sky. Kahlo chose the potent moment when the newly created sun and moon hang immobile

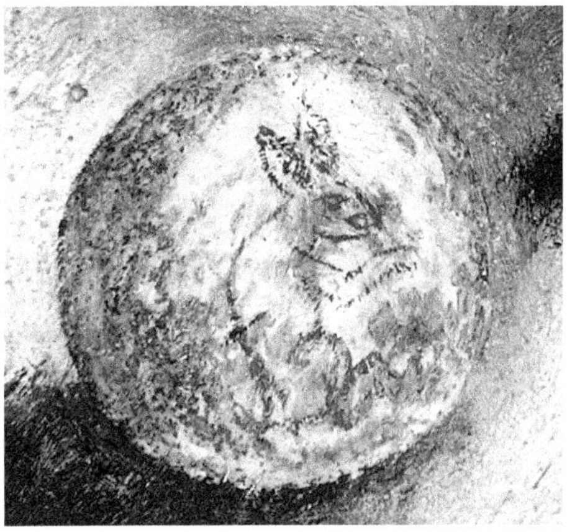

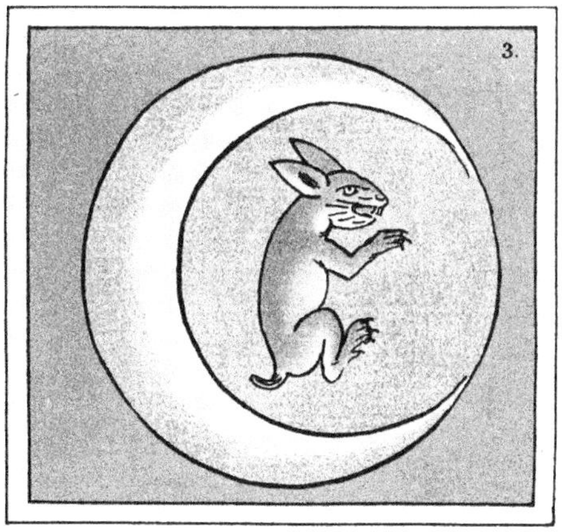

Fig. 44. Frida Kahlo, detail of the moon in *La niña, la luna y el sol*, 1942. Reproduction authorized by the Instituto Nacional de Bellas Artes y Literatura, 2015.

Fig. 45. Rabbit in the moon from the *Florentine Codex* (after Sahagún, *Florentine Codex*, facsimile edition published by Paso y Troncoso, ca. 1905).

in the sky waiting for the breath of the wind god to set them in motion. In this painting Kahlo has merged mythic time with present time.

Kahlo's manner of rendering the rabbit in the moon comes from an illustration in the *Florentine Codex*, the same book that records the myth of the creation of the Fifth Sun at Teotihuacan (fig. 45). The original sixteenth-century manuscript is in Florence, Italy, but sometime between 1905 and 1907 a luxurious facsimile edition was published by the Mexican government under the direction of Francisco del Paso y Troncoso. Kahlo based her depiction of the rabbit in the moon on the image reproduced in the facsimile or a later illustrated version of the codex.[13]

In the 1980s Dolores Olmedo, a longtime friend of Rivera and the director-for-life of the Museo Frida Kahlo, stated that the museum contained a box of facsimiles of the Precolumbian and early colonial codices that Rivera cited in his paintings.[14] When the archives of the Museo Frida Kahlo finally became accessible to scholars around 2010, they revealed that Rivera's collection of codices was indeed substantial. One of Rivera's three representations of Quetzalcoatl on the north wall of the stairway of the National Palace is a pertinent example of how he employed images from the codices in his own work (fig. 46). Rivera based this version of Quetzalcoatl on an illustration from the *Florentine Codex* (fig. 47). Rivera meticulously copied all the details of the god's costume from this source then diverged from tradition by showing the god sailing across the sky in a snake-shaped boat.

Images from the *Florentine Codex* frequently have been used to illustrate other publications. The rabbit in the moon appears in José Juan Tablada's *Historia del arte en México* (History of Art in Mexico) of 1927 (fig. 48). Using the sun and moon as examples, Tablada demonstrated how Precolumbian hieroglyphs evolved into European naturalism after the Conquest.[15] In central Mexico the Precolumbian glyph for the moon combined a crescent-shaped bone, the symbol for water, and a rabbit. Tablada compared a Precolumbian glyph of the moon to the sixteenth-century depiction of the rabbit in the moon from the *Florentine Codex*, which represents an early stage in the process of adapting to European forms of representation. Thus Kahlo's depiction of the rabbit in the moon is a sixteenth-century representation of a Precolumbian concept. She may have used the colonial image as a way of temporally linking the Precolumbian legend to the modern girl or representing the lunar rabbit in a style that unobtrusively blended with the naturalistic style of the painting.

While Kahlo alluded to the past in her representation of the moon, she depicted the sun as seen through a modern telescope. Art historian Rita Eder notes that Kahlo used a

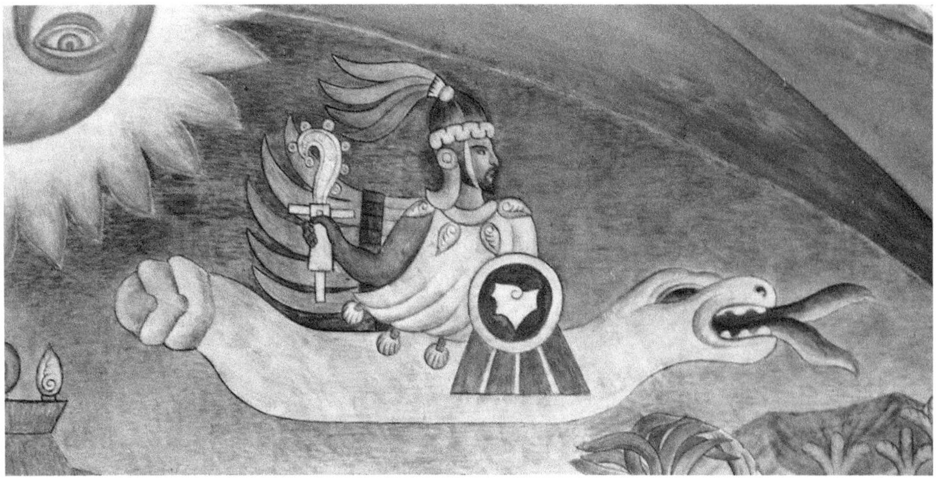

Fig. 46. Diego Rivera, detail of Quetzalcoatl in *México prehispánico* (known in English as *The Aztec World*), 1929, fresco, north wall of the stairway at the Palacio Nacional, Mexico City. Photograph by Dirk Bakker, courtesy of the Detroit Institute of Arts. © 2014 Banco de México Diego Rivera Frida Kahlo Museums Trust, Mexico, D.F./Artists Rights Society (ARS), New York. Reproduction authorized by the Instituto Nacional de Bellas Artes y Literatura, 2015.

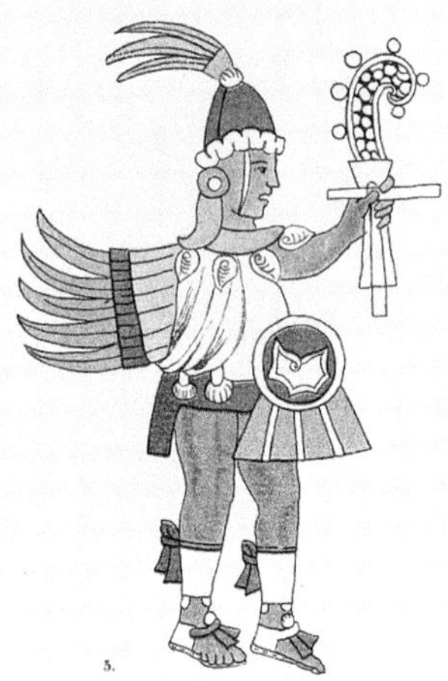

Fig. 47. Quetzalcoatl from the *Florentine Codex* (after Sahagún, *Florentine Codex*, facsimile edition published by Paso y Troncoso, ca. 1905).

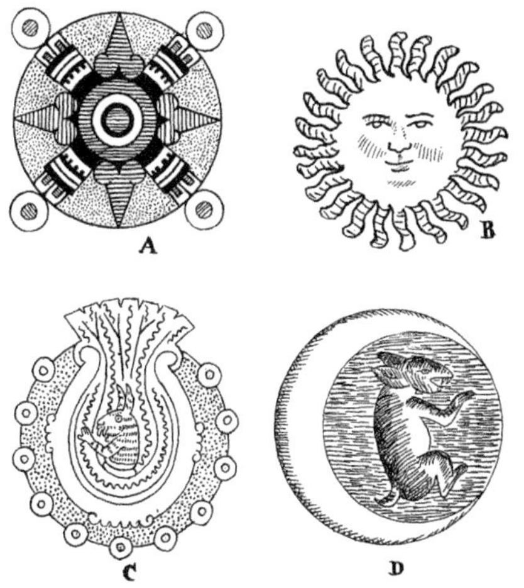

Fig. 48. José Juan Tablada's example of the "evolution of hieroglyphs into realism": A. Mesoamerican glyph for the sun; B. colonial representation of the sun; C. Mesoamerican glyph for the moon; D. colonial depiction of the rabbit in the moon (after Tablada, *Historia del arte en México*, fig. 23).

postcard from the American Museum of Natural History as her source for representing sunspots as seen through a powerful telescope.[16] The postcard survives in the archives of the Museo Frida Kahlo. This mixing of ancient culture and modern technology is a recurring theme in the painting, evident not only in the background but in the painting's main subject as well.

The Girl and the Airplane

Although the girl seated at the center of the painting is indigenous, she does not wear native dress. This is interesting because Kahlo, whose father was German and whose mother was mestiza, adorned herself with traditional indigenous clothing in her daily life and depicted herself attired in *huipiles* and rebozos in her self-portraits. The girl in the painting wears a plain white dress and a sweater with a bold black and white geometric design. The sweater is from Chiconcuac, a village near Texcoco famous for its hand-knit sweaters.[17] While the sweater comes from a traditional village, its style is modern not Prehispanic. The clothing that Kahlo chose for her model prevents the viewer from mistaking this painting for a historical scene. The girl's modern clothing and toy airplane irrefutably assert that the painting is about the twentieth century.

The girl holds the model airplane in a way that provides an unobstructed view of it. The toy's surface is embellished with a peculiar olive green and ocher pattern that may represent camouflage, possibly alluding to the painting's creation during World War II. Or the design, which resembles both feathers and snakeskin, may imply that the airplane is a metaphor for the Feathered Serpent, a Precolumbian deity portrayed in high-relief sculpture on the façade of the Temple of the Feathered Serpent at Teotihuacan.

Flight, freedom of movement, and physical restriction are persistent themes in Kahlo's work. Though she might have been inspired by the desire to fly under any circumstances, the almost fatal accident in her youth that permanently affected her health made this dream distressingly relevant. To combat her physical limitations, Kahlo made images that expressed her desire for movement, especially flight. She created over twenty-five paintings and drawings that include one or more birds: alter egos that could fly. In her self-portraits she exaggerated her heavy eyebrows just enough for them to form one undulating dark line, a pictograph of the wings of a bird in flight. In addition to the birds and her avian eyebrow, she also included airplanes or toy airplanes in two early works: *Autorretrato* (Self-Portrait) of 1929 and *Piden aeroplanos y les dan alas de petate* (They Ask for Airplanes and They Only Get Straw Wings) of 1938.

Kahlo's fascination with flight was shared by other Mexican artists with whom she was close. Her good friend Juan O'Gorman painted a three-panel mural entitled *La conquista del aire por el hombre* (The Conquest of Air by Man) in 1937–1938, which he dedicated to her.[18]

A mural by Diego Rivera which includes an image of a boy with a model airplane offers a particularly revealing comparison with *La niña, la luna y el sol*. Rivera's representation of the boy appears in the mural *Allegory of California*, which he painted at the Pacific Stock Exchange in San Francisco in 1931 (fig. 49). The composition revolves around an enormous allegorical female figure of California surrounded by elements and figures that exemplify the state's riches. At the exact center of the composition Rivera depicted "a young California boy facing the sky with a model airplane in his hands," whom he considered "a symbol of the future."[19]

Fig. 49. Diego Rivera, detail of *Allegory of California*, 1931, fresco, City Club, Stock Exchange Tower, San Francisco, Bridgeman Art Library. © 2014 Banco de México Diego Rivera Frida Kahlo Museums Trust, Mexico, D.F./Artists Rights Society (ARS), New York. Reproduction authorized by the Instituto Nacional de Bellas Artes y Literatura, 2015.

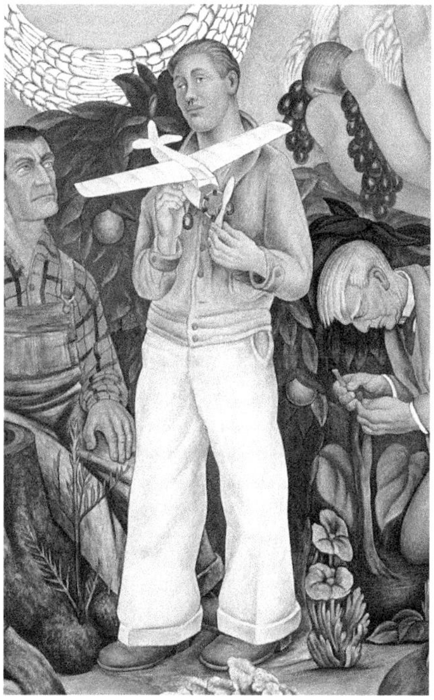

Can we extrapolate that Kahlo's young indigenous girl facing "relentless and marvelous space" with a model plane in her hands also symbolizes the future? Without either mentioning Rivera or quoting Kahlo, two of her former students have interpreted this painting in ways that confirm and amplify this idea. Guillermo Monroy observed that "the girl of the airplane, she is Mexico. The sun and the moon . . . day and night; Mexico, with the zeal for the pyramids of Teotihuacan. In the background the ancient world and [in the foreground] the girl holding in her hands the modern era."[20] Another former student, Arturo García Bustos, said: "In the back can be seen the pyramids of Teotihuacan, and in her hands she holds the little airplane, as if to show the modern world in the hands of the Mexican."[21]

In his murals Rivera repeatedly glorified the Precolumbian past and honored the indigenous people and campesinos of Mexico. He was probably the person most responsible for the rising appreciation of Precolumbian art after the Mexican Revolution. In the context of the *Allegory of California*, however, his child of the future is a blond California boy whose environment encompasses all the vegetable, mineral, and industrial wealth of California. For Kahlo the child of the future is a skinny, barefoot indigenous girl whose environment offers her the austere beauty of the Precolumbian past. Kahlo chose to entrust the future to a child who was female, indigenous, and poor. The gifts that the artist gave her for her quest were not physical riches but the architecture, mythology, and cosmic concerns of her ancestors, along with an airplane whose speed "equals that of imagination-reason."

One issue raised by the reception of this remarkable painting is the degree to which art historians and critics appear to trust text over image. After Marta Zamora provided the important information about the message on the back of the painting, the word "tehuacana" seems to have caused most writers to fail to see—or be unwilling to acknowledge—the site of the painting. As the work slowly entered the body of works by Kahlo that are known to a wide audience, the few scholars who have published texts that identify the site of the painting are myself (2005), Eduardo Matos Moctezuma (2007), and Rita Eder (2012).[22]

La niña, la luna y el sol was exhibited twice during Kahlo's life and only three times between her death and its appearance in the catalogue for Sotheby's auction of Latin American art on November 16, 2004. Sotheby's did not sell the painting.[23] There are several possible explanations for why a work by Kahlo would fail to sell, including an asking price of $800,000 for a work that was still relatively obscure and the painting's legal status as a *monumento nacional* (national monument), which prohibits its export from Mexico.[24] Nevertheless, it is safe to assume that a self-portrait by Kahlo would have sold. The relative lack of interest in this painting that lasted until the beginning of the twenty-first century is due in part to the way in which biographical methodologies have dominated Kahlo scholarship and contributed to the emphasis on her self-portraits, while other parts of her work have received less attention.

In early 2007 the art collector Juan Antonio Pérez Simón bought the painting in a private sale. In the short time between Sotheby's auction and the painting's purchase, it was exhibited in solo shows of Kahlo's art at the Tate Modern in London and the Museo de Arte de Ponce (Museum of Art of Ponce) in Puerto Rico. In the first six years after Pérez Simón's acquisition it was exhibited thirteen times, in Paris, Biarritz, Berlin, Vienna, Quebec City, Los Angeles, San Francisco, Philadelphia, Mexico City, Monterrey, and elsewhere. The once obscure painting is emerging from the shadows.

La niña, la luna y el sol is a vital part of Kahlo's oeuvre. It is central to comprehending her admiration of Precolumbian culture, her belief that ancient Mexican art was the root of modern Mexican art, her way of unobtrusively blending Precolumbian elements into twentieth-century contexts, and her insistence on the role of women—in this case a girl—in the formation of Mexican national identity.

5

Mother of the Maize

Izquierdo's Images of Rural Gardens with Granaries

In the 1940s María Izquierdo created a series of canvases that represent rural gardens with granaries. On the surface these paintings appear bland, bucolic, peaceful, and apolitical. Nevertheless, these works are political, in terms of both national politics and gender politics: in this series Izquierdo addressed gender issues in relation to national identity. As a woman painter working in postrevolutionary Mexico, Izquierdo was confronted with the challenge of working at a time and place where national identity was paramount and was constructed as masculine identity.[1]

The so-called Mexican School's concept of important art, especially as expressed by Siqueiros in the forties, demanded that it be "heroic," "monumental," and "public." The muralists frequently conveyed these concepts through enormous images of powerful historical and mythological males: Emiliano Zapata, Miguel Hidalgo, Prometheus, Quetzalcoatl, and Karl Marx. While the uncritical reverence for male heroes presented a serious challenge for women artists, other aspects of the Mexican School's agenda were not gendered, were less heavily gendered, or were potentially gendered as female.

The valorization of indigenous traditions was one of the areas where artists could assert national identity without necessarily linking it to male identity. The valorization of indigenous traditions usually took the form of positive representations of Precolumbian art and culture, affirmative portrayals of indigenous people, and appealing presentations of artisan objects. Both male and female artists frequently addressed these subjects. For women artists it was one of the areas where they had considerable flexibility to negotiate identity by, for example, portraying themselves and other women in traditional Mexican clothing or depicting artisan objects with indigenous associations. Kahlo's repeated representations of herself with Precolumbian artifacts from West Mexico (see chapter 3) and her portrayal of an indigenous girl at Teotihuacan in a 1942 painting (see chapter 4) fall into this category. This chapter examines an unusual approach to staking claim to indigenous traditions: Izquierdo's repeated representations of rural gardens with granaries. The links among the granaries, indigenous traditions, and gender and how Izquierdo turned the seemingly bland subject of a rural garden into a site to negotiate the gender of the nation are the subject of this chapter.

In the early forties Izquierdo initiated her series of paintings of gardens with granaries with *Los gallos* (The Roosters) of ca. 1942 (fig. 50). The painting represents a woodland scene with a low rectangular hut, presumably the home of a campesino family, and an oddly bulbous structure known as a *coscomate*, which is used for storing corn. In the foreground a rooster and hen perch on a felled tree, two chicks forage for food, and a tiny goat stands below a towering tree. The hut is depicted in dramatically foreshortened perspective, and the hen and rooster are inexplicably larger than the goat. The peculiar perspective and illogical scale endow the image with a naïve quality that reinforces the rustic subject matter.

The buildings and animals are located in a tiny clearing amid old growth trees that are so tall that their crowns extend beyond the limits of the picture. While at first glance the scene might be considered a forest landscape, it is in fact the garden around the home of a campesino. Although this image and others in the series do not conform to prevailing notions of what constitutes a garden in the United States, the paintings represent gardens in the sense of depicting the spaces immediately around a home which have been shaped by the people who live there.[2]

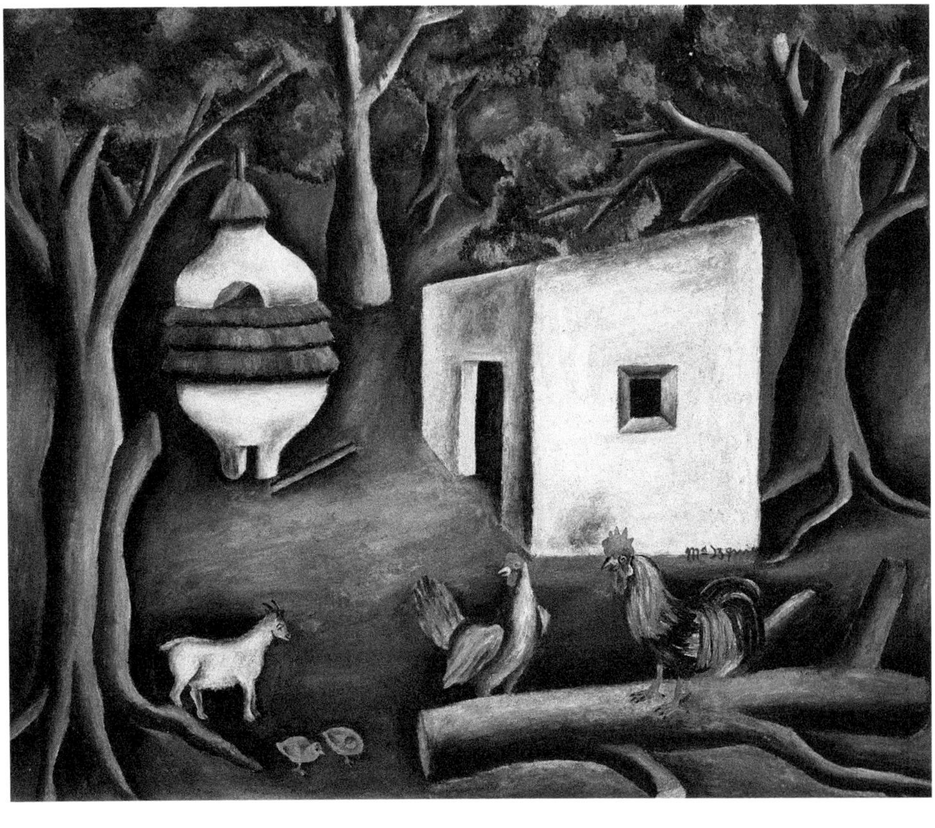

Fig. 50. María Izquierdo, *Los gallos* (The Roosters), ca. 1942, oil on canvas, 20 × 24 inches (51 × 61 cm), collection of Galería de Arte Mexicano, Mexico City. Photograph by Francisco Kochen. Reproduced with the permission of María Rosenda López Posadas, legal representative of the intellectual property of María Izquierdo.

Between 1943 and 1945 Izquierdo painted at least eight other canvases that repeat the essential elements of *Los gallos*: a curvaceous *coscomate*, a simple rectangular hut, a few well-fed farm animals, and trees with lush foliage (some of which are fruit trees, though not currently bearing fruit). The other paintings in the series include *La troje* (The Granary) of 1943, *Troje* (Granary) of 1943, *Paisaje de Cuautla* (Cuautla Landscape) of 1943, *Los gallos* (The Roosters) of 1944, *Paisaje tropical* (Tropical Landscape) of 1943, two paintings titled *Coscomates* (Granaries) both of 1945, and an unpublished 1945 work whose title is unknown.[3] In 1945 she also represented a *coscomate* in a study for the mural project for the Departamento del Distrito Federal. The following year she decorated a folding screen with a panoramic tropical landscape that includes a *coscomate*. The reiteration of this subject matter testifies to Izquierdo's fascination with *coscomates* and the popularity of the images with collectors.[4]

Coscomates

Coscomate is a Hispanicized version of the Nahuatl word *cuezcómatl*. In *Diccionario de aztequismos* Luis Cabrera notes that *coscomate* is an incorrect variant of *coztomate* and *cozcomate*; he defines *cozcomate* as "big pot of clay, basket of wicker, or wood granary to store ears of corn."[5] Despite Cabrera's objection to the Hispanicized version of the word, I persist in using it, because it is commonly used in Mexico and (in the plural) is the title by which two of Izquierdo's paintings are known.[6]

The type of *coscomate* that Izquierdo depicted is essentially a gigantic clay pot in which an individual family stores the season's harvest of maize. *Coscomates* are filled through an aperture at the top. The maize is removed as needed from a small hole at the base, which is normally kept covered. This type of *coscomate* is used by peasants in the state of Morelos and in some parts of the states of Puebla and Tlaxcala.[7] Other types of granaries are found elsewhere in Mexico. Traditional *coscomates* are used by indigenous people and by campesinos who may no longer be ethnically and linguistically pure Indian but have deep indigenous roots.

Izquierdo's images of *coscomates* were based on ones that she had seen during her visits to the countryside near the provincial city of Cuautla. Her daughter Aurora remembered seeing the granaries with her mother on several occasions, buying food from the owners, sometimes eating with them, and always speaking with them.[8]

Most of Izquierdo's representations of *coscomates* show the structure as a wide hourglass form with a three-tiered ruffle of thatch at the waist and a tiny cap of thatch at the top. Some of her depictions include a semicircular opening at the top, and most display the exit hole at the base in a way that makes the structure appear to have short legs (fig. 51). The exceptions are the two paintings titled *Coscomates* (fig. 52) and the unpublished work whose title is unknown; each of the three paintings represents two *coscomates* that are wide at the center, narrow at the base, and crowned with conical hats of thatch. Although the shapes of the granaries in these three paintings are less common in Izquierdo's oeuvre, they are in fact more typical of the *coscomates* of Morelos. Similar granaries are documented in numerous photographs (fig. 53).

Even within Morelos the shapes of *coscomates* vary locally and individually. The precise form that Izquierdo repeatedly represented, with its wide hourglass shape, is atypical of *coscomates* but highly evocative of the female body. It also suggests that the structure

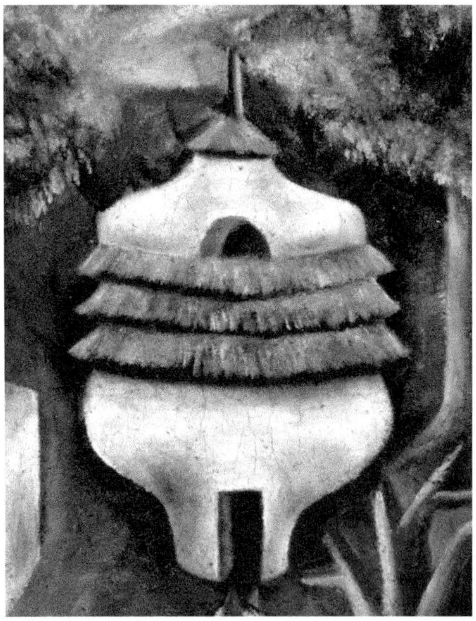

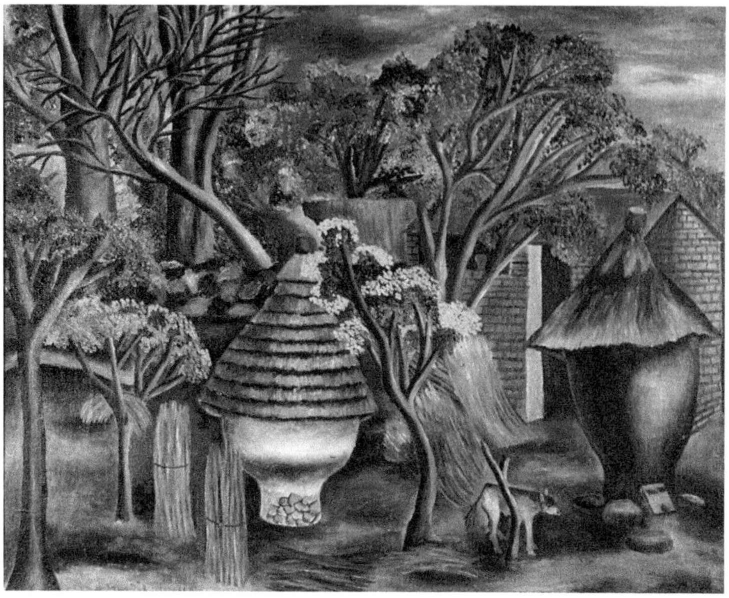

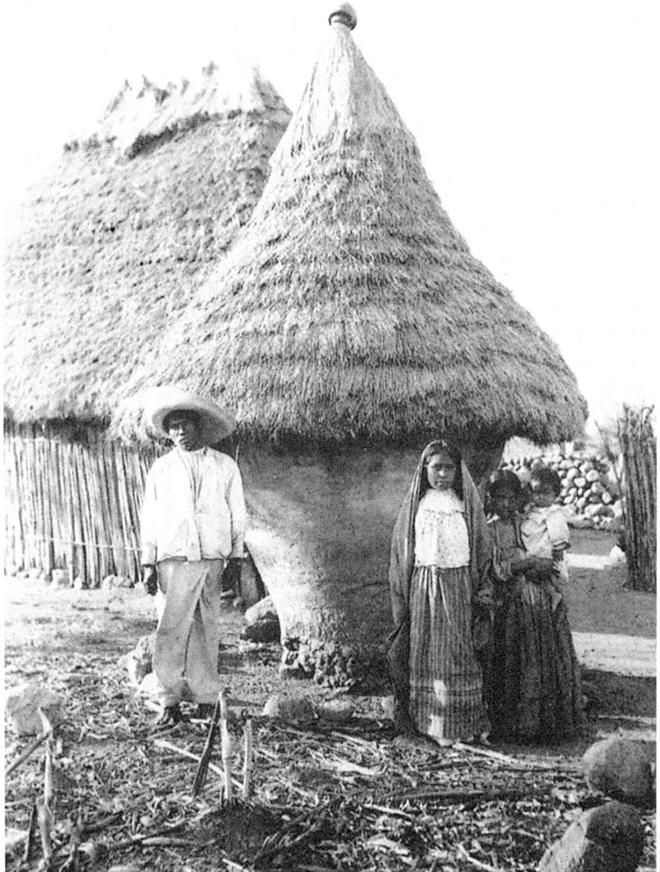

Fig. 51. (*top left*) María Izquierdo, detail of the *coscomate* in *Paisaje tropical* (Tropical Landscape), 1944. Reproduced with the permission of María Rosenda López Posadas, legal representative of the intellectual property of María Izquierdo. Reproduction authorized by the Instituto Nacional de Bellas Artes y Literatura, 2015.

Fig. 52. (*top right*) María Izquierdo, *Coscomates* (Granaries), 1945, oil on canvas, 23 ⅝ × 31 ½ inches (60 × 80 cm), private collection. Reproduced with the permission of María Rosenda López Posadas, legal representative of the intellectual property of María Izquierdo. Reproduction authorized by the Instituto Nacional de Bellas Artes y Literatura, 2015.

Fig. 53. (*left*) Postcard of a *coscomate* and an indigenous family, probably in Morelos. Courtesy of Ana Garduño.

is bulging with grain, that the harvest has been abundant, and that the family's future is therefore secure. Izquierdo's *coscomates* imply a connection of women, fecundity, and abundance.

There are striking formal similarities between Izquierdo's images of granaries and Max Ernst's *Celebes* (also known as *Elephant of the Celebes*) of 1921 (fig. 54). Ernst, who painted *Celebes* during his Dadaist period, modeled the bulbous gray elephantine form on a photograph of an African corn crib reproduced in an English anthropological journal.[9] In addition to the zoomorphic quality of Ernst's figure and the anthropomorphic quality of most of Izquierdo's depictions of granaries, both artists made the granary the central focus of the painting. As art historian Kim Grant notes, Izquierdo's granaries stand out like idols at the center of the composition, much as in Ernst's image. Grant astutely observes that Izquierdo's rather "primitive" modernist style makes the granaries into the absolute focus of the paintings: "They are odd, distinctive, mysterious as well as symbolic of fertility [and] abundance."[10] Grant adds that this is quite different from naturalizing these forms in a realistic style, where viewers would immediately know that they were farm structures even if they had never seen them before.

While the visual similarities between Ernst's and Izquierdo's paintings are compelling and reveal how both artists used formal elements to construct meaning, it is not known whether Izquierdo had seen Ernst's *Celebes*. Izquierdo possessed considerable knowledge of surrealism, especially after 1936 when she befriended Antonin Artaud, but information about Dada and surrealism arrived in Mexico in an uneven fashion. Less information about Ernst was available in Mexico than about other artists who participated in the surrealist movement or who, like Giorgio de Chirico, were appropriated by the surrealists.[11]

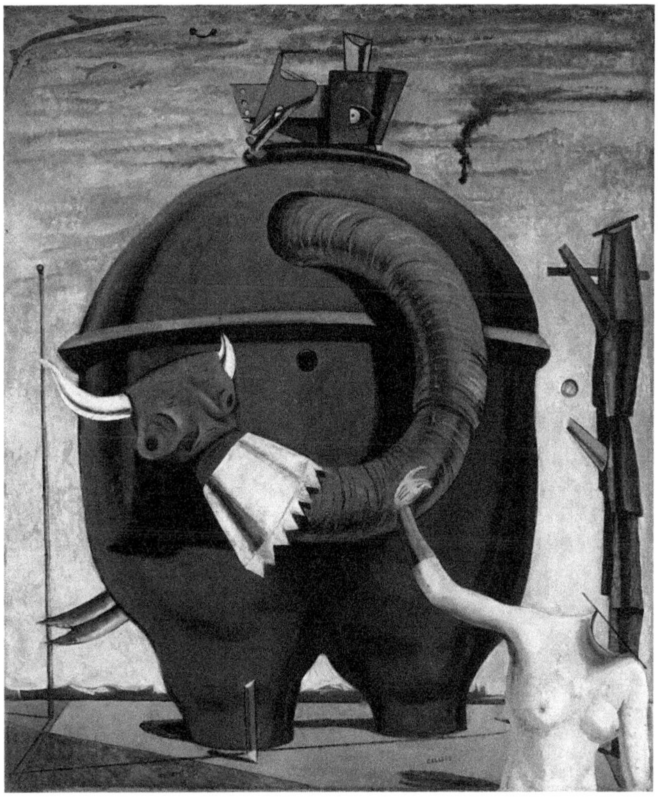

Fig. 54. Max Ernst, *Celebes* (also known as *Elephant of the Celebes*), 1921, oil on canvas, Tate Modern, London. © 2014 Artists Rights Society (ARS), New York/ ADAGP, Paris.

Coscomates of Morelos in Modern Mexican Art

Izquierdo, who rarely explained her images, left no record of what her paintings of rural gardens with *coscomates* meant to her, and the series has not attracted serious analysis from critics and art historians. But Izquierdo's contemporary colleagues in the arts were fascinated with the indigenous granaries. The type of *coscomate* typical of Morelos has been depicted by Diego Rivera, Leopoldo Méndez (1902–1969), Alfredo Zalce (1908–2003), and other artists.[12] The structures have been the subject of numerous photographs, most notably in the work of Mariana Yampolsky (1925–2002). In 1931 Rivera drew a busy village with indigenous women shucking corn in the foreground, a *coscomate* in the middle distance, and another in the background.[13] In the mid-forties Alfredo Zalce and Leopoldo Méndez made many images of *coscomates*.[14] These artists knew each other and would have been aware of at least some of the others' representations of granaries. Izquierdo had met Zalce when they were both students at the Escuela Nacional de Bellas Artes; and Izquierdo, Zalce, and Méndez had participated in Liga de Escritores y Artistas Revolucionarios together, before Zalce and Méndez became founding members of the Taller de Gráfica Popular in 1937.[15]

Zalce's images of *coscomates* include drawings, prints, and paintings, many of which, like *Coscomates* of 1945 and *Paisaje de Cuautla* (Landscape of Cuautla) of 1947, were created in the mid-forties. At the time Zalce taught at La Esmeralda. During the annual three-month vacation he went to Cuautla, where he painted and drew in the surrounding countryside. In a 1997 interview Zalce recalled that he was intrigued by the *coscomate* because it has "a very strange and very peasant form, very indigenous, because it is a strange construction. It looks more like an object of adornment, a cup."[16] He explained that *coscomates* are made of clay; although reeds and sticks are used to strengthen the structure, they are essentially handmade clay objects. While they have an absolutely practical function, they are also artisan objects, almost works of art, that express individual sensibilities and "very good indigenous taste." Although the basic form is the same, people make them in their own way: "some [of the *coscomates*] are wider, others are narrower, some are very tall, it depends."[17] In his *Coscomates* of 1945 two distinctly shaped granaries in close proximity exemplify the personal variation involved in their construction (fig. 55). Zalce observed: "The peasants make [the *coscomate*] as a personal object, with taste, because it is for them. It isn't for anyone else."[18] This insistence that the structures are not made for anyone else places them in opposition to tourist art and emphasizes their authenticity.

Mariana Yampolsky, a generation younger than Izquierdo and Zalce, came to Mexico in 1944 to join the Taller de Gráfica Popular, where she participated as an engraver for several years before becoming a photographer. Her encyclopedic photographic documentation of Mexican vernacular architecture includes an extensive record of granaries throughout the republic. In 1997 Yampolsky said: "I have always been fascinated with corncribs. There are many kinds, each state has their own way of storing grain."[19] Yampolsky regarded *coscomates* as "remnants of Precolumbian times that have come down to us almost without any modifications, especially the ones that are found in Morelos. They have been drawn in Mexican codices." She added that she particularly liked "the ones in Morelos that are so beautiful because they are like enormous jugs."[20]

Yampolsky confirmed that *coscomates* are located on relatively small plots of land, are designed to store grain for one family, and are constructed near the house. "Usually if the

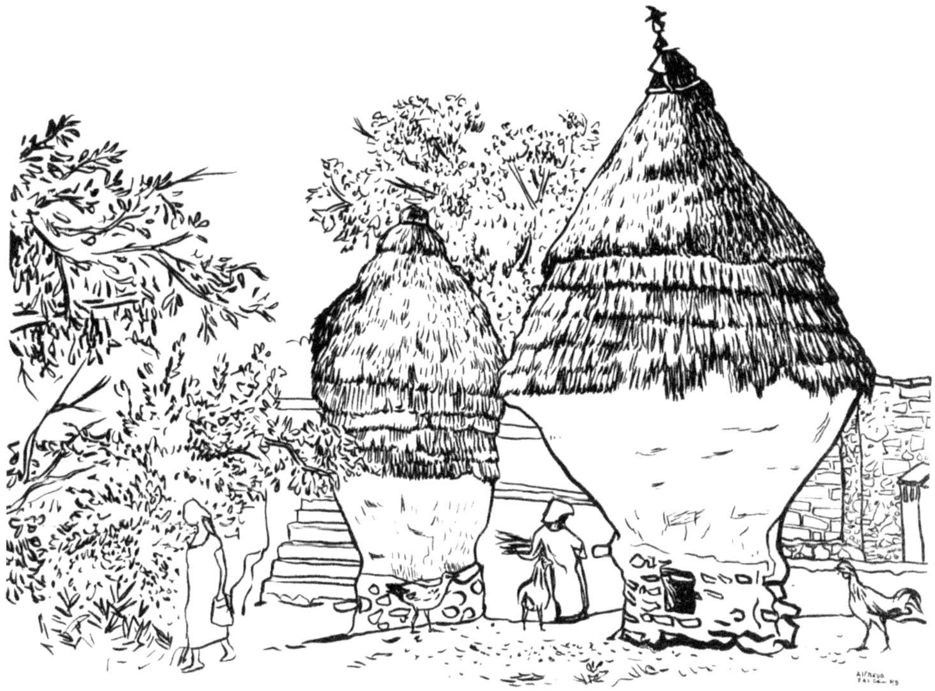

Fig. 55. Alfredo Zalce, *Coscomates*, 1945, ink on paper, 16 ⅛ × 20 ⅞ inches (41 × 53 cm), reproduced with the permission of Beatriz Zalce de Guerriff.

bin is full it is enough to tide [the family] over [for] the whole season until the corn flowers again." She observed that "corn is the staple food in Mexico, and it has been for time without end."[21] Because the well-being of peasant families depends on the harvest and the safe storage of grain, the *coscomates* have a sacred aspect. The corncribs have a cross, and when the priests visit the villages they bless them. The *coscomate* "is a holy place, more so than the house . . . because the corn is more important than the place [where] you sleep. . . . [The *coscomate*] is always blessed. It is a blessed place, it is a sacred place."[22]

It is clear that Izquierdo represented *coscomates* as curvaceous forms that evoke the female body. It is probable that she understood them in a way quite close to that of Zalce, her contemporary, former classmate at the Escuela Nacional de Bellas Artes, and fellow teacher at the Escuela de Pintura y Escultura. If so, she would have admired their forms, seeing them as artisan objects and as examples of the sensitivity and taste of indigenous people. She probably also knew—through reading, formal analysis, logic, or intuition—that the granaries have Precolumbian origins. Because many *coscomates* have a cross (and Izquierdo talked to the people who made and used them), she may also have apprehended their sacred quality.

Coscomates, Land, and Labor

Taking a panoramic view of representations of *coscomates* in modern Mexican art and considering what Zalce and Yampolsky have said about their own images, we can extrapolate several things about their significance and why they became popular in the forties. First, the *coscomates* assert Mexican national identity. In the same way that representations of the volcanic mountains Popocateptl and Iztaccihuatl locate a landscape in the Valley of Mexico, the heartland of the Mexican Republic, the *coscomate* nationalizes a landscape. Because the type of *coscomate* depicted by Izquierdo, Zalce, and Méndez is recognizably from Morelos, these images also identify a specific region of Mexico. Second, the *coscomate* links the land to the indigenous people and by extension to the Precolumbian past. Third, it associates land with labor. One of the slogans of the agrarian movement during the Mexican Revolution was "Liberty, Work, and Land!"[23] In 1929 Anita Brenner claimed: "The only recognized native law about possession of land is the ancient tenet sung by Netzahualcoyotl: "'The land belongs to him who works it with his hands.'"[24] In twentieth-century Mexican art the *coscomate* testifies to the farmer's labor. Fourth, because *coscomates* belong to individual families, the images are not about teeming anonymous masses of peasants. They are about families and villages. This is true by implication whether or not people are actually depicted.

The images of *coscomates* already discussed portray rural life in an idyllic manner. They may include representations of hard work, but the land is fertile, the harvests are abundant, and the scenes are peaceful. This is not always the case, however, in the art of Leopoldo Méndez. In 1949 Méndez created a disturbing image of village life in a lithograph titled *Cuando nace un hombre* (When a Man Is Born) (fig. 56). In the foreground blackbirds peck at a few remaining ears of corn on dry plants. Behind the ravaged corn is a village with three *coscomates* and a hut with one missing wall that reveals a room in which a baby has just been born. An owl-faced priest, accompanied by an owl-faced acolyte, knocks at the door, an ominous image: owls have been considered harbingers of death in Mexico since the Precolumbian era. A buzzard leans out of the window of the upper story of an adjacent structure. In the right foreground a farmer on a ladder empties a big sack of corn into the upper aperture of a *coscomate*, while a dog-faced creature at the base of the granary surreptitiously empties grain into a large bag; behind him a burro

Fig. 56. Leopoldo Méndez, *Cuando nace un hombre* (When a Man Is Born), 1949, lithograph, 16 ⅝ × 12 inches (42.3 × 30.5 cm), reproduced with the permission of Pablo Méndez.

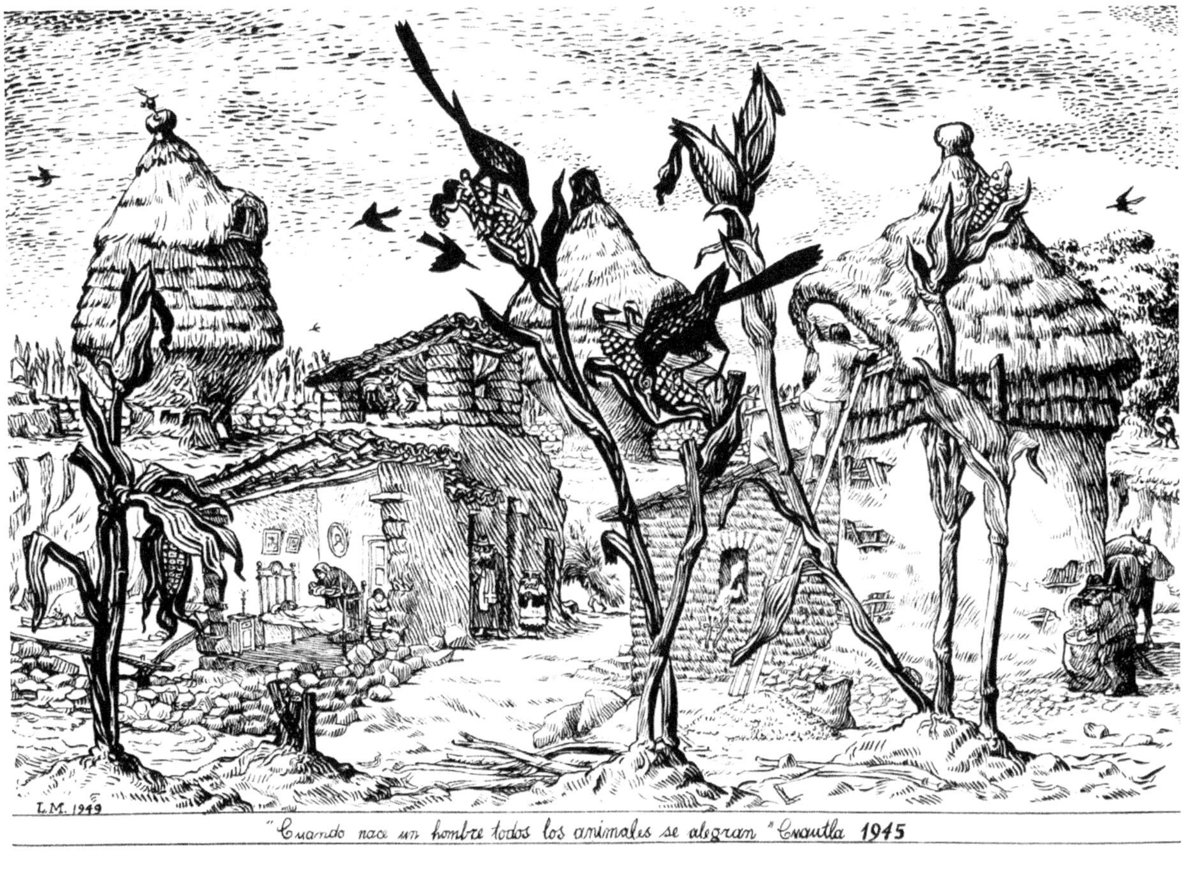

laden with sacks waits to facilitate his escape. A thin horizontal border at the bottom of the print carries the message: "'Cuando nace un hombre todos los animales se alegran.' Cuautla 1945" (When a man is born all the animals are happy. Cuautla 1945). The first part of the message in quotation marks must be a citation, though its source is now unknown. The print depicts a dog-faced thief, an owl-faced priest, an owl-faced acolyte, and a buzzard, who all stand on two legs and wear clothing, so presumably the animals alluded to in the quotation are human: the print critiques the predatory nature of the human species. It almost certainly also protests a specific historical, political, or social situation in Cuautla, although, like the source of the citation, this information resists retrieval.[25]

With the exception of Méndez's lithograph of 1949, all other images of *coscomates* by him and his contemporaries extol the virtues of the Mexican countryside. Yampolsky's photographs document many different types of *coscomates* throughout the Republic of Mexico, but most other artists depict the type used in the state of Morelos, and many of the titles mention Cuautla.[26]

Coscomates, Morelos, Emiliano Zapata, and Agrarian Reform

Beyond these elements of the *coscomates* based on artists' statements, formal and iconographic analysis of the art, and information about the construction, use, and geographic distribution of the granaries, I believe that the eloquence of these images and their popularity in Mexico rest on a vast amount of shared knowledge and cultural memory about the central place of maize in Mexican civilization, the roots of agrarian reform in Morelos, the connection between Emiliano Zapata and the state of Morelos, and the centrality of agrarian reform to the Mexican revolution and the ideals of postrevolutionary Mexico. While none of these issues is overtly dealt with in the images, the importance of maize and the associations of Morelos, Zapata, and agrarian reform are such common knowledge in Mexico and so central to national identity that this information forms the cultural bedrock of the images.[27]

The diverse groups that fought in the Mexican Revolution (1910–ca. 1920) had different agendas. Agrarian reform was the priority for the campesinos. The man whose name is most closely linked to agrarian reform is Emiliano Zapata, the leader of the Revolution of the South, who came from the heart of Morelos. In 1911 Zapata and Otilio Montaño drew up the Plan de Ayala, the most famous agrarian document of the Mexican Revolution. It called first for the lands, woods, and water that had been usurped by the *hacendados* (owners of haciendas) and other property owners to be returned to the pueblos and citizens who held the proper deeds. Villages and individuals with the true titles were urged to reclaim their lands immediately and hold them by force. Because the vast majority of villages and citizens owned nothing, not even deeds to usurped land, the Plan de Ayala also proposed that a third of the land monopolized by the *hacendados* and other owners would be expropriated with compensation so that pueblos and citizens could use it. This land was to become "*ejidos*, colonies, *fundos legales*, or fields for planting and tillage, and improve in every way and for everyone the lack of prosperity and well being of Mexicans."[28] Enrique Krauze summarizes the significance of the Plan de Ayala for the Zapatistas: "The dream of Zapatista redemption was to create a mosaic of small autonomous holdings whose owners would be united by a strong sense of community. For the Zapatistas, the Plan de Ayala was the means to this goal and it would always retain the character of Holy Writ, of a messianic promise."[29]

A few other observations about representations of rural scenes with granaries may be added. Izquierdo's images of rural gardens—which lack humans, and usually contain just one *coscomate* and a few animals—appear to represent the small private lots of individual families. In contrast, Zalce's and Méndez's images—which usually include people and often show several *coscomates*—suggest the types of agrarian reform that involve an entire community: *ejidal* (communal land) grants, agricultural colonies, and town sites. The fact that all three artists make a point of locating the images in the vicinity of Cuautla may be due in part to the town's importance during the Mexican Revolution.[30]

One odd, unexplained fact remains in regard to Izquierdo's, Zalce's, and Méndez's images of *coscomates*: they were created during Manuel Ávila Camacho's term as president from 1940 to 1946. Izquierdo made her depictions of *coscomates* between ca. 1942 and 1946. Zalce and Méndez began to create their images of Morelos-style granaries around 1945 and continued to produce them over a longer period. The greatest redistribution of land took place under the leadership of Lázaro Cárdenas, who was president from 1934 to 1940. After Ávila Cámacho took office in 1940, the pace of land redistribution was significantly reduced. The production and popularity of these works in a period of decreased land distribution raises a serious question about why these images became so prevalent in the early forties. One possibility is that they express nostalgia for a recent past and evoke an endangered authenticity.

Izquierdo's 1943 retrospective at the Palacio de Bellas Artes included the painting *Paisaje tropical*, but the catalogues to her other exhibitions in the forties do not record any of the titles by which her paintings of rural gardens with *coscomates* are now known. This could mean either that most of this series was not exhibited in the forties or that these paintings were shown under different titles. (A surprisingly large number of Izquierdo's paintings are now known by titles other than the ones under which she originally exhibited them.) The catalogue to her solo show at the Instituto Peruano Americano in Lima in 1944 lists an oil painting titled *Paisaje de la tierra de Emiliano Zapata* (Landscape of the Land of Emiliano Zapata).[31] The small catalogue lacks reproductions, but *Paisaje de la tierra de Emiliano Zapata* was one of three works reproduced in an article titled "La exposición de María Izquierdo" (María Izquierdo's Exhibition) in the Lima newspaper *La Crónica* on August 28, 1944.[32] The reproduction reveals that *Paisaje de la tierra de Emiliano Zapata* is the work known in Mexico as *Paisaje tropical*. Izquierdo may have renamed this canvas for her exhibition in Lima so that the title explicitly tied the garden and *coscomate* to the land of Zapata because she realized that a Peruvian audience did not bring the same cultural memory to the work as a Mexican audience.

Izquierdo created another work in which Zapata's name appears in the title. *Tumba de Zapata* (Zapata's Grave) of 1945 shows the heaped earth of a freshly dug grave within a barren landscape in which all the elements of nature seem to mourn Zapata's death (fig. 57). A solitary bird perches on a branch of a leafless, heavily pruned tree before a yellow sky streaked with red. Two horses visit the grave; the one on the right lowers his head; the one on the left pulls his head away, an equine gesture of fear.[33] Zapata was known to be the "*Charro* of *Charros*—the finest of horsemen."[34] After his death many people swore that they saw him riding through the country at night.

In *Tumba de Zapata* Izquierdo pays homage to Zapata, and by implication to agrarian reform, without participating in the usual visual rhetoric about male heroes. The agrarian leader is simultaneously present and absent from the painting. The focus of the painting

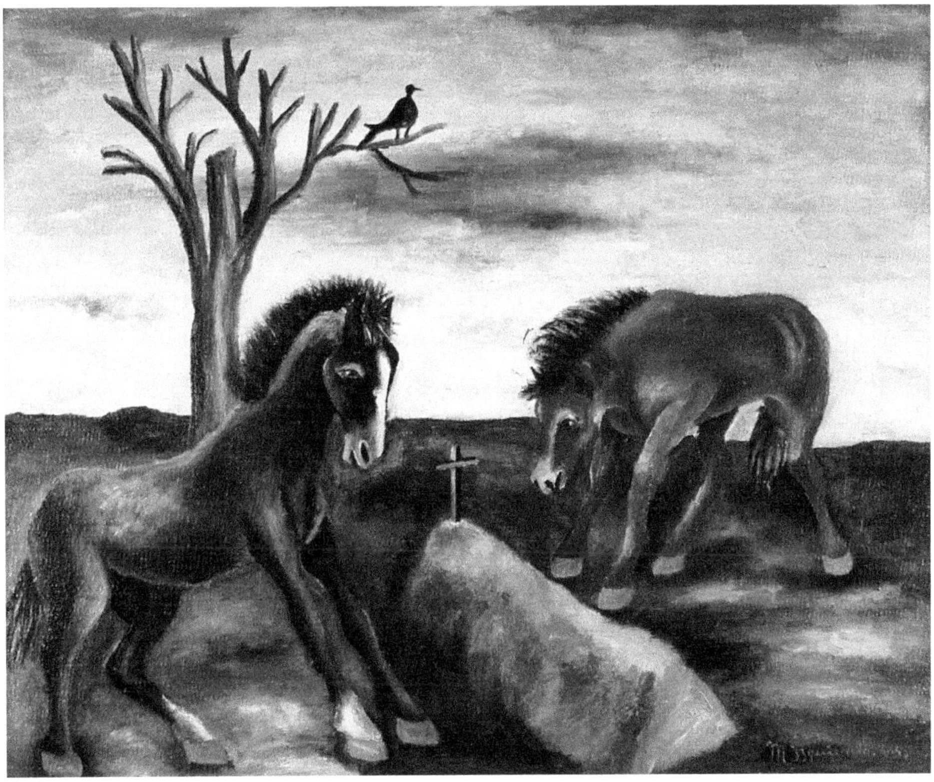

Fig. 57. María Izquierdo, *Tumba de Zapata* (Zapata's Grave), 1945, oil on canvas, 16 ⅛ × 20 1/16 inches (41 × 51 cm), collection of Andrés Blaisten. Reproduced with the permission of María Rosenda López Posadas, legal representative of the intellectual property of María Izquierdo.

is the heaped earth of his fresh grave. Zapata is represented not as a revolutionary leader but as the land itself.

In Izquierdo's oeuvre no *coronelazo* assaults the viewer's space with a clenched, foreshortened fist; no Prometheus rises to the heavens in a burst of flame in the hallowed architectural space of a dome; no revolutionary martyr is enveloped in a full-body halo. Izquierdo consistently avoided contributing to the idealization of male heroes. She repeatedly affirmed Mexican national values in ways that posited feminine alternatives to the masculine revolutionary images of Mexico.

Land and Gender

Izquierdo represented the land as female, a view implied by the hourglass-shaped *coscomates* in the rural gardens and made explicit by *La tierra* (Earth) of 1945, in which a nude earth-toned indigenous or mestiza woman rises out of the land, one leg still embedded in the earth and one arm raised with her hand in a closed fist (fig. 58). Izquierdo's association between land and women was shared by the campesinos of Morelos. Enrique Krauze writes: "Zapata fought religiously for the land that was, to the Zapatistas as to all peasants in traditional cultures, 'the mother who nourishes us and cares for us.' . . . The word *patria*, in his manifesto issued in Nahuatl to the Indian people of Tlaxcala, becomes 'our beloved Mother the Earth, which is called the Fatherland.'" Krauze believes that Zapata was looking "for a mythical place, for the breast of his mother earth and her constellation of symbols."[35]

In 1967 the Mexican historian Alfredo López Austin published a study of Nahuallatolli, the form of Nahuatl used by witches, healers, and diviners in incantations. López Austin, who based his study on words used in the seventeenth century in the area that is

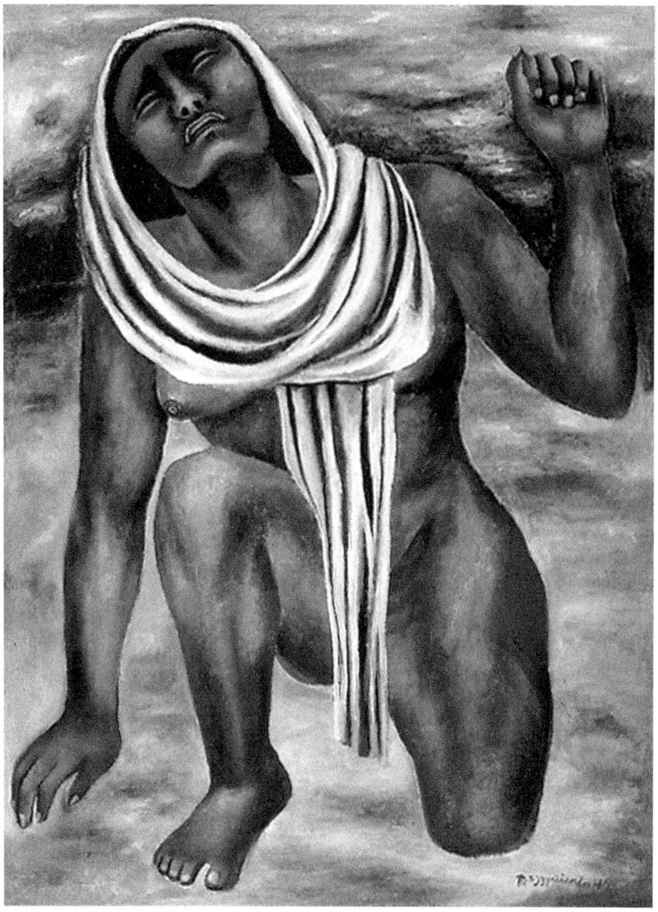

Fig. 58. María Izquierdo, *La tierra* (Earth), 1945, oil on canvas, 35 3/16 × 26 7/8 inches (89.3 × 68.3 cm), collection of Andrés Blaisten. Reproduced with the permission of María Rosenda López Posadas, legal representative of the intellectual property of María Izquierdo.

now Morelos, defined the Nahuallatolli word *monantzin* as "the granary, as the mother of the maize who guards it in her bosom."[36] Obviously López Austin's scholarship of 1967 cannot be directly linked to Izquierdo's paintings of the 1940s, yet the Nahuallatolli language and the modern artist interpret the granaries in the same way. Izquierdo's representations of the *coscomate* as a wide hourglass form that seems to bulge with grain depict the granary as the mother of the maize who guards it in her bosom. We can only wonder how Izquierdo arrived at a visualization of granaries that portrays or parallels the native concept of the granary as it is expressed in an indigenous magical language.

However she arrived at this visual solution, Izquierdo has returned to a tradition much older than the twentieth-century rhetoric that constructs national identity as masculine. She cites the venerable authority of indigenous tradition that can be traced back through the campesinos to the Precolumbian era. In this tradition the land is predominantly female.[37] By linking land and women in her series of rural gardens in the heartland of agrarian reform, a state where "even the stones are Zapatista,"[38] Izquierdo lobbies for national values that acknowledge women's contributions and accept women as full partners.

In the paintings discussed in this chapter Izquierdo developed a subtle but highly effective strategy for gendering the land and by extension the nation as female. She utilized the indigenous traditions of Morelos—the land of Zapata and agrarian rights—to build a corpus of paintings that construct the land as female and thereby offer an alternative to the aggressive masculinity of the muralists. These paintings contribute to a more balanced view of the gender of Mexico.

PART THREE

The Wall of Resistance

María Izquierdo wanted to paint a mural and tried repeatedly to do so. In 1942 the governor of Veracruz, Jorge Cerdán, invited her to paint frescos in the Palacio de Gobierno del Estado (Palace of the State Government) in Jalapa. During short research trips to the region Izquierdo made numerous drawings, now lost, in preparation for painting thirty panels about the crafts, industries, fiestas, dances, and clothing of the Totonac people. The mural was never created because Cerdán's tenure as governor ended before Izquierdo began painting in the palace. The new governor was not interested in the project.[1] (Public projects in Mexico need to be completed during the term of office of the politicians who initiate them.) In 1945 Izquierdo signed a contract to paint frescos in the monumental staircase of the building of the Departamento del Distrito Federal (Department of the Federal District) in the heart of Mexico City. She undoubtedly calculated that she had sufficient time to complete the murals before key government officials changed office and surely felt confident in her ability to carry out the prestigious project. She did not foresee the vehement objections from some of her colleagues that soon prevented her from painting the murals.

Art historians and critics usually write about the successes of the art world. We write about art that has been deemed worthy by major museums, chosen by important collectors, shown in trendy galleries, and inaugurated in public spaces. Chapter 6 recounts a defeat. In the process it lays bare the gap between the dominant discourse of the Mexican art world and one woman's convictions about the purpose of art and ideas about better ways to represent women.

6

What Sex Is the City? Izquierdo's Aborted Mural Project

On February 14, 1945, journalist Carlos Denegri announced in an article in the newspaper *Excélsior* that María Izquierdo had been commissioned to paint murals in the building of the Departamento del Distrito Federal (Department of the Federal District). Denegri proclaimed that Izquierdo was "the first woman in America to succeed in breaking the pictorial tradition that requires that only male painters be commissioned for monumental murals." He also observed that "Diego Rivera and David Alfaro Siqueiros, among the most renowned, until now have monopolized this rough work of painting."[1] Denegri's claim that Izquierdo was to be the first female muralist in the Americas was inaccurate: Aurora Reyes, Marion Greenwood, and Grace Greenwood had already painted murals in Mexico, albeit in locations less prestigious than the Departamento del Distrito Federal. Although the claim was not true, it reveals the degree to which muralism was popularly perceived as a male domain.

The contract for the murals was signed by Javier Rojo Gómez, the governor of the Federal District, and María Izquierdo on February 9 or February 19, 1945 (both dates have been published, but the original contract has not been located).[2] She was to paint frescoes about "The Progress of Mexico" on the wall of the monumental staircase and about "The Arts" on the plafonds (the coffered ceiling) above the staircase. The mural was to cover 154.86 square meters. She was to be paid 34,843.50 pesos, which was 225 pesos per square meter. This was equivalent to 7,184.23 U.S. dollars or 46.39 U.S. dollars per meter. From this sum Izquierdo was responsible for paying for materials, scaffolding, and the salaries of her assistants. The agreement stipulated that the work must be completed by December 15, 1945,[3] a date that would have allowed ample time for the project to be presented to the public before President Ávila Camacho's term of office ended on November 30, 1946.

The building in which Izquierdo was to paint the frescoes was a graceful colonial structure (fig. 59) on the south side of the Zócalo, the main plaza of Mexico City, also known as the Plaza de la Constitución (Constitution Square) and the Plaza Mayor (Great Square). The building is located between the streets Cinco de Febrero and Veinte de Noviembre. Today it is known as the Antiguo Palacio del Ayuntamiento (Old Palace of the City Hall). The location of Izquierdo's mural commission in an important government building on the Zócalo—the place of maximum political and spiritual power in Mexico since the founding of Tenochtitlan in 1325 CE—is central to the events that later unfolded. The site that she had claimed for her first murals embodied power and prestige. Unfortunately, the walls that Izquierdo was commissioned to paint remain without murals.

Despite Izquierdo's joy and pride in obtaining a major mural commission, her project was quickly aborted, painfully and publicly. When she fought to keep the commission, a major scandal erupted. Opinions, then and now, have always been polarized. A large segment of the Mexican art world vigorously supported her. Her detractors dismissed her style as unsuitable for murals and claimed that she was unprepared technically to paint frescos. While there were elements of truth in the arguments for and against Izquierdo's undertaking, the story of what happened is significantly more complex than has ever been acknowledged. The degree to which gender issues affected the outcome of the project was ignored until four decades after her commission was revoked, when Mexican writer Carlos Monsiváis briefly broached the subject in 1986.[4]

This chapter examines numerous factors that led to the abrogation of Izquierdo's commission, including the inherent power of the location, the fierce competition among the muralists for walls, and the lack of mural commissions for Rivera and Siqueiros in the years immediately preceding Izquierdo's commission. Although Izquierdo never painted the murals, she created studies in pencil, ink, and watercolor. After she lost the battle to keep the commission, she painted two large portable panels in fresco to prove her

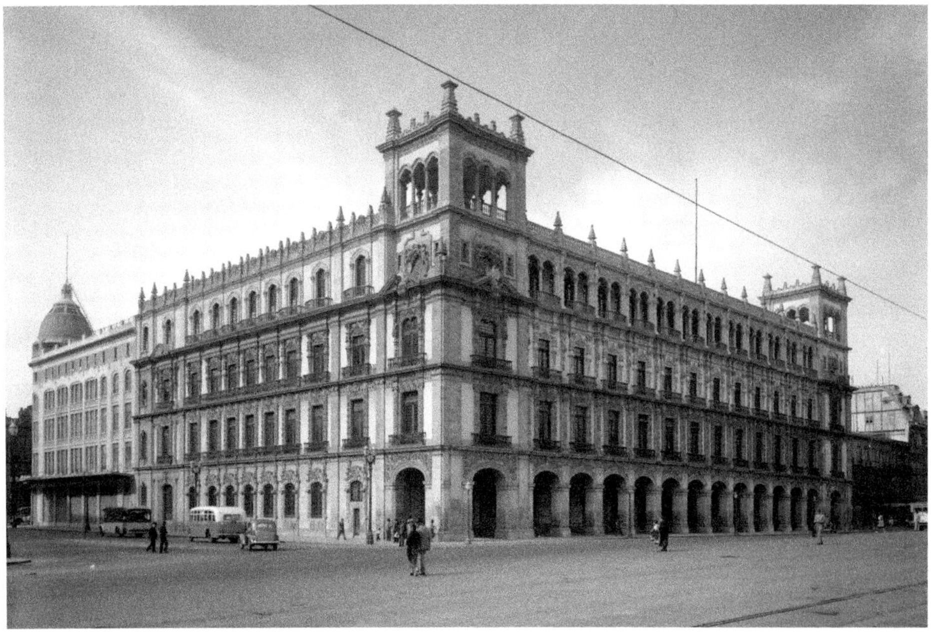

Fig. 59. Photograph of the Departamento del Distrito Federal ca. 1940. This building, which is now known as the Antiguo Palacio del Ayuntamiento, is located on the Zócalo between the streets Cinco de Febrero and Veinte de Noviembre. Photograph from the Casasola Archive of the Fototeca Nacional, Mexico. © 88671 CONACULTA.INAH. SINAFO.FN.MEXICO.

technical ability in this demanding medium. Izquierdo's studies for the murals feature women in leading roles, a choice that deviates from the usual postrevolutionary practice of celebrating male heroes and relegating women to secondary roles. Hence her images of women as protagonists challenge the usual construction of Mexican national identity as masculine.

Mexican art historian Teresa del Conde has dismissed Izquierdo's loss of the commission with the comment that "María Izquierdo was not gifted for painting 'with a message' and so we should not lament too much that her mural projects for the staircase and the plafonds of the Central Department were not completed."[5] Based on the studies that survive, I do not believe that the murals would have been as aesthetically pleasing as her best paintings if the completed murals simply reproduced the studies. But substantially more was at stake than just aesthetics: Izquierdo's images would have presented women as leaders. In 1945 this was a bold departure from the usual representation of women in Mexican murals. The last part of this chapter discusses the transgressive nature of Izquierdo's imagery and the consequences of the cancellation of the mural project. The focus on aesthetics by Conde and others only serves to obfuscate the real issues of power at play in the cancellation of the project.

History of the Mural Project

According to Izquierdo, the initial steps toward her mural project took place during her travels in South America in 1944, when Peruvian artists and intellectuals expressed interest in having a Mexican muralist come to Lima to paint a mural. The Peruvians proposed an exchange in which Izquierdo would paint a mural in Lima and a Peruvian artist would paint a mural in Mexico. Izquierdo returned from her trip intending to consult Jaime Torres Bodet, the minister of education, about the possibility of an artistic interchange between the two countries. At the end of January 1945 she spoke to Javier Rojo Gómez, the govenor of the Departamento Central del Distrito Federal, about her aspirations and the Peruvians' proposal, adding: "Nevertheless, I would prefer to do my first mural in Mexico."[6] Izquierdo recounts that Rojo Gómez responded by offering her walls to paint.

Reactions to Izquierdo's mural commission began soon after it was announced in the newspaper. According to Antonio Rodríguez, Luis Islas García, a critic for *La Nación*, wrote Javier Rojo Gómez a letter that began with the following words:

> You will be told that we have reactionary prejudices against the work of the painting [*sic*]. We respond simply that it is not reactionary prejudice to demand that a painter possess a minimum of drawing, of modeling, of skill in the handling of oil. Do you believe that one who is not even capable of resolving the few problems posed by the background of a portrait is going to know how to find the answer to the immense problems of a monumental decoration? Do you believe that one who does not even have an average reputation as a portrait painter might have the mastery required to confront the more serious problems of a mural?[7]

Islas García, the man responsible for the original complaint, was a minor figure in the Mexican art world. In 1929 he had written a long and largely negative critique of Izquierdo's first solo exhibition, at the Galería de Arte Moderno in the Teatro Nacional, the building now known as the Palacio de Bellas Artes.[8] Ironically, this exhibition of Izquierdo's work was instigated by Diego Rivera because, according to Izquierdo, he considered her art to be the only good work being done by any student at the Escuela Nacional de Bellas Artes when he first took over the directorship in 1929.[9] Rivera's intention was to convert the prestigious but obsolete academy into a truly modern art school. While many students had greater technical facility in rendering than Izquierdo, her work was vigorous and modern. Being singled out as the only talented student at the academy by the most famous artist in Mexico had major consequences for Izquierdo's career: it led to her first solo exhibition, for which Rivera wrote cautiously positive praise appropriate for a talented emerging artist.[10] As Izquierdo tells the story, however, Rivera's attention also provoked bitter envy, hostility, and rivalry on the part of fellow students who did not understand why Rivera admired her work and not theirs. A group of students literally drove her out of the academy within days after Rivera first praised her work, thus truncating her formal art education.[11]

In Islas García's review of her 1929 solo show, he revealed that he had seen her earlier work in a group show (probably the exhibition that was organized so that Rivera could see the student work at Escuela Nacional de Bellas Artes, though this is not explicitly stated). Based on this early work, Islas García "did not have the least confidence in her artistic future."[12] In his 1929 review Islas García claimed to be pleasantly surprised by her current work. He praised her use of color but complained about the compositions of several paintings. According to him, her principal defect was her lack of knowledge of composition and drawing. He concluded that she could be considered "the best female painter among all of the students of painting at [the Escuela Nacional de Bellas Artes]."[13] In addition to the sexism imbedded in the wording of his evaluation, it is also a backhanded compliment, considering that she had already left art school. Islas García's review of Izquierdo's first solo exhibition suggests that, like her classmates, he failed to understand what Rivera saw in her work.[14]

Sixteen years later Islas García's scathing letter provoked conversations behind closed doors (to which we will never have access) and other reactions (discussed below).

Meanwhile Izquierdo dedicated her time to setting up scaffolding and testing fresco techniques. She hired a team of workers who had assisted Diego Rivera, including the chemist Andrés Sánchez Flores and the mason and painter David Barajas. But by the time she had completed the designs and was ready to start work, other obstacles had arisen. Ignacio Martínez, the Federal District government employee in charge of the project, discovered that the scaffolding was poorly constructed. Work was suspended so that it could be reinforced, but the carpenter who was to make the repairs was fired before they were requested, leaving no one to do the work.

Izquierdo was told to create "false walls" (*falsos muros*) so that her murals could be moved in case the building was remodeled. She later told the writer Loló de la Torriente: "I was convinced that the building would not suffer such changes, but I could not accept the idea that they were plotting to obstruct my work."[15] She recalled that she waited calmly and communicated with the officials closest to Rojo Gómez. Then one day she discovered that her cans of paint had been covered with garbage. "I began to realize that they were sabotaging me."[16] After a few weeks, when she believed that the problems were about to be favorably resolved, Martínez refused to allow her to paint and told her that the orders had come from higher up.[17] In October work was officially suspended: she was locked out of the room where she stored her materials.[18]

While Izquierdo was encountering obstacles at the site, the political side of the problem mushroomed. After Rojo Gómez received Islas García's letter, he allegedly consulted

Rivera, Siqueiros, and Orozco about the commission, a conference that the press later referred to as a *junta secreta* (secret meeting). The meeting took place in private, so we do not know its date or what was said. But Rivera later confirmed that Rojo Gómez contacted him about the mural.[19]

In the early 1950s Izquierdo told a journalist her version of how the project unraveled. "As soon as Siqueiros and Rivera saw that the work was really going forward, they began to criticize the subject and set up thousands of obstacles; in other words, to fight in every possible way against the execution of the mural that I had been commissioned to do."[20] Commenting on the role of Rivera and Siqueiros, she observed:

> They had two attitudes: one public, let's say official, in which they maintained that because this building was colonial it should not be painted in fresco because "it would spoil the building." (They had these scruples for the first time. Diego painted the Palace of Cortez in Cuernavaca, which could not be any more colonial, and Siqueiros [painted] other buildings of this type.) Along with this they argued that I had not painted in fresco before and that in doing so for the first time everything would be spoiled. (There is a first time for everything. I believe that even Rivera and Siqueiros did some murals before others, and no one stopped them then.) Along with these attitudes and public arguments there was something much deeper: Siqueiros and Rivera wanted to dictate the subject, wanted to oblige me to give them political content, something that I never accepted, for two reasons: I have never belonged to any political party and I have never wanted my painting to be a poster or social proclamation.[21]

Izquierdo considered her work to be aesthetically revolutionary but insisted that as a painter she had only one goal: "to give my people, whom I sincerely love, the best of my artistic sensibility, color, form, poetry, and Mexican art, to deliver to them part of my being in the form of paintings, so that they have an authentic aesthetic delight. I will never give them an artistic lie, a camouflage, or a mixture of demagogic color and flag-waving." She added: "Siqueiros and Rivera knew this and know it very well, and because of this they fought me and won temporarily."[22]

Soon after the project was halted, Rojo Gómez offered Izquierdo another contract to paint in any of the less important government buildings. She refused, later explaining: "I did not accept painting in another building out of artistic pride and above all because I did not want the muralist monopoly to do and undo at their whim."[23]

After the suspension of the project was announced in the press, a group of approximately one hundred artists and intellectuals signed a letter in support of Izquierdo. The letter, dated December 26, 1945, and addressed to Rojo Gómez, requested "on behalf of the artistic prestige of María Izquierdo, her valuable national work, and the honor she has won for Mexico in other nations, the restitution of the contract that the government of the Federal District signed."[24] The people who signed the letter represented a spectrum of artistic tendencies and political affiliations. In early January an article in *Esto* listed the names of those who had signed the letter and identified each by profession.[25] If a visual artist had painted a mural, that information was noted in order to emphasize the signer's qualifications to judge Izquierdo's potential for painting frescos. Those who signed the letter included Emilio Portes Gil, president of Mexico from 1928 to 1930, and José Vasconcelos, minister of education from 1921 to 1924, who had initiated the Mexican muralist movement by commissioning young and mid-career artists to paint murals in important government buildings in the early 1920s. Visual artists who signed the letter included

Jesús Guerrero Galván, Fernando Leal, Leopoldo Méndez, Pablo O'Higgins, Clarita Porcet, Víctor Reyes, Manuel Rodríguez Lozano, Antonio Ruiz, Juan Soriano, and Alfredo Zalce. Among the writers who signed were Graciela Amador, Alfredo Cardona Peña, León Felipe, Justino Fernández, Álvaro Gálvez y Fuentes, Andrés Henestrosa, Efraín Huerta, Margarita Michelena, Carlos Pellicer, Alfonso Reyes, Xavier Villaurrutia, and Adelina Zendejas. Others signers included gallery director María Asúnsolo.

To demonstrate her ability to work in a monumental scale and prove her technical competence in fresco, Izquierdo created two large portable fresco panels: *La tragedia* (Tragedy) and *La música* (Music), both from 1946.[26] Each panel was just over eight feet tall, making them the largest works that she ever created. The Galería de Arte de María Asúnsolo (GAMA) issued invitations to the exhibition of the fresco panels, which opened on May 22, 1946. Due to the size and weight of the panels, the exhibition was held at the Izquierdo-Uribe home on Kepler Street, where Izquierdo had painted them, rather than in the Galería de Arte de María Asúnsolo on Reforma Avenue.[27] The exhibition received mixed reviews. Margarita Michelena, who was a close friend of Izquierdo, extolled the work and praised the technical excellence of the frescoes, obviously attempting to refute complaints that a major commission had been awarded to an artist who had not yet painted in fresco.[28] Other critics were less enthusiastic. Loló de la Torriente wrote: "It cannot be said that the work completed—and which she only exhibited in part—is as powerful as required for mural painting. Something is missing: the touch of genius, the spark of greatness, epic transcendence, and universal harmony."[29] A journalist writing under the cloak of anonymity for *Futuro* claimed that the panels looked like they were made by a high school student for a graduation ceremony and should never have been exhibited.[30]

Izquierdo's exhibition of the fresco panels kept the controversy alive throughout the summer of 1946. Loló de la Torriente's article "Murales que desataron pasiones" (Murals That Unleashed Passions), published on June 5, 1946, focused less on the fresco panels than on the controversy surrounding the commission. Torriente interviewed Izquierdo and Rivera and included both of their accounts of what led to the cancellation of Izquierdo's contract. She stated that on more than one occasion she heard Rivera say: "It's fair that she be offered an opportunity; when I painted the Ministry of Education I tried mural painting for the first time [*sic*], and in the end it didn't turn out so badly."[31] However, she also reported that Izquierdo's husband, Raúl Uribe, came to Rivera's studio to ask him to sign the petition supporting Izquierdo's right to paint the frescos. Rivera refused, offering the excuse: "I think it is useless. Rojo has already formed his opinion and no one will change it: he is a very firm man."[32] Rivera snidely remarked to Torriente: "I believe María has a screw loose."[33] He argued that Izquierdo should have accepted Rojo Gómez's offer to decorate a less important building. To promote this idea he recounted how Orozco with his "magnificent attitude" abandoned his controversial murals at the Suprema Corte de Justicia (Supreme Court of Justice) in order to paint in the Hospital de Jesús (Hospital of Jesus) in Guadalajara. Rivera concluded: "When Rojo called me, I asked for María's sketches: there were no sketches. Later I could not judge by what was on the walls: there wasn't anything. . . . Nevertheless I told him that she should be allowed to work to see what she would do."[34] If what Rivera said to Rojo Gómez was similar to what he said to Torriente, then he helped kill the project with lies, contradictions, condescension, and scorn, all the while mouthing the words that she should be allowed to paint.

Siqueiros wrote an open letter to Izquierdo that was published in *Excélsior* on July 25,

1946, in which he insisted that he wanted to end rumors about his position in regard to her "professional problem." He assured her that when consulted by the mayor's secretary he had said that revoking a signed mural contract would set a bad precedent.[35] Siqueiros argued that the problem was the result of a lack of a fine arts commission, which allowed government officials to grant and cancel contracts at their whim. He claimed that no *junta secreta* ever took place and added that he had suggested that painters with more experience in mural painting could assist her in the project. Siqueiros concluded that other easel painters were also capable of painting murals and that the Mexican government ought to provide more artists with opportunities to paint murals.[36]

On the day that Siqueiros's letter appeared in *Excélsior*, he and Izquierdo happened to meet at a reception at the Colombian Embassy. He greeted her with a big smile; she called him a hypocrite.[37] Whether Siqueiros was a hypocrite is a matter of opinion; but, like Rivera, he damned her with less than wholehearted support. His open letter did not argue that she should be allowed to paint the murals because she was a good painter; he merely observed that it would establish a bad precedent to rescind a signed mural contract. His allusion to her "professional problem" and recommendation that more experienced painters could help her suggest condescension. Based on later developments, it seems likely that Siqueiros's letter was primarily motivated by his desire to win the support of other painters for a mural commission by dangling before them the promise of more mural contracts for everyone.

Factors behind the Opposition

The reasons behind Rivera's and Siqueiros's opposition to Izquierdo's murals are complex and involve a variety of issues, some of which have never been openly discussed. Both Rivera and Siqueiros had gone through extended periods in which they had been unable to obtain commissions to paint public walls in Mexico. From 1937 through 1941 Rivera received no public mural commissions in Mexico.[38] According to Rivera's biographer, Bertram Wolfe, the late 1930s and early 1940s were a difficult time for Rivera because his opportunities to paint murals were shrinking.[39] In 1942 Rivera returned to the Palacio Nacional, where he began to paint a series about Precolombian cultures for the second floor courtyard. In 1945 he created *La Gran Tenochtitlan* (The Great City of Tenochtitlan) at the National Palace. Even though Rivera was painting murals in 1945, his enormous capacity for work and ravenous appetite for walls exceeded his commissions. Siqueiros received no public walls in Mexico from 1940 until 1944, when he painted *Nueva democracia* (New Democracy) of 1944–1945 in the Palacio de Bellas Artes.[40] Rivera and Siqueiros were acknowledged masters of muralism at the height of their fame. The problem was that they invariably provoked controversies. As Wolfe observed, politicians had learned too much from tangling with Rivera over the previous two decades to risk involvement with him. "His reputation was too great, public notice too sure; in any war of words in the press he had demonstrated that he was a master of sharp retort."[41] Siqueiros's lack of mural opportunities in Mexico began after he led an armed assault on the home of Leon Trotsky on May 23, 1940. Trotsky escaped harm, but his secretary, Robert Sheldon Harte, was kidnapped and murdered. Siqueiros was captured in September 1940 and sent to Lecumberri Penitentiary, where he was incarcerated for seven months then discreetly released on the condition that he leave the country.[42]

Rivera was capable of enormous generosity but acted ruthlessly when asserting his dominance in the art world. In postrevolutionary Mexico artistic dominance was determined through the creation of monumental murals on the walls of important public buildings. When ego, artistic power, and prestige were at stake, Rivera's sense of solidarity with his colleagues was unreliable. For example, developing a high-quality version of *buon fresco* (true fresco) that worked well in Mexico proved difficult for the first muralists, including Rivera. When he began using fresco at the Secretaría de Educación Pública in 1923, his assistant Xavier Guerrero made substantial refinements in the technique. Guerrero, whose father had painted on plaster, started with a family recipe, made trips to Teotihuacan to compare his experiments with Precolumbian murals, and finally presented Rivera with a successful solution. Rivera was initially delighted and declared: "We will save this sample, embed it in the finished work, and next to it paint your portrait with the date of the discovery."[43] Guerrero asked Rivera to let him remove the sample from its container, but Rivera insisted on doing it and hammered the sample to bits, crushing the last large chunk with his foot. The commemorative portrait of Guerrero was forgotten.

Other instances of Rivera's drive for artistic hegemony occurred a few months later at the same location. When José Vasconcelos commissioned the murals for the Secretaría de Educación Publica, he assigned Rivera to work in the first court of the building, while Xavier Guerrero, Amado de la Cueva, and Jean Charlot were to work in the second court. Guerrero, de la Cueva, and Charlot worked full-time as Rivera's assistants, so they made slow progress with their own murals. While Rivera painted the first court, with many walls yet to paint, he praised the work of his younger colleagues to the press. Defending their style to a public that was not yet accustomed to modern art, Rivera told a reporter: "Xavier Guerrero has realized an ornamentation of great simplicity and purity and of a Mexicanism indisputably modern, devoid of picturesque or archaeological compromise." Rivera praised Charlot for having "entered into the Mexican mode of feeling and the good and firm expression of French plasticity, doing things that take their place among those of the highest character and quality executed here." Finally, Rivera proclaimed that Amado de la Cueva had painted "two frescoes that will remain for all time among the best references on the initiation of the movement; they possess simplicity, an intonation of great delicacy, and a clear sense of decorative composition."[44] When Rivera had finished painting all the walls in the first court and the second court was only partially painted, however, his craving for walls overcame his feelings of solidarity with his fellow artists. Rivera began painting in the second court, not only on unpainted walls but also over his young colleagues' frescoes, obliterating Charlot's *Danza de los listones* (Dance of the Ribbons) and two panels by Guerrero. After he had painted over their frescoes, he spoke disparagingly of their art to the press, alleging that the three artists had failed to achieve unity in their work.[45]

Rivera's destruction of his collegues' murals and other acts of artistic aggression are documented in Charlot's *The Mexican Mural Renaissance,* 1920–1925.[46] Similar behavior on the part of Siqueiros at a later date has gone virtually unnoticed. Before Siqueiros painted *Apología de la futura victoria de la ciencia médica contra el cáncer* (Apology from the Future Victory of Medicine over Cancer) at the Centro Médico in Mexico City in 1958, Leonora Carrington had signed a contract to paint murals at the site and had prepared detailed studies, now in a private collection. Many years later Carrington recalled that "Siqueiros made a tantrum" and got the commission.[47]

Beginning in 1922, when José Vasconcelos commissioned a small group of young and mid-career artists to paint the walls of the Escuela Nacional Preparatoria, until at least the late 1950s, muralism was central to artistic prestige in Mexico. Rivera, Siqueiros, and Orozco wrote as well as painted. Through the combined force of their murals, writings, and success in obtaining prestigeous government commissions, they largely set the standards for art in Mexico.[48] They defined the highest artistic achievement as work that was monumental, public, didactic, and ideological. The manifesto issued by the Sindicato de Obreros Técnicos, Pintores y Escultores glorified art that was collective and public, renounced easel painting as aristocratic, and urged artists to "promote an ideological focus" that would help the people.[49] The murals that Orozco, Rivera, Siqueiros, and others created often presented panoramic views of history. To a large extent the Mexican muralists reasserted the old hierarchies of the Italian Renaissance, in which history painting was at the top, portraiture and landscape were of lesser importance, and still-life painting was at the bottom. The major difference was that in Mexico history painting needed to be presented on a wall in a public space, preferably in a major government building, rather than on canvas or in a palace or a church. Rivera, Siqueiros, and Orozco created an environment in which artistic status was directly linked to an artist's ability to obtain mural commissions and successfully complete monumental murals in important public buildings.

One of the principal factors behind the opposition to Izquierdo's murals was the paramount location of the Departamento del Distrito Federal on the Zócalo at the center of the capital (fig. 60). As noted above, this location had been the site of political and spiritual power in Mexico since the founding of Tenochtitlan in 1325 CE. After the Conquest of Mexico, the plaza and principal buildings of the new capital of Nueva España (New Spain) were constructed over the ruins of the Aztecs' sacred precinct at the center of Tenochtitlan. Consequently, the site has been continually the center of maximum political and spiritual power since the fourteenth century. When the colonial city was founded, the Cathedral of Mexico was placed at the north end of the plaza. Hernán Cortés's residence and headquarters were constructed on the east side of the plaza; the building subsequently became the Palacio Virreinal (Viceregal Palace). After Independence it was renamed the Palacio Nacional (National Palace). The Antiguo Ayuntamiento (Old City Hall, the building that was called the Departamento del Distrio Federal in 1945) was located to the southwest. Finally, the Portales de los Mercaderes (Arcades of the Merchants) were situated on the west side.

Since the sixteenth century numerous architectural changes have been made to all the buildings on the Zócalo, and the names of most of the buildings have changed repeatedly. The Antiguo Ayuntamiento was destroyed in the riots of 1692. Its reconstruction was not completed until 1724. The current façade of the building dates from 1910. In 1942 construction was begun on a second building, located on the southeast of the Zócalo, which was designed to resemble the Departamento del Distrito Federal. Both buildings have always housed urban authorities. The building that was called the Departamento del Distrito Federal in 1945 is now known as the Antiguo Palacio del Ayuntamiento.

What has not changed is the convergence of political, spiritual, and economic power at the heart of the city. The Zócalo is where major buildings representing the power of the nation, the capital, the church, and commerce unite. The social and the spatial are intertwined. Geographer Tim Cresswell convincingly argues that physical location needs to be considered along with issues of race, class, and gender.[50] Cresswell's assertion is highly relevant to the present study, in which issues of space, power, and gender collide.

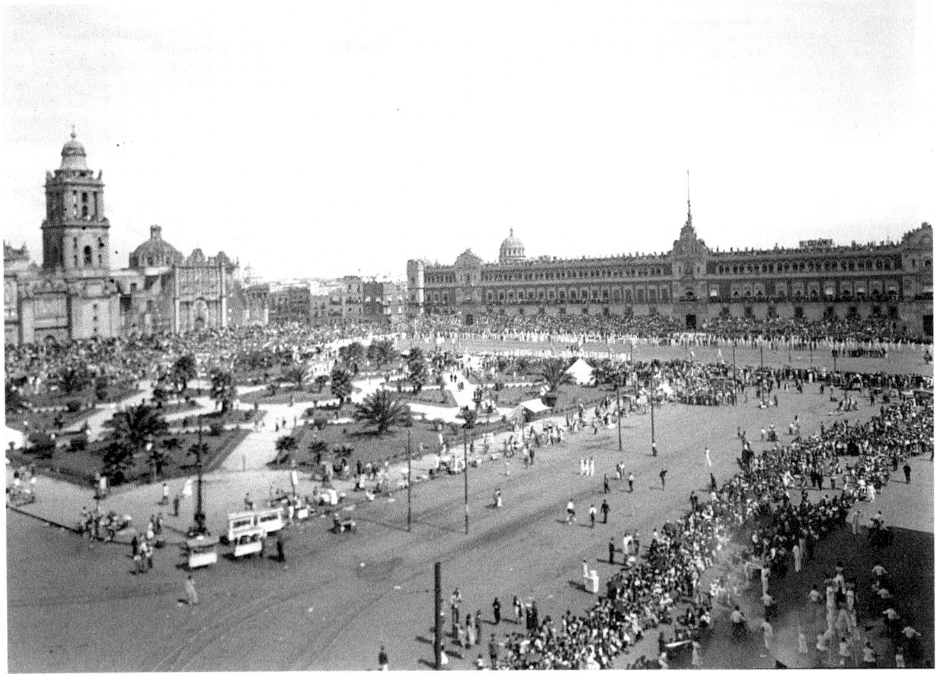

Fig. 60. Photograph of the Zócalo, showing the cathedral (*left*) and the National Palace (*right*), 1935 to 1940. The photograph was taken from the southwest corner of the Zócalo. Consequently, the Antiguo Palacio del Ayuntamiento, which was the building of the Departamento del Distrito Federal in 1945, is not visible in the photograph. Photograph from the Casasola Archive of the Fototeca Nacional. © 50668 CONACULTA.INAH. SINAFO.FN.MEXICO.

When Izquierdo encountered resistance to her mural project in 1945, Rivera was the only muralist who had painted murals in a building on the Zócalo. He painted *Historia de México* (known in English as *History of Mexico: From the Conquest to the Future*) on the main stairway of the Palacio Nacional from 1929 to 1930 and in 1935. In 1943 he returned to the Palacio Nacional, where he began a series of fresco panels on the corridor of the second floor, a project that he would complete in 1951. In 1941 José Clemente Orozco painted murals in the Suprema Corte de Justicia, which is located just off the southeast corner of the Zócalo on Pino Suárez street. Several other buildings with important murals, such as the Secretaría de Educación Pública and the Escuela Nacional Preparatoria, are located within a radius of a few blocks. The historic center of Mexico City is the cradle of the Mexican muralist movement, but only Rivera had painted murals in a building that was literally on the Zócalo. The magnificence of the architecture on the Plaza de la Constitución and the power inherent in the site endowed any mural painted there with dramatically greater importance than it would have had in any other location.

The degree to which issues of power underlie the revoking of Izquierdo's commission is revealed in a conversation between art critic Margarita Michelena and politician Alfonso Corona del Rosal. Michelena claimed that Rivera did not have previous mural experience when he created his first murals; but, she added, sooner or later a doctor had to be given an opportunity to perform his first operation. Corona del Rosal retorted: "Fine, but not one that entrusts him with the health of the President of the Republic."[51]

Tim Cresswell asserts that place is "a powerful force in hegemonic and counterhegemonic struggles."[52] I argue that Izquierdo's bid to paint murals in a government building on the Zócalo challenged assumptions about who had the right to paint murals at the center of power. What Izquierdo intended to paint at this location transgressed gendered expectations regarding how Mexico should be represented. Her attempt to paint these images constitutes a counterhegemonic struggle against the way in which the Mexican nation was gendered.

Izquierdo's Studies for the Murals

Izquierdo's surviving studies make it possible to establish what she intended to paint, where the images would have been situated within the building, and what the murals would have communicated, both individually and as an ensemble, if she did not make significant changes as she worked on the project. We will never know for certain what Izquierdo would have painted if she had been given the opportunity. The watercolor and the drawings that survive may or may not have been her final designs. Even if Izquierdo intended these studies to be final, the history of muralism contains numerous instances of artists painting something quite different from what were supposedly the definitive designs. Changes that muralists have made after the plans have been approved have often led to more dynamic murals or to problems with the patron or both. What Izquierdo intended to paint is directly related to the problems that developed, so the images must be carefully examined.

Inside the Palacio del Departamento del Distrito Federal, the sweeping monumental staircase branches at the landing into two stairs that lead in opposite directions, an arrangement that leaves only one wall for a mural (fig. 61). The wall is bilaterally symmetrical and six-sided. Dominating the wall, at the top center, is an enormous bas-relief escutcheon inscribed with the message: "GOBERNAR A LA CIUDAD ES SERVIRLA" (to govern the city is to serve her). Izquierdo created two studies—an ink drawing and a watercolor—that are designed to wrap around the escutcheon and conform to the unusual shape of the wall. The studies are nearly identical in subject and design. But additional details in the watercolor suggest that it is the more developed, so that is the version discussed except where otherwise noted (fig. 62).

Izquierdo used the division in the wall created by the large escutcheon to establish a temporal divide. On the left side she embodies the Aztec capital Tenochtitlan through the figure of a *tlatoani* (ruler), who holds a sixteenth-century plan of the city. On the right she personifies the modern capital as a woman holding a map. At the center, immediately below the escutcheon, a small hourglass communicates the passage of time, a device that simultaneously links and separates the two sides of the composition.

On the left the *tlatoani*, who wears the *xiuhuitzolli* (turquoise diadem or royal headdress) and whose body is turned slightly toward the center of the composition, holds out a schematic plan of Tenochtitlan. The plan comes from the frontispiece of the sixteenth-century Codex Mendoza (Bodleian Library, Oxford University). At the center is an eagle perched on a cactus in front of a large turquoise X. According to tradition, the Aztec cult deity Huitzilopochtli told his followers to look for an eagle on a cactus on an island as a divine sign of where to found their city. The turquoise X suggests the canals that crisscrossed the Aztec capital, the division of the city into four barrios, and the significance of the four directions in the Mesoamerican worldview. Other elements on the Precolumbian side of Izquierdo's composition include an ancient pyramid, a maguey plant, a man in a boat (which refers to Tenochtitlan's location on an island in Lake Texcoco), an Aztec sculpture of a serpent head, and a kneeling man who reaches up with his right hand to help support the plan of Tenochtitlan.[53]

Modern Mexico City is personified on the right side of the composition as a young woman whose body is turned slightly toward the center of the composition and who holds up a map. Her size, position, posture, and map make her the counterpart of the

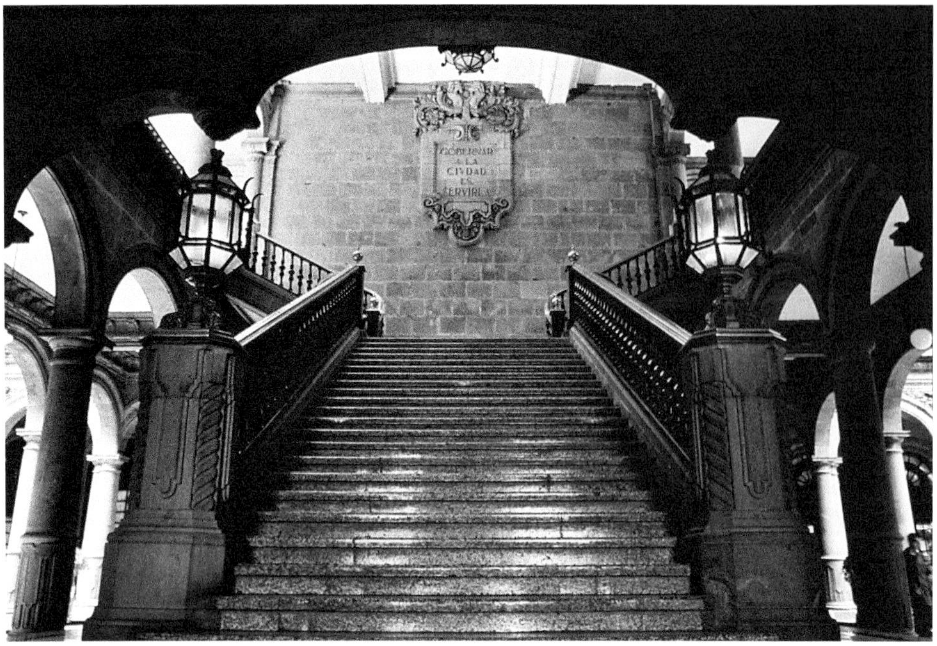

Fig. 61. Photograph of the monumental staircase in the building formerly known as the Departamento del Distrito Federal.

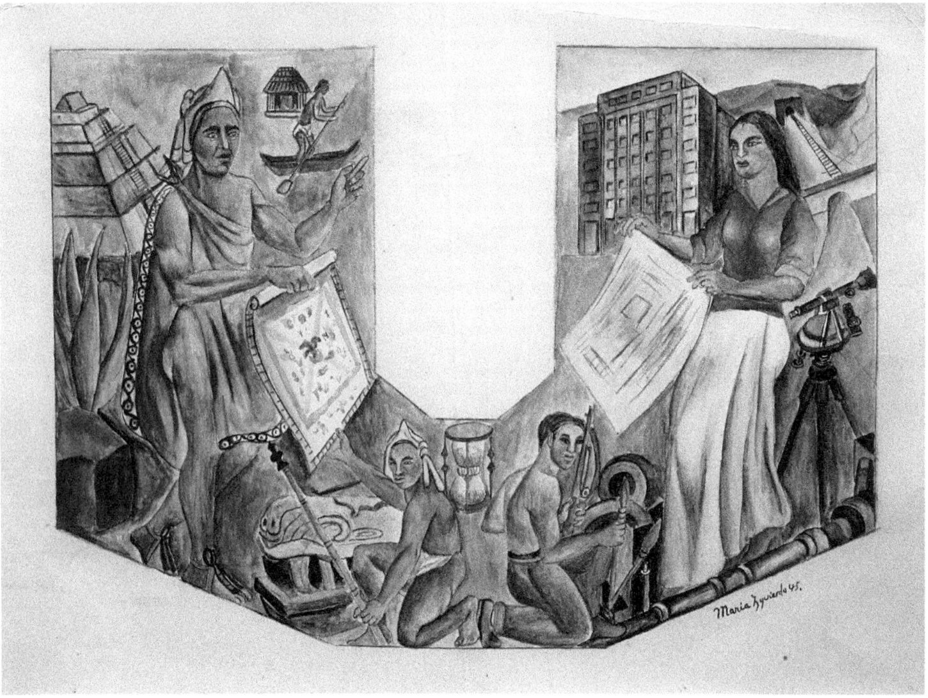

Fig. 62. María Izquierdo, study for the mural for the monumental staircase at the Departamento del Distrito Federal, 1945, watercolor on paper, 11 ⅞ × 16 ⅛ inches (30 × 41 cm), collection of the Museo de Arte Moderno, Mexico City. Photograph by Francisco Kochen. Reproduced with the permission of María Rosenda López Posadas, legal representative of the intellectual property of María Izquierdo. Reproduction authorized by the Instituto Nacional de Bellas Artes y Literatura, 2015.

tlatoani, although nothing in her appearance suggests elite status. Her red blouse and long white skirt are neither traditional indigenous clothing nor assertively modern attire. By modern standards she is dressed quite modestly. In the black-and-white drawing the paper she holds is labeled "plano de la Ciudad de México (actual)" or "map of (present-day) Mexico City." In the watercolor the map of the modern city is less clearly drawn and less recognizable than the sixteenth-century map held by the *tlatoani*. The background of the right side of the composition includes a tall modern building and a railroad track leading to a tunnel or mine in a mountain, while the foreground contains machinery and a kneeling male worker, who mirrors the kneeling man on the Precolumbian side.

In the presumably earlier black-and-white version of the image the woman wears her hair in braids, while in the watercolor her hair is loose. This small change suggests that Izquierdo originally represented an indigenous woman but later switched to a hairstyle without ethnic connotations. In other words, she first envisioned Mexico City as an indigenous woman and then later decided to portray the city as a mestiza, a woman of mixed Spanish and indigenous ancestry.

Izquierdo also created preliminary studies for the plafonds, which are located on the ceiling above the staircase and consist of nine rectangles arranged in three rows. In her studies for the plafonds, she featured allegorical figures of the arts, thus paying tribute to Mexico City's role as the cultural capital of the nation. Her choice of subject matter was inspired in part by Rufino Tamayo's mural *El canto y la música* (The Song and the Music) of 1933 in the Escuela Nacional de Música (National School of Music).[54] (The building is now used by the Coordinación Nacional de Arqueología.) In one drawing, which represents an overview of the plafonds, a single figure personifying one of the arts appears in each of the nine coffers (fig. 63). Izquierdo also made individual sketches for the panels *La literatura* (Literature) and *La tragedia* (Tragedy) and a joint study for *La música y la pintura* (Music and Painting). The drawings for the individual panels and the adjacent panels are more developed (and presumably done after the group study), while the ensemble provides a holistic view.

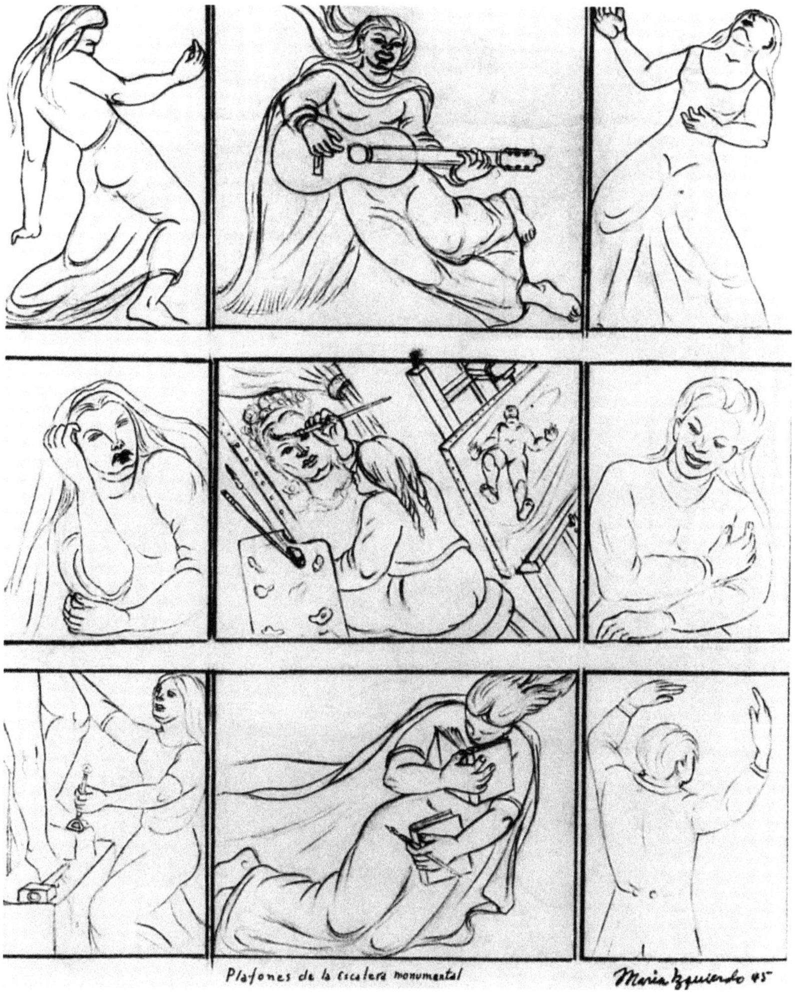

Fig. 63. María Izquierdo, study for the plafonds above the monumental staircase at the Departamento del Distrito Federal, 1945, pencil on paper, 13 15/16 × 11 1/16 inches (34 × 28 cm), private collection. Reproduced with the permission of María Rosenda López Posadas, legal representative of the intellectual property of María Izquierdo. Reproduction authorized by the Instituto Nacional de Bellas Artes y Literatura, 2015.

In the group study for the plafonds, a female musician playing a guitar floats diagonally across the central horizontal rectangle of the top row, while a woman representing modern dance occupies each of the flanking vertical rectangles. The central panel in the middle row depicts a female artist painting a portrait of a woman. The artist's twin braids imply that she is indigenous or a campesina, while the subject of the portrait wears her hair in an elegant coiffure. The artist works at her easel, and a painting to her right depicts a monumental foreshortened female figure similar to the one that Izquierdo later created for the fresco panel *La tragedia*. The panels on either side contain figures personifying the theater: tragedy on the left, comedy on the right. In the central image of the bottom row, the floating figure of Literature clasps a book in each hand. The rectangle to the left shows a female sculptor at work, while the panel on the right features a male conductor, whose back is toward the viewer. His raised hands and baton suggest that he is directing a symphonic orchestra. The nine figures may be understood as allegories of the arts and testimonies to the cultural wealth of the capital.[55]

Izquierdo's studies for the wall and plafonds of the monumental staircase correspond to what she agreed to paint in the contract as reported in the first newspaper articles and in her letter of February 21, 1946, to President Ávila Camacho. A study for an additional mural for the Departamento del Distrito Federal was first published in May 1945 (fig. 64).[56] Izquierdo probably created this study after completing the other designs in response to criticism that her designs were not related to the history of the building. An undated newspaper clipping from the María Izquierdo Archive reveals that art critic Antonio Rodríguez wrote: "It is not known whether she has the necessary historic documentation to conceive a pictorial work that reflects, as it must, the extraordinary dramas, the heroic deeds, that this city experienced—precisely in the Plaza de Armas—of which that building is truly the seat."[57] In the colonial era the portals of the Antiguo Ayuntamiento (Old City Hall) on the southeast corner of the Zócalo were used as a grain and vegetable

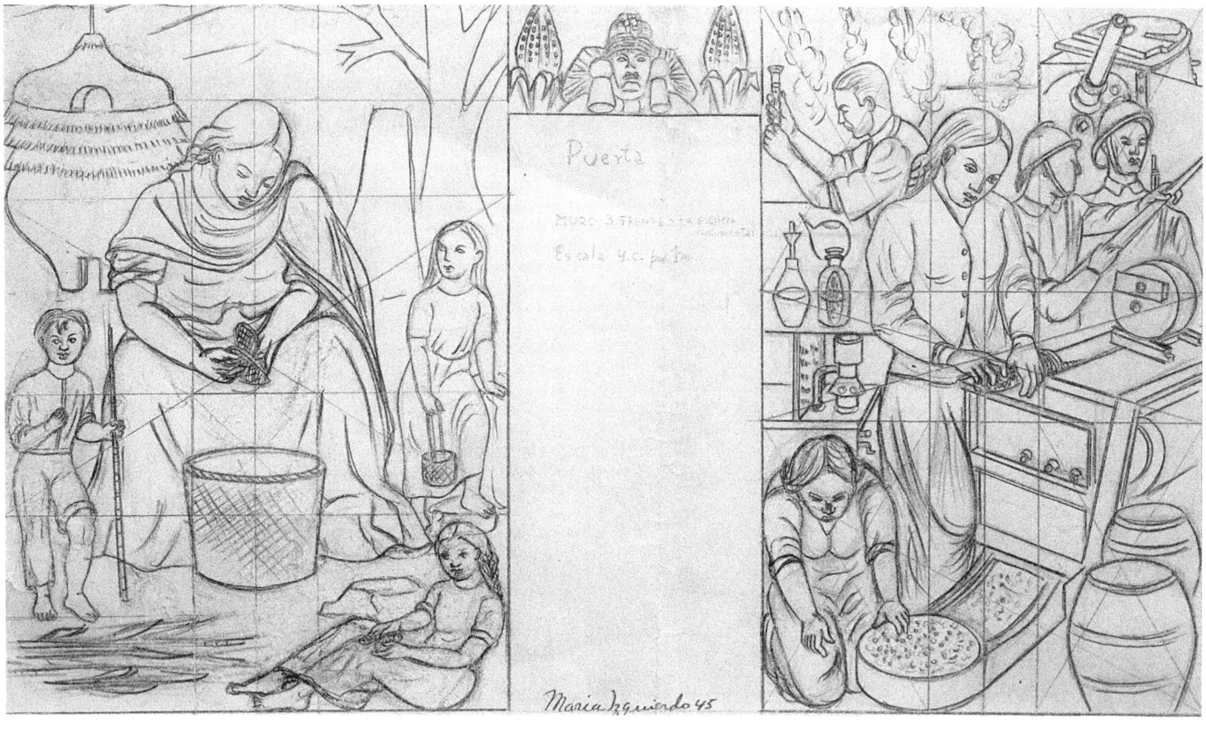

Fig. 64. María Izquierdo, design for a mural that was in addition to those originally commissioned for the Departamento del Distrito Federal, 1945, pencil on paper, 9 ½ x 16 ½ inches (24 x 42 cm), collection of the Museo de Arte Moderno, Mexico City. Photograph by Francisco Kochen. Reproduced with the permission of María Rosenda López Posadas, legal representative of the intellectual property of María Izquierdo. Reproduction authorized by the Instituto Nacional de Bellas Artes y Literatura, 2015.

market, so the theme of corn in this composition anchors the later design to the history of the site.[58]

The composition of the mural design is divided into two major sections that are intended to flank a door and are connected by a small panel above the door. According to an article in *Esto*, the mural was intended for the second floor.[59] The spaces on the second floor that conform to this shape are limited to a section of the north wall (which the viewer would see immediately after emerging from the staircase and turning toward the north) and a section of the south wall directly above the monumental staircase (which is not visible from the staircase).

On the left side of the composition a monumental indigenous woman who is stripping corn from the cob personifies traditional rural Mexico.[60] She is surrounded by three disproportionately small children who are helping or playing. The background contains a *coscomate* (traditional indigenous granary), which Izquierdo has drawn as a voluptuous bulging form. The woman, who is bent intently upon her work, uses a tool called an *olotera* to strip the grain from the cob, which she holds between her legs at crotch level, while a large basket is placed between her feet to catch the grain.[61] The charcoal study is drawn over a visible grid that includes two diagonals that intersect at the center of the composition, which is precisely where Izquierdo has positioned the woman's hands and the *olotera*. The combination and placement of the woman, corn, hands, *olotera*, basket, and granary suggest a conflation of corn, nourishment, work, woman, and womb.

The right side of the mural is busy, active, and crowded, as befits a representation of modern urban Mexico City. The main figure is a woman whose features are similar to those of the matriarch on the left but who wears modern clothing and works in a factory, probably processing corn with the help of a conveyer belt. Her hands are also at the precise center of the composition. A second woman kneels in the foreground to gather the product emerging from the machine. The background includes images of a male chemist with lab equipment and two soldiers with heavy artillery. The soldiers and female factory workers reflect the creation of the design at the end of World War II, when war had been constantly in the news for six years and middle-class women were a novelty in the Mexican workplace.

The panel above the door that connects the traditional and modern sides of the mural represents an Aztec maize deity flanked by two large ears of corn. There may be a trace of self-reference in the subject. Writing about Izquierdo's appearance, Rivera once observed that "she might have posed for an ancient sculptor, author of an image of [the maize deity] Centeotl."[62]

The three sections of the mural function together as a tribute to the fundamental importance of maize since the Precolumbian era and the enormous value of women's work in Mexico. The image of the traditional woman on the left reminds the viewer that Mexican women have always worked, albeit in ways that may have been underacknowledged. The image on the right asserts the changing role of women in the 1940s and the interest in utilizing technology to increase corn production during this period.[63] I consider this design to be the most successful of Izquierdo's mural studies. The more detailed drawing and the use of a grid suggest that this study is more developed than the others and that Izquierdo was beginning to do the advanced planning necessary for a successful mural program. Her usual method of painting was to paint directly on the canvas without preliminary studies, so this was a significant change.

Images and Issues

What Izquierdo planned to paint on the walls of the Palacio del Departamento del Distrito Federal is central to the problems she encountered. According to her, Rivera and Siqueiros wanted to force her to add political content to her murals.[64] In terms of the way in which politics were viewed in 1945, her preparatory studies for the murals were apolitical. They are, however, profoundly political in terms of gender issues.[65]

Jean Franco has observed that national identity in postrevolutionary Mexico was constructed as male identity. According to Franco, the Mexican Revolution of 1910–1920 promised social transformation and promoted a messianic spirit that transformed mortal men into supermen. During the postrevolutionary period the national discourse associated virility with social transformation and marginalized women just as they were supposedly obtaining greater rights.[66]

The association between virility and social transformation is manifested in the murals of Rivera, Orozco, Siqueiros, and others through the glorification of heroes. Canonical works of Mexican art include Rivera's figures of Emiliano Zapata and Lenin, Orozco's images of Quetzalcoatl and Prometheus, and Siqueiros's portrayals of Cuauhtemoc and himself as the *coronelazo*. Yet the representation of heroes in Mexican art was not limited to rulers, deities, and famous warriors. At the end of his life Rivera told art historian Raquel Tibol that for the first time in history monumental painting "ceased to employ as its central heroes the gods, kings, chiefs of state, heroic generals, etc. For the first time in art history, I repeat, Mexican mural painting made the masses the hero of monumental art, that is, the man from the country, from the factories, from the cities to the towns. When the hero appears among them, he is part of them and the result is clear and direct."[67] Rivera's concept of the nonelite hero is clearly exemplified in his figure of the unnamed leader featured in the first four panels dedicated to the theme of social transformation on the west wall of the former chapel at the Universidad Autónoma de Chapingo (Autonomous University of Chapingo) (fig. 65).

On the other hand, the muralists almost always represented women in secondary roles: as helpers, teachers, flower vendors, grieving mothers, or *soldaderas* trailing behind the troops. When women were featured in a mural they were either nudes epitomizing fertility and nature or allegorical figures of democracy or corruption.[68]

In some ways the images that Izquierdo planned to paint on the wall of the monumental staircase and on the second floor resemble Rivera's vision of the nonelite hero. Although Izquierdo planned to epitomize the city's past with the figure of an Aztec ruler in the mural for the monumental staircase, she intended to symbolize the city's present with a young mestiza whose attire does not suggest elite status. For the murals on the second floor, Izquierdo proposed to represent traditional, rural Mexico with an indigenous woman stripping corn from the cob and modern Mexico with a female factory worker. In the majority of these images, Izquierdo made common people the heroes of monumental art, in which she featured women from the country, from the factories, from the city. There was, of course, one significant difference between Rivera's vision of nonelite heroes and Izquierdo's: she intended to make her nonelite heroes women.

Izquierdo's plan to depict women as protagonists throughout the mural program and as the embodiment of Mexico City would have been a unique contribution to Mexican art. Her murals would have engendered the city as female. Of course, in the Spanish language

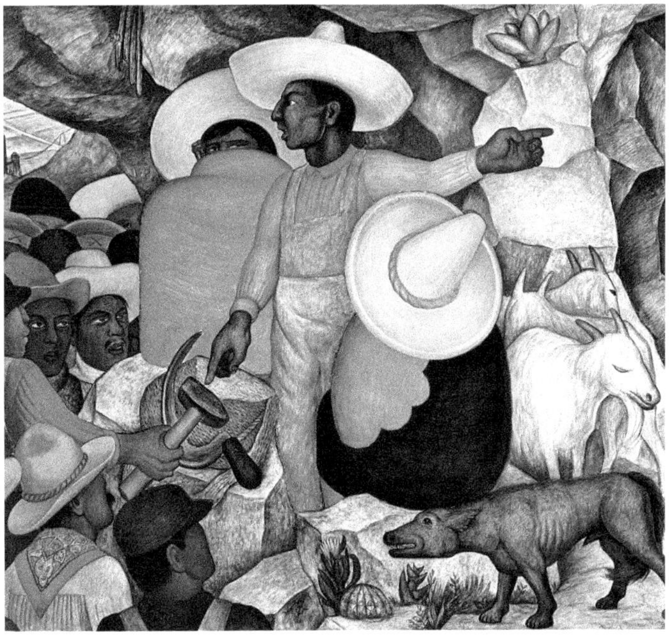

Fig. 65. Diego Rivera, detail of *El agitador* (The Agitator), also known as *Birth of Class Consciousness*, 1926, the first of five panels representing *La transformación social* (known in English as *Social Revolution*) on the west wall of the former chapel at the Universidad Autónoma de Chapingo, Mexico. Photograph by Rafael Doniz. © 2014 Banco de México Diego Rivera Frida Kahlo Museums Trust, Mexico, D.F./Artists Rights Society (ARS), New York. Reproduction authorized by the Instituto Nacional de Bellas Artes y Literatura, 2015.

la ciudad (the city) is grammatically feminine. But during the postrevolutionary period the construction of the nation was masculine, and in Mexico the capital was and is the political, economic, and cultural heart of the nation. Mexico has a centralist government: on a symbolic level, capital and country converge.[69] Ultimately, Izquierdo's murals were not lacking in political content; to the contrary, they were too political. Or perhaps it would be more accurate to say that they were political in the wrong way for 1945. Izquierdo's studies for the wall of the monumental staircase and the second floor challenged the construction of national identity as male and did so at the center of power.

Discussions at the time ignored the ways in which gender issues played a part in Izquierdo's loss of the mural commission. To my knowledge, the first person to state that gender was a factor was Carlos Monsiváis, who in 1986 observed that when Izquierdo returned from her travels in South America and embarked on her mural "the greatest disappointment occurred, the big encounter with the machismo that is moral and artistic discrimination."[70]

While the images that Izquierdo planned to paint did not express themes that Rivera and Siqueiros were willing to support, they did not publicly criticize the themes of the proposed murals. Discussion of the content of her mural studies did not appear in the press at the time when the commission was being debated because this type of discussion would have raised uncomfortable questions about censorship. Rivera and Siqueiros had vehemently protested when their murals were censored and destroyed in the United States in the early 1930s, so they could not afford to be perceived as trying to dictate subject matter to another artist.

This analysis of the multiple factors that contributed to Izquierdo's loss of the mural commission shows that the story as it has usually been told (which reduces the issues to her lack of experience painting in fresco and the supposed inappropriateness of her style) obscures other factors at work. The potency of the geographical location of the Departamento del Distrito Federal on the Zócalo provoked covetous competition for prestigious walls at the center of political, spiritual, and economic power in Mexico. Izquierdo's attempt to forefront images of monumental modern women in a major public building on the Zócalo constituted a form of transgression. Her subject matter prompted Rivera and Siqueiros to censor her work. Previous oversimplifications of the unraveling of her commission have obfuscated issues related to power and the gendering of the capital and thus the nation.

Consequences

In 1947 Fernando Gamboa, the director of the Instituto Nacional de Bellas Artes, had conversations with Rivera, Siqueiros, and Orozco in which the three muralists presented him with proposals. The proposals prompted Gamboa to invite a group of artists to exchange ideas about "current problems" in the art world, "principally in mural creation."[71] On July 28, Gamboa met with sixteen artists: Miguel Covarrubias, Jesús Guerrero Galván, Xavier Guerrero, Guillermo Meza, Leopoldo Méndez, Juan O'Gorman, Pablo O'Higgins, José Clemente Orozco, Máximo Pacheco, Gonzalo de la Paz Pérez, Feliciano Peña, Julio Prieto, Everardo Ramírez, Aurora Reyes, Diego Rivera, and Alfredo Zalce. María Izquierdo was conspicuously absent. But Aurora Reyes, the only Mexican woman to have painted a mural, was part of the gathering, and four artists who had signed the petition in support of Izquierdo painting the frescoes at the Departamento del Distrito Federal were present. The group passed a resolution with a number of provisions, including the establishment of a commission for mural painting, composed of Rivera, Siqueiros, and Orozco, who at their discretion could invite two additional painters to join the committee. The agreement became effective upon its publication in the *Diario Oficial* of the federal government, which took place on September 1, 1947.

The mural commission was known as the Comisión Impulsora y Reglamentadora de la Pintura Mural (Commission for the Promotion and Regulation of Mural Painting); its purpose was to stimulate and regulate the production of murals in Mexico. Although in theory it could have consisted of five painters, in practice it was initially composed exclusively of the three most famous muralists, who were often referred to as *los tres grandes* (the three great ones). Even before the commission was officially in effect, complaints arose that it was a de facto monopoly. In August 1947 Fernando Leal observed:

> If in the Renaissance a now irrefutable genius such as Michelangelo, or anyone else, had been named arbiter of artistic production, the Renaissance would have failed because even he would not have recognized the talent of Leonardo. The low opinion that El Greco had of Michelangelo, which a writer of his times transmits to us, is equally well known. On being asked if he met Michelangelo during his stay in Rome, Teocópulos said, "Yes, I met him. He was a good man, but the poor man did not know how to paint."
>
> All of these things I cite to demonstrate that not even the true geniuses, no one, can be the arbiter of art, and this is especially true in the case of *los tres grandes*.[72]

The Comisión Impulsora y Reglamentadora de la Pintura Mural consisted exclusively of the original three muralists until Orozco's death in 1949, at which time his position went to Jorge González Camarena. When Rivera died in 1957, Federico Cantú took his place. The degree to which the commission affected or did not affect the history of Mexican muralism is unclear. Juan O'Gorman, who was appointed to the commission in 1959, claimed that only two meetings of the commission could be verified, which did not produce any result.[73]

In 1981 art historian Shifra Goldman noted that between 1905 and 1969 only 289 artists were involved in the creation of 1,286 murals in Mexico, making it "apparent that commissions have not been diffused among the growing artistic community."[74] If we were to count only the artists who painted murals in important buildings in desirable locations in Mexico City between 1922 and 1955 (the year of Izquierdo's death), the number would plummet. While the Commission for Mural Painting that emerged out of the controversy surrounding Izquierdo's mural commission may not have had any impact on these statistics, the fierce competition for walls and the willingness of some artists to prevent other artists from painting murals undoubtedly contributed to the relatively limited number of artists who successfully completed mural commissions.

After the debate over the Comisión Impulsora y Reglamentadora de la Pintura subsided, the controversy over María Izquierdo's aborted mural project completely faded from public discussion and ceased being an issue for virtually everyone except the artist herself. For her, it remained a salient issue—and an open wound—for the rest of her life. In 1953 she told a newspaper reporter that Siqueiros should give up being "the boss of the mural painting monopoly" and go back to painting "portraits, which is what he does best."[75] The following year she told the journalist Bambi (nom de plume of Ana Cecilia Treviño) that for some of the great muralists choosing an individual path in art—one different from theirs—"is a true crime" that the independent artist must atone for by being excluded from mural painting.[76] As proof that these exclusionary practices still continued, Izquierdo cited recent maneuvers to prevent Rufino Tamayo from painting a mural at the Ciudad Universitaria (University City), the new campus of the Universidad Nacional Autónoma de México (National Autonomous University of Mexico). The maneuvers proved effective: Tamayo never painted a mural there.

Epilogue

In 1949 María Izquierdo donated the portable fresco panels *La música* (fig. 66) and *La tragedia* (fig. 67) to the Basilica of San Juan de los Lagos, her hometown. The panels were hung in the church and blessed on March 21, 1954. In 1961 Carmen Barreda, the director of the Museo de Arte Moderno, acquired them for the Instituto Nacional de Bellas Artes,[77] and at an unknown date they were moved to a museum in Aguascalientes.[78] The panels disappeared from public view.

Around 1975 the two panels were transported to the Centro Nacional de Conservación de Obras Artísticas (National Center for Conservation of Artistic Works) in Mexico City, where their state of conservation was evaluated before they were placed in storage.[79] At the beginning of the twenty-first century the two panels were cleaned and restored by the mural painting workshop at the Centro Nacional de Conservación y Registro del Patrimonio Artístico Mueble (National Conservation Center and Register of Moveable Artistic Patrimony) in Mexico City, under the supervision of Eliseo Mijangos.[80] While the surfaces of the frescos required little more than cleaning, more extensive restoration was needed for the frameworks of the panels. The wooden frames, which had deteriorated, were removed, and the panels were made level. Lightweight honeycombs of paper impregnated with resin were installed to strengthen the framework of the panels. New exterior frames were created. According to Mijangos, the design and materials that Izquierdo used for the construction of the supports of the heavy panels had proven to be inadequate.[81]

While the fresco panels were being restored, they were seen and admired by Fernando Serrano Migallón, the director of the School of Law at the Universidad Nacional Autónoma de México. Serrano Migallón, who built an impressive collection of monumental paintings for the School of Law during his tenure as director, secured a 99-year loan of the two panels and obtained financial support from the alumni of the School of Law to pay for the cost of transporting and installing the panels.[82] In 2003 the panels were installed in the Ius Semper Loquitur Auditorium of the School of Law.[83] The panels flank the stage: *La tragedia* is on the audience's left, and *La música* is on the right. While the subjects of these works are not directly related to the theme of justice, Serrano Migallón observes that it is important to represent the arts in public spaces. He notes that the presence of *La tragedia* and *La música* in this auditorium means that thousands of people see them daily.[84] Izquierdo would almost certainly have perceived an element of justice in the installation of her fresco panels in an auditorium at the most prestigious university in Latin America.[85]

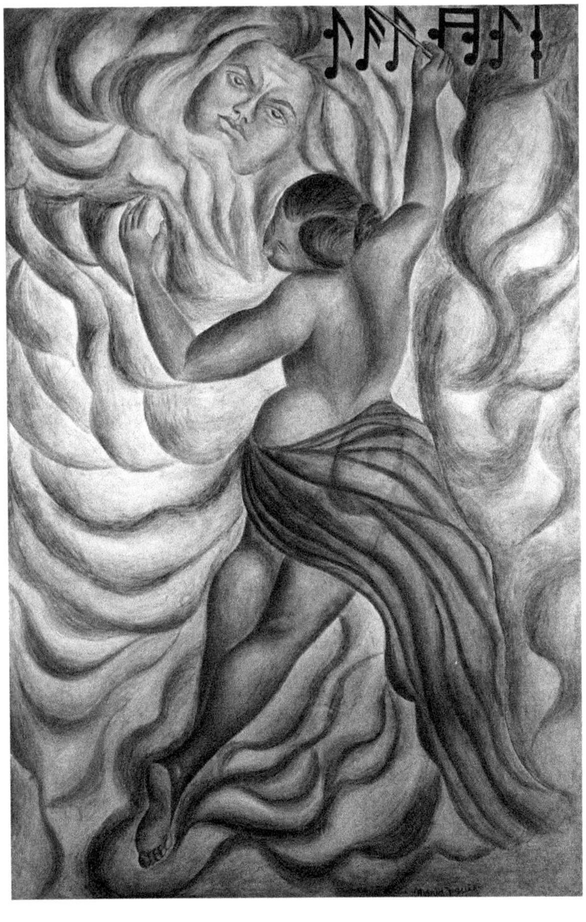

Fig. 66. María Izquierdo, *La música* (Music), 1946, fresco, 98 7/16 × 68 1/8 inches (250 × 173 cm), in the Ius Semper Loquitur Auditorium in the Facultad de Derecho, Universidad Nacional Autónoma de México, Mexico City. Photograph by Javier Hinojosa. Reproduced with the permission of María Rosenda López Posadas, legal representative of the intellectual property of María Izquierdo. Reproduction authorized by the Instituto Nacional de Bellas Artes y Literatura, 2015.

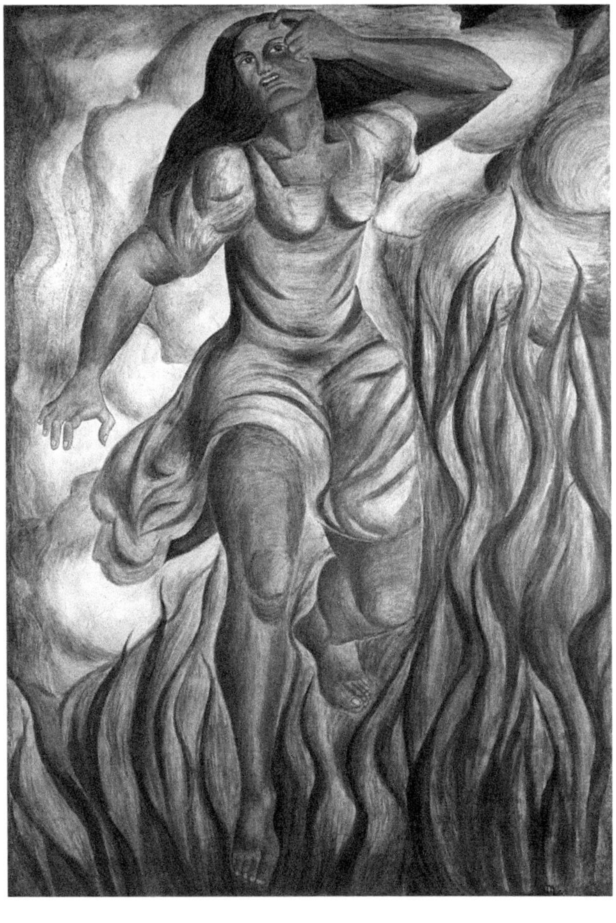

Fig. 67. María Izquierdo, *La tragedia* (Tragedy), 1946, fresco, 94 9/16 × 66 15/16 inches (240 × 170 cm), in the Ius Semper Loquitur Auditorium in the Facultad de Derecho, Universidad Nacional Autónoma de México, Mexico City. Photograph by Javier Hinojosa. Reproduced with the permission of María Rosenda López Posadas, legal representative of the intellectual property of María Izquierdo. Reproduction authorized by the Instituto Nacional de Bellas Artes y Literatura, 2015.

PART FOUR

Still-Life Paintings

María Izquierdo and Frida Kahlo created still-life paintings at a time and place in which the genre partook of a rich and distinctive national heritage, but its status was undermined by factors beyond the remnants of outdated hierarchies. Mexico's still-life tradition, which began in the colonial era and flourished after independence, has roots in Spanish, Dutch, and Flemish still-life painting but is distinct from its European predecessors. The best-known nineteenth-century practitioner, José Agustín Arrieta (1803–1874), depicted table tops laden with Mexican fruits, vegetables, and flowers displayed in serving vessels that provide a dazzling array of textures. Many of his works include fish, fowl, or bread. Often a live parrot perches on a basket or a cat sits beside the food. The flora that appears in his work and in other Mexican still-life paintings looks exotic to foreign eyes, but mameys, prickly pears, and dahlias are no more exotic in Mexico than apples, pears, and daisies in the United States. The parrots that show up in Agustín Arrieta's work and in many other nineteenth-century still-life paintings are a favorite pet in Mexico and equally nonexotic there. Consequently, elements such as parrots, dahlias, and marigolds, which in a seventeenth-century Dutch still life would connote exotic lands and colonial power, are devoid of such implications in Mexico and must be understood in context.

The status of still-life painting in Mexico in the twentieth century was affected by the theory and ideology of the muralist movement, which glorified art that was monumental, public, and political and denigrated easel painting. Neither the "Manifiesto del Sindicato de Obreros Técnicos, Pintores y Escultores" nor *No hay más ruta que la nuestra* specifically mentions still-life painting, but the muralist movement effectively reasserted the hierarchies of the Renaissance, in which history painting reigned and still life lacked status. The degree to which muralism revived old hierarchies is demonstrated by the oeuvres of Orozco, Siqueiros, and, after 1922, Rivera. As a young artist in Europe, Rivera created numerous still-life paintings, especially during his cubist period. But after embarking on his first mural he rarely worked in the genre (exceptions include *Las tentaciones de San Antonio* [The Temptations of St. Anthony] of 1947 and *Las sandias* [The Watermelons] of 1957). While Rivera almost completely stopped producing still-life paintings after 1922, he sometimes incorporated still-life compositions within portraits and in scenes in murals. I interpret his inclusion of still-life elements within other types of paintings as a testament to his enduring affection for a genre that had become a political liability among the ideologically driven muralists. Siqueiros only created a few still-life paintings in his entire career. Orozco's forays into the genre are similarly rare.[1]

The muralists' abstinence from still-life painting goes beyond their preference for murals over easel painting. Despite their rhetoric about easel painting being a bourgeois art form, they all created quantities of easel paintings for a variety of reasons (including financial incentives), especially during the periods when they lacked mural commissions. In Mexico the kitchen and hearth were indisputably women's realm. We can only wonder about the degree to which the associations of still life, food, and the kitchen prevented still-life painting from being an important art form at a time when Mexican national identity was a fundamental issue and that identity was constructed as male.

Orozco, Siqueiros, and Rivera's rejection of still-life painting did not mean that this type of painting ceased or even that it stopped being a site of creativity in Mexico during the postrevolutionary period—quite the contrary. Rufino Tamayo and Alfonso Michel, who held views about art that were dramatically different from those of the most famous muralists, dedicated substantial portions of their oeuvres to still-life painting. Tamayo's images of bright pink and red wedges of watermelon are among his best-known works. Numerous other artists with a range of viewpoints about art, such as José Chávez Morado, Juan O'Gorman, Jesús Reyes Ferreira, Juan Soriano, and Alfredo Zalce, occasionally painted still lifes and sometimes produced highly innovative work. Several women artists other than Izquierdo and Kahlo produced still-life paintings, most notably Olga Costa (1913–1993), who also created one of the canonical works of Mexican modernism with *Vendedora de frutas* (Fruit Vendor) of 1951, a market scene that could be considered a monumental still life.

Despite the unique and vital tradition of still-life painting in Mexico, it was not a highly competitive arena during the decades in which Izquierdo and Kahlo were active. Tamayo, for whom still-life painting was of fundamental importance, moved to New York in 1936. Still-life painting was not the site where the most visible artists in Mexico asserted dominance. The ferociously competitive muralists battled for hegemony on the walls of public buildings and in the press, leaving the field of still-life painting alone. In this peaceful, unguarded space Kahlo and Izquierdo quietly created work that challenged prevailing views about life and still-life painting, as they transformed an apparently innocuous genre into a viable space for expressing their thoughts on everything from eroticism to spirituality.

Kahlo and Izquierdo dedicated significant portions of their oeuvres to still-life painting. Kahlo created over twenty-five still lifes and numerous related works that are difficult to categorize. Izquierdo painted at least fifty-five still lifes; it was the only subject that rivaled her circus paintings in quantity. Both artists embarked on the genre at the beginning of their careers and pursued it assiduously till the end. Chapter 7, "*Picantes pero sabrosas*," takes a panoramic view of Kahlo's still-life paintings and examines the recurring themes of national identity and eroticism. Rather than discussing every painting in the genre, I analyze key works that exemplify salient themes in her still lifes and related works. I have not attempted an overview of Izquierdo's still-life paintings, which could be the focus of an entire book. Instead I examine one small part of her still-life production: the images of ephemeral home altars to the Virgin of Sorrows that she created in the 1940s. In this series Izquierdo combined gender issues and *mexicanidad*, spirituality and popular culture. In different ways Izquierdo and Kahlo employed the seemingly bland genre of still-life painting as a forum for discourse on serious, vital, and unexpected issues.

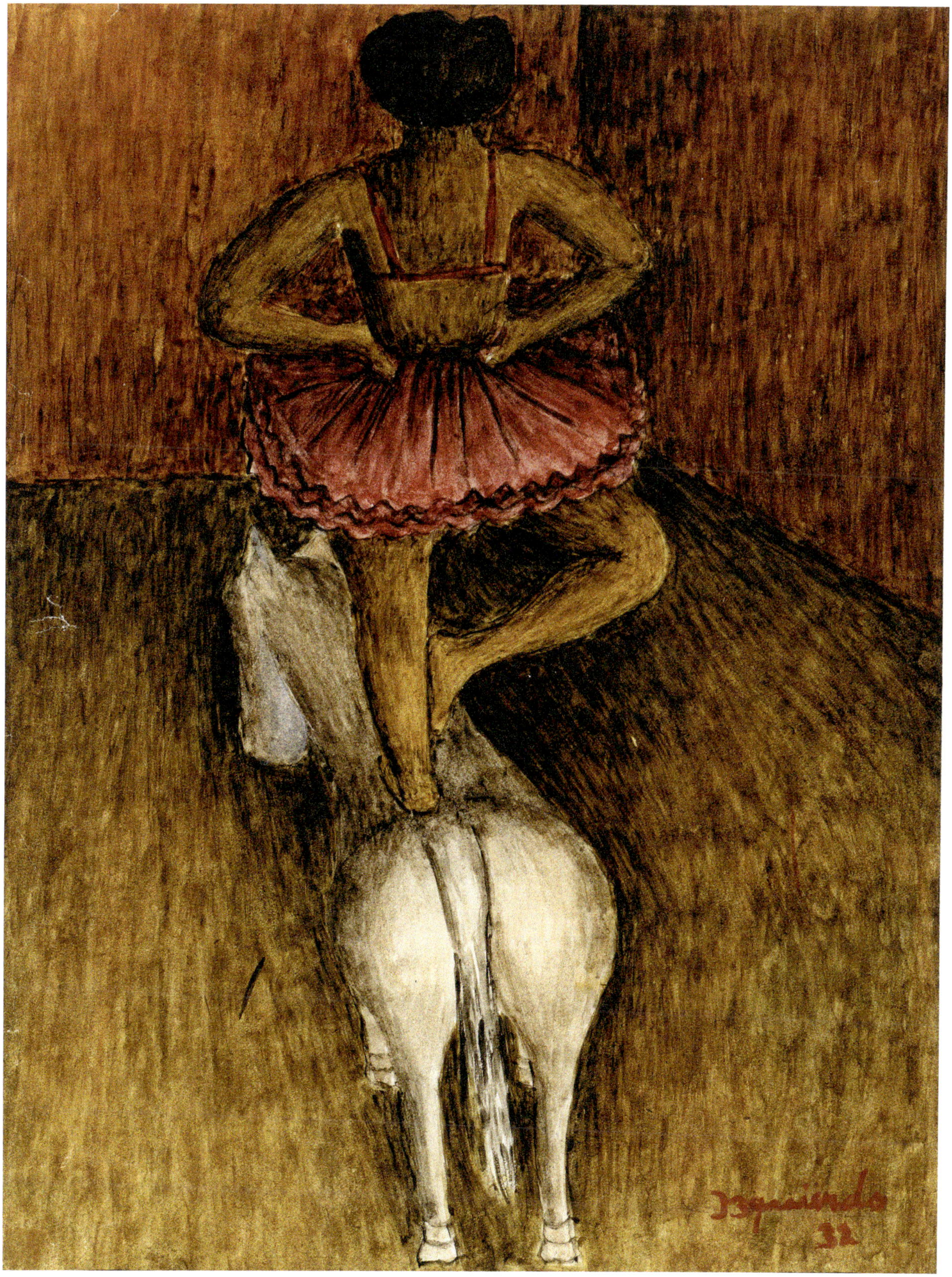

1

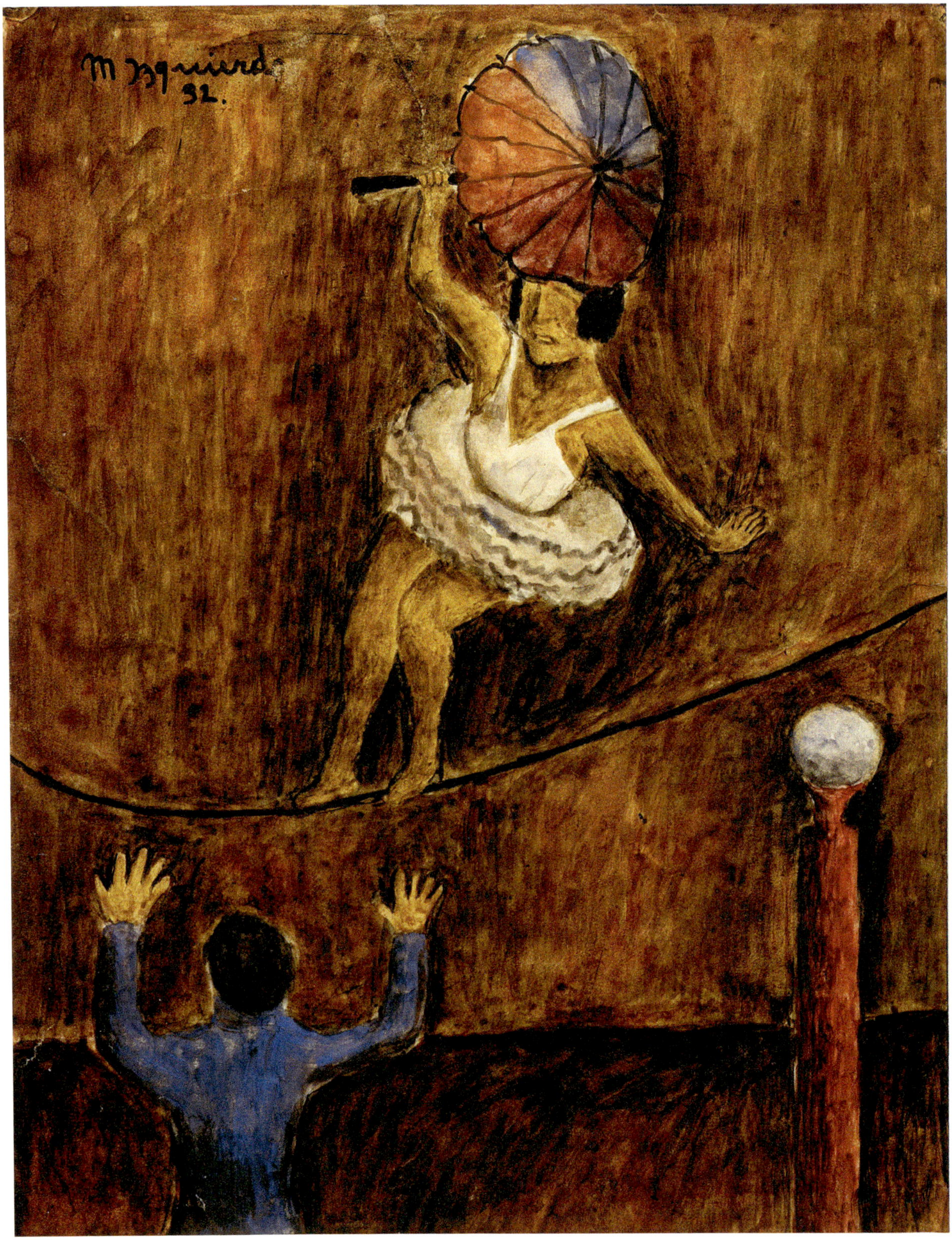

2

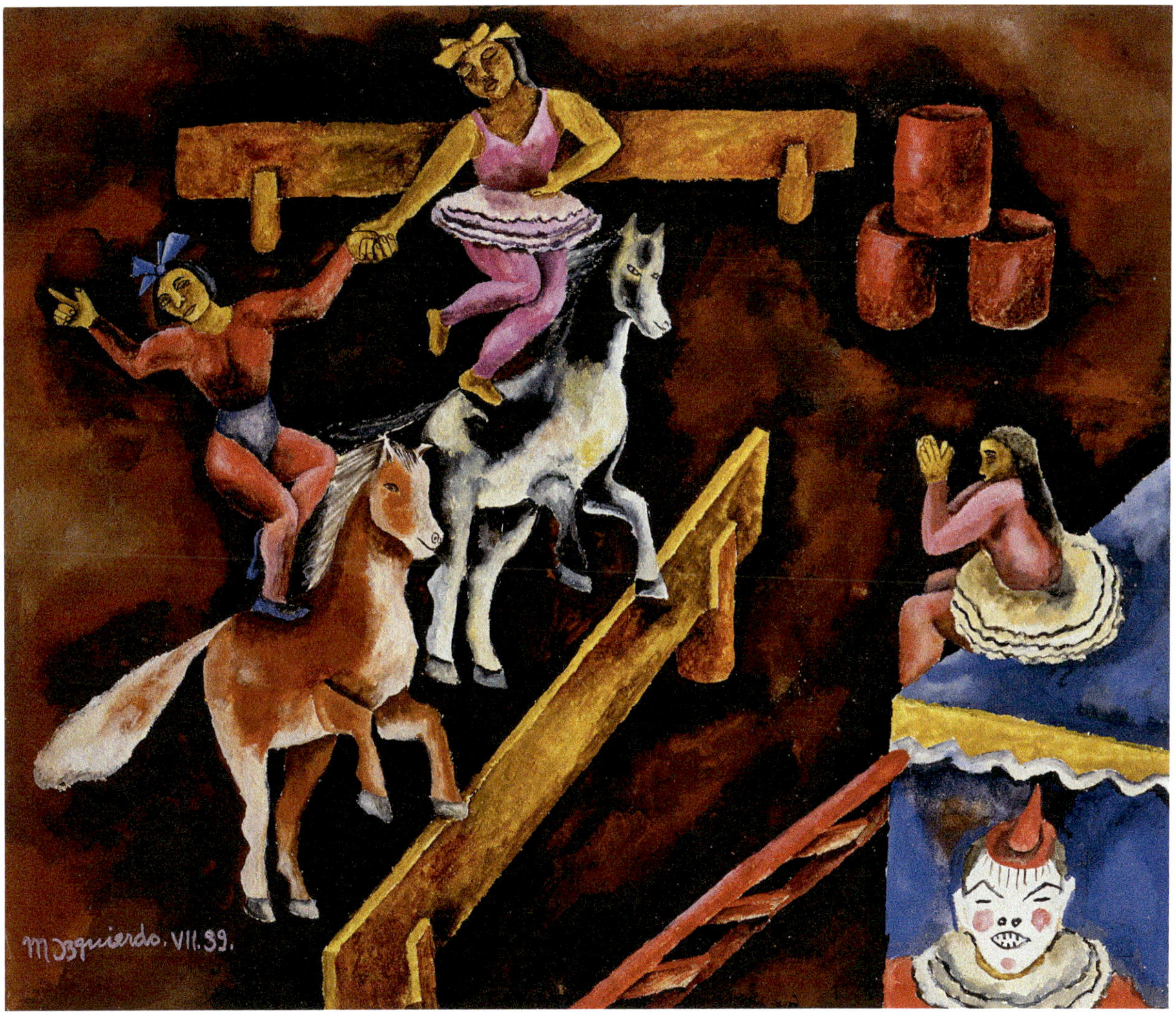

3

Plate 1. María Izquierdo, *Bailarina ecuestre* (Horseback Dancer), 1932, watercolor, 10 ¼ × 8 ¼ inches (26 × 21 cm), collection of Museo de Arte Moderno de Gómez Palacios, Durango, Mexico. Photograph by Francisco Kochen. A virtually identical watercolor titled *La Cirquera* (The Circus Performer or The Circus Woman), 1932, belongs to the Banco Nacional de México. Reproduced with the permission of María Rosenda López Posadas, legal representative of the intellectual property of María Izquierdo. Reproduction authorized by the Instituto Nacional de Bellas Artes y Literatura, 2015.

Plate 2. María Izquierdo, *Equilibrista* (Rope Walker), 1932, watercolor on paper, 10 ⅝ × 8 ¼ inches (27 × 21 cm), collection of the Museo de Arte Moderno de Gómez Palacio, Durango, Mexico, and the Instituto Nacional de Bellas Artes. Photograph by Francisco Kochen. Reproduced with the permission of María Rosenda López Posadas, legal representative of the intellectual property of María Izquierdo. Reproduction authorized by the Instituto Nacional de Bellas Artes y Literatura, 2015.

Plate 3. María Izquierdo, *Les écuyères* (The Equestriennes), 1939, gouache on paper, 16 ⅛ × 24 inches (41 × 61 cm), collection of Mariana Pérez Amor. Photograph by Francisco Kochen. Reproduced with the permission of María Rosenda López Posadas, legal representative of the intellectual property of María Izquierdo.

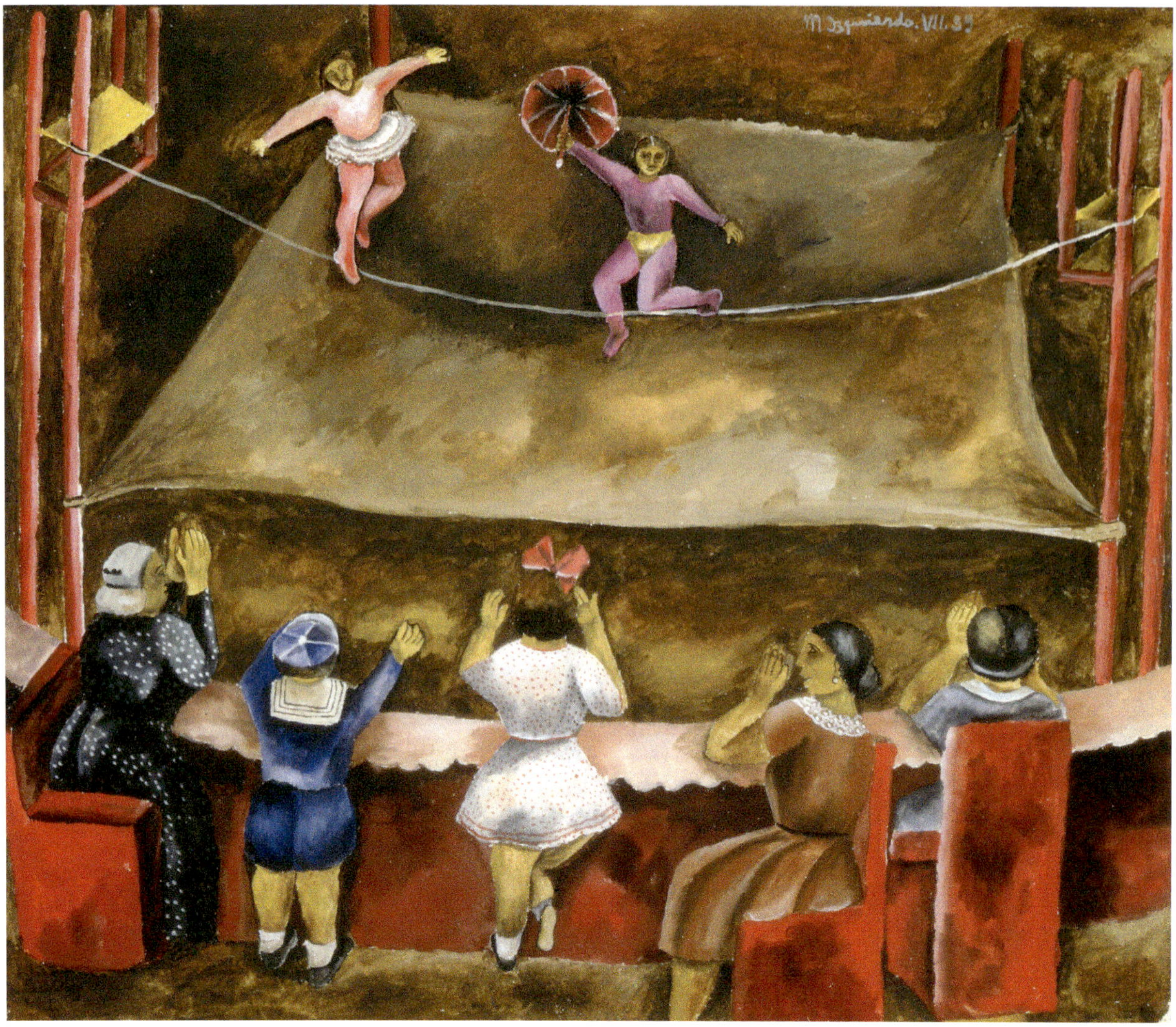

4

Plate 4. María Izquierdo, *En el circo* (At the Circus), 1939, watercolor and tempera on paper, 16 ⅛ × 19 11/16 inches (41.5 × 50 cm), private collection, USA. Photograph courtesy of Mary-Anne Martin Fine Art, New York. Reproduced with the permission of María Rosenda López Posadas, legal representative of the intellectual property of María Izquierdo. Reproduction authorized by the Instituto Nacional de Bellas Artes y Literatura, 2015.

Plate 5. María Izquierdo, *Autorretrato* (Self-Portrait), 1940, oil on canvas, 55 ⅛ × 34 ¼ inches (140 × 87 cm), collection of Andrés Blaisten.

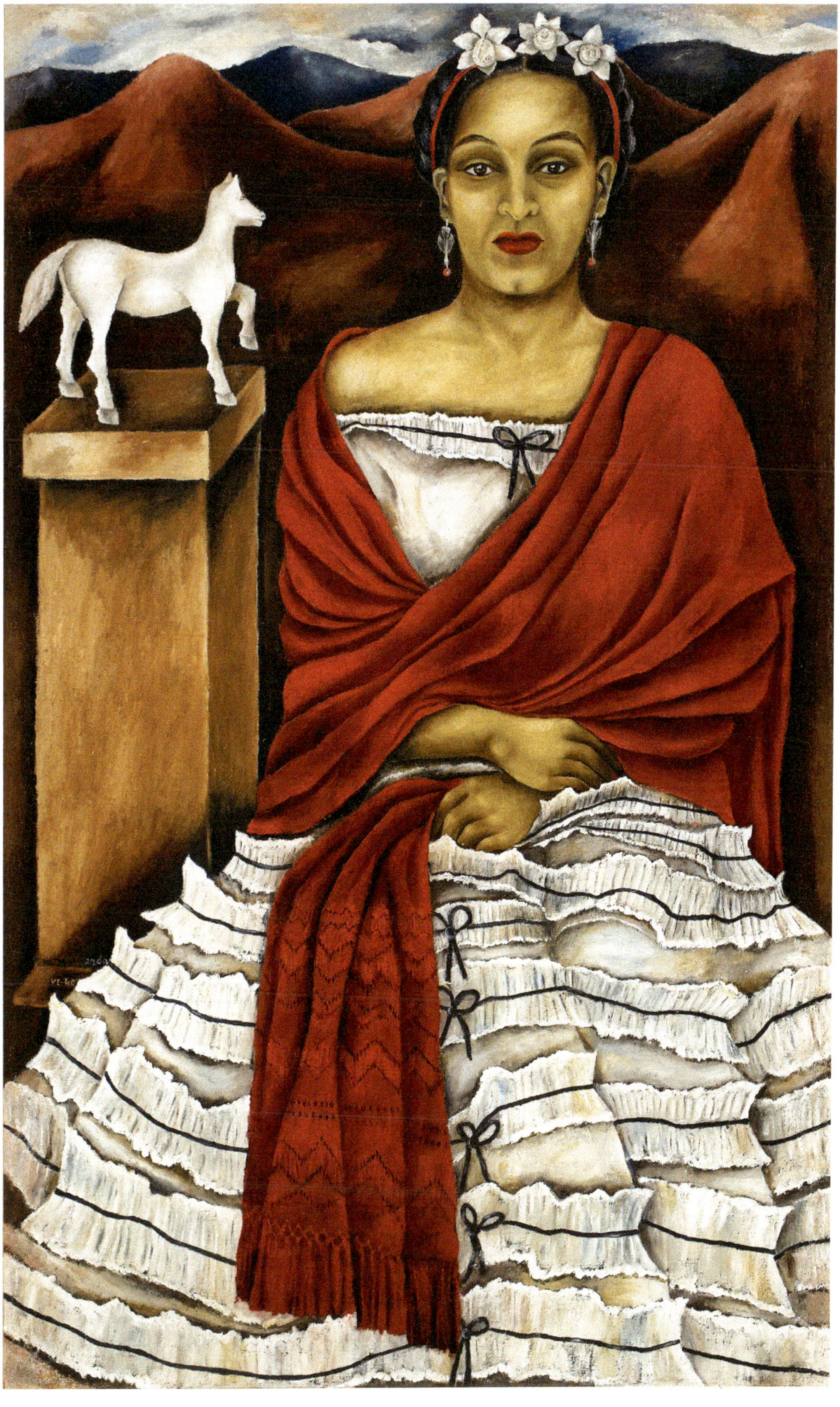

5

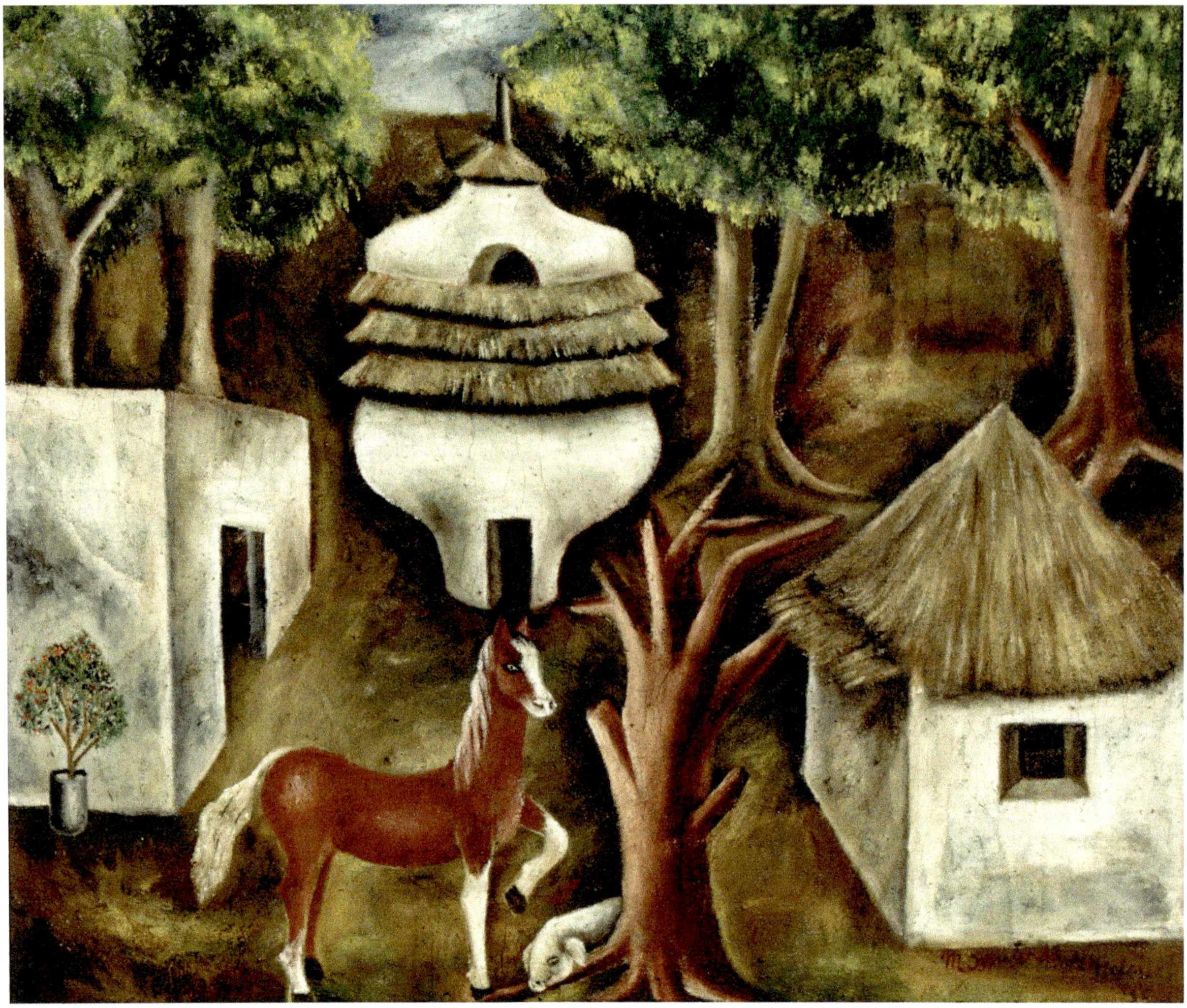

6

Plate 6. María Izquierdo, *Paisaje tropical* (Tropical Landscape), 1944, oil on canvas, 23 5/8 × 27 3/16 inches (60 × 69 cm), private collection. In 1944 Izquierdo exhibited this painting under the title *Paisaje de la tierra de Emiliano Zapata* (Landscape of the Land of Emiliano Zapata) at a solo show in Lima, Peru. Reproduced with the permission of María Rosenda López Posadas, legal representative of the intellectual property of María Izquierdo. Reproduction authorized by the Instituto Nacional de Bellas Artes y Literatura, 2015.

Plate 7. María Izquierdo, *Ofrenda del Viernes del Dolores* (Offering for the Friday of Sorrows or Offering for the Friday of the Virgin of Sorrows), 1943, oil on Celotex, 23 5/8 × 19 3/4 inches (60 × 50 cm), originally in the collection of María Asúnsolo. Photograph courtesy of Galería de Arte Mexicano. Reproduced with the permission of María Rosenda López Posadas, legal representative of the intellectual property of María Izquierdo. Reproduction authorized by the Instituto Nacional de Bellas Artes y Literatura, 2015.

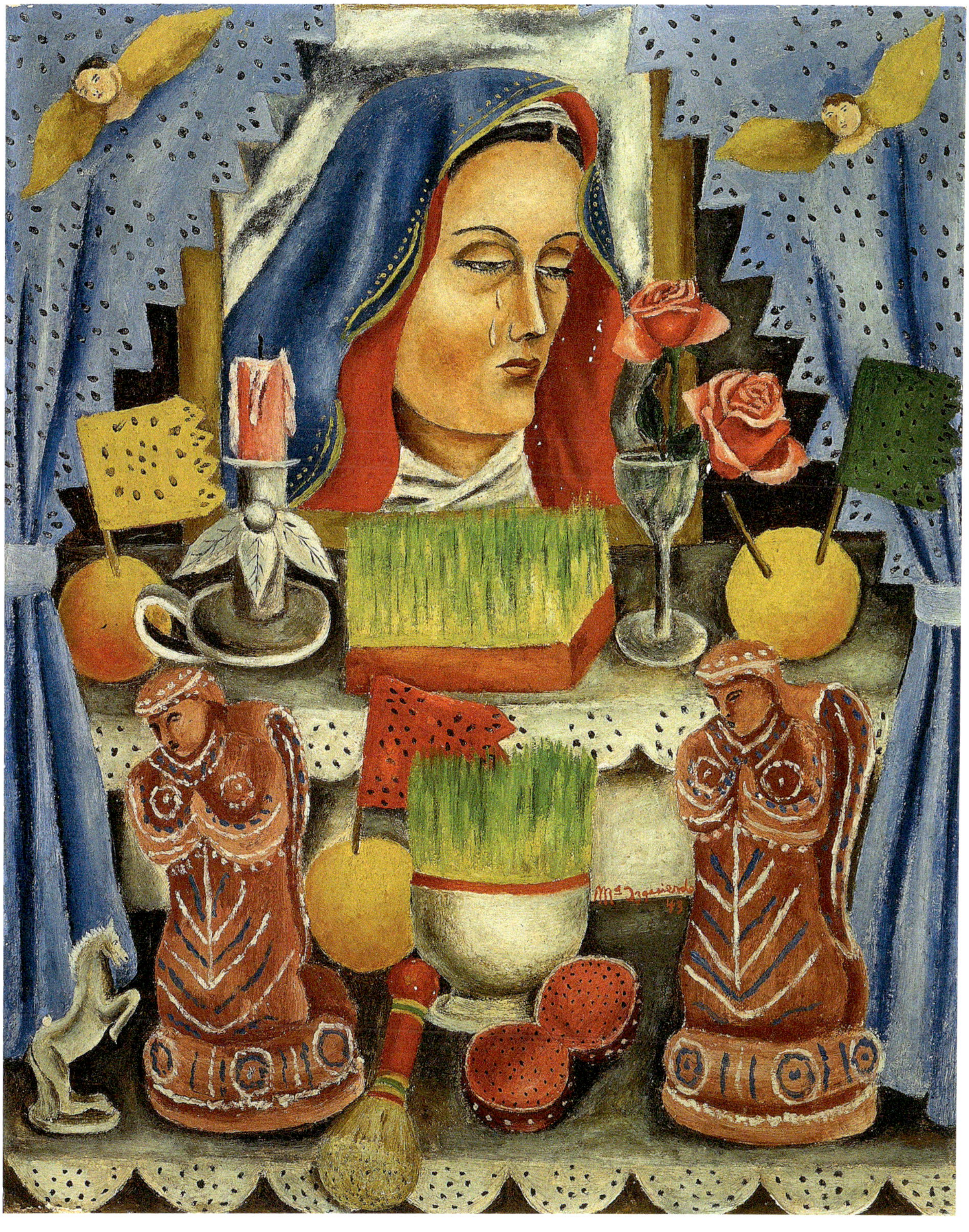

7

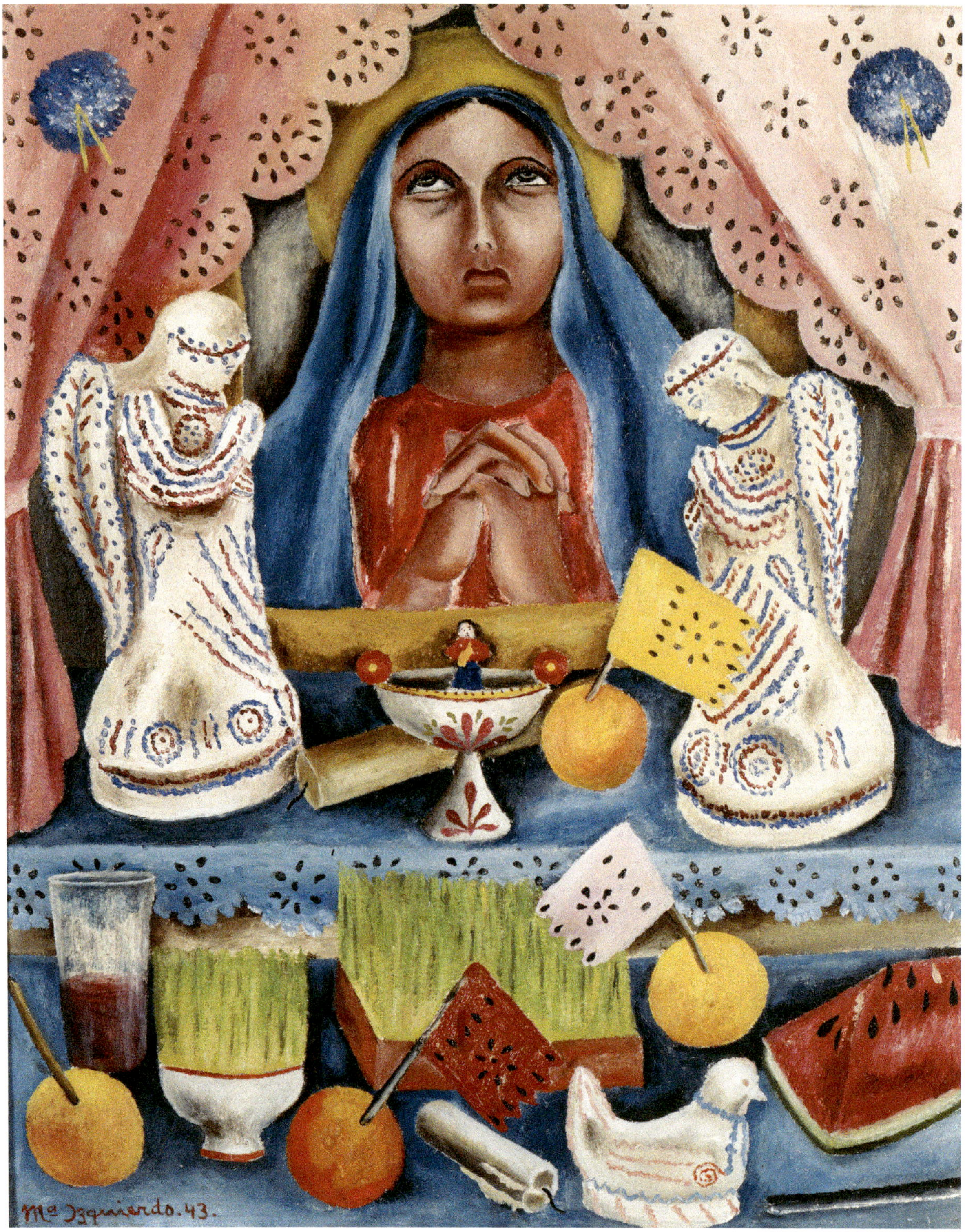

Plate 8. María Izquierdo, *Altar de Dolores* (Altar [for the Virgin] of Sorrows), 1943, oil on board, 23 3/4 × 19 1/2 inches (60.3 × 49.8 cm), private collection, USA. Photograph courtesy of Mary-Anne Martin Fine Art, New York. Reproduced with the permission of María Rosenda López Posadas, legal representative of the intellectual property of María Izquierdo. Reproduction authorized by the Instituto Nacional de Bellas Artes y Literatura, 2015.

Plate 9. María Izquierdo, *La tragedia* (Tragedy), 1946, fresco, 94 9/16 × 66 15/16 inches (240 × 170 cm), in the IUS Semper Loquitur Auditorium in the Facultad de Derecho, Universidad Nacional Autónoma de México, Mexico City. Photograph by Javier Hinojosa. Reproduced with the permission of María Rosenda López Posadas, legal representative of the intellectual property of María Izquierdo. Reproduction authorized by the Instituto Nacional de Bellas Artes y Literatura, 2015.

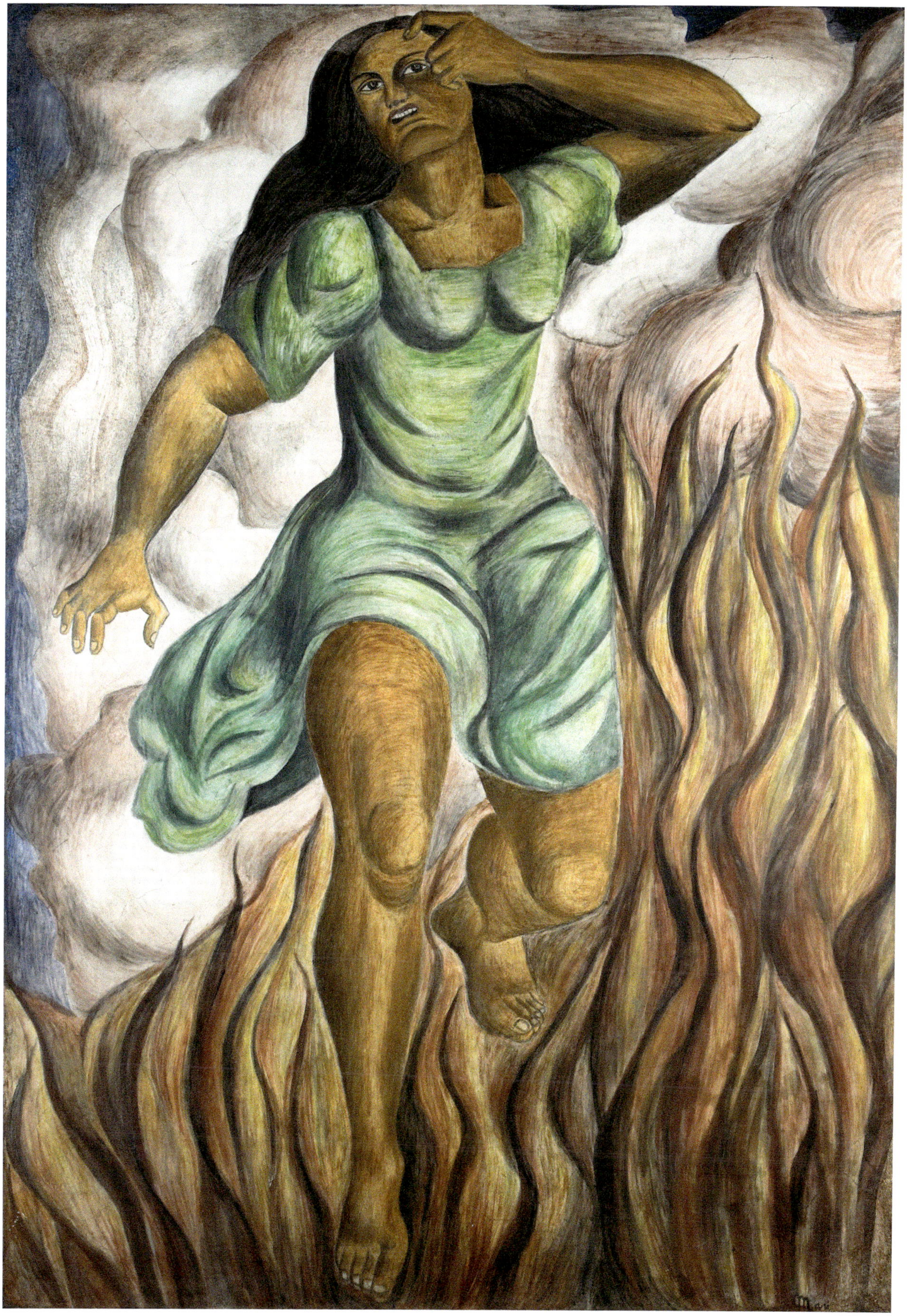

9

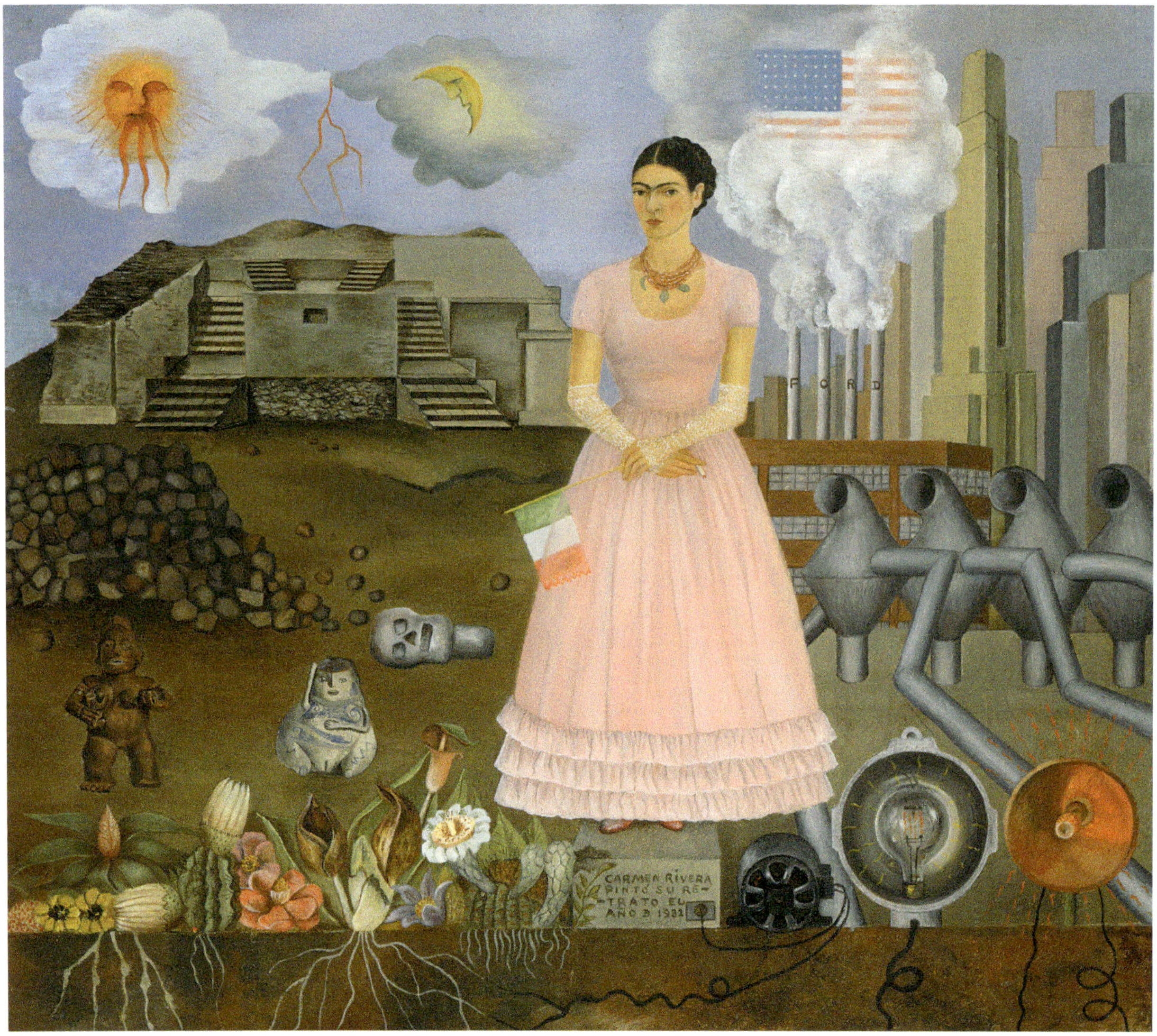

10

Plate 10. Frida Kahlo, *Autorretrato en la frontera entre México y los Estados Unidos* (Self-Portrait on the Border between Mexico and the United States), 1932, oil on metal, 12 1/2 × 13 3/4 inches (31.8 × 34.9 cm), collection of María Rodríguez de Reyero, New York.

Plate 11. Frida Kahlo, *El superviviente* (The Survivor), 1938, oil on tin, 6 5/8 × 4 3/4 inches (17 × 12 cm), without frame, and 16 3/4 × 14 3/4 inches (45.5 × 37.5 cm) with the original tin frame from Oaxaca, Pérez Simón collection, Mexico City. Photograph courtesy of Christie's Images Limited.

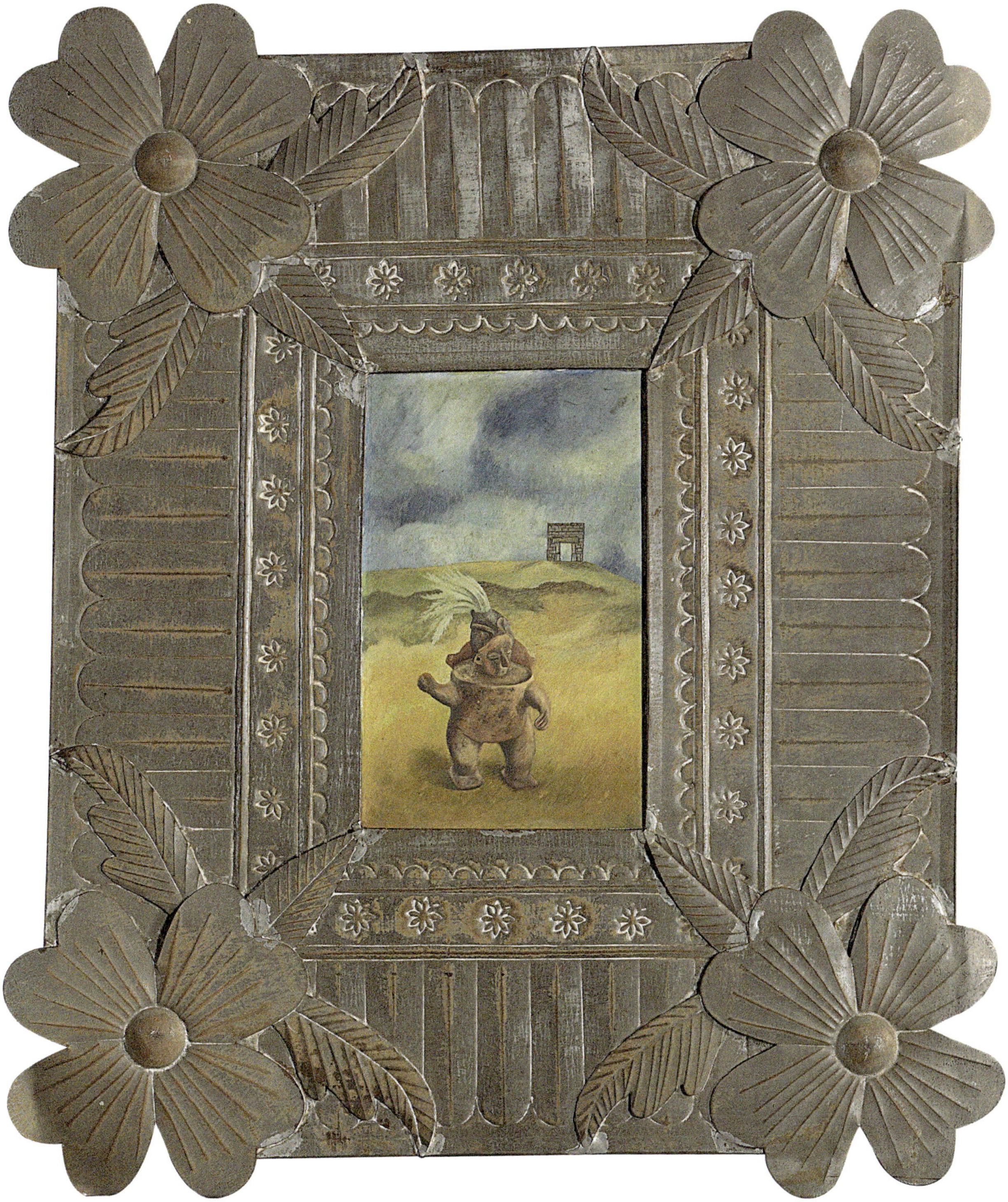

11

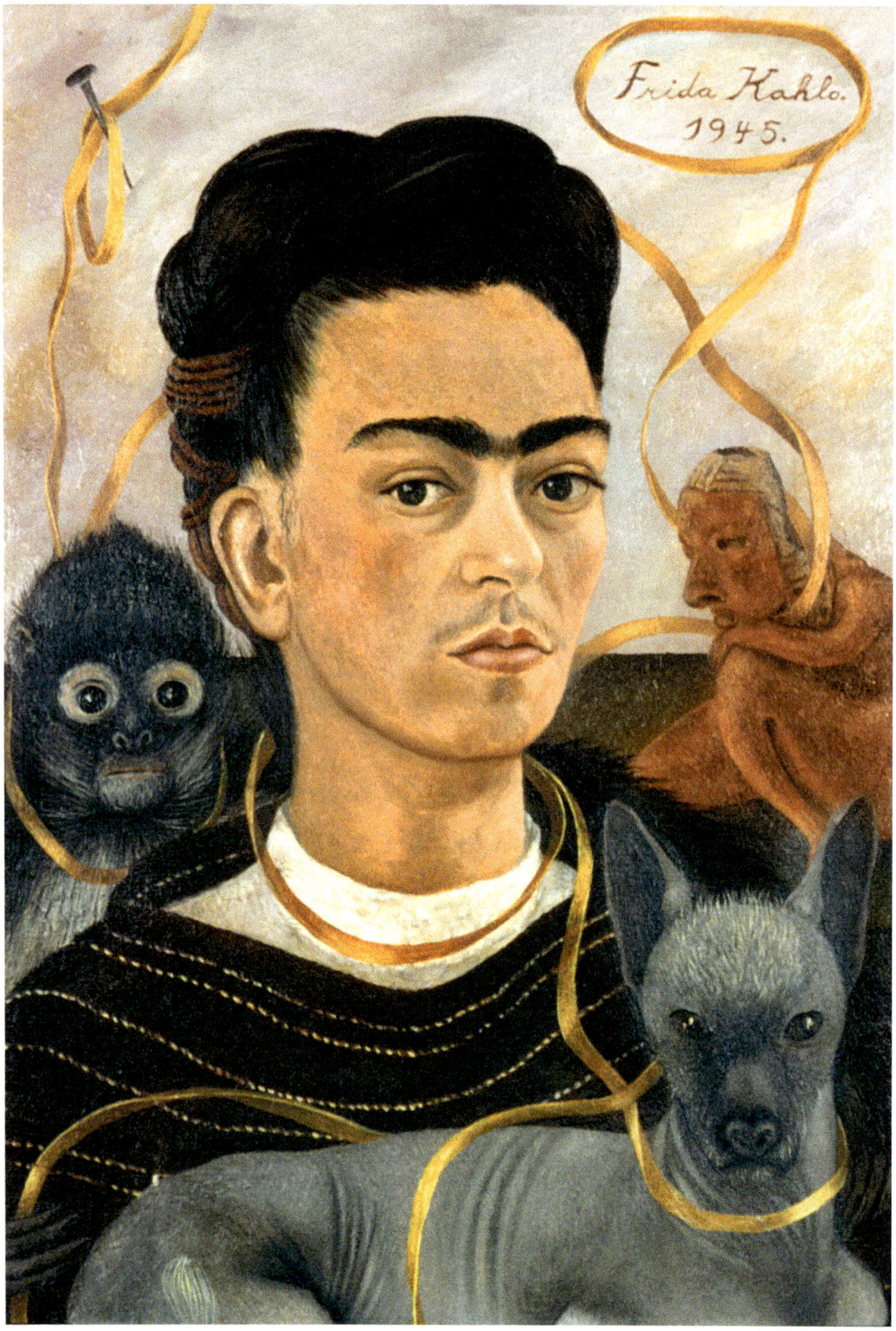

12

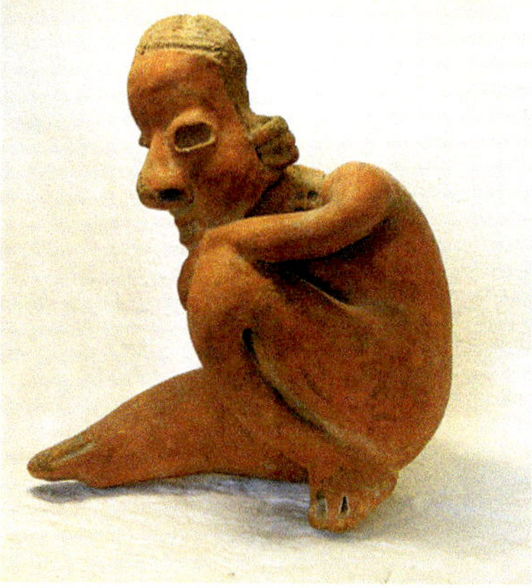

13

Plate 12. Frida Kahlo, *Autorretrato con changuito* (Self-Portrait with Small Monkey), 1945, oil on Masonite, 22 1/16 × 16 3/8 inches (56 × 41.5 cm), collection of the Museo Dolores Olmedo, Xochimilco, Mexico, D.F. © 2014 Banco de México Diego Rivera Frida Kahlo Museums Trust, Mexico, D.F./Artists Rights Society (ARS), New York. Reproduction authorized by the Instituto Nacional de Bellas Artes y Literatura, 2015.

Plate 13. Precolumbian figure from Nayarit, collection of Diego Rivera, on display at Anahuacalli.

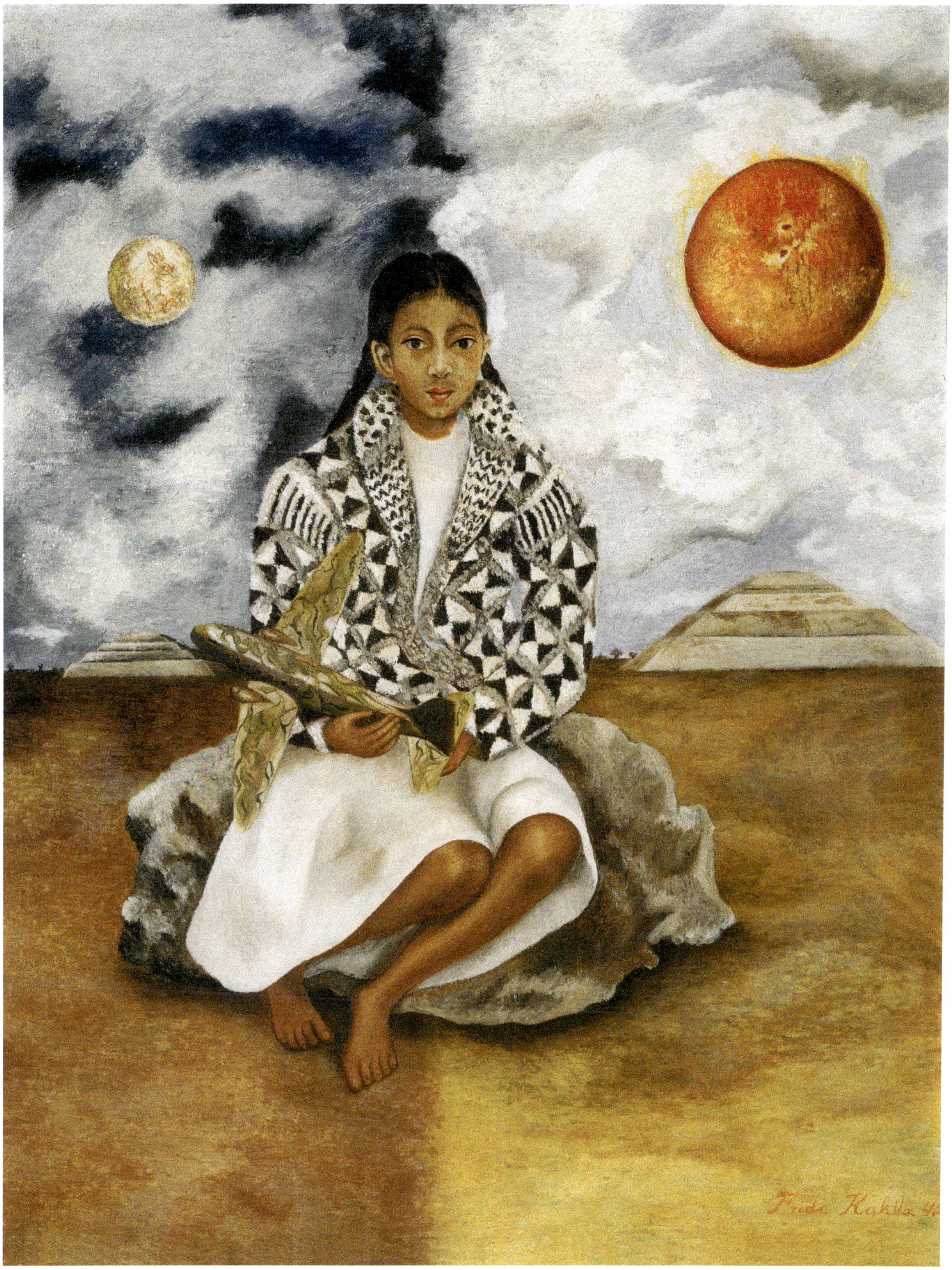

14

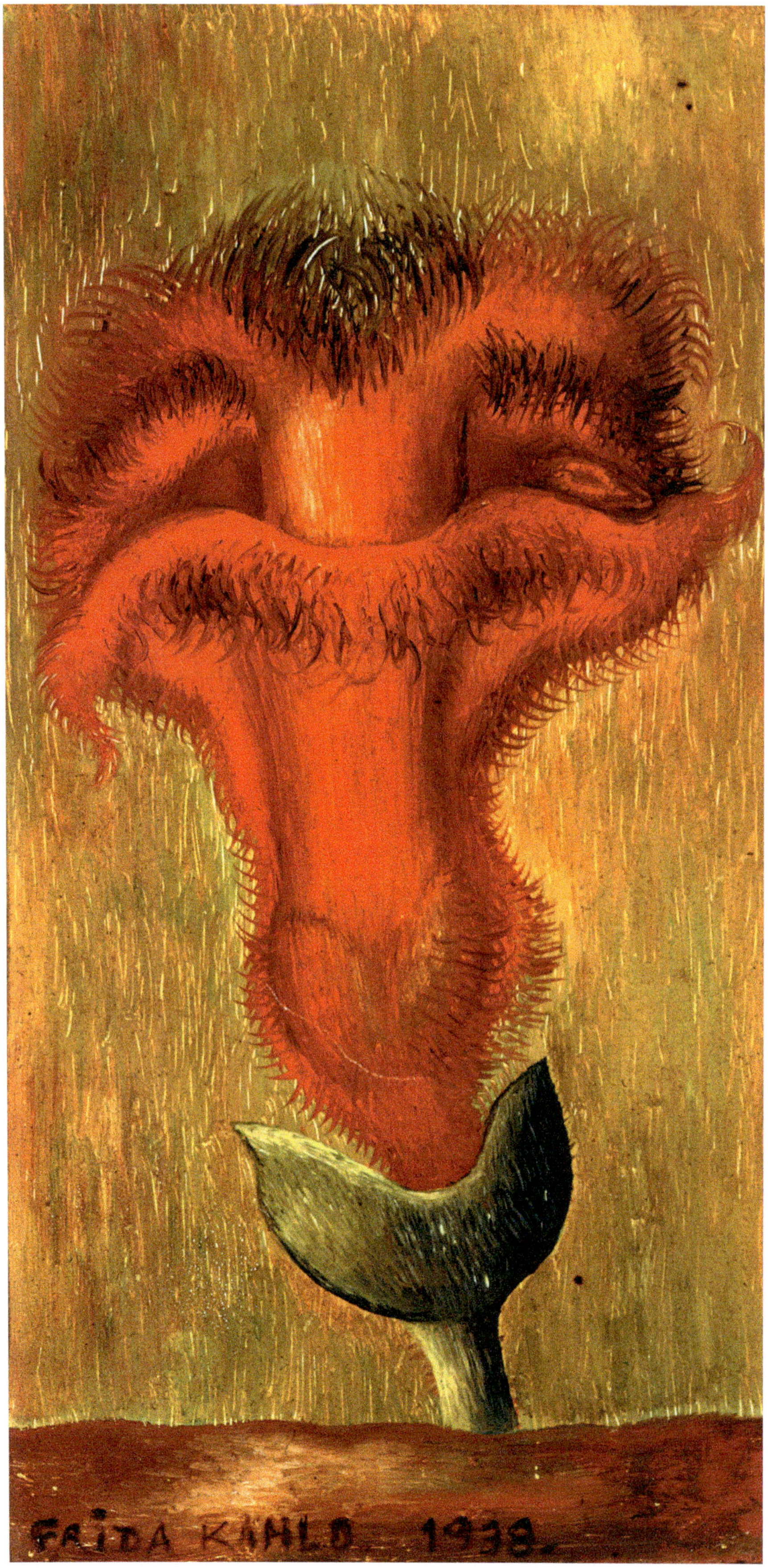

15

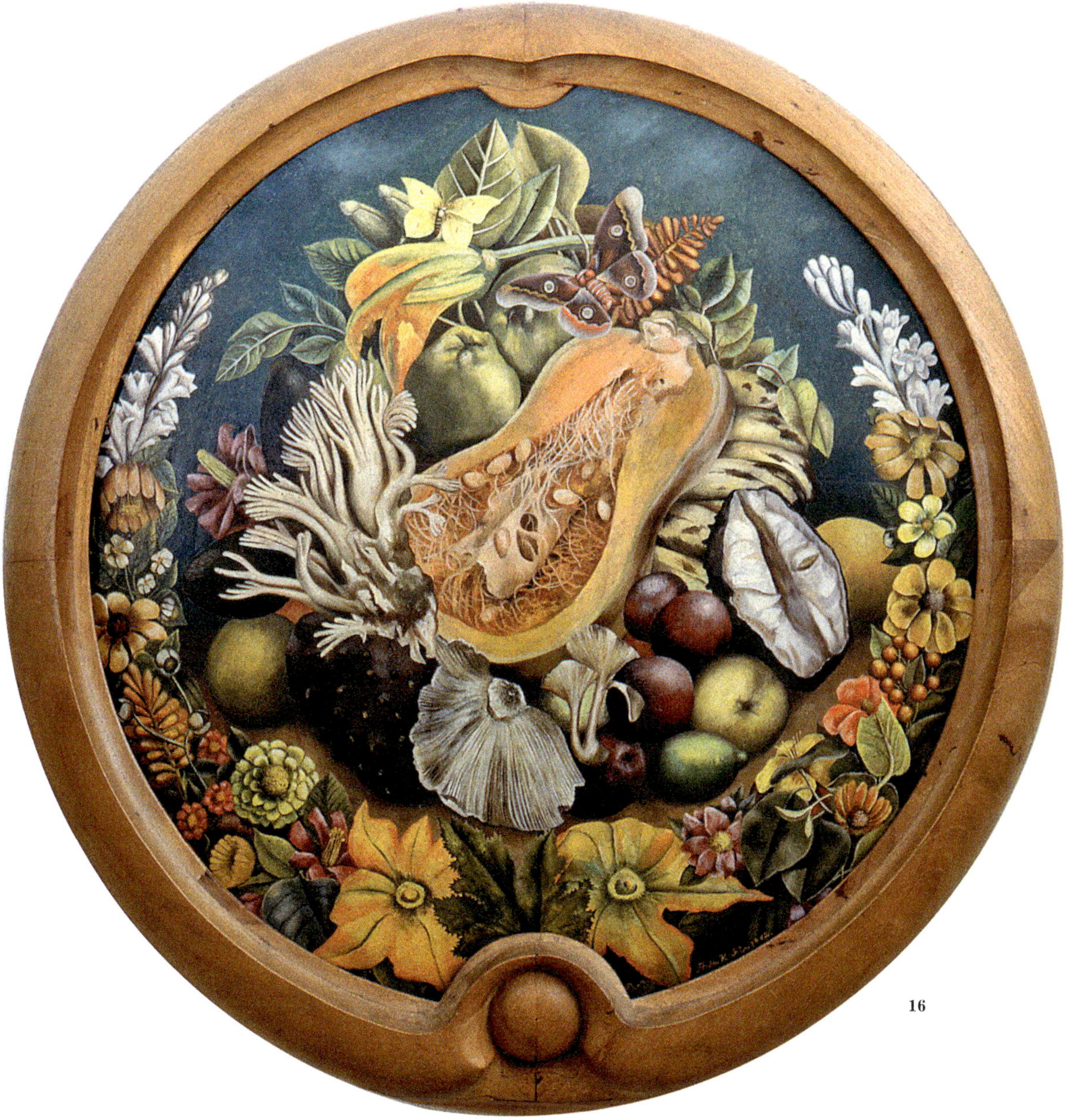

16

Plate 14. Frida Kahlo first exhibited this painting under the title *La niña, la luna y el sol* (The Girl, the Moon, and the Sun), 1942, at the Biblioteca Benjamin Franklin in Mexico City in 1944. Since 1987 the painting has been known as *La tehuacana Lucha María* (The Tehuacana Lucha María) or *El sol y la luna* (The Sun and the Moon). Oil on Masonite, 21 1/2 × 17 inches (54.6 × 43.1 cm), Pérez Simon collection, Mexico City. © 2014 Banco de México Diego Rivera Frida Kahlo Museums Trust, Mexico, D.F./Artists Rights Society (ARS), New York. Reproduction authorized by the Instituto Nacional de Bellas Artes y Literatura, 2015.

Plate 15. Frida Kahlo, *Xochitl*, 1938, oil on metal, 7 1/8 × 3 3/4 inches (18 × 9.5 cm), collection of Dr. Rodolfo Gómez, Mexico City. Photograph by Rafael Doniz. © 2014 Banco de México Diego Rivera Frida Kahlo Museums Trust, Mexico, D.F./Artists Rights Society (ARS), New York. Reproduction authorized by the Instituto Nacional de Bellas Artes y Literatura, 2015.

Plate 16. Frida Kahlo, *Naturaleza muerta* (Still Life), 1942, oil on metal, 24 13/16 inches in diameter (63 cm in diameter), collection of the Museo Frida Kahlo. © 2014 Banco de México Diego Rivera Frida Kahlo Museums Trust, Mexico, D.F./Artists Rights Society (ARS), New York. Reproduction authorized by the Instituto Nacional de Bellas Artes y Literatura, 2015.

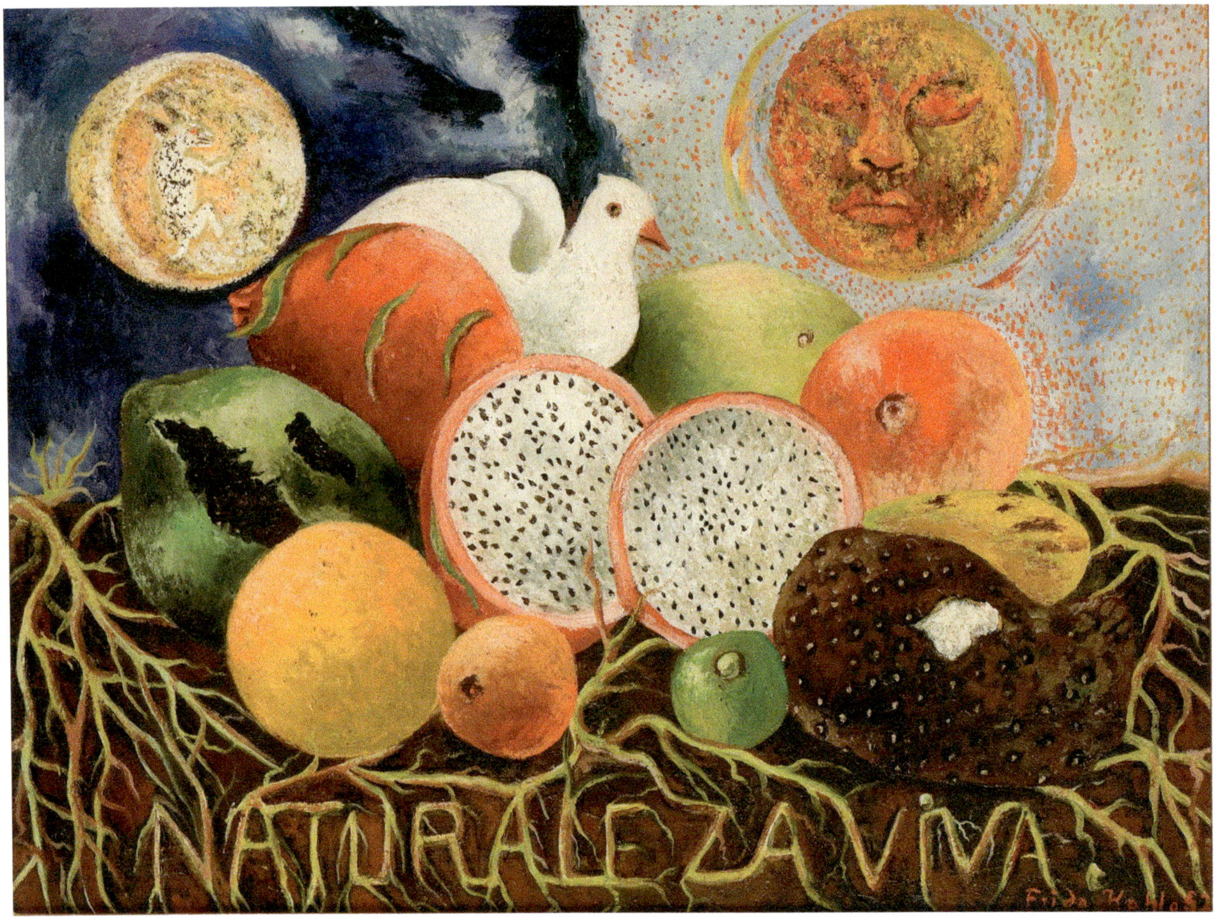

17

Plate 17. Frida Kahlo, *Naturaleza viva* (Living Nature), 1952, oil on canvas, 17 1/4 × 23 5/8 inches (44 × 60 cm), private collection. Photograph courtesy of the Museo de Arte Contemporáneo de Monterrey (MARCO).

7

Picantes pero sabrosas

Kahlo's Still-Life Paintings and Related Images

Yo soy como el chile verde, Llorona,
picante pero sabroso.

I am like the green chile, Llorona,
hot but full of flavor.

FROM THE TRADITIONAL MEXICAN SONG "LA LLORONA"

Kahlo created over twenty-five still-life paintings, two still-life photographs, and several remarkable works that defy categories but use vegetal imagery in ways that both link them to and separate them from traditional still lifes. Considering the number of still lifes that Kahlo produced, relatively little has been written about this aspect of her art. While scholars frequently discuss individual still-life paintings, until recently they have rarely considered them as a group, thus ignoring her significant contribution to the genre. The scarcity of studies devoted to Kahlo's still lifes probably stems from scholars' overwhelming reliance on biographical and psychological methodologies that have prioritized her self-portraits.

In *Looking at the Overlooked*, art historian Norman Bryson observes that still life is perhaps "the genre at the furthest remove from narrative."[1] Kahlo's still lifes actively resist the biographical interpretations that have been habitually applied to her self-portraits. Despite the non-narrative nature of the still-life genre, two authors who have written about Kahlo's still-life paintings impose biographical interpretations on these works. In "Wissenschaft und Pflanzen, Liebe, Tod und Teufel," Helga Prignitz-Poda extends biographical interpretations to these paintings with unfortunate results. Incredibly, Prignitz-Poda literally sees Diego Rivera in the watermelons in *Viva la vida* (Long Live Life) of 1954 and asserts that in all the slices of melon he "turns around himself as if in a macabre dance of dismemberment," a vision that rather ingeniously facilitates her conclusion that "for Kahlo there is no more room in the world."[2] In a 2004 article titled "Frida Kahlo's Still Lifes," Salomon Grimberg declares: "Kahlo's still lifes often read like pages in a diary."[3] To illustrate his claim, he alleges that a small piggy bank represents Rivera while a figurine of a horse stands for Kahlo in *Still Life with Piggy Bank and Black Horse* of ca. 1928. Later in the article he sights Rivera in a slice of watermelon and a prickly pear. The title of Grimberg's later book *Frida Kahlo: The Still Lifes* (2008) implies that it is entirely about Kahlo's still-life paintings, even though it is in fact a biography that discusses all of her still-life paintings along with numerous works not connected to the genre. Grimberg invariably applies psychobiographical interpretations to every still-life painting. Constructing an argument on nothing more than the representation of a vase and three blossoms in the juvenile work titled *Still Life with Roses* of 1924, he claims that the painting represents the love triangle in the artist's life.[4] As these examples clearly indicate, the habit of applying biographical and psychological methodologies to Kahlo's art can lead to unwarranted conclusions that limit and distort our understanding of her work.

The following discussion of Kahlo's still-life paintings considers her approach to the genre in its cultural context and in relation to her beliefs and personal philosophy. While her still lifes do indeed stand at the furthest remove from narrative, they are nonetheless rich in her personal iconography and address an eclectic group of themes that include daily life, eroticism, Precolumbian culture, and *mexicanidad.* In fact she often addressed more than one of these disparate themes in a single work.

Still Life, Daily Life, and Popular Culture

Kahlo seldom explained her imagery. Little survives concerning her thoughts on still-life painting, but one of her students distinctly remembers an incident that gives a sense of her approach to still-life painting. As a teacher she used an oblique but vivid manner to communicate to her students the ties of still life, daily life, and popular culture in Mexico. Guillermo Monroy remembers being invited, along with other students, to eat breakfast in the garden of the *casa azul.* As two domestic employees brought fruit and dishes into the garden, Kahlo set the table, saying: "These things are precious; it's necessary to give them a pretty arrangement. So I'm going to arrange them like this. How does it look, guys?"[5]

Monroy, who was hungry, replied: "It looks very pretty, *maestra.* You feel like eating it very fast."[6]

Kahlo, seemingly oblivious to the ravenous appetite of the teenage boy, responded, "Good. Now you. I'm going to mess it up for you. Now you arrange it. Let's see what arrangement you give it. . . . The fruits are beautiful, and it shouldn't be hard for you because for sure your mother arranges things very nicely at your house when she comes from the market."[7]

Monroy concurs: "What she said was true; of course relatively, because I came from a very poor family."[8] He recalls that his mother was a traditional Mexican woman who would come from the market with her basket of purchases and arrange an embroidered cloth, fruit, a *molcajete* (a basalt mortar, often used to serve salsa), guacamole, avocados, *papaloquilitl* (an aromatic herb), tortillas, and little clay plates so that the family could eat comfortably. When Kahlo said, "Let's see what arrangement you give it," Monroy believes that she wanted to see her student's taste. Instead of doing the expected thing—placing the fruit in a composition and telling her students to paint it—Kahlo did the unexpected—asking him to arrange the fruit and dishes as if he were going to paint them.[9]

The lesson implies not only that Kahlo found beauty and took pleasure in fruit and domestic objects but that she also considered the way in which people display simple things in Mexico a valuable aesthetic tradition in its own right. It includes the ways in which Mexican women set out food and cooking utensils as well as the manner in which vendors in the market stack fruit in ingenious displays of color and form. The writer Anita Brenner, a good friend of Kahlo, expressed a similar appreciation for quotidian aesthetic practices: "Several deeply marked and unmistakable characteristics emerge over and over again in Mexican art throughout many thousands of years of history, of which the most enviable, in modern terms—and the secret of its vitality—is its instinctive identification with day-to-day living and human use."[10]

Kahlo's still-life lesson also defied gender stereotypes. She seems to have intentionally chosen a male student—the one who at that moment was in the greatest hurry to eat—and made him slow down enough to think about how fruits and dishes should be arranged on the table, a subject that Mexican men were not normally required to consider. The group of students who went to Kahlo's home often included Fanny Rabel and occasionally Lidia Briones, so Kahlo's choice of a male student for this experiment was probably not due to a lack of options.

Interestingly, Monroy states that both Kahlo and Rivera arranged tables beautifully. According to Trotsky scholars, in 1937 Diego Rivera designed a special table setting for Leon Trotsky's birthday, which coincided with the anniversary of the Russian Revolution.[11] Rivera's daughter, Guadalupe Rivera Marín, recalls that it was actually Kahlo who decorated the dining room table with leaves and flowers that spelled out "VIVA TROTSKY" (Long live Trotsky) and "ARRIBA LA CUARTA INTERNACIONAL" (Up with the Fourth International).[12]

Kahlo's Still Lifes

Kahlo created still-life paintings over a period of thirty years, beginning with the round *Charola de amapolas* (Tray with Poppies) of ca. 1924, which she made for an aunt, and ending with her last completed work, *Viva la vida* (Long Live Life) in 1954. During many of these years she produced both traditional still-life paintings and works that defy expectations about the genre.

Frida Kahlo and Diego Rivera admired nonacademic nineteenth-century portraiture and still-life painting, especially the work of regional artists, who were often anonymous. Among the regional painters who signed their work, Kahlo and Rivera greatly esteemed Hermenegildo Bustos (1832–1907), a self-taught artist from the state of Guanajuato who primarily practiced portraiture but also created two unforgettable still-life paintings, *Bodegón con frutas, alacrán y rana* (Still Life with Fruits, Scorpion, and Frog) of 1874 and *Bodegón con piña* (Still Life with Pineapple) of 1877. The Riveras owned several anonymous nineteenth-century still-life paintings, and two or three hung in the dining room of the *casa azul*.[13]

Guadalupe Rivera Marín remembers accompanying her stepmother to the Lagunilla flea market, where Kahlo would look for anonymous still-life paintings. "The more popular [folkloric] they were, the better she liked them."[14] Kahlo gave her stepdaughter one of these found treasures and had a frame especially made for it (fig. 68). The small painting, which appears to be from the nineteenth century, is in fact from 1920, testifying to the continuity of the tradition in the popular art of Mexico.

Rivera Marín affirms that nineteenth-century still-life paintings had an influence on Kahlo's art.[15] Indeed, some of Kahlo's still-life paintings closely follow the popular nineteenth-century still-life traditions of Mexico in their simple compositions that represent native fruits and flowers and include birds. Parrots appear in innumerable anonymous nineteenth-century still-life paintings and in the work of regional artists such as the Puebla-based José Agustín Arrieta (fig. 69). Kahlo's *Naturaleza muerta* (Still Life) of 1951, which features her pet parrot, pays homage to this tradition (fig. 70). As this chapter demonstrates, Kahlo turned the still-life tradition on its head in numerous other works.

Early in her career Kahlo demonstrated an innovative approach to still life, and by 1938 she was pushing the limits of the genre. She continued to challenge conventional expectations about still-life painting for the next fifteen years. Still lifes became her preferred subject in the last years of her life, but after 1952 her execution deteriorated, along with her health.

In April 1929 Kahlo produced two remarkable photographic still lifes. One of the photographs is a low-key vertical composition of carpenter's tools (fig. 71), which reveals the influence of a series of politically charged photographic still lifes that her friend Tina Modotti created in 1927. Modotti's *Guitarra, maíz y correa de cartucho* (known in English as *Bandolier, Corn, Guitar*) unites three objects associated with the Mexican Revolution and voices her solidarity with it. Such an overt expression of political convictions within a still life is highly unusual for the genre. Kahlo's elegant arrangement of carpenter's tools addresses the theme of labor and, by extension, Marxism. This choice suggests that she followed Modotti's lead in rethinking and expanding the possibilities of still life. Kahlo's

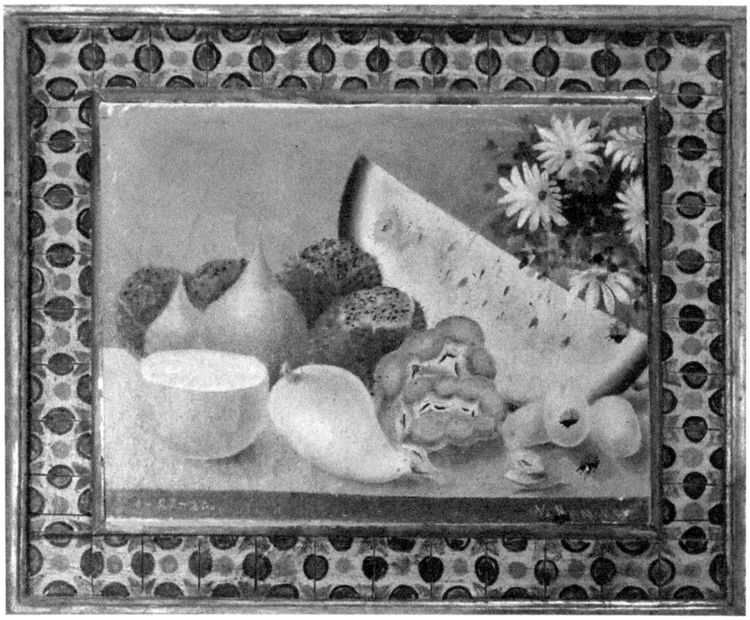

Fig. 68. V. Ramírez, untitled, 1920. Frida Kahlo gave this still life to Guadalupe Rivera Marín. Photograph courtesy of the Galería Pablo Goebel, Mexico City.

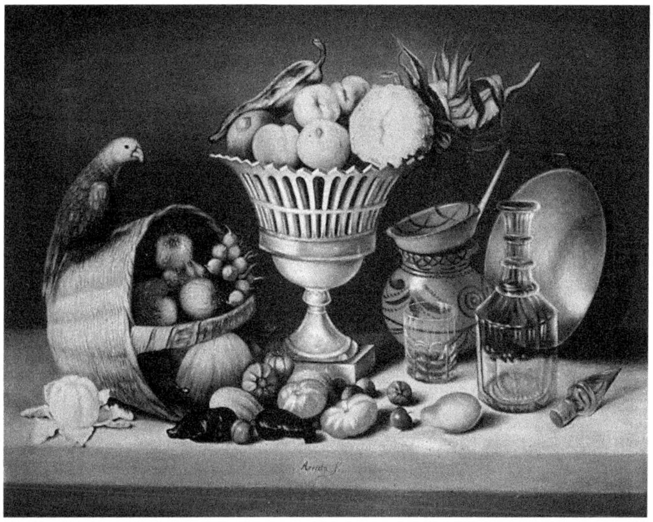

Fig. 69. José Agustín Arrieta, *Cuadro de comedor* (Dining Room Painting), nineteenth century, oil on canvas, 25 ¼ × 35 ⅞ inches (64 × 91 cm), private collection. Photograph courtesy of Instituto de Investigaciones Estéticas.

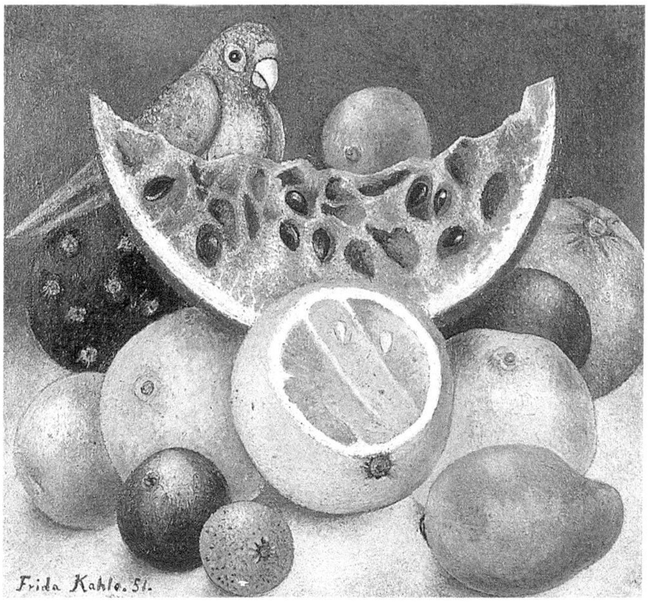

Fig. 70. Frida Kahlo, *Naturaleza muerta* (Still Life), 1951, oil on canvas, 10 ⅛ × 11 ⅛ inches (25.7 × 28.2 cm), iconography collection, Harry Ransom Humanities Research Center, University of Texas at Austin. © 2014 Banco de México Diego Rivera Frida Kahlo Museums Trust, Mexico, D.F./Artists Rights Society (ARS), New York. Reproduction authorized by the Instituto Nacional de Bellas Artes y Literatura, 2015.

other photographic still life displays a rag doll, toy horse, and cart that have collided, scattering the elements of the composition diagonally across a *petate* (straw mat). The image participates in the Mexican artistic discourse of the time by featuring objects of popular art.

Kahlo began creating her most original still-life paintings in 1937/1938, when she started to question the nature of still life and challenge its boundaries. In *Tunas* (Prickly Pears) of 1937 or 1938, a small work painted in oil on metal, Kahlo defied assumptions about the decorous subject matter, sumptuous textures, and aesthetic refinements usually associated with the tradition (fig. 72).[16] *Tunas* depicts three peeled prickly pear cactus fruits on a white plate with a plain green rim; the plate sits on a surface covered with a rumpled bluish-white cloth. The different colors of fruit represent the green and red varieties, rather than degrees of ripeness, though the fruit on the right is noticeably overripe. With their skins removed the two red *tunas* resemble human organs; the one on the right is beginning to split open, so that the form of the fruit mimes the shape of the human heart. Crimson juice smudges the plate and bloodies the cloth.

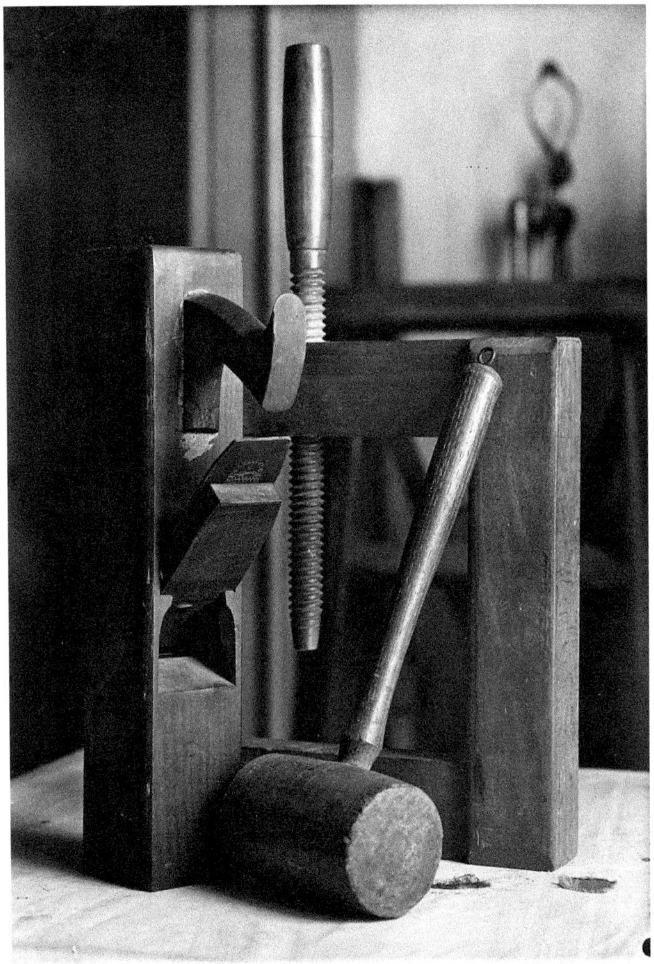

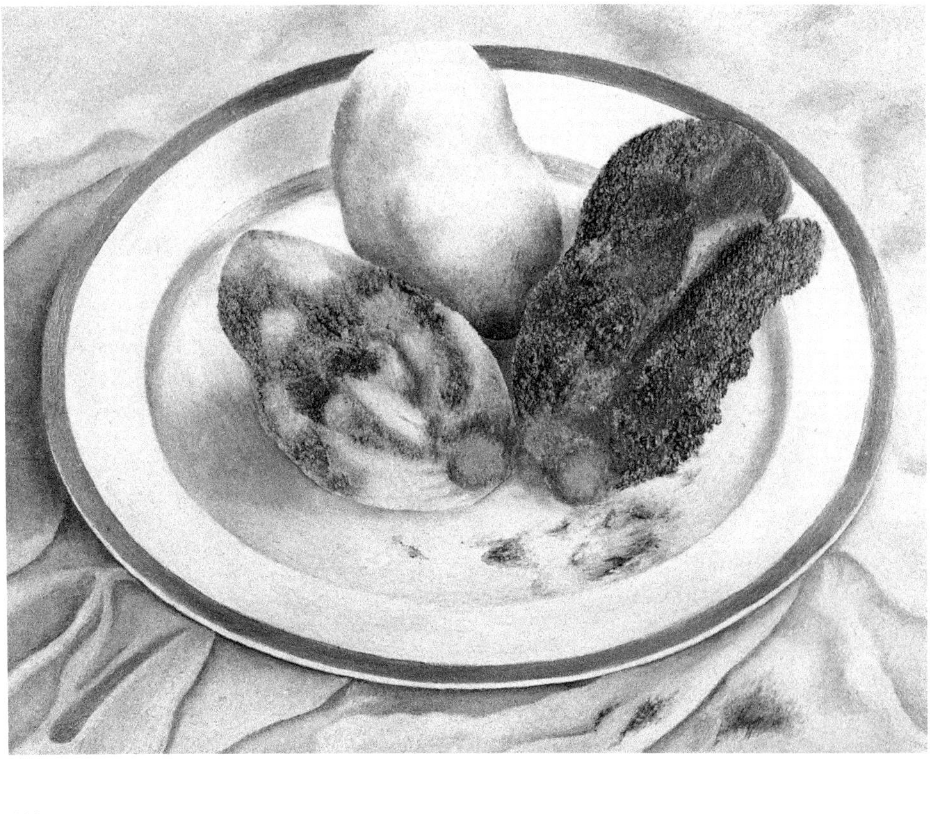

Fig. 71. Frida Kahlo, untitled, photograph of carpentry tools, 1929. The photograph is dated and signed on the back, "2° Abril 1929/ Foto. Frieda Kahlo" (April second, 1929/ Photo. Frieda Kahlo). © 2014 Banco de México Diego Rivera Frida Kahlo Museums Trust, Mexico, D.F./Artists Rights Society (ARS), New York. Reproduction authorized by the Instituto Nacional de Bellas Artes y Literatura, 2015.

Fig. 72. Frida Kahlo, *Tunas* (Prickly Pears), 1937 or 1938, oil on metal, 7 15⁄16 × 9 ½ inches (18.5 × 24 cm), Robert Holmes a Court collection, Australia. © 2014 Banco de México Diego Rivera Frida Kahlo Museums Trust, Mexico, D.F./Artists Rights Society (ARS), New York. Reproduction authorized by the Instituto Nacional de Bellas Artes y Literatura, 2015.

Among the Aztecs the *tuna* was a metaphor for the sacrificial heart. As Irene Nicholson observed in a study of Nahuatl poetry and symbolism, "The fruit of the nopal cactus is heart-shaped and suggested a heart nesting whole and red with the blood of life, surrounded by the pricks of suffering."[17] In Aztec sacrificial rituals the extracted heart was called *quauhnochtli*, "eagle-cactus-fruit."[18] The toponym for the Aztec capital, Tenochtitlan, is an eagle perched on a nopal cactus. The emblem may be understood as the eagle/sun feasting on *tunas*/hearts, an image that embodies the Aztec belief that the survival of the world depends on human sacrifice.

Kahlo was knowledgeable about Precolumbian symbolism. In a passage in her diary about color, she associated reddish-purple (*solferino*) with "Aztec *tlapalli*. Old blood of the prickly pear. The most alive and ancient."[19] Hence in *Tunas* Kahlo drew on the metaphorical language of ancient Mexico to transform prickly pears into sacrificial hearts, alive yet ancient.

In addition to disregarding expectations that still-life paintings should be decorative and decorous, Kahlo repeatedly used the genre to create works that were covertly or overtly erotic. In 1942, probably soon after president Manuel Ávila Camacho met with a small group of artists including Kahlo at the Galleria de Arte Mexicano, the president and his wife, Soledad Orozco de Ávila Camacho, commissioned Kahlo to create a still-life painting for the dining room of Los Pinos, the official presidential residence. In response, Kahlo painted *Naturaleza muerta* (Still Life) of 1942, an exquisitely rendered tondo that intertwines themes of *mexicanidad* and sexuality (fig. 73). In *Naturaleza muerta* Kahlo represents a variety of primarily indigenous flowers, fruits, mushrooms, and vegetables in a clear expression of eroticism within a traditional still-life format. At the center of the composition she features half a winter squash that has been sliced longitudinally to reveal a uterus-shaped form; the firm saffron flesh surrounds a capacious interior cavity with a network of fiber and seeds. Nestled up to the squash are an array of edible fruits and fungi, including a guanábana (soursop) with its creamy pulp exposed and three types of white mushrooms with intriguing textures and exotic forms.[20] The coral mushroom, whose branching segments seem to be living tentacles, may suggest fallopian tubes and fimbriae. A moth and a butterfly hover at the top of the painting near an unopened squash blossom. Encircling most of the composition is a wreath of squash blossoms, dahlias, zinnias, tuberoses, and other flowers. The star of the show, the heroine of the painting, is the humble squash.

Making a squash the central focus of the painting pays homage to its role in Mexican culture and cuisine. Squash was one of the earliest plants to be cultivated in Mesoamerica; maize, beans, squash, and chiles formed the basis of the Mesoamerican diet and remain central in modern Mexican cooking.[21] The technical virtuosity with which Kahlo painted the still life of 1942 demands that we pay attention to a common vegetable that we might normally ignore. Handled in this way, the still life becomes a vehicle for expressing national pride by emphasizing the diversity, beauty, and usefulness of Mexican plants.

Despite the *mexicanidad* conveyed by *Naturaleza muerta* of 1942, the erotically charged painting was not well received at Los Pinos. Soledad Orozco de Ávila Camacho found the organic quality and biological metaphors disturbing. She considered the work indecent, took personal offense, and demanded that it be returned immediately.[22] The painter Héctor Xavier believed that Kahlo intentionally created a work that would provoke the first lady, who had a reputation for being sanctimonious.[23]

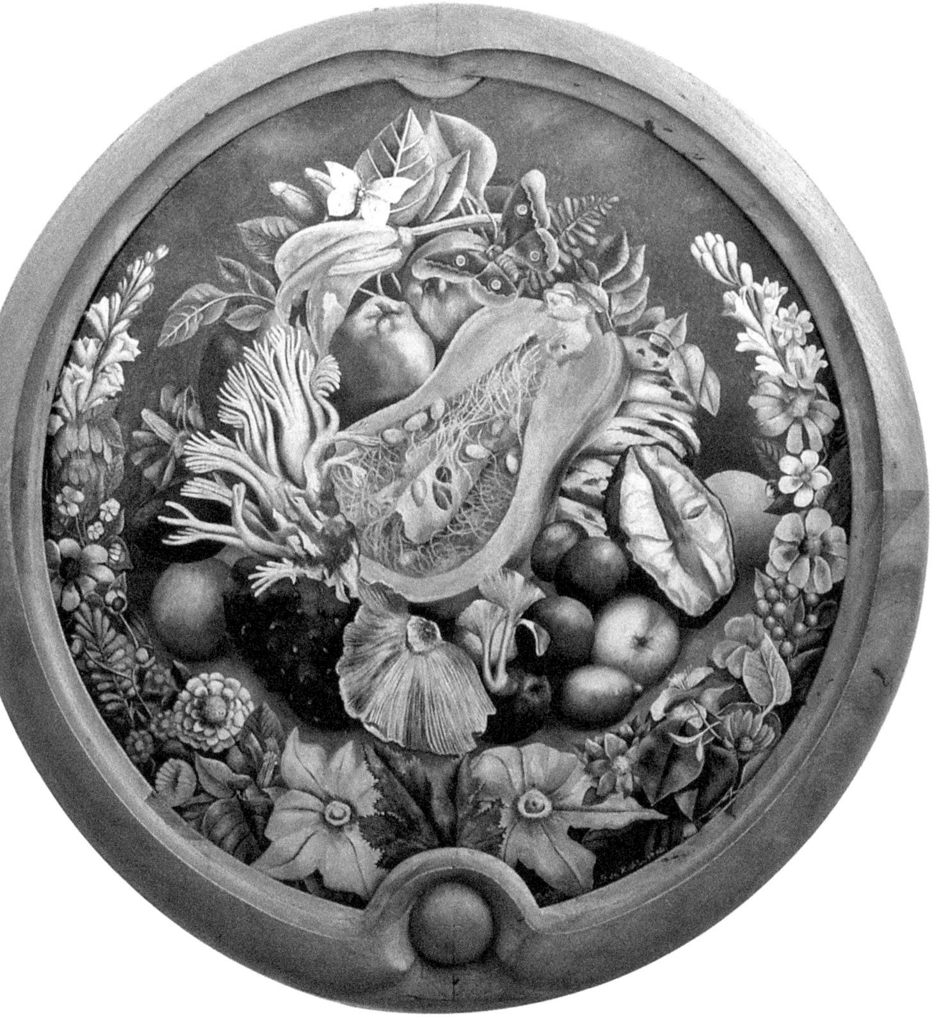

Fig. 73. Frida Kahlo, *Naturaleza muerta* (Still Life), 1942, oil on metal, 24 13/16 inches in diameter (63 cm in diameter), collection of the Museo Frida Kahlo. © 2014 Banco de México Diego Rivera Frida Kahlo Museums Trust, Mexico, D.F./Artists Rights Society (ARS), New York. Reproduction authorized by the Instituto Nacional de Bellas Artes y Literatura, 2015.

Naturaleza muerta of 1942 is one of the most technically accomplished and labor-intensive works that Kahlo ever created, rivaling *Lo que el agua me ha dado* (What the Water Has Given Me) of 1939 for skillful rendering and invisible brushwork. This is remarkable: while Kahlo often exercised great ingenuity in conceiving the ideas for her still lifes, as a group these works are the most casually (and sometimes crudely) executed part of her work. We can imagine Kahlo taking extreme care with all aspects of the conception, composition, and rendering of *Naturaleza muerta* so that Soledad Orozco de Ávila Camacho could not reject it on any grounds other than its sensuality and sexuality.[24]

David Alfaro Siqueiros's *Tres calabazas* (Three Squashes) of 1946 (fig. 74) presents an interesting contrast to Kahlo's *Naturaleza muerta* of 1942. The exaggerated forms of Siqueiros's three squashes twist toward each other and seem to project beyond the picture plane in much the same way that his fist invades the spectator's space in his self-portrait *El coronelazo* (1945). Although *Tres calabazas* is merely a medium-sized easel painting commissioned for a bourgeois dinning room, it conveys the aggressive, heroic quality of Siqueiros's murals. His squash are pumped and full of testosterone. *Tres calabazas* projects Siqueiros's agenda and contributes to his construction of national identity as male.[25] Both Siqueiros and Kahlo offer the squash as a symbol of national identity, but they gender the country's identity differently.

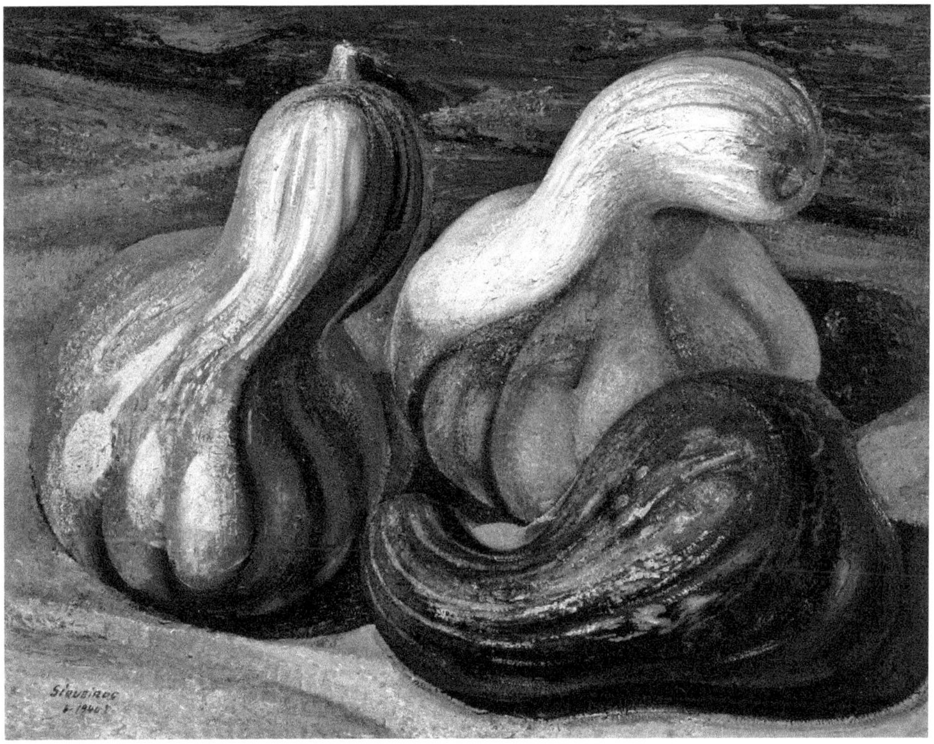

Fig. 74. David Alfaro Siqueiros, *Tres calabazas* (Three Squash), 1946, pyroxylin on pressed wood, 35 ⅞ × 47 ¾ inches (91 × 121 cm), collection of the Museo Carrillo Gil, Mexico City. Photograph by Francisco Kochen. © 2014 Artists Rights Society (ARS), New York/SOMAAP, Mexico City. Reproduction authorized by the Instituto Nacional de Bellas Artes y Literatura, 2015.

Not-So-Still Lifes

While Kahlo created many true still-life paintings, she also created several works that defy categorization but employ close-ups of vegetation that connect them—however loosely—to still-life paintings. In these works Kahlo utilizes anthropomorphic plant forms to invent a new type of erotic art that does not depend on the display of the nude female body. This trajectory in her work begins subtly with *Xochitl* of 1938, whose title comes from the Nahuatl word for flower (fig. 75). The painting represents a single fleshy red flower on a short green stem emerging from a strip of brown earth and silhouetted against a muted ocher ground. A large exterior petal covers, clings to, and reveals the interior phallic shaft of the flower, the base of which appears to be the glans of a penis. The top of the flower has three segments with a darker, hairy patch growing at the center and petals curving down on each side. The flower combines male and female genitalia in a way that implies their conjunction during sexual intercourse.

In addition to its erotic anthropomorphic references, the shape of the flower is loosely based on the Aztec day sign *xochitl*, which, like Kahlo's flower, has three sections at the top (fig. 76). The patron of the day was Xochiquetzal, goddess of flowers, love, and pregnancy.[26] According to the sixteenth-century friar Diego Durán, the day was associated with artisans. Those born on this day were destined to be painters, metalworkers, weavers, sculptors, and carvers. Women born on the day were to become fine weavers and laundresses, who would love embroidered clothing and enjoy beautifying and adorning themselves.[27]

In Mexico "Xochitl" is also a female given name of indigenous origin, which Kahlo adopted as her private identity during an intense love affair. During 1938 and early 1939 she was romantically involved with Nickolas Muray, a Hungarian-American photographer

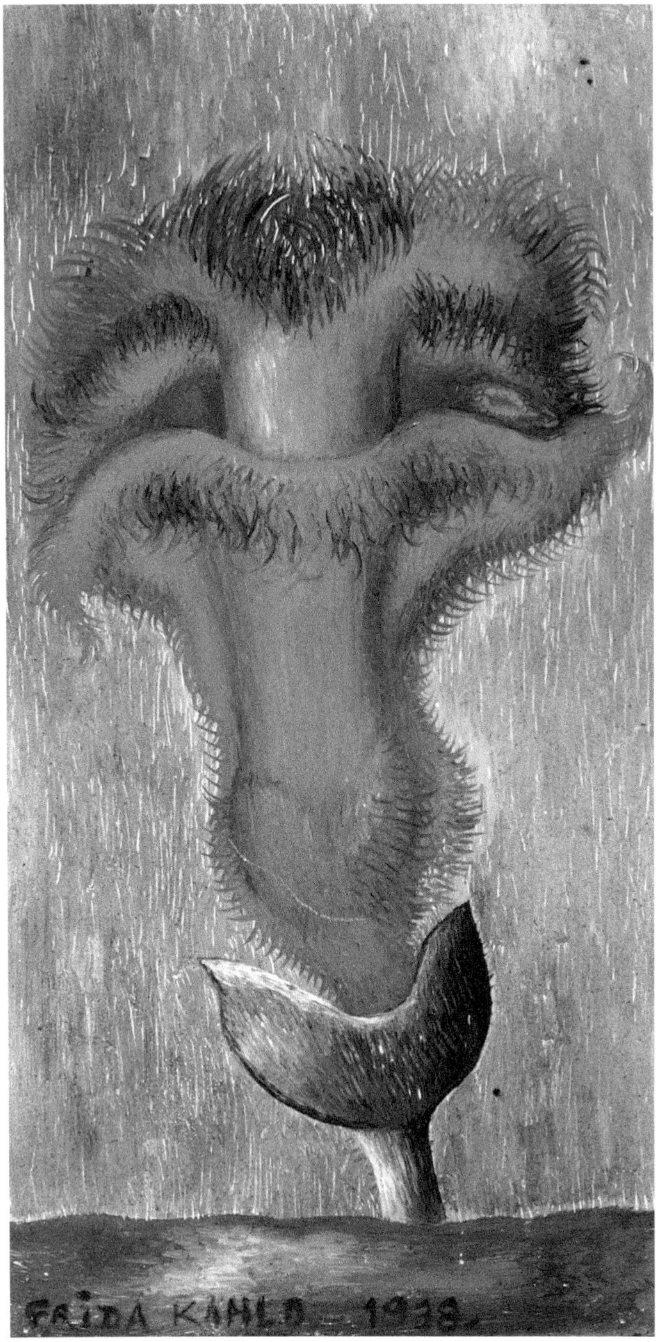

Fig. 75. Frida Kahlo, *Xochitl*, 1938, oil on metal, 7 ⅛ × 3 ¾ inches (18 × 9.5 cm), collection of Dr. Rodolfo Gómez, Mexico City. Photograph by Rafael Doniz. © 2014 Banco de México Diego Rivera Frida Kahlo Museums Trust, Mexico, D.F./Artists Rights Society (ARS), New York. Reproduction authorized by the Instituto Nacional de Bellas Artes y Literatura, 2015.

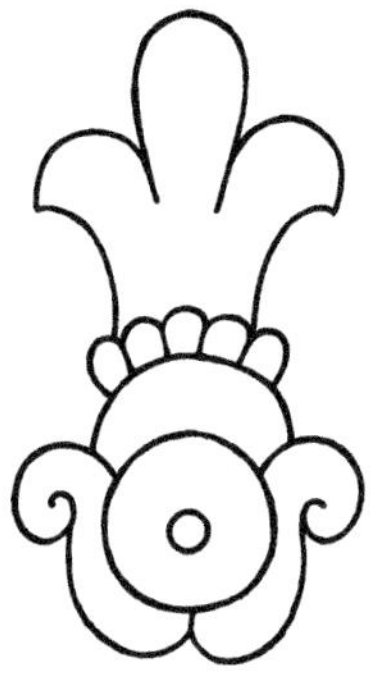

Fig. 76. Aztec day sign *xochitl* (flower).

who lived in New York. They met in Mexico around 1931, and later he helped her plan her solo show at the Julien Levy Gallery in New York and photographed her paintings, including *Xochitl*. Writing to him from Paris in February 1939, she referred to herself as "Xochitl" in one letter and signed another in the same way.[28] But no one can say whether the love affair inspired the painting or the painting prompted the alias.

Six years after creating *Xochitl*, Kahlo again used plant forms to suggest human sexuality. But this time she made a clear break with the still-life genre. In *La flor de la vida* (Flower of Life) of 1944 she hybridizes a plant with the reproductive system of a human female by depicting a uterus rising out of a radiating skirt of red leaves that glow like live coals (fig. 77). (The painting was originally titled *Flame Flower*.)[29] Fallopian tubes extend from both sides of the form and end in hand-like fimbriae. From the flower-like opening at the top, a shape barely emerges, which can be interpreted, alternately, as a baby's head partially covered by a burst of exploding pollen or as the glans of an ejaculating penis. A sun and a flash of lightning occupy the upper corners of the painting, representing the sunshine and rain necessary for vegetal growth. The sun and bolt of lightning may also function as visual analogies for an ovum and spermatozoon, thus creating a parallel between macrocosm and microcosm. Or the sun and lightning may allude to sexual heat and the lightning-like power of orgasm. *La flor de la vida* links human and vegetal fertility, merges themes of sexual passion and reproduction, and manifests correspondences between the microcosm and the macrocosm.

When Kahlo's friend Fernando Gamboa saw *La flor de la vida*, his first reaction was to exclaim, "*Caramba*, congratulate Diego for me!"[30] Hayden Herrera observes that the overt sexual symbolism of *La flor de la vida* must have been surprising to the flower-loving public who attended the "Salon de la Flor" in which Kahlo exhibited the work.[31] In fact, few visitors to the exhibition ever saw the painting, because it was relegated to a separate room that was unpublicized and opened to the public only upon request.[32]

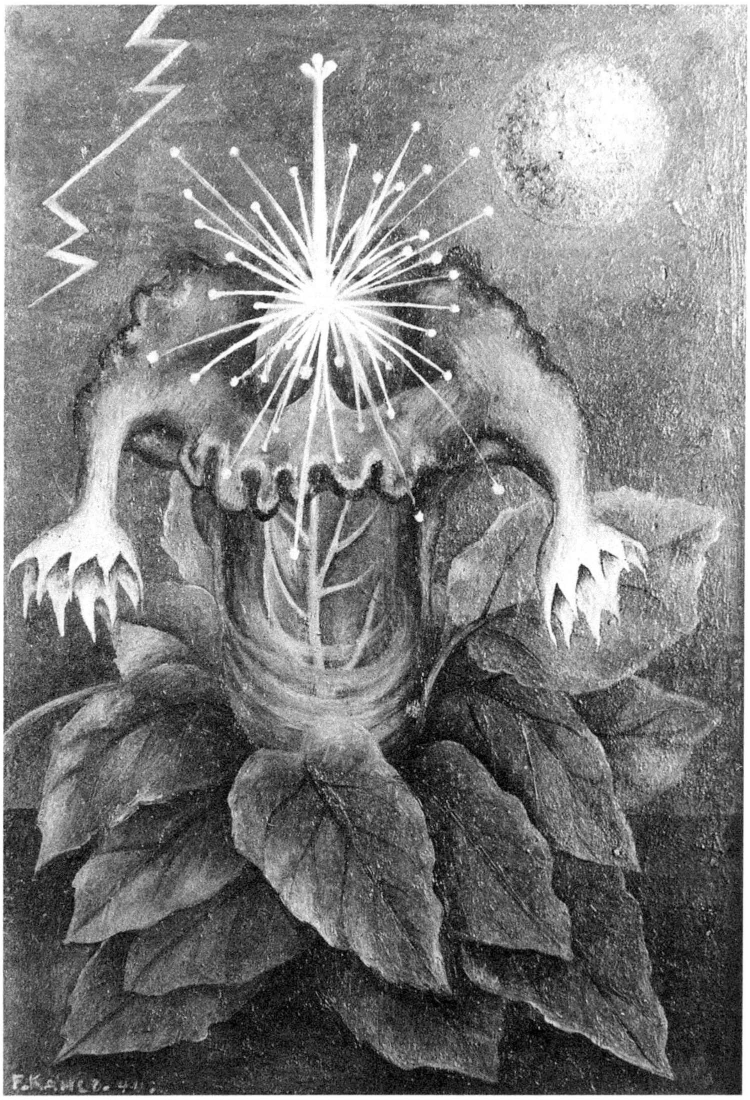

Fig. 77. Frida Kahlo, *La flor de la vida* (Flower of Life), 1944, oil on Masonite, 11 × 7 13/16 inches (27.8 × 19.7 cm), collection of Museo Dolores Olmedo, Xochimilco, Mexico, D.F. © 2014 Banco de México Diego Rivera Frida Kahlo Museums Trust, Mexico, D.F./Artists Rights Society (ARS), New York. Reproduction authorized by the Instituto Nacional de Bellas Artes y Literatura, 2015.

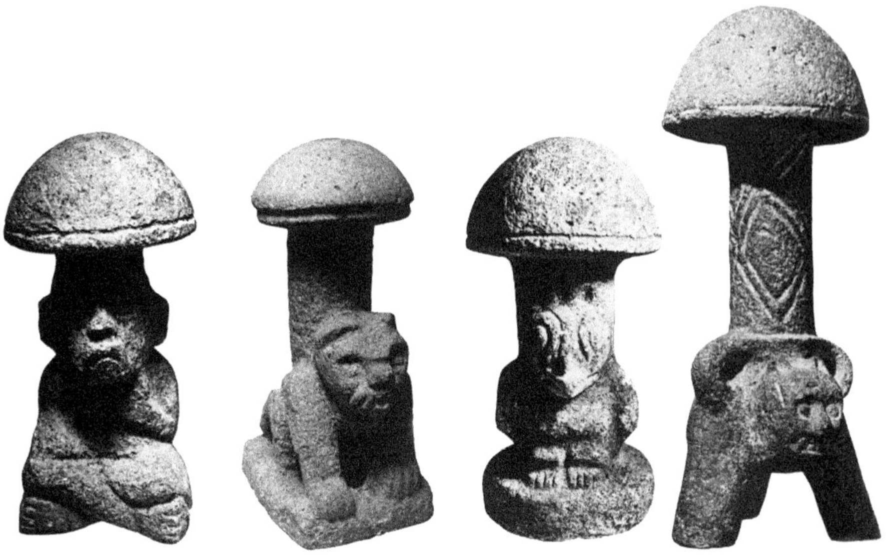

Fig. 78. Precolumbian stone sculptures from southern Mexico, Guatemala, or El Salvador. Kahlo saw similar sculptures in the "secret collection" of the old Museum of Anthropology in Mexico City on Moneda Street (after Richard Evans Schultes, *Plants of the Gods: Origins of Hallucinogenic Use*, 148).

Kahlo knew of Precolumbian precedents for erotic representations of plants. Fernando Gamboa recalled discussing the symbolism of mushrooms with her after seeing the "secret collection" in the old Museum of Anthropology on Moneda Street. The secret collection consisted of phallic sculptures of different sizes, primarily in stone, many of which were phytomorphic (fig. 78). Gamboa remembered that Kahlo objected to the museum's policy, exclaiming: "It's stupid that people don't get to see this. This is life! Although it is wrapped up in a vegetal form, like the mushroom, it is the masculine penis. Look at the different forms! What extraordinary interpretations!"[33] Gamboa associated this conversation and their visit to see the Precolumbian phallic sculptures at the anthropology museum with *La flor de la vida.*

El sol y la vida (Sun and Life) of 1947 portrays a sun with a human face and a third eye amid dense tropical vegetation. The upper canvas is filled with pairs of cream-colored petal-like spadices with each pair cupped around an ejaculating phallic form. Leaves with engorged veins emerge from the stems, while some of the veins extend beyond the edges of the leaves, where they turn into slender aerial roots. Though more metaphorical than real, the anthropomorphic forms are nonetheless loosely based on the florescence of several types of Araceae.

With these paintings of anthropomorphic plants, Kahlo invented a form of erotic art that unites sexuality and fertility. Her erotic imagery does not depend on the display of the nude female body or its objectification. Instead she bypassed the Western tradition of the female nude created primarily for a male audience and took as her closest artistic model the fertility-related phytomorphic sculptures of Precolumbian Mesoamerica.

Mexicanidad, Life, and Death

A high percentage of the fruits and vegetables that Kahlo depicted were indigenous, while the remainder were naturalized. In several canvases in the early 1950s a small red, white, and green banner waves from a stick that pierces the flesh of a fruit. The banners are miniature reminders of the tricolor Mexican flag and proclaim the national origin of the fruit.

In three still-life paintings from the same period, Kahlo combines ripe fruits, a dove, earth, and sky.[34] *Naturaleza viva* (Living Nature) of 1952 features Mexican fruit, both native and naturalized, heaped directly onto the bare earth (fig. 79). At the center of the composition is a pitahaya fruit cut open transversally to reveal a multitude of tiny black seeds dotting its pearly flesh encircled by fuchsia skin, making the twin circles of fruit look like life forms viewed through a microscope.[35] The pitahaya is surrounded by a variety of whole tropical and semitropical fruits with a white dove of peace nestled among them. The sky is divided into a night sky with the moon on the left and a day sky with the sun on the right. The orange sun contains human facial features, while the sky around it is sprinkled with tiny particles of orange light that visually echo the pitahaya seeds. An image of a rabbit appears on the moon, a reference to the Aztec myth of the creation of the Fifth Sun, our world, at Teotihuacan. According to the myth, when the sun and moon were first created they appeared in the sky simultaneously and provided equal levels of illumination. One of the gods hurled a rabbit at the moon, darkening its face so it would not outshine the sun. Then the wind god set both the sun and moon into motion.[36] Thus, when Kahlo depicted the sun and moon in the sky togther with an image of a rabbit on the moon, she explicitly referred to the creation of the Fifth Sun. This is the same creation myth that she referenced in *La niña, la luna y el sol.*

In the lower half of *Naturaleza viva* the earth around the fruit is filled with restless roots that form the words *Naturaleza viva* (living nature). *Naturaleza viva* is a pun on the

Fig. 79. Frida Kahlo, *Naturaleza viva* (Living Nature), 1952, oil on canvas, 17 ¼ × 23 ⅝ inches (44 × 60 cm), private collection. Photograph courtesy of the Museo de Arte Contemporáneo de Monterrey (MARCO). © 2014 Banco de México Diego Rivera Frida Kahlo Museums Trust, Mexico, D.F./Artists Rights Society (ARS), New York. Reproduction authorized by the Instituto Nacional de Bellas Artes y Literatura, 2015.

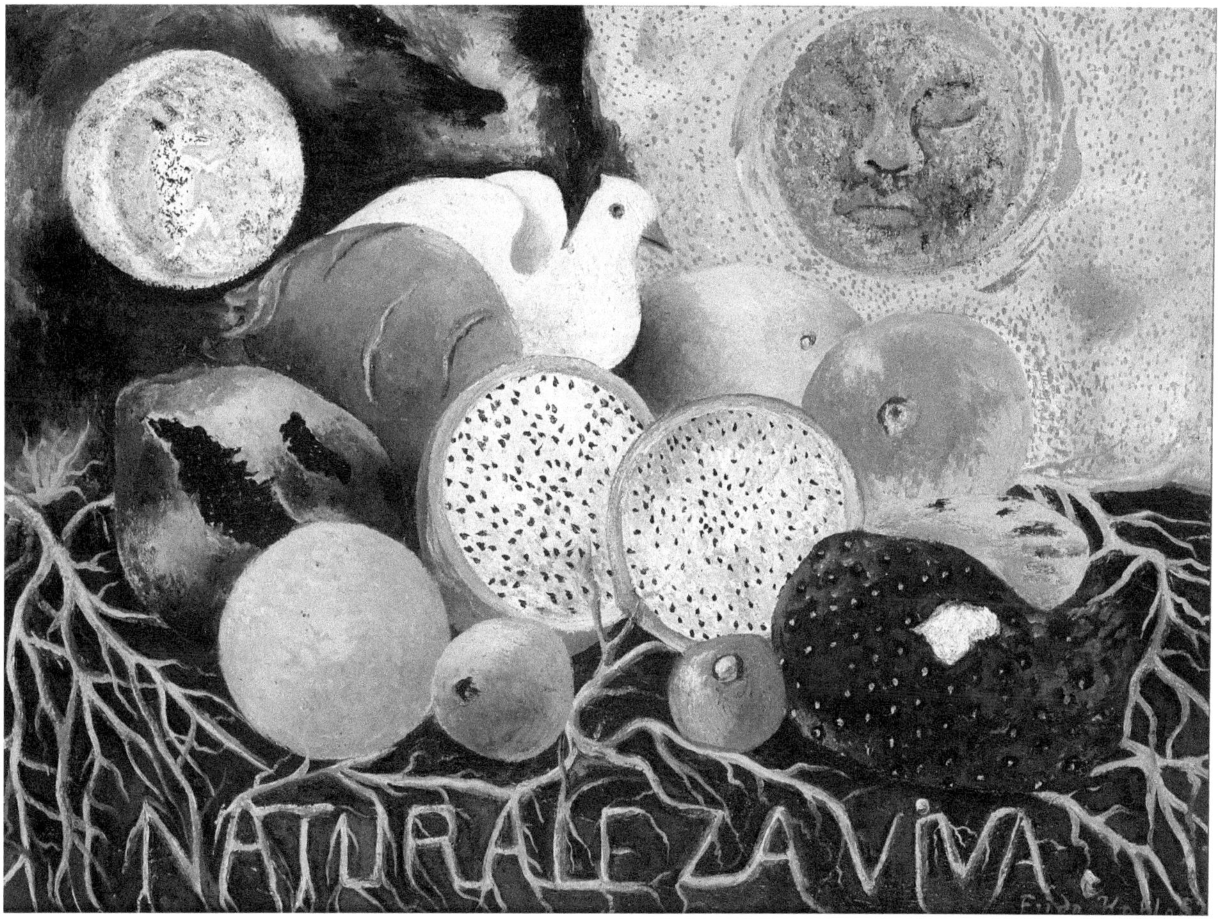

Spanish term for still life, *naturaleza muerta* (dead nature). The wordplay, which was also employed by Izquierdo in the titles of several still-life paintings, insists that the subject of the painting is alive and animate.[37] In this work Kahlo juxtaposed the microcosm, represented by the pitahaya that doubles as microscopic life forms, against the macrocosm of the Mesoamerican cosmos.

In 1940 Kahlo told her long-term lover Jesep Bartolí, who was a fellow painter and a Spanish exile, "I paint flowers so they will not die."[38] This rare statement about artistic intent testifies to Kahlo's conscious connection of plants, life, and death. Death is one of the major themes of traditional still-life painting and the principal theme of seventeenth-century Dutch still-life painting.

Kahlo never created a true *vanitas* painting. As a Marxist who thought that people invented or imagined gods out of fear, she would never have produced a painting whose principal goal was to meditate upon the transitory nature of worldly pleasures and the need to prioritize the salvation of the soul. Nevertheless, she did create at least one still-life painting that addresses the theme of death. In 1951 she painted *Naturaleza muerta* for her dentist, Samuel Fastlicht (fig. 39). At the center of a rainbow of fruits and vegetables stands a small gray-brown ceramic figurine of a dog. The ceramic dog, which is still in the Museo Frida Kahlo, is a Precolumbian figure from Colima (fig. 40). In ancient Mexico both real dogs and ceramic effigies of dogs were placed in tombs so that the dog could guide its owner through the arduous four-year journey to the underworld. The dog from Colima reminds us of the transience of life, but Kahlo's message is to enjoy life's pleasures while we can rather than an admonishment to save our souls.

The last painting that Kahlo completed was *Viva la vida* (Long Live Life) of 1954, which depicts a whole green watermelon encircled by an array of six other melons, five of which are sliced into different shapes. The melons sit on the ground in front of a bright blue sky divided—as in so many of her other works—into light and dark halves. Seeds freckle some of the slices, while others lack seeds. The watermelon, though not native to Mexico, frequently appears in Mexican still-life painting. Its popularity is due in part to its colors—red, white, and green—which are those of the Mexican flag. Eight days before Kahlo's death, she wrote her last painted message on the slice of melon in the center foreground: "Viva la vida. Frida Kahlo. Coyoacán, Mexico."[39]

Kahlo's still lifes range from works that fit snugly within the still-life traditions of Mexico to canvases that turn still-life painting on its head. They affirm daily life and quotidian aesthetic practices, celebrate eroticism and sexuality, draw on Precolumbian art, and pay homage to Mexican nature and culture. Her images often combine elements that a viewer would not expect to encounter in a single work, such as her frequent conflation of Precolumbian symbolic language and sexual themes. Her still lifes are a vital part of her artistic production that must be considered along with the better-known parts of her work. Because of her consistent and prolonged attack on the more conservative conventions of still-life painting, she should be regarded as a major innovator in the genre.

8

Grain of Memory

Izquierdo's Paintings of Altars to the Virgin of Sorrows

In the 1940s María Izquierdo continued to paint most of the same subjects that she had depicted in the previous decade, but she also introduced new subjects. Some of these conformed to mainstream ideas about *mexicanidad* in a way that had not been true of her earlier work. In 1943 she initiated a series of images of altars to the Virgin of Sorrows. While the Virgin of Sorrows is venerated throughout the Catholic world, erecting ephemeral altars to her on the day called Viernes de Dolores is a tradition deeply rooted in the folk Catholicism of Mexico. Izquierdo utilized these images of altars to the Mater Dolorosa to assert a powerful female presence within an expression of *mexicanidad*. This chapter examines the creation, patronage, context, iconography, and significance of these paintings.

Viernes de Dolores, the Friday of the Virgin of Sorrows

In Mexico the sixth Friday of Lent is called Viernes de Dolores, the Friday of the Virgin of Sorrows. On this day, exactly one week before Good Friday, devotees of the Dolorosa erect ephemeral altars in homes, gardens, streets, plazas, and churches and at the entrances to mines.[1] The day commemorates the seven sorrows of the Virgin, and its timing in the religious calendar emphasizes her suffering during Christ's Passion. While the altars are a prelude to Holy Week, they are also tied to the agricultural cycle of central Mexico, where seeds are sown soon after Candelaría (Candelmas), on February 2. By Viernes de Dolores, which usually falls in late March, the seeds have sprouted. The Virgin's tears are thought to fertilize the earth and irrigate the young plants.[2]

The custom of erecting ephemeral domestic altars to the Virgin of Sorrows on Viernes de Dolores began in Nueva España (New Spain) during the colonial era. The custom probably began near the capital or in what is now the state of Jalisco and reached its height of popularity in the nineteenth century.[3] The altars are not now (and never were) as common, as geographically widespread, as well known, or as thoroughly documented as Day of the Dead altars. Nevertheless, the tradition of making ephemeral altars on Viernes de Dolores had a wide geographical distribution in the late-eighteenth and nineteenth centuries. The custom persists in some parts of Mexico City (fig. 80) and Guadalajara and in sections of the states of Guanajuato, Oaxaca, Puebla, Querétaro, and elsewhere. It is strongest in the Bajío (lowlands), the region that was Mexico's breadbasket during the eighteenth century.[4]

While regional differences and individual preferences are expressed in the altars, most have multiple levels. The requisite image of the Dolorosa—which can be a sculpture, a painting, or a print—occupies pride of place at the top. Purple is usually the predominant color because it expresses the mourning appropriate for this prelude to Holy Week. A typical altar is adorned with candles, flowers, citrus fruit spiked with small flags, pots of sprouted wheat, containers of colored water, and mirror-coated globes.

In the nineteenth century Frances Calderón de la Barca noted in *Life in Mexico* that the Virgin of Sorrows was equally popular with the rich and the poor.[5] This is still true. The objects included on these altars depend on the economic resources of the people who build them. People who can afford to do so use gold-leaf flags. When the thin gold-leaf

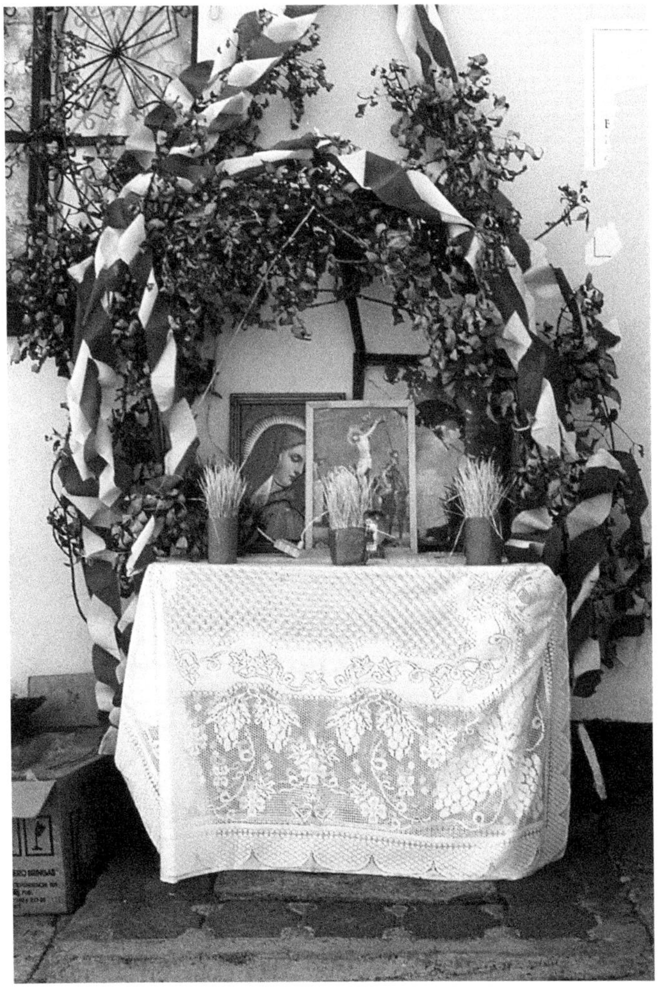

Fig. 80. Ephemeral altar for the Virgin of Sorrows, erected on March 29, 1996, on the sidewalk of a street in the El Rosal neighborhood of the Magdalena Contreras Delegation, Mexico City.

flags are placed on an altar ablaze with candles, the variations in temperature on the altar cause the flags to vibrate. This combination of light and movement reflects the baroque aesthetics of the colonial origin of the altars.[6] When gold leaf is beyond the altar maker's means, gold paper or *papel picado* (cut paper) flags are used instead. Light and its reflections off different types of reflective surfaces—mirrors, glass, water, and metal—are an integral part of the visual tradition of these altars.

The pots of wheat have both eucharistic and agricultural associations. The altars may also include pots of sprouted barley or terra-cotta animals covered with chia sprouts. Glass and crystal vessels containing brightly colored water form an essential part of the altars. The water represents the tears shed by the Virgin over the death of her son. The most lavish altars have special containers called *lágrimas* (tears) that have spherical compartments filled with water of different colors: fuchsia, purple, scarlet, and indigo. Some altars include an *alfombra* (carpet) of sand, colored sawdust, multicolored seeds, or flowers. The carpet usually includes the monogram of the Virgin or a floral pattern, which is often created with a stencil.

Izquierdo's Images of Altars for Viernes de Dolores and Related Works

Between 1943 and 1948 Izquierdo created six paintings that represent the type of ephemeral home altar made for Viernes de Dolores.[7] This chapter looks at the series in conjunction with three other works: *Trigo crecido* (Sprouted Wheat) of 1940, which preceded the series by three years; *Viernes de juguetería* (Friday of the Toy Shop) of 1952, which trailed behind the series by four years; and *Hacia el paraíso* (Toward Paradise) of 1954, which emerged last. *Trigo crecido* and *Viernes de juguetería* are obviously connected to the series of altars, while *Hacia el paraíso* visualizes spirituality via abstraction.

The unusual combination of objects placed on the tabletop in *Trigo crecido* could suggest either a still life or a domestic altar.[8] The objects include a bowl of sprouted wheat, a violet mask, a lily in a goblet, a *papel picado* religious image, a clown's head, and half of a large winter squash. A curtain partially hides the *papel picado* religious image; the visible side contains a figure with the full body halo of the Virgin of Guadalupe and the sacred heart of Christ.[9] The mask and clown's head are objects that occasionally function as *memento mori* elements in still-life paintings, while the religious image, sprouted wheat, and lily signify the sacred. *Trigo crecido* probably commemorates the entire Lenten season: the mask and the clown's head evoke Carnival, the squash alludes to the Lenten diet, the sprouted wheat refers to Friday of Sorrows, and the lily symbolizes Easter.[10]

Three years after creating *Trigo crecido*, Izquierdo began the Viernes de Dolores series and completed three works dedicated to this theme in the first year. Typical of the series, *Ofrenda del Viernes de Dolores* (Offering for the Friday of Sorrows or Offering for the Friday of the Virgin of Sorrows) of 1943 depicts the upper portion of a domestic altar that features a framed image of the Virgin of Sorrows (fig. 81). The image is probably based on a reproduction of an Italian baroque painting, one of the many chromolithographs that circulated in inexpensive editions in Mexico.[11] The print shows the Virgin's face in a three-quarter view, with two tears falling from her half-closed eyes and her head covered with a blue and red mantle. The offerings on the top tier of the altar include a tray of bright green sprouted wheat, a candlestick with an unlit candle, two pink roses in a wine glass, and two oranges with colorful *papel picado* flags. The lower shelf holds a bowl of sprouted wheat, two cocoa-colored *alfeñique* (molded sugar paste) angels, an orange with a red paper flag, a small figurine of a white horse, a brush, and a pitaya cactus fruit cut open to reveal red flesh dotted with tiny black seeds. The altar is framed by blue *papel picado* curtains held aside by sashes.

Other works in the series feature a similar color print of the Virgin, display the same type of offerings, contain minor variations in composition, and employ equally intense colors.[12] The altar depicted in *Altar de Dolores* (Altar [for the Virgin] of Sorrows) of 1943, for example, presents a picture of a dark-complected Virgin wearing a red dress and blue mantle, whose hands are clasped in prayer and whose eyes gaze upward (fig. 82). Objects on the altar are a wedge of watermelon, a glass of *agua de jamaica* (hibiscus-flower water), an incense burner from Metepec, a white *alfeñique* hen, a pair of white *alfeñique* angels, two unlit candle stumps lying on the shelves, oranges spiked with *papel picado* flags, and containers of sprouted wheat. In a later work, *Altar de Dolores* (Altar [for the Virgin] of Sorrows) of 1946, the offerings include celery and jícama, in addition to the ubiquitous wheat, fruit, flags, and candles.

Patronage was a major factor in the creation of these paintings. The series exists in large part because more than one collector saw a painting, wished to purchase it, learned that it was already sold, and requested that Izquierdo paint another. The original owners of the paintings included the artist's good friends María Asúnsolo and Elías Nandino, who each owned one.[13]

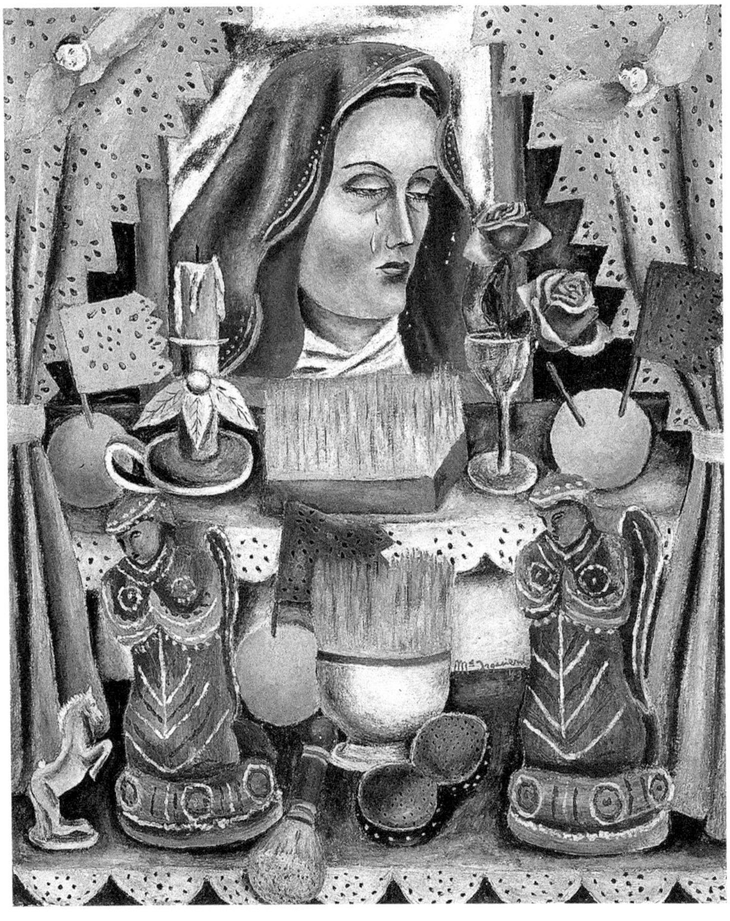

Fig. 81. María Izquierdo, *Ofrenda del Viernes de Dolores* (Offering for the Friday of Sorrows or Offering for the Friday of the Virgin of Sorrows), 1943, oil on Celotex, 23 ⅝ × 19 ¾ inches (60 × 50 cm), originally in the collection of María Asúnsolo. Photograph courtesy of Galería de Arte Mexicano. Reproduced with the permission of María Rosenda López Posadas, legal representative of the intellectual property of María Izquierdo. Reproduction authorized by the Instituto Nacional de Bellas Artes y Literatura, 2015.

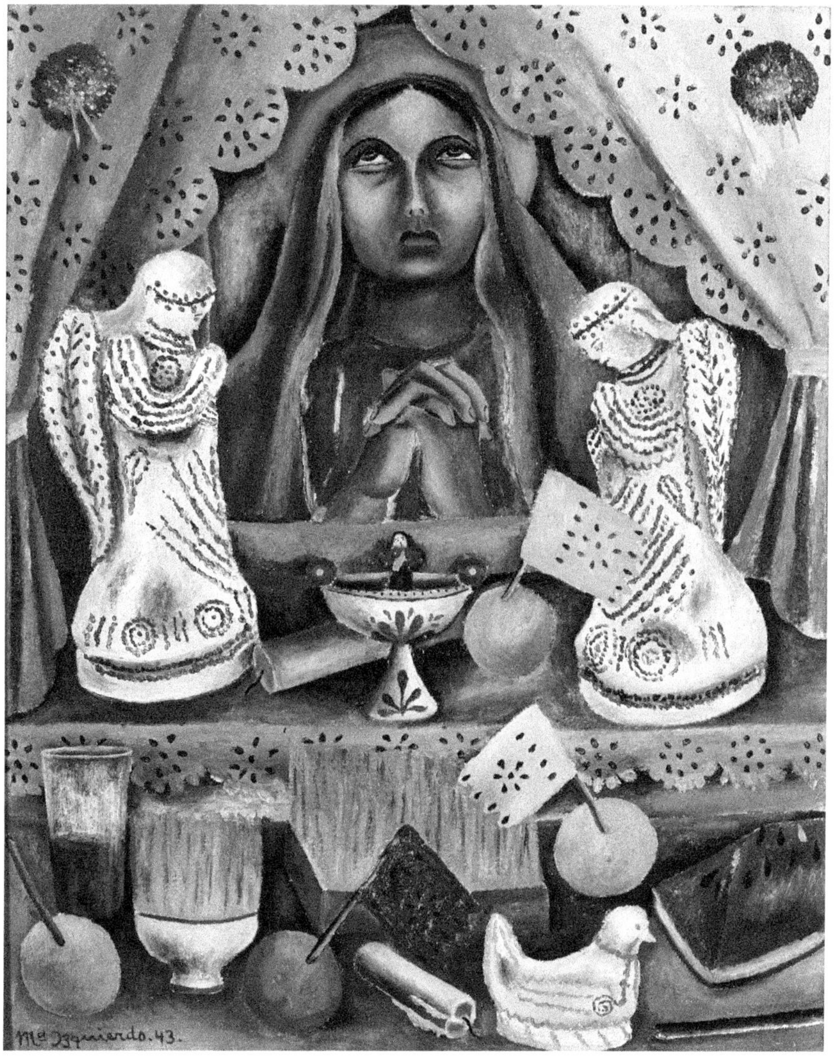

Fig. 82. María Izquierdo, *Altar de Dolores* (Altar [for the Virgin] of Sorrows), 1943, oil on board, 23 ¾ × 19 ½ inches (60.3 × 49.8 cm), private collection, USA. Photograph courtesy of Mary-Anne Martin Fine Art, New York. Reproduced with the permission of María Rosenda López Posadas, legal representative of the intellectual property of María Izquierdo. Reproduction authorized by the Instituto Nacional de Bellas Artes y Literatura, 2015.

The Viernes de Dolores paintings can be interpreted as homages to Mexican popular arts, as expressions of popular devotion, or as both. The positive reception of these works may be due in part to their encouragement of open-ended interpretations that permit their enjoyment by people with diverse views. The ambiguity of the images may reflect either the problematic status of religious imagery among avant-garde artists in postrevolutionary Mexico or Izquierdo's own complex views about religion.

Religion and Modern Mexican Art

From the early 1920s to the late 1950s most Mexican artists, like the majority of their counterparts in Europe and the United States, displayed a strong preference for secular subjects. In addition to the reasons shared by modern artists regardless of nationality, in Mexico the avoidance of religious art may have been related to its association with colonialism and with the anticlerical and Marxist views of the most visible, vocal, and respected muralists. When artists made images that involved religion in any way, the art reflected the views of individual artists and patrons. In modern Mexico art that treats religious themes usually falls into one of five categories. First, some works portray the role of the Catholic church in Mexican history. These carry didactic messages and interpret the deeds of individual priests and the church according to secular nationalistic values, such as Rivera's depiction of an auto-da-fé in his mural in the Palacio de Cortés in Cuernavaca. Second, some images employ Catholic iconography for secular purposes. Many modern Mexican artists drew on the potency of Catholic symbolism and its ability to communicate on a deep level through familiarity, authority, and clarity. The innumerable instances of the secularization of sacred iconography include Kahlo's allusions to Christ's crown of thorns in *Autorretrato* of 1940 and Saint Sebastian in *La columna rota* of 1943.[14] Third, some contain images of individual expressions of spirituality that are not related to a religious institution or an organized religion. This category is illustrated by Orozco's figures of Prometheus. Fourth, some representations of popular devotion could be interpreted as religious subjects or as homages to the popular and artisan traditions of Mexico, especially rural Mexico. This category, which is often ambiguous in its intent, is exemplified by María Izquierdo's *Calvario* (Calvary) of 1933, *Mujer y cruz* (Woman and Cross) of 1933, and the series of altars discussed in this chapter. Fifth, some artists depict unequivocally religious topics, as in the work of Chucho Reyes and Federico Cantú. The last category is relatively rare. Individual artists often created work that could exemplify more than one of these categories, but none produced art that could illustrate all of them.

In this overwhelmingly secular context María Izquierdo painted a significant number of works with religious themes that fall into the fourth category of imagery, about folk Catholicism or popular art or both.[15] This chapter examines a small group of Izquierdo's many paintings that deal with popular devotion and popular art.

Izquierdo, Religion, and Spirituality

Izquierdo was born in the town of San Juan de los Lagos, which is an important pilgrimage site. The eighteenth-century basilica of the Virgin of San Juan de los Lagos dominates the town, whose economy is driven by the commerce that springs up at pilgrimage sites. Both of her parents worked at jobs that required them to travel. During the first five years of Izquierdo's life she was raised primarily by her maternal grandparents and an aunt, who were extremely devout Catholics. Even as a small child she was not completely in accord with all of their forms of religious observance. By the time she was three years old, her grandmother and aunt required her to attend mass at five o'clock every morning. This exercise in forced devotion so displeased Izquierdo that she occasionally doused herself with cold water so that she would catch cold and could stay in bed. She also noticed that her aunt Bartola, who taught her how to offer flowers to the Virgin, was hypocritically sweet to her in public and cruel in private.[16]

Despite or perhaps because of her strict Catholic upbringing, as an adult Izquierdo rarely attended church. Her younger daughter, Aurora Posadas Izquierdo, recalls that her mother was "very much a believer, without being fanatical. From an early age . . . I believe that she was very spiritual and liked perhaps to dream and be near something. As an adult she followed a philosophy that completely pulled us away from religion, but . . . she liked and respected religion."[17] She remembers her mother reading the Bible and books about traditions outside of Catholicism: Freemasonry and Buddhism.[18] Izquierdo's husband Cándido Posadas was a Mason, and she was especially interested in Freemasonry and theosophy.[19]

In a 1941 newspaper article María Izquierdo made the following statement about her work and her beliefs:

> I frequently feel attracted by SOMETHING that, without being able to assign it with its own name, inspires my talent and makes me act without hesitation or fears about what other people think; I confidently deliver myself to my painting, and I feel most satisfied when I am sure that I'm not imitating any one, but obeying my own intuition. "I believe that in the 'other dimension' a community of incorporeal beings exists, atoms of a universal soul that move the souls of earthly individuals. And those beings, extremely subtle, group themselves in kindred families, together with the human sectors that, at the same time, find themselves in well-determined planes of a selective scale. And I believe, finally, that one of these groups or cells of the universal soul is from one of those who were my ancestors, the ones from the precolonial era of my country, and that they are the ones who inspire me."[20]

This statement, which to my knowledge is unique in the scant documentation of Izquierdo's beliefs, reveals that she was interested in esoteric spiritual traditions and believed in a higher dimensional consciousness.[21] Izquierdo was one of several Mexican artists interested in esoteric religions. In his 2008 book *La máquina de pintar* (The Painting Machine), Mexican art historian Renato González Mello documents Orozco's and Rivera's extensive use of secret Masonic and Rosicrucian codes in their early murals that coexist with the public symbolic meanings in the same works.[22]

While Izquierdo's beliefs differed from orthodox ideas of the Catholic church, she maintained emotional ties to the Virgin. In 1943 when her daughter Aurora, who was about thirteen years old, became critically ill with typhoid, Izquierdo vowed that if her daughter recovered she would walk barefoot to the shrine of the Virgin of Guadalupe; she kept her promise but only walked barefoot for the last block of the pilgrimage.[23] Throughout her life Izquierdo was critical of religious excesses. Izquierdo began her series of images of altars to the Virgin of Sorrows two years after making the statement revealing her interest in esoteric spiritual traditions and the same year she walked to the shrine of the Virgin of Guadalupe.[24]

In the 1940s Izquierdo was the only prominent painter who portrayed the type of ephemeral home altars made for Viernes de Dolores, but she was not the only artist interested in the day. Chucho Reyes, Luis Barragán, Juan Soriano, and, somewhat later, Rodolfo Morales constructed Viernes de Dolores altars in their homes.[25] Chucho Reyes was famous for his annual altar, which filled an entire room, featured a colonial painting of the Virgin, was lit by numerous candles, incorporated many reflective surfaces (especially mirror-coated glass spheres), and included a carpet of rose petals.[26]

Gender, Race, Class, and *Mexicanidad*

Izquierdo was interested in the altars because they were an aspect of traditional Mexican customs. Both of Izquierdo's daughters have independently expressed the opinion that these paintings were motivated primarily by their mother's interest in the customs of the people of Mexico, which was of greater importance than their religious aspect.[27]

Izquierdo's altars prominently display many of the traditional elements of the altars, yet they differ from the dominant tradition in significant ways. Izquierdo depicted the Virgin with a darker complexion than is normal for images of the Dolorosa, who is typically represented with fair skin. In Izquierdo's images, the Virgin's complexion ranges from that of a relatively fair mestiza in *Ofrenda del Viernes de Dolores* (1943) to a dark mestiza or indigenous woman in *Altar de Dolores* (1943). This alteration of skin color stresses the *mexicanidad* of the Virgin and associates her with all the women of Mexico. Izquierdo's linking of the Virgin of Sorrows with Mexican womanhood suggests that she perceived and empathized with difficulties in the lives of her female compatriots.

In Izquierdo's paintings the images of the Virgin are popular chromolithographs rather than more costly paintings or sculptures, and the altars never include gold flags or gold of any kind. Izquierdo's use of prints and her avoidance of sumptuous materials reveal that she never portrayed altars of the wealthy.

Izquierdo is best known for her exquisite use of color, and she was probably originally drawn to the altars in part because of their colorful appearance.[28] Traditionally the Viernes de Dolores altars are dominated by purple, which is associated with mourning, but the objects on the altars provide an opportunity for altar makers to include a range of colors. In Izquierdo's depictions of the altars, she used a brighter palette, especially red and blue, which are colors associated with the Virgin but not with the Virgin of Sorrows. Izquierdo's kaleidoscopic colors give the altars an exceptionally festive quality.[29] Her altars often include artisan objects, such as the decorative ceramic incense burner and *alfeñique* angels on *Altar de Dolores* of 1943. Artisan objects are not usually included on altars to the Virgin of Sorrows, but the *alfeñique* angels are made for this and other holidays.

Memory, Gender, and Spirituality

Izquierdo painted most of her images from memory. Her friend the poet Margarita Michelena recalled that they often went to the country together, and Izquierdo dedicated herself to looking—just looking. She did not sketch or paint while she was in the country. Nor did she paint still lifes with a model in front of her. "She really knew [her subjects] from memory, from always. And she made them return to life."[30] Izquierdo applied this method to her depictions of altars. She never set up an altar to the Virgin of Sorrows and painted from it. Nor did she own any of the images of the Virgin that are depicted on the altars.[31]

Izquierdo evoked memory in her paintings in two ways. First, she used formal means to create a sense of time past. Prior to 1940 she employed loose brushstrokes and avoided detail. Throughout her life she created paintings that lack the directional light and cast shadows that would suggest a specific time of day. Second, after 1940 she portrayed traditional aspects of Mexican culture that were known to be vanishing, such as *coscomates* (granaries) and altars to the Virgin of Sorrows. The tradition of making Viernes de Dolores altars began to vanish in the 1940s.[32] This is precisely the decade in which Izquierdo painted her series of Viernes de Dolores altars.

Izquierdo's friend the author Agustín Yáñez, who was also from Jalisco, wrote about three Viernes de Dolores altars in his novel *Al filo del agua* (*The Edge of the Storm*) of 1947. The story takes place in a small town in the Bajío in 1910–1911, during the final months of the dictatorship of Porfirio Díaz and the first months of the Mexican Revolution. In Yáñez's novel the Viernes de Dolores altars contribute to the author's portrayal of a conservative, staid, closed society on the eve of the cataclysmic revolution that changed the lives of virtually all Mexicans. Two of the altars were life-sized scenes rather than multi-level tabletop altars. One consisted of a sculptural scene of Mount Calvary. The other communicated the archconservative political and religious views of its maker, a pampered former seminary student with an over-the-top imagination. The former seminary student painted life-sized figures on cardboard, which he divided into two groups. One group was clustered around heaven, personified as the Bosom of Abraham. The other was grouped around hell. Hernán Cortés, Maximilian, Miguel Hidalgo, and Porfirio Díaz appeared on the side of heaven. The hell side included Pontius Pilate, Martin Luther, and Benito Juárez. Juárez, who usually epitomizes integrity in Mexico, was presumably cast into hell for his role in the creation of the Constitution of 1857, which put an end to Catholicism as the official state religion, and for his successful efforts to establish a liberal secular state. Cortés, who is almost never viewed as a benevolent figure in Mexico, could only have been aligned with heaven because the Spanish Conquest brought Catholicism to Mexico.

The degree to which past time is a factor in Izquierdo's paintings of Viernes de Dolores altars is less obvious than in Yáñez's novel. Unlike his portrayal of the altars, hers do not contribute in an obvious way to a broader critique of society. Yet time, tradition, and gender are crucial to the meaning of these paintings. She brought the altars back to life in order to employ them to assert the female side of *mexicanidad.*

According to Aurora Posadas Izquierdo, the period in which her mother began the Viernes de Dolores series was a peaceful and pleasant time in her life. The twin themes of sorrow and hope embodied in the altars were not connected to any specific event or unusual trauma in her life.[33] The paintings corroborate this. They are cheerful, partly because of the selection of offerings, which, in addition to the standard elements, include festive artisan objects. Izquierdo's most effective way of shifting the emphasis toward hope is her use of a rainbow palette rather than the traditional purple of mourning.

In 1948 the themes of sorrow and hope took on more personal significance. In February 1948 Izquierdo suffered a stroke that left her completely paralyzed on the right side and unable to talk. She was right handed. During the next year she struggled to relearn how to speak, write, paint, and walk; progress was slow. The first work she painted after her stroke was *Dolorosa con trigo* (Dolorosa with Wheat) of 1948. When she spoke to a newspaper reporter about her illness and this painting, she said: "It is my first painting after I have returned to life. I painted it still with much effort, helping my right hand with the left." In a wordplay with her last name, which means "left," she added, "It is the most *izquierdo* painting that I have."[34]

Four years after Izquierdo painted *Dolores con trigo* she painted *Viernes de juguetería* (Friday of the Toy Shop) of 1952, which includes all of the elements of her altars except the image of the Virgin (fig. 83). In the place where she had previously placed a picture of the Virgin is a tiny window that looks to the sea and sky. The deep inset of the frame and the perspectival effect created by the diagonal lines where the sides of the frame join draw the viewer backward in space to another plane. Unexpected windows are a recurring motif in Izquierdo's work. Her granddaughter, María Rosenda López Posadas, observes that in *Viernes de juguetería* the window functions technically as a vanishing point, but on another level it is metaphysical, "a quiet pool of tranquility or of hope."[35]

Viernes de juguetería, like the series of paintings of altars to the Virgin of Sorrows, is a cheerful image, full of color and charm. Izquierdo titled the painting *Viernes de juguetería* after discussing the work and its title with her younger daughter. Izquierdo considered the painting an *alacena* (a still-life painting of a cupboard) rather than an altar.[36] Despite

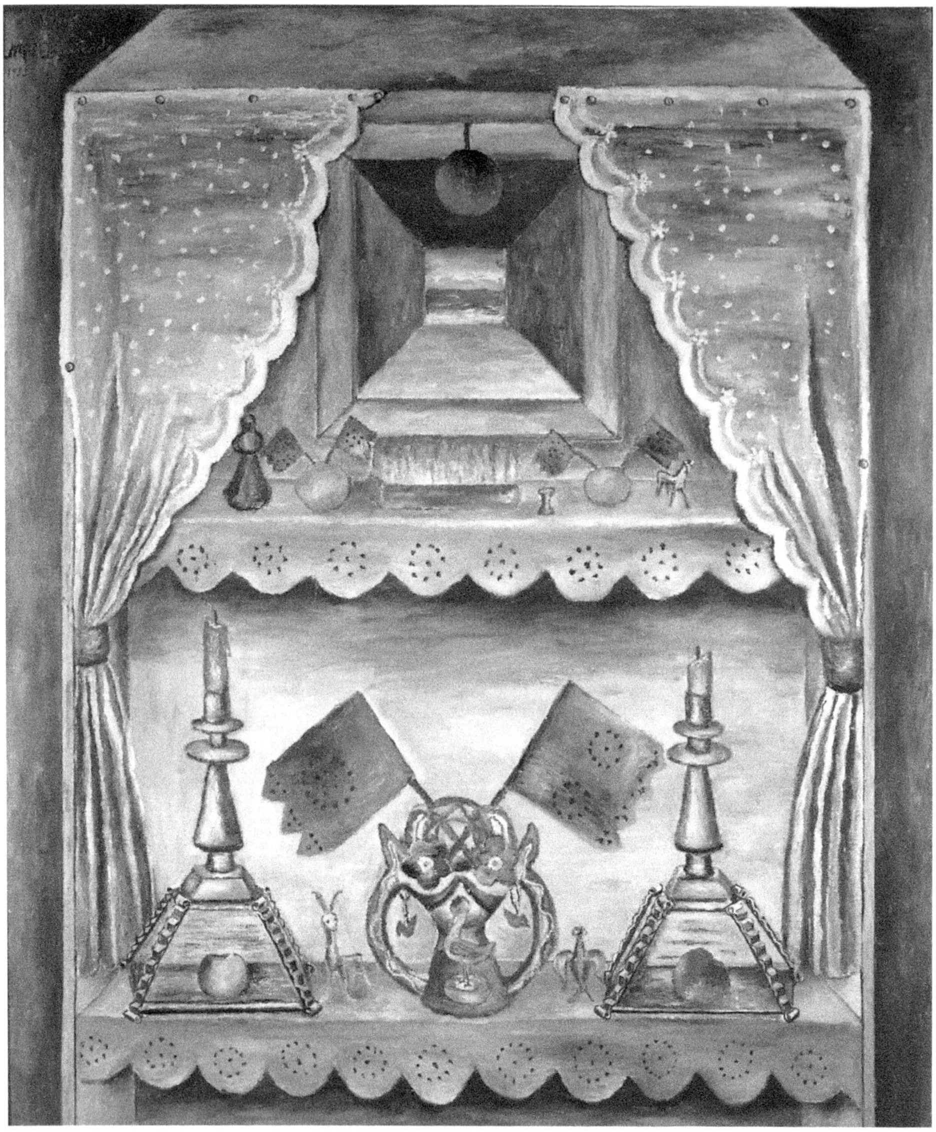

Fig. 83. María Izquierdo, *Viernes de juguetería* (Friday of the Toy Shop), 1952, oil on canvas, 30 × 26 inches (76 × 66 cm), collection of the Museo de Arte Moderno, Mexico City. Reproduced with the permission of María Rosenda López Posadas, legal representative of the intellectual property of María Izquierdo. Reproduction authorized by the Instituto Nacional de Bellas Artes y Literatura, 2015.

the secular title and the artist's perception of the work as a still-life painting, the composition contains all of the elements of the altars except an image of the Virgin, a shift that might or might not indicate that the artist's beliefs had changed.

Two years later, in 1954, Izquierdo painted *Hacia el paraíso* (Toward Paradise), the most abstract painting of her career (fig. 84). The painting consists of only a few elements: an orange flame appears slightly below the center of the canvas. The lower two-fifths of the ground is a streaky orange; the upper three-fifths is mottled blue and white, suggesting a cloudy sky. A small rectangle floats at the top. The rectangle is divided internally into four triangles, thereby creating perspectival lines that cause it to shift between a receding and a projecting form. The combination of the title and image conveys a metaphysical quality. Art historian Elizabeth Ferrer regards this canvas as "a hopeful symbol of life, death and renewal, and ultimately a Promethean vision of spiritual purification."[37]

Izquierdo's *Hacia el paraíso* is akin to Orozco's *Paisaje metafísico* (Metaphysical Landscape) of 1948. Orozco's and Izquierdo's abstract paintings appear suddenly at the end of careers dedicated to figurative work. Orozco is known for his scathing criticism of the clergy as well as for addressing spiritual concerns in his work. Izquierdo's work never includes criticism of the church, but her paintings with religious themes all deal with aspects of private, personal devotion that take place outside any religious institution. *Hacia el paraíso* seems compatible with Izquierdo's 1941 assertion of belief in another "dimension with a community of incorporeal beings, . . . atoms of a universal soul." *Hacia el paraíso* and these ideas are linked by their abstraction and their metaphysical qualities, yet her words preceded her painting by thirteen years.

Between 1943 and 1954 Izquierdo's imagery shifted from altars to the Virgin of Sorrows to the virginless, ambiguous *Viernes de juguetería* and then to the abstract *Hacia el paraíso.* It could be argued that Izquierdo's religious ideas changed from lapsed but nevertheless traditional Catholicism to doubts and subsequently to more esoteric beliefs. Based

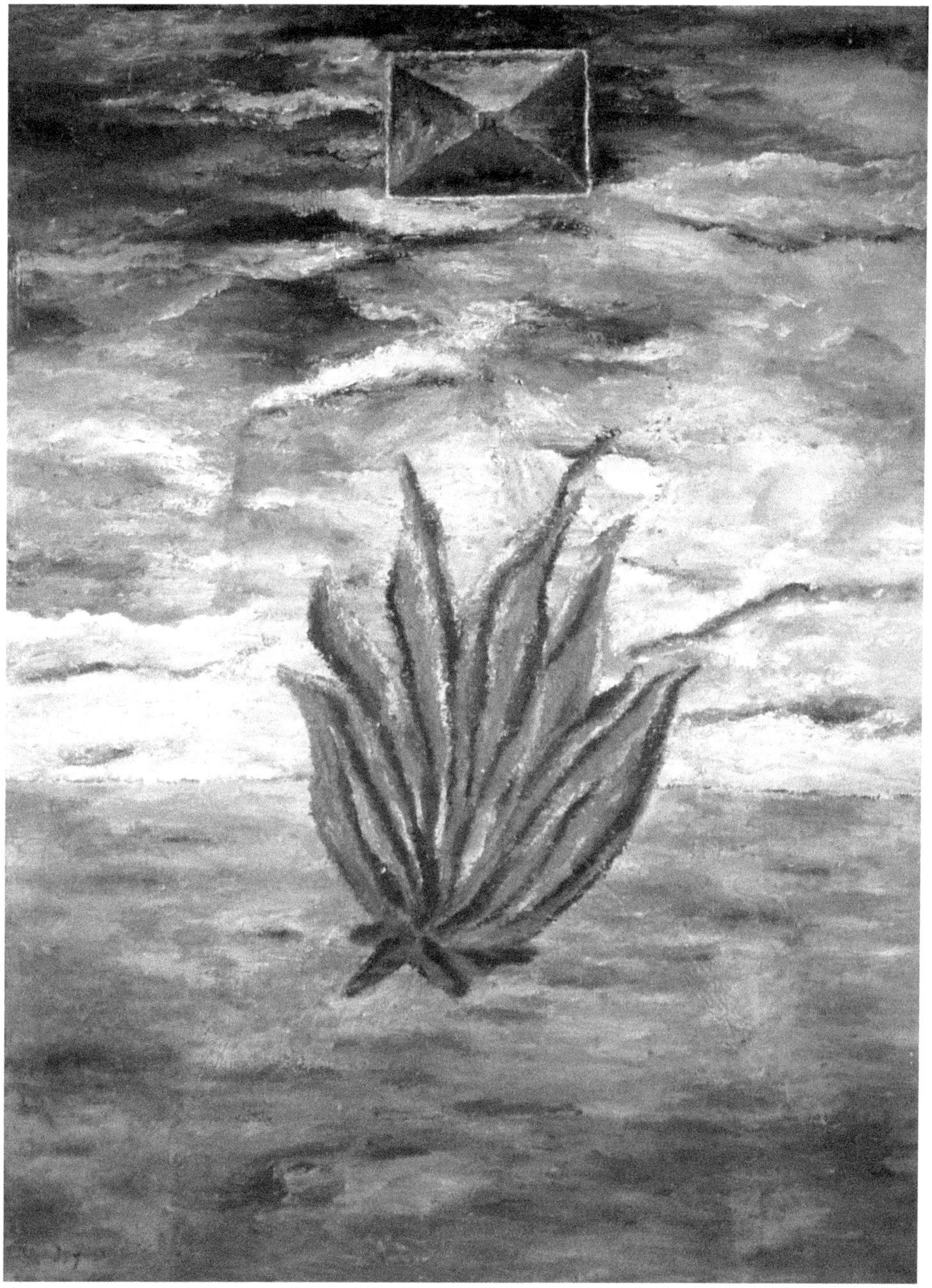

Fig. 84. María Izquierdo, *Hacia el paraíso* (Toward Paradise), 1954, oil on canvas, 35 ½ × 27 ½ inches (90 × 70 cm), collection of Sr. and Sra. Akle. Reproduced with the permission of María Rosenda López Posadas, legal representative of the intellectual property of María Izquierdo. Reproduction authorized by the Instituto Nacional de Bellas Artes y Literatura, 2015.

on purely visual evidence this is the logical conclusion. Yet other interpretations are possible if we consider her 1941 statement about her belief in another dimension with "atoms of a universal soul." Izquierdo expressed these thoughts two years before she embarked on her series of paintings to the Virgin of Dolores and thirteen years before she created *Hacia el paraíso*. This chronology suggests that she may have been receptive to a variety of ways of understanding spirituality.

Izquierdo's paintings of altars to the Virgin of Sorrows, which obviously depict a religious subject, may have less to do with her personal beliefs than the elusive *Viernes de juguetería*—with its escape through the picture frame to a "quiet pool of tranquility or of hope"—and the abstract *Hacia paraíso*. While the images of altars for Viernes de Dolores may or may not express her own religious beliefs, they are irrefutably related to memory and gender. The paintings are in a sense documents, personalized through memory, of a Mexican tradition that was invented in Jalisco, her *patria chica* (home state), or the Distrito Federal, her home as an adult. The representations of altars affirm popular customs in a way that pointedly stresses gender. At a time when much of the so-called Mexican School asserted the virility of the nation, Izquierdo insisted that the national heritage was also profoundly linked to Mexican women, whom she embodies in images of mestiza and indigenous Virgins of Sorrows.

Ironically, *Viernes de juguetería* and *Hacia el paraíso*, which contain no obvious visual references to religion, may more accurately express Izquierdo's spiritual convictions. Although little is known of her beliefs, the scant information that exists suggests that she, like many twentieth-century artists in Mexico, Europe, and the United States, explored esoteric spiritual ideas and believed in a higher dimensional consciousness. The nine paintings discussed in this chapter demonstrate a complex interplay between the celebration of national heritage, the insistence that Mexican national identity include the female gender, the evocation of personal and communal memories, and the artist's assertion of her own modern spiritual eclecticism.[38]

PART FIVE

Women's Rights in Modern Mexico

Many people in the United States presume that Frida Kahlo was a feminist. Anyone who has read Mexican art historian Luis-Martín Lozano's essay "María Izquierdo: Regarding Modern Mexican Painting" may recall the vehemence with which he insists that Izquierdo was not a feminist and his stern warning not to attempt to turn her into one.[1] The last chapter of this book documents what Izquierdo and Kahlo said and wrote about women's rights. The story that emerges contradicts simplistic categories that cast Kahlo in the role of feminist and Izquierdo in the role of nonfeminist.

One of the reasons for previous oversimplifications of Izquierdo's and Kahlo's ideas about women's rights is trouble with the terms "feminist" and "feminism." Their connotations vary considerably according to time and place. Feminist ideas have entered the mainstream in the United States since the 1970s, and the feminist label ceased being acutely controversial, except among conservative segments of society. This was not true in Mexico during the 1930s and 1940s. Conservatives have always opposed feminism, but in Mexico the left also raised objections. Mexican historian Gabriela Cano writes that by the 1930s the term "feminism" had fallen out of favor. The dominant currents of Marxism considered feminism a bourgeois reform movement that was contrary to the interests of workers. The most important organization promoting women's rights, the Frente Unico Pro-Derechos de la Mujer (Unified Front for Women's Rights), which was founded in 1935, did not use the term "feminist" because of opposition from the left, even though the rights that it promoted had been previously described as feminist.[2]

Izquierdo and Kahlo lived during a period when women's rapidly changing role in society provoked anxiety. According to Jocelyn Olcott, as revolution, civil war, and nascent industry pulled women out of their homes and upset prescribed gender roles, concern arose about threats to traditional femininity. Both men and women responded by extolling Mexican femininity, whose qualities included abnegation, maternity, piety, modesty, and domesticity. The virtues of traditional Mexican women were considered a national treasure envied by other countries. If a woman dared to question the value of self-sacrifice, she was labeled "a *marimacho*, a tomboy of dubious sexuality (dyke or butch in more contemporary parlance)."[3] One effect of the idealization of old-fashioned feminine virtues and the taboo against questioning them is that women who worked for greater rights for women often insisted that increased rights would not diminish their ability to be good wives and mothers.

9

Beyond the Canvas

Izquierdo, Kahlo, and Women's Rights

Before concluding this book, I wish to examine whether Izquierdo and Kahlo contributed to the struggle for equal rights for women in Mexico beyond the imagery that they created and the examples that they set as professional artists and teachers. I am particularly interested in what, if anything, they said, wrote, or did in relation to the sociopolitical movement to increase women's opportunities and legal rights.

The literature about Izquierdo and Kahlo provides different types of information about the two artists. Extensive biographical information is available about Kahlo in Herrera's *Frida* and numerous other publications that focus on the artist's life, yet these texts contain almost no information about her spoken or written comments about women's rights. Either Kahlo did not speak or write about the topic or her biographers have neglected this aspect of her political commitments. For Izquierdo the reverse is true. Existing publications contain a reasonable amount of information about her earliest childhood and her life after her mid-twenties but only sketchy, undocumented information about her life between the ages of approximately six, when she moved with her mother and father to Aguascalientes, and twenty-five, when she enrolled in the art academy in Mexico City in 1928. In spite of this gaping hole in the biography of Izquierdo, abundant documentation survives about her views on a variety of women's issues. She first spoke publicly about women's rights in the mid-thirties and continued to address this issue for almost two decades. Her thoughts about women's rights and gender issues survive in her published articles in magazines and newspapers, the text of a speech that she gave on the radio, and quotations of her words in articles about her. The types and quantities of information on

Izquierdo's and Kahlo's ideas and convictions about women's rights are thus dramatically different: abundant documentation exists for Izquierdo, almost nothing for Kahlo.

The goal of this chapter is to document and examine any material beyond the paintings and lifestyles of Izquierdo and Kahlo that testifies to their commitment to women's rights. This means acknowledging lacunae and telling a story that is not always politically correct by today's standards. Before discussing specifics about each artist, I must first provide historical context.

A Brief Overview of Women's Rights in Mexico

María Izquierdo and Frida Kahlo never voted in a presidential election. Mexican women did not obtain full suffrage until 1953 and first voted in a presidential election in 1958, three years after Izquierdo's death and four years after Kahlo's death.[1] In Mexico, as in France, the fear that women would overwhelmingly vote for church-endorsed candidates delayed women's suffrage.[2] Despite the late date at which women won the right to vote in national elections, the struggle for women's rights has a long history in Mexico. We could argue that Mexican feminism began when the seventeenth-century nun Sor Juana Inés de la Cruz (1648–1695) composed her famous poem "Hombres necios" (Foolish Men), in which she admonished men for maintaining a double standard and acting hypocritically with regard to sexual relations between men and women.[3] A significant movement to win greater rights for women (involving thousands of women of every social class) developed from approximately 1890 to 1940.[4] The term *feminismo* (feminism) was used in Mexico with both positive and negative connotations by the first decade of the twentieth century.[5] Between 1916 and 1923 the Yucatan was a center of social reform and women's emancipation under the leadership of two socialist governors, Salvador Alvarado and Felipe Carrillo Puerto. The first two feminist congresses in Mexican history were held in Mérida, Yucatan, in 1916. After 1924 the center of the struggle for female emancipation shifted to Mexico City.[6] Five more feminist congresses, organized by women, were held in the twenties and thirties.

Suffrage was only one of a number of issues for which women struggled. Before 1910 women prioritized literacy, access to education, and the right of married women to administer and dispose of their property. Because the effective use of the vote had not been a reality for men prior to the Mexican Revolution (1910–ca. 1920), it was only after Francisco Madero's insistence on "effective suffrage and no reelection" that women became seriously interested in the vote. In *La mujer y la ley* (Women and the Law) of 1921, Sofía Villa de Buentello asserted that without the vote women would continue to be stigmatized as inferior beings. In 1917 President Carranza's Law of Family Relations granted married women the right to draw up contracts, participate in legal suits, and act as guardians. These rights were implemented in the Federal District with the Civil Code of 1927, which also permitted single women to leave their parental home at the same age as men. Married women, however, still needed their husbands' permission to work outside the home.[7]

The prominent anthropologist Manuel Gamio accused feminists of being unfeminine in *Forjando patria* (Forging the Fatherland) of 1916, a seminal work in the construction of Mexican national identity.[8] Feminists were seldom supported and often ridiculed in the press. The major newspaper in Mexico City, *Excélsior*, was fiercely antifeminist from 1916 through the early 1930s.[9]

The struggle for women's rights met with stubborn resistance from several different powerful sectors in Mexico, sometimes from individuals and institutions that would have agreed on little else. Although the church was in conflict with the state during the first forty years of the twentieth century, it continued to exert enormous influence on most Mexicans. The church hierarchy consistently discouraged even moderate gains in freedom and equality for women. The Catholic church in Mexico refused to countenance the establishment of any women's organizations that it did not control. In the 1920s and 1930s powerful, articulate priests such as José Cantú Corro and José Castillo y Piña condemned feminist ideas as destructive to traditional values. Consequently, most pious women of all classes avoided feminism. As historian Ana Macías notes, "the ranks of Mexican feminism were filled with women who came from families that generally departed from traditional religious values. A large number of Mexican feminists were liberal anticlericals, Protestants, agnostics, freethinkers, atheists, anarchists, Socialists, and Communists."[10] While some of Mexico's leading advocates of women's rights, such as the singer-songwriter Concha Michel and the author Adelina Zendejas, were Communists, this did not mean that the Mexican Communist Party supported feminism. In the thirties the Mexican Communist Party regarded feminism as a bourgeois tactic that diverted women from the struggle to liberate the proletariat. The most powerful women's organization of the late thirties, the Frente Unico Pro-Derechos de la Mujer (Unified Front for Women's Rights), was composed mostly of socialist and Communist women.[11] However, in *Marxism and Communism in Twentieth-Century Mexico*, Barry Carr testifies to the remarkably slow acceptance of feminism within the party. It took until 1981 for the Mexican Communist Party to recognize in theory "the historically specific problems of female oppression" and acknowledge that "revolutionary changes in the relations of production did not by themselves liberate women from their oppressed condition."[12]

During Izquierdo's and Kahlo's lives, feminist activity peaked between 1930 and 1940. For a while it appeared that women would win the vote during Lázaro Cárdenas's administration (1934–1940). In 1937 Cárdenas introduced a bill that would award full political rights to women by adding the three words "men and women" to article 34 of the constitution. By May 1939 the women's suffrage amendment had been ratified by every state in the Mexican Republic, and "all that remained to be done was for Congress to formally declare that, the states having ratified the amendment, it was now in force."[13] This never happened. Despite considerable pressure from feminists and repeated promises from members of Congress, the amendment was allowed to die.

The penultimate year of Cárdenas's administration was 1939, and the political campaign for the next president of Mexico was underway. Cárdenas's radical reforms and encouragement of workers and peasants to unite against the propertied classes had alienated both men and women in large sectors of the population. In early 1939 a well-financed Partido Femenino Idealista (Feminine Idealist Party) was established that supported a conservative candidate for president, General Juan Andreu Almazán. Andreu Almazán waged an effective campaign that frightened the official party, then named the Partido de la Revolución Mexicana (Party of the Mexican Revolution, PRM). The move to grant women the right to vote was halted for fear that the majority of women would vote for the pro-Catholic candidate Andreu Almazán. Cárdenas, who feared that his reforms would be undone, chose a moderate presidential candidate to represent the PRM, Manuel Ávila Camacho, rather than his close friend, Francisco J. Múgica, whose liberal convictions more closely matched his own and whose feminist ideas had influenced him. To calm the fears of religious Mexicans, Ávila Camacho declared during the campaign that he was a believer and won the election by a wide margin. His statement and his election were pivotal in Mexican history. Most political observers agree that the government moved to the right in 1940, and the conflict between church and state was reduced. Consequently, the term "postrevolutionary" is usually employed for the period from the end of the Mexican Revolution through Cárdenas's administration: 1920 to 1940.

Women gradually obtained voting rights in Mexico. In 1946 they were granted the right to vote and hold office at the municipal level. In 1954 women voted in congressional elections, and in 1958 they voted in the presidential election for the first time. When women finally received suffrage, the conflict between church and state had been defused; the government no longer feared that women would swing elections toward pro-Catholic candidates.

Frida Kahlo

Specific comments on the feminist movement and the right to vote are absent from Kahlo's diary, her two published essays, and the published collections of her letters. According to her long-time friend Adelina Zendejas (1909–1993), a writer and feminist activist, Kahlo was interested in women's rights.[14] Thirty years after Kahlo's death, Zendejas recalled Kahlo's support for the struggle to gain legal equality for women: "She made many declarations. She supported all of the actions that we carried out." Zendejas added that Rivera supported Kahlo in this: "They both participated in all of the popular struggles."[15] In a discussion of the women's rights group Frente Único Pro-Derechos de la Mujer, which was founded in 1935, the U.S. historian Shirlene Soto stated that Frida Kahlo was one of the mostly socialist and Communist women who worked closely with its leader, Cuca García.[16] Despite Zendejas's unequivocal statement and Soto's inclusion of Kahlo's name as a supporter of the most important women's rights organization of the late thirties, Kahlo's participation in feminist activities has not been recorded by any of her biographers. The accounts of Zendejas and Soto lack specific examples of where, when, and how Kahlo supported women's rights and have not been verified with archival documentation. It is possible that biographers have ignored a significant political commitment or, conversely, that Kahlo was either not a member or not an active member of Frente Único.[17]

Kahlo's Marxist beliefs and membership in the Communist Party have received more attention. She joined the Young Communist League when she was nineteen or twenty, enrolled in the Mexican Communist Party at the age of twenty-one, and maintained her membership throughout her life.[18] Despite her long-term membership, she rarely attended Party meetings or showed up at the office to help, claiming ill health as her reason for not participating. As writer Martha Zamora notes, during the years when Kahlo used poor health as her excuse for not going to party meetings, she attended concerts, went to movies, and visited friends. Kahlo's good friend Concha Michel, who was both an advocate of women's rights and a Communist, conjectured that Kahlo "abandoned active participation in the party because of the secondary roles women played as typists, assistants, or messengers, tasks that would not have interested her."[19]

María Izquierdo

Starting in the mid-thirties, María Izquierdo voiced her opinions on women's rights to the press, in her own articles, and on the radio. She knew from personal experience how difficult it was for a woman to earn a living in Mexico during the second quarter of the twentieth century. Izquierdo was married twice (three times if reports are true that her first husband was not Cándido Posadas), and Posadas continued to support the children after their divorce. Nevertheless, throughout much of her adult life Izquierdo earned a living selling her paintings and teaching art. In the forties she also wrote art criticism for magazines and newspapers. She was painfully aware of the pervasive resistance to women working outside the home. Izquierdo expressed her opinions on women's issues with a large dose of pragmatism about the real needs of average women in Mexico.

Izquierdo was not entirely consistent in what she said and wrote about women's rights. Part of what she communicated is uncomfortable for a twenty-first-century feminist to read. Variations in what she said and wrote cannot be explained by changes in her ideas over time (a problem with the dating of a key text is discussed below). Her perceptions of her audiences may have affected what she said and wrote, and her desire to persuade a very traditional audience to embrace a more liberal position was probably also a factor. The distance between some of her views and those frequently held by twenty-first-century feminists reveals more about societal pressures in Mexico during her life than a more comfortable concordance of beliefs then and now would provide.

The first time Izquierdo was cited on women's rights was in 1935 during a trip to Guadalajara for the opening of an exhibition of posters by women artists. In response to a question posed by a leftist journalist about the role of women in the revolutionary struggle, she replied: "Above all women must unite and fight together strongly to improve their condition. Women have to cease being luxury objects and transform themselves into a factor within the class struggle; they ought to evolve socially and participate directly in the revolutionary struggle."[20] This is the only time that Izquierdo argued for group action.

Izquierdo's Radio Presentation "Woman and Mexican Art"

At an unknown date Izquierdo presented a lecture on national radio titled "La mujer y el arte mexicano" (Woman and Mexican Art). Aurora Posadas Izquierdo believed that her mother gave the speech on XEW, the radio station with the most powerful transmitters in Latin America at the time.[21] A typed six-page manuscript of the lecture survives in the María Izquierdo Archive. At the top of the first page a handwritten note by someone other than Izquierdo states that the text was broadcast on national radio in July 1934. This date is unlikely: the text is signed María Izquierdo de Uribe, and she did not meet her last husband, Raúl Uribe, until 1938. When I wrote about this radio presentation in my doctoral dissertation (University of Texas at Austin, 2000), I believed that the real date was 1939. At the time, I thought the handwritten date could be read as 1939 as well as 1934.[22] Luís-Martín Lozano and Adriana Zavala also date the text to 1939.[23] Izquierdo and Uribe married in Chile on May 31, 1944. I now think that Izquierdo probably presented "La mujer y el arte mexicano" soon after she and her new husband returned to Mexico (in 1944, not 1934).[24]

Izquierdo communicated mixed messages in "La mujer y el arte mexicano." She began ominously by dividing modern women into three groups: feminists, pseudointellectuals, and authentic women. In the first half of the text she devalued feminists and pseudointellectuals, while idealizing "authentic" women. According to Izquierdo, feminists considered themselves superior to men, believed that they could replace them, regarded them as enemies, and imitated their dress and gestures: "The feminists have not conquered anything for humanity or for themselves. Instead of helping to elevate woman (for so many centuries the slave of everyone), they slow down her emancipation."[25] She then referred disparagingly to pseudointellectuals, whom she called *intelectualoídes* (intellectualoids). In contrast, the "authentic woman" was profoundly feminine, spiritual, self-sacrificing, and happy to be a mother because she possessed a creative force within herself. She had good sentiments, a pure soul, and a clean sexual life. She knew how to love with passion and sweetness, loved her husband, and adored her children. Izquierdo asserted that the majority of these qualities existed in all authentic women and permitted them to conquer everything for the good of humanity and culture.[26] In this section of the text Izquierdo reinforced negative stereotypes of feminists, disparaged women with intellectual pretensions, and promoted authentic women, whom she described in ways that conformed to traditional ideas about positive female qualities and acceptable behavior.

The idea of dividing women into groups was undoubtedly adopted from Manuel Gamio's chapter about Mexican women in his seminal book *Forjando patria* of 1916, a similarity that has been noted by Zavala.[27] Gamio's chapter, "Nuestras mujeres" (Our Women) divided women into categories: Aztec women, women serfs, feminists, and feminine women. Not surprisingly, he preferred feminine women and proudly concluded that Mexico had more feminine women than female serfs and feminists.

After Izquierdo positioned herself against feminists, criticized pseudointellectuals, and allied herself with authentic women, her argument took a surprising turn. In the second half of the lecture she began to expound her views on the emancipation of women and expressed her "concerns and ambitions in the struggle definitively to incorporate women into civilization."[28] In what seems to be a total reversal of the first half of the presentation, she stated:

> *I think that for a woman to achieve success, she cannot be bound by religions or prejudices or political parties.* She ought to have an ample spirit of self-criticism and of struggle, and never lose her femininity, always feel physically and spiritually like a woman, feel with force in order to create, never feel inferior or superior to man, and always consider him a companion in equal conditions. All this is difficult to attain, but if a woman achieves consciousness, has ambition, directs her forces, knows what she wants to conquer—in what field and in what situation—then I am really sure that she will triumph as long as she can overcome the obstacles that arise.[29]

This is an extraordinary statement. Having already positioned herself as a traditional Mexican woman who was not a feminist, she then argued that women should not be bound by religion or politics and that women and men were equal. These issues are crucial for women's rights, so this could be seen as a feminist viewpoint. By aligning herself with traditional values, however, Izquierdo positioned herself as a moderate but then claimed equality as the moderate position of authentic women.

In the middle of her presentation Izquierdo confided to her listeners that the people who organized the program had asked her to speak about painting, but "it is difficult to speak about artistic expression, which is born from emotion and sensitivity and which is destined to stimulate the spirit and the finest sensations of individuals."[30] She explained that, despite the challenge, she would express her opinion in order to participate in the debate about women as artists.

> Many times I have heard it said that women never will equal the great masters of painting. It is true that so far no woman has emerged with the creative force of a Michelangelo (which, moreover, is not needed in our era), but there are explainable reasons. Is it not a fact that primitive women, of the Middle Ages, or of the Renaissance, were completely excluded from artistic and intellectual work? Everyone knows that only in our century are women beginning to be given opportunities to study and work at what they like. Before, women were not permitted to do anything other than cooking, embroidering, and attending to their husbands. Have you forgotten about the condition of women during the Middle Ages? Women are only now being given opportunities to develop their talent. For this reason, it does not seem strange to me that women have not yet equaled the immortal masters of painting. But I believe that if women continue winning greater and greater freedom of expression, they will achieve such heights in the visual arts. Why not? Are not good women painters already arising everywhere, who even mark out new directions in art?[31]

Izquierdo's explanation of why there has been no female equivalent to Michelangelo predated Linda Nochlin's famous essay "Why Have There Been No Great Women Artists?" by more than a quarter century.[32] Izquierdo argued that the lack of famous women artists in the past was caused by their exclusion from artistic and intellectual work. As women gain greater freedom of expression they will grow in stature as artists. Izquierdo did not compile the detailed historical context or weave the elegant argument that Nochlin (a scholar with a doctoral degree in art history) later did, but the core of her argument is essentially the same, as independently noted by María González and myself.[33]

Immediately after her explanation of why there has been no female equivalent to Michelangelo, Izquierdo discussed her own work:

> I paint because I feel the need to do so. The very fact of painting produces an emotion that makes me happy. My only teacher is my own sensitivity. I do not belong to any pictorial school, nor am I interested in defining my style, because I do not paint for the egotistical pleasure of enjoying my own paintings. I like for others to enjoy and feel emotion too, whether agreeable or of another nature. I do not copy nature as it is, because with that I would not have the sensation of creating. I do not imitate other painters because I believe that all of us artists ought to express what personally stirs our emotion. We must suggest our own manner of seeing and feeling the beauty that surrounds us, contributing something new to the world of art. I cannot explain to you how much color affects me emotionally, but I strive to make others feel color in my painting. . . . Nothing in the visual arts moves me more than color: I feel it marvelous, magic, indescribable![34]

She then observed: "Many people say that Mexico is currently the foremost country in the world in painting. Comparing the modern movement of Europe with that of Mexico, undoubtedly something more interesting is being done here. . . . I dare to say that the movement that Picasso initiated is already in decadence, whereas Mexico is opening new paths for current painting." Despite her enthusiasm for current trends in Mexican art, Izquierdo disagreed with the "almost universal" idea that "Mexico is a country of painters, and that the quantity and quality of painters [in Mexico] is grandiose." She protested,

"Not all Mexicans are painters, nor are all Mexican painters good." She warned her listeners that the exaggerated estimation of Mexican art has deterred young painters from investing the hard work necessary to become serious artists. "There are Mexicans who calculate there are two hundred good painters here. I absolutely disagree with these figures. Frankly, I do not believe there are ten!"[35]

Izquierdo concluded her presentation: "I sincerely appreciate the attention given to my words. Good night. María Izquierdo de Uribe."[36] From the time she entered the Escuela Nacional de Bellas Artes in 1928, she used the name María Izquierdo for all professional activities rather than her full name as recorded on her birth certificate or her married name.[37] Identifying herself as María Izquierdo de Uribe was a unique gesture. Married women who choose to use their husband's surname in Spanish often link it to their maiden name with "de." By referring to herself as María Izquierdo de Uribe (literally María Izquierdo of Uribe), she communicated that she was a married woman, thus positioning herself as a respectable matron who believed in women's rights rather than as a single or divorced woman. She presumably made this choice because she believed that she could more effectively argue for women's rights as a married woman.

Izquierdo's speech about women and Mexican art is, on the surface, an odd composite of seemingly contradictory viewpoints. After distancing herself from feminists and pseudointellectuals, she then argued passionately for women's emancipation, asserted that women wanted success, insisted that they should not be limited by church or state, explained that historical situations have limited the rise of women artists, and declared that women artists will succeed if given liberty. The reader is left wondering about several issues. Why did Izquierdo have such a negative opinion of feminists? Did she really object to feminism as she understood it? Or did she intentionally distance herself from feminism because she perceived it to be such an unpopular movement in Mexico that it was a political liability?

Anthropologists have long noted a tendency for people not to identify with disenfranchised groups.[38] Izquierdo's disavowal of feminism was probably related to a desire to distance herself from a group that she believed was perceived as marginal by most Mexicans. Even in recent decades in the United States the phrase "I'm not a feminist, but" has been frequently employed by people who want the benefits of women's rights without being labeled feminists.

Another major factor undoubtedly contributed to the way in which Izquierdo presented her ideas about female emancipation. As anthropologist Ramona Pérez notes, "Many anthropologists and other social scientists working in Mexico and throughout Latin America have demonstrated women's resistance and outright refusal to identify with feminism or as feminists, while at the same time fighting for women's rights." Pérez adds that women in Latin America "struggled for recognition and equality but did so within their own cultural framework."[39]

What Izquierdo said in "La mujer y el arte mexicano" may have been affected in more than one way by the media in which it was presented. Radio reached and continues to reach a broad spectrum of the population: everyone from the highly educated to the illiterate. Communication historian Joy Elizabeth Hayes observes that radio was "one of the first mass media to communicate across the social lines of race, class, and gender." By the early 1930s in Mexico "radio reached professionals and the upper class, as well as urban dwellers of all classes in public places such as bars, restaurants, community centers, and schools."[40] If "La mujer y el arte mexicano" was broadcast on XEW as Izquierdo's daughter believed, then the station's high-power transmitters would have carried it to most of the nation.

Beginning in 1926 the federal government regulated radio in Mexico. The commencement and development of radio coincided with the postrevolutionary period. The Mexican government effectively employed radio to promote national unity and political consolidation by promoting an official version of national culture. All stations were required to include some government programming and to devote at least 25 percent of each day's broadcasts to *música típica* (typical Mexican music). Laws prohibited any transmissions that attacked public order, state security, or the government. Programs of a political or religious nature were barred from the airways.[41]

What Izquierdo said in her radio presentation about women and Mexican art may have been heavily influenced by the media in which she delivered it. She probably tailored her lecture for a more diverse audience than the educated urban public who read her reviews of art exhibitions in the early 1940s. No record survives of who invited her to speak, but Izquierdo's younger daughter recalled that many of the invitations that Izquierdo received to speak on the radio came from Álvaro Gálvez y Fuentes.[42] In her presentation Izquierdo said that she was asked to talk about painting, which she discussed at the end after dedicating substantial attention to the role of women in Mexican society. She based the first half of her speech on Gamio's chapter about "Nuestras mujeres" in *Forjando patria*, presumably because of the anthropologist's prestige and the importance of his book to the construction of national identity in Mexico. She may have done this to establish credibility, to begin with familiar ideas before developing an original personal statement, or to evade laws prohibiting political programs on the airwaves. We will probably never know what caused her to give a lecture with such profound internal contradictions. Nonetheless, with one exception (discussed below), all of her subsequent public statements argue for greater rights for women without criticizing feminists.

Izquierdo as a Writer

Beginning in 1942 Izquierdo wrote articles for the magazine *Hoy* (Today) and later for *Excélsior* and other newspapers. Between January 1942 and July 1943 she wrote nineteen articles for *Hoy*, most of which reviewed individual and group exhibitions. She usually wrote about lesser-known artists or foreign artists temporarily working in Mexico; sometimes her subjects fit into both categories. She wrote three reviews of solo shows by women artists: the Chilean painter Mireya Lafuente, the Russian American artist Ann Medalie, and the Italian American photographer Tina Modotti.[43] Izquierdo also devoted half of an article to a young Haitian painter, Andrée Malebranche, who exhibited her canvases in a dress shop, and a full article to the influential Inés Amor, who directed the prestigious Galería de Arte Mexicano.[44] Izquierdo's reviews of women's exhibitions and her article about Amor demonstrate solidarity with female colleagues. For the purposes of this chapter, the most pertinent of these texts is her 1942 article about Lafuente. In a passage subtitled "La mujer que pinta" (The Woman Who Paints), Izquierdo observed:

> The first obstacle that the woman painter has to overcome is the old belief that the woman only serves for the home and its related obligations. When she succeeds in convincing society that she also can create, she encounters a big wall of incomprehension formed by the envy

or superiority complexes of her colleagues. Later come the eternal improvised art critics who, upon judging a work by a woman painter, almost always exclaim, "For a feminine painting it's not bad!" As if color, line, volumes, landscape, or geography had a sex. Male painters almost never see in the woman who paints one more colleague, who dedicates herself to the same creative work with the same seriousness as they do. No. On the contrary, they see in her an obstructing and inferior competitor whom they attack venomously.[45]

Izquierdo complained that women who are not artists assume that women painters need to create an aura of neglected bohemia, which for the nonartist signifies laziness, disorder, anarchy, and libertinism. She concluded:

The path that the woman who paints must travel is terribly hard! Thus, when a woman achieves renown as a great painter or wins a name in the artistic universe, her personality moves me to fervent respect and admiration.

A talented Central American art critic once said to me, "Face the facts, friend, the woman who paints is understood and supported only by intelligent men and women . . . and they are scarce!"[46]

Given Izquierdo's clear support of women's rights in her essay about Lafuente, it would be tempting to claim that her criticism of feminism in her radio broadcast "La mujer y el arte mexicano" was a unique aberration, but it was not. Soon after returning from South America, Izquierdo wrote fifteen articles about her trip, which were published in *Excélsior* between October 1944 and April 1945. In the sixth installment she wrote that in Chile women have the same rights as men and attributed this achievement to Chile having fewer feminist organizations than Mexico.[47]

In 1950 Izquierdo returned to the topic of women's rights in a newspaper article titled "Carta a las mujeres de México" (Letter to the Women of Mexico). In her open letter to the women of Mexico she defended the reputation of young working women against critics' assumptions that they were less moral than traditional women who did not work outside of the home. Izquierdo insisted that, for the most part, modern women possessed traditional values. She emphasized the need for women to be able to support themselves and their children if necessary. She contended that the modern young woman would be better prepared to chose and understand a husband because she had male companions from work who were real friends:

When she marries, she will not be converted into a slave. Because she knows how to earn her living, she will not feel inferiority complexes before her husband. These complexes are felt by the woman of antiquated or provincial mentality who is worn away waiting for the man who will marry her to fall from the sky or from the next city. She will obey or follow this man blindly because she knows or perceives intuitively that if he abandons her she will be converted into a useless being, incapable of supporting herself, much less her children, if she has them.[48]

In previous texts Izquierdo had discussed the professional struggles of women artists, but in the letter she emphasized the importance of economic independence for all women. This was (and still is) a crucial issue for the emancipation of women.

Notable similarities and differences exist between Izquierdo's radio broadcast "La mujer en el arte mexicano," whose date is uncertain (1934, 1939, or 1944), and her open letter to the women of Mexico (1950). In her radio presentation she let her listeners know that she was married by identifying herself as María Izquierdo de Uribe, the form of her name that communicates married status. In the open letter to the women of Mexico she was more explicit. She wrote that she spoke as a happily married woman who did not feel animosity toward men, a piece of personal information clearly intended to assuage skeptical readers and facilitate their acceptance of increasingly independent women. In the letter she stated, "I am not a feminist of the classic type,"[49] which, while still separating herself from feminists, did so in a much gentler fashion than she had done in her radio address. Her wording in the letter opened up the possibility that she might be a feminist of some other type. The radio broadcast and open letter were different in tone but shared a strategy. Both argued for emancipation for women while trying to reassure a broad popular audience that Mexican women could gain independence and still be loving, feminine wives. Historian and feminist scholar Asunción Lavrín has noted that in Latin America female feminists "coaxed men's opinions: they acted persuasively, not aggressively."[50] While this is not how Izquierdo perceived feminists, it is how she approached promoting greater rights for women.

Izquierdo and Female Suffrage in the Early Fifties

Izquierdo's last published statement about women's rights appeared in a newspaper article written by an anonymous journalist in 1952. The article, which focused on the problems that Izquierdo encountered with her 1945 mural commission, was published just before Mexican women finally gained the right to vote in all elections. Izquierdo spoke about the positive changes that were taking place during the presidency of Adolfo Ruiz Cortines: "I believe that in the present no one will suffer an injustice as I did. It seems that now it will not be a crime to be born woman."[51]

The following year Izquierdo expressed similar ideas about the changing political and social situation of women in Mexico. In her memoirs, which she dictated to a secretary, she recalled being pressured to leave art school by a gang of hostile male students who were envious of Rivera's admiration of her paintings. She explained that during that period women were relegated to a lower status than men. Only the most talented men—like Rufino Tamayo, Diego Rivera, Manuel Toussaint, and Alfonso Caso—promoted and helped women, especially those gifted artistically. In her opinion, in those days mediocre men still held ideas from the Middle Ages and followed customs from the Inquisition. Izquierdo perceived great advances between the late twenties and the early fifties, when women attained full suffrage. Remembering her early difficulties, she asserted, "In those days, it was a *crime to be born a woman*, and if the woman had artistic abilities, it was much worse."[52]

A Feminist by Any Other Name

Izquierdo experienced discrimination, empathized with other women—especially women artists—who shared the struggle for equality, and wrote in favor of women's rights for almost two decades. Was she a feminist? Not by her own definition. Quite the contrary, on two occasions, once in a radio presentation (which I now believe took place in 1944) and once in an article in *Excélsior* in 1944, she wrote about feminism in ways that uncritically accepted and promoted damaging stereotypes. For those of us who equate feminism with the belief in the equality of women and men and reject demeaning stereotypes, Izquierdo's unflattering typecasting of feminists and her equally troubling praise of authentic women are highly problematic. Except for the radio presentation and the 1944 article, however, Izquierdo was firmly and passionately in favor of equal rights for women. She argued that women should be able to support themselves financially, promoted women's rising reputations in the visual arts, and insisted that religion and politics should not interfere with women's development. After the debacle of her failed mural project of 1945, she never again spoke with the same harshness about feminism, though she never embraced the label either. While I am uncomfortable with Izquierdo's low opinion of feminists and idealization of self-sacrificing, pure, maternal women, I consider the conservative passages in her writings to be clear indicators of the extraordinarily traditional environment in which she lived and worked. Precisely because her words are at times unsettling, they reveal the degree to which the society in which she worked was conservative in regard to gender issues. The discomfort that I and presumably most readers of this book feel about some of her comments marks the changes in commonly held beliefs in Mexico, the United States, and elsewhere between the second quarter of the twentieth century and the first quarter of the twenty-first century.

Izquierdo's and Kahlo's commitment to women's rights and their concern with gender issues are irrefutably central to the bodies of visual work that they created. Both artists were professional women who exhibited, traveled, and wrote. They led modern, independent lives. Kahlo may also have been an active member of the Frente Único, though documentation for this has yet to be offered. Izquierdo—despite her two published criticisms of feminists—spoke and wrote about issues related to women's lives for nearly two decades. In her writings Izquierdo addressed the crucial issues of women's liberation with energy, force, and conviction.

In *The Power of Identity* sociologist Manuel Castells writes that "the essence of feminism, as practiced and narrated, is the (re)definition of woman's identity." Castells describes the "cultural polyphony of feminism." Whether proponents of women's rights advocate equality, difference, or separation, he asserts, "[i]n all cases, . . . what is negated is women's identity as defined by men, and as enshrined in the patriarchal family."[53] In their visual work Izquierdo and Kahlo de/re/constructed women's identity in Mexico. They used a variety of strategies that ranged from creating strong female protagonists that rivaled the male heroes to legitimating female power by linking women to ancient traditions. Castells sees the self-construction of identity as a way of mobilizing women toward their goals. "Claiming identity is power-making."[54] Claiming identity is one of the major recurring themes in Izquierdo's and Kahlo's art. It is there, in their visual work, that Izquierdo and Kahlo most articulately and assiduously asserted their beliefs in women's rights.

Conclusion

This book has explored Izquierdo's and Kahlo's strategies for representing women and negotiating the gender of the nation in an artistic environment that prioritized a virile image of Mexico. During the years when Izquierdo and Kahlo were active, the muralists and other artists who held similar views about art constructed national identity as male. While the two women occasionally portrayed men or children, they overwhelmingly represented women, creating strong female personages that counterbalanced the ubiquitous images of male heroes in Mexican art. Izquierdo and Kahlo developed distinct approaches to meeting the challenges of representing women as more central than other artists of their era.

Kahlo's self-portraits are the opposite of the master narratives of muralism. In her self-portraits she articulated her views in a first person singular voice, insisting on the subjective viewpoint of a specific woman. By accentuating the idiosyncrasies of her appearance (penetrating gaze, conjoined eyebrows, faint mustache) and the specific circumstances of her life (artist, wife of Rivera, childless woman, invalid) she stressed her singularity. The individuality of her face and the details of her personal narrative preclude reading her self-portraits as symbols of "Woman with the capital letter, the *representation* of an essence inherent in all women."[1] Kahlo's emphasis on her individuality was especially remarkable during a time when Siqueiros and others were relentlessly attacking bourgeois individualism.

Izquierdo took another tactic. She represented a range of women and children, primarily Mexican, mostly mestiza, some indigenous, a few of European descent, an occasional foreigner, and a score of images of herself.[2] Her strategy was to be inclusive.

Izquierdo and Kahlo represented themselves and other women in ways that sometimes affirmed and sometimes refuted the ideas of the dominant art movement in Mexico. Kahlo's many citations of Precolumbian culture fit seamlessly into mainstream ideas about Mexican art, especially as practiced by her husband, who created numerous idealized images of Precolumbian cultures. Kahlo utilized references to ancient Mexican culture to recount her story in a way that placed her within the Mesoamerican world view and thus within the trajectory of Mexican history. Izquierdo's depictions of altars for Viernes de Dolores also present positive images of women within the existing construction of *mexicanidad.*

The two artists frequently created images that questioned the construction of gender. Izquierdo's landscapes with indigenous granaries imply an association of women, abundance, maize, and land in a way that genders the nation as female, which was a radically different projection of national identity than was promulgated by the muralists. Nevertheless, Izquierdo conveyed her alternative vision with such subtlety and finesse that the paintings slipped gracefully into Mexican modernism without causing controversy.

In Izquierdo's extended series of female circus performers, she testified to the women's bravery, strength, balance, physical prowess, and power to command attention. These assets did not match conventional ideas of the time about the qualities of Mexican women, whose virtues were stereotypically thought to include self-sacrifice, submission, and modesty. In fact, the qualities required of a circus performer are remarkably similar to those present in a hero: courage, daring, strength, and charisma. Izquierdo upset established gender roles by repeatedly representing women circus performers with these attributes.

Izquierdo and Kahlo also resisted the spaces usually assigned to women artists. At the Departamento del Distrito Federal, Izquierdo intended to feature women in leading roles in ways that would have constructed the gender of the capital, and by extension the nation, as female. She was prevented from doing so by Rivera, Siqueiros, and others. Neither muralist would have publicly admitted to censoring someone else's art, but they censored her aesthetic and political vision under the guise of objecting to her lack of experience painting in fresco and the supposed inappropriateness of her style for muralism.

Kahlo took a dramatically different approach to challenging the spaces assigned to women artists in her still-life paintings. She employed the seemingly ladylike genre for a wide variety of purposes that included creating erotic art. Thus she converted the type of painting considered the most suitable for lady painters into a site that contested the conventions of gender and genre. During the quarter century in which she produced still-life paintings, she continually pushed at and expanded the boundaries of the art form.

Izquierdo's failed fight to carry out her mural commission and her spoken and written words about women's rights make it clear that women had not achieved full equality in Mexico. Nevertheless, based on the bodies of work that Kahlo and Izquierdo created and their related professional accomplishments (exhibitions, teaching, awards, and honors), it is clear that they achieved high levels of professional success. The challenges that Izquierdo, Kahlo, and other women artists encountered in Mexico were not greater than those that women artists faced in almost every country during the same period. As noted in the introduction, more Latin American women than North American women became well-known artists between 1915 and 1975.[3] Based on the number of women artists producing interesting work in Mexico, it appears that in the early and mid-twentieth century only Russia and Brazil provided more favorable environments for women artists.

Some of the challenges that Izquierdo, Kahlo, and their female colleagues faced were specific to Mexico. During the postrevolutionary period the Mexican art world had clear-cut hierarchies. The most famous and powerful artists—Rivera, Orozco, and Siqueiros—had established muralism as the measure of true artistic success. A by-product of the exalted status of muralism and the prevailing belief in the positive value of nationalism was the reinstatement of the old hierarchies of the Renaissance: history painting reigned, landscape and portraiture were respectable but less prestigious genres, and still-life painting was devalued.

While a few women managed to paint murals in provincial towns or in a dimly lit market in Mexico City, women were marginalized in the muralist movement. Muralism was a men's club, and the leaders of the club wanted as few new members of either gender as possible. As demonstrated in chapter 6, Rivera and Siquieros were ruthless about obtaining the best walls for themselves. In terms of opportunities for women artists in postrevolutionary Mexico, muralism was the glass ceiling.

According to Tibol, Kahlo was eager to work in fresco when she began painting, but Rivera advised her, "Your will has to lead you to your own expression."[4] In this version of the many entwined stories about their courtship and first conversations about art, Kahlo got the hint, began to paint images that Rivera considered suitable for her talents, and won his admiration and love. Except for diverting her away from muralism, Rivera supported her as an artist with enthusiasm, sincerity, and steadfastness. Even if he had not stifled her desire to paint frescoes, Kahlo's health would have precluded the hard physical labor and long hours necessary to paint monumental works. With the exception of *Moisés*, Kahlo's paintings are dramatically different in design from mural painting. Beginning with Juan O'Gorman in 1966, many people have noticed that *Moisés* looks like a miniature mural. O'Gorman believed that the monumental quality of this painting demonstrates that she could have been a great muralist.[5] *Moisés* was one of the three paintings Kahlo displayed in the national exhibition at the Palacio de Bellas Artes in 1946, and she was awarded a major national prize for the painting that year by a jury whose members included O'Gorman.[6] Kahlo painted *Moisés* the same year that Izquierdo embarked on her mural project for the Departamento del Distrito Federal. She won the prize at about the time that Izquierdo's commission was revoked. It seems unlikely that these events were entirely coincidental.

Women artists were accepted in Mexico, as long as they did not tread on the sacrosanct territory of muralism. The prestige of muralism and the gendering of the nation as male by the so-called Mexican School were salient features of the Mexican art world during the years in which Izquierdo and Kahlo were active. This was the artistic space within which they functioned, and they used a variety of tactics to turn the obstacles of this environment into opportunities.

While I have divided this book into five parts that address different themes, some of the ideas spill across these divisions. The issue of the hero, which I discussed in part one, crops up again in part three. In the introduction I quoted Kahlo's observation that the adulation of heroes is motivated by "fear of life and fear of death."[7] Izquierdo never made a comparable verbal statement about heroes, but her studies for the mural project at the Departamento del Distrito Federal contest the practice of always gendering the hero as male. She intended to break with this convention, which was one of the reasons she lost the commission. A little-known oil painting titled *La muerte del héroe* (Death of the

Hero), whose location is unknown, may provide additional information about Izquierdo's thoughts about heroes. The painting depicts a man, a child, and a dozen women gathered around the closed coffin of a fallen hero. In the foreground the figures gesture broadly toward the coffin or kneel in grief before it, while the seven women behind the casket clasp their hands in prayer, grimace, and implore the heavens. The facial expressions and body language are so exaggerated that the characters look like bad actors in a play. Izquierdo portrayed sorrow in earlier works, especially in her allegorical female nudes ca. 1933 to 1938, but never in such a gauche fashion. The catalogue to Izquierdo's retrospective dates *La muerte del héroe* as ca. 1945 and claims that it was part of the mural project, but the painting is an oil on canvas that was not published until 1952.[8] Rather than being part of the original project, I believe that this work was painted after 1946, when Izquierdo realized that she had lost the fight to create murals in the prestigious building on the Zócalo. In this painting she comments ironically on the exaggerated importance of the hero in Mexican art. *La muerte del héroe*, in my opinion, is the visual equivalent to Kahlo's disavowal of the cult of heroes.

Paradoxes

Several paradoxes emerge from this study. Izquierdo and Kahlo are the two women who forcefully and consistently challenged the dominant discourses of modern Mexican art in their work. They were also dramatically more successful than other Mexican women artists of the time in terms of their inclusion in important group exhibitions, the frequency with which major critics, art historians, and poets wrote about their art, the appeal of their work for collectors, and their work as teachers. Izquierdo's and Kahlo's imagery contributes to the rich diversity of modern art in Mexico. Despite Siqueiros's fervent belief that there was only one route in modern art, a significant part of the art-loving public wanted and still wants choices.

During Izquierdo's life, writers seemed unable to resist commenting on her indigenous appearance and the native component of her mestiza ancestry. This was true whether the writer was from Europe, the United States, or Mexico. Izquierdo did not seem to be bothered by this obsession with her ethnicity. In fact she considered Antonin Artaud, who believed that her paintings were "in communication with the true force of the Indian soul," to be one of the writers who best understood her work.[9] Yet during the first decade of her career she virtually ignored *mexicanidad* as it was construed by the so-called *escuela mexicana*. Instead she concurred with the ideas of the Contemporáneos, who wanted Mexican culture to be understood and appreciated as part of Western culture. Throughout the 1930s she created relatively few works that could be considered especially Mexican by the standards of the dominant art movement. In the 1940s she embarked on new subjects that fit within popular notions of *mexicanidad*, while continuing to pursue most of the same subjects that she had painted in the thirties. Most of her paintings with overtly Mexican themes, including the representations of indigenous granaries and ephemeral home altars, also function as vehicles for promoting a vision of Mexico that was less exclusively masculine.

Writers frequently commented on Kahlo's mestiza ancestry, although they did not make the kind of essentializing statements about her that were imposed on Izquierdo. But Kahlo assiduously asserted ties to Precolumbian and indigenous culture. She did this in ways that were obvious, such as wearing traditional Mexican clothing and including ancient artifacts from West Mexico in several paintings. And she did this with subtlety when she depicted an Aztec glyph on her *huipil* in two self-portraits in the early 1940s. Kahlo affirmed the nationalist agenda of the so-called Mexican School in ways that were personal and individualistic.

Izquierdo and Kahlo were modern and secular. They were the polar opposite of the traditional Mexican Catholic woman who would vote for a conservative political candidate on religious grounds, the stereotype that was used to justify blocking women's suffrage in 1939. Despite their secular lives and nontraditional ideas about religion, in different ways each artist created a significant number of works that convey spirituality. Izquierdo produced many more paintings about popular expressions of faith than have been individually discussed in this book. Her images of altars for Viernes de Dolores and other manifestations of devotion are ambiguous in their intent. They are positive images, but whether they are homages to Mexican folkways or to popular religiosity or to both is left to each viewer's imagination. What can be stated with certainty is that Izquierdo depicted images of folk Catholicism with greater frequency than most Mexican artists of the period and that women figure prominently in these images.

Kahlo used Christian and Mesoamerican iconography in her art in dramatically different ways. She employed Catholic symbolic visual language to present herself as if she were a Virgin, a saint, or a martyr. When she portrayed herself as a secular saint, she co-opted the power of Catholic symbolism to communicate with the Mexican people and, at the same time, undermine the authority of the church with irony. Her use of Precolumbian symbolism is more subtle and never ironic. She appropriated Precolumbian symbolism to valorize the ancient cultures of Mexico and to inscribe her story into the Mesoamerican worldview. This is one of the recurring themes in her art and an aspect of her art that has not been fully acknowledged until now.

Dolorosa

Izquierdo and Kahlo were very different painters who met the challenges of being a woman artist in modern Mexico in distinct ways, but they shared a special interest in the Dolorosa. The manner in which they employed references to her epitomize their similarities and differences. In *Mi nacimiento* of 1932 Kahlo portrayed a picture of a weeping Virgin of Sorrows hanging above the bed where she was born and where her mother died, fictitiously presented as if the two events occurred simultaneously. That same year she depicted herself crying in *Henry Ford Hospital* and *El aborto*, works about her miscarriage in Detroit. From this time onward she intermittently represented herself with tears. Kahlo is the Dolorosa.

Izquierdo's images of the Virgin of Sorrows are externalized rather than internalized. In her series of paintings of altars for the Virgin of Sorrows, Izquierdo portrayed her with a darker complexion than is normal for images of the Dolorosa, who is usually represented with fair skin. In Izquierdo's work the Dolorosa may be a fair mestiza, a dark mestiza, or an indigenous woman. Izquierdo's utilization of a range of skin tones representative of the women of Mexico suggests that she has nationalized the Virgin of Sorrows. For Izquierdo, the Dolorosa is associated with all the women of Mexico.

In 1946 Kahlo's major patron, Eduardo Morillo Safa, wrote from Venezuela to ask her to paint an image of an altar to the Virgin of Sorrows. She replied that she would paint the altar with little pots of green wheat and barley and recalled that her mother had set up this type of altar every year and that the altars were wonderful. She reported that she had already planted the chia and other seeds and promised to begin the painting as soon as she finished *Árbol de esperanza mantente firme* (Tree of Hope, Stand Firm) of 1946.[10] Despite her initial enthusiasm, she never represented an altar to the Virgin of Sorrows. Perhaps she determined that such an image was too traditionally Catholic for a Marxist to paint in an uncritical way. Or she may have decided not to paint a subject that Izquierdo had already preempted. Regardless of the reason, Kahlo did not fulfill a commission that would have reconfigured the way in which she employed the iconography of the Virgin of Sorrows.

Izquierdo's series of altars for Viernes de Dolores and Kahlo's long-standing identification with the Dolorosa are especially interesting because the Virgin of Guadalupe is a much more popular advocation of the Virgin in Mexico. Referencing the Virgin of Guadalupe would have been the expected choice for a twentieth-century Mexican artist. While we will probably never know all the reasons behind Izquierdo's and Kahlo's preference for the Dolorosa, it was probably in part because elements of pain were inherent in the gender issues that they addressed in their art.

Challenges

From the point of view of 1970s-style feminism, Kahlo's current international recognition and entry into popular culture is a phenomenal advance toward more egalitarian representations of women in the visual arts. From the point of view of contemporary feminist and Latin American scholarship, many of the publications and much of the media coverage that have encouraged her fame are problematic. To the degree to which Kahlo's international reputation is based on the merits of her work and appreciation of her paintings, the changes that have taken place in the art world and beyond are cause for celebration. Unfortunately, a significant part of Kahlo's fame is the product of the popular taste for soap opera, especially when it is dressed up in seemingly respectable trappings. *El superviviente* (1938) surfaced after a seventy-two-year absence. It is not a self-portrait and was originally described as symbolizing "the survival of Mexico in a shaky world."[11] But this did not stop the writer who penned the essay for Christie's auction catalogue from claiming that the painting was about her personal life. Although the author quotes the line that connects the painting to the political uncertainties of the time, he gives it no importance. Instead he brings up Rivera's affair with Kahlo's sister three years before the work was created; a separation, also three years before the piece was produced; Rivera's request for a divorce at an unspecified date; and alleged suicidal thoughts.[12] This tally of personal information is intentionally used to divert the reader away from interpreting the painting as political commentary, despite strong indications that the work is related to political and historical events in Mexico in the late 1930s. The tiny painting, which was never photographed prior to 2010, sold for over a million dollars.[13] To what extent have flamboyant fixations on Kahlo's personal life affected her popularity and the market for her art? More importantly, why are women artists still sometimes written about in the twenty-first century in ways that would be considered risible and unacceptable if applied to male artists?

Despite the vast literature about Kahlo, scholarly work still needs to be done on her art. Publications that provide insightful analyses of her paintings are still greatly outnumbered by less useful ones. Kahlo and her oeuvre need to be rethought and repositioned. The belief that she was a victim whose emotions flowed onto her canvases without her making intellectual decisions or inserting social critiques should be regarded as outdated, obtuse, and misogynistic. A wide range of methodologies similar in diversity to those that have been used in the study of Velázquez, Caravaggio, Cézanne, and Picasso must be employed.

The literature on Kahlo lacks at least one fundamental study. No one has written an in-depth scholarly study about the patronage of Eduardo Morillo Safa, who was Kahlo's major collector during her lifetime. Morillo Safa bought over thirty works by Kahlo, including many of the paintings upon which her reputation rests and ones that address taboo subjects and gender issues in bold and innovative ways: *Henry Ford Hospital* of 1932; *El aborto* (The Miscarriage) of 1932; *Unos cuantos piquetitos* (A Few Small Nips) of 1935; *Mi nana y yo* (My Nurse and I) of 1937; *El difunto Dimas Rosas* (The Deceased Demas Rosas) of 1937; *Raices* (Roots) of 1943; *Pensando en la muerte* (Thinking of Death) of 1943; *Flor de la vida* (Flower of Life) of 1943; *La columna rota* (The Broken Column) of 1944; *Autorretrato con changuito* (Self-Portrait with Monkey) of 1945; and *Árbol de la esperanza mantente firme* (Tree of Hope, Stand Firm) of 1946. In the mid-forties Kahlo portrayed every member of Morillo Safa's family either individually or in a double portrait, in the case of his wife and son. How did Kahlo become one of the most written about women artists of all time without anyone conducting a serious study of Morillo Safa's patronage?

Completely different challenges exist in the scholarship on Izquierdo. To date most of the texts have been overviews. Her work needs focused studies about the distinct themes and genres within her oeuvre. Her still-life paintings, which are spectacular and represent almost a quarter of her work, deserve an in-depth study. (This book deals only with a small part of them.) An exhibition of the art that Tamayo and Izquierdo created during the years when they shared a studio in the heart of the historic center of Mexico City has not yet taken place. While Olivier Debroise and María González have written about this topic, it is one thing to read about Izquierdo and Tamayo's shared visual language in texts with limited illustrations and something altogether different to see it played out with an abundance of prime examples of each artist's paintings and drawings.[14]

Remarkably little is known about the years between Izquierdo's departure from San Juan de los Lagos, when she was about six years old, and her enrollment in the Escuela Nacional de Bellas Artes in 1928. This lacuna of approximately twenty years is unacceptable. Basic information such as the date of her first marriage and whether it was to Cándido Posadas (as long believed) or to someone else (as asserted by Lozano) needs to be determined through archival research. Also missing are the dates when she studied at the Ateneo Fuente in Saltillo, the dates when she lived in Aguascalientes, Torreón, and Saltillo, and the dates and places of her three children's births. Although it is unlikely that more than a few basic facts can be culled from public records, whatever can be retrieved should be recovered in order to expand our knowledge of Izquierdo's life.

In early 2014 the *Archivo María Izquierdo del Museo de Arte Moderno* (María Izquierdo Archive of the Museum of Modern Art of Mexico City) was published. It contains short essays by Teresa Arcq and Gustavo Martínez, reprints of one text by Antonin Artaud and another by Pablo Neruda, facsimiles of most of Izquierdo's articles, reproductions of select correspondence, and the previously unpublished text of her radio speech "La mujer y el arte mexicano." The publication makes crucial primary sources available.[15]

The *Archivo María Izquierdo del Museo de Arte Moderno* does not contain María Izquierdo's memoirs, which once were part of the archive but disappeared before the Museo de Arte Moderno acquired the archive in 2005. The unpublished memoirs are fascinating but highly problematic. In 1953 a secretary recorded Izquierdo's memories of her early childhood, studies at the Escuela Nacional de Bellas Artes, and trip to New York. By 1953 Izquierdo had suffered at least two strokes and presumably acquired the secretary because she had lost the manual dexterity to write efficiently.[16] Aurora Posadas Izquierdo was not certain of the secretary's identity but thought that he may have been José Sendra.[17] The secretary made the mistake of not recording Izquierdo's own words or producing a manuscript that closely adhered to her exact words. The text is written in third person singular rather than first person singular. Although it covers the period from 1902 to 1934, it barely mentions Tamayo, who was her partner during her formative years as an artist. The manuscript contains some saccharine passages that are not credibly by Izquierdo, who never showed a trace of excessive sentimentality in her other writings.[18] Aurora Posadas Izquierdo stated that the secretary interpreted what her mother said "in a 'novelesque' fashion."[19] While Izquierdo's younger daughter generously shared the manuscript with some scholars, she did not want it to be published because of the secretary's unfortunate choice to use his own words rather than those of her mother.[20] Irrespective of its serious problems, the manuscript contains information that has not been published elsewhere, so it is of great interest to people who wish to know more about Izquierdo. If the memoirs are ever published, the text would require a substantial introductory essay that discusses the circumstances of its production and warns the reader about changes, missing information, the temporal limits, and the loss of Izquierdo's true voice.

Despite my suggestions about scholarship that still needs to be done for Izquierdo and Kahlo, I do not mean to imply that monographs about individual artists are the best way to write about art. Studying the work of more than one artist, especially discrete groups of closely related artists, facilitates better understanding of the artistic, social, political, and historical contexts in which art is created, circulated, and received.

The cult of celebrity, which pervades the fine arts as well as popular culture, promotes stars and superstars. The excessive focus on a few of the most famous artists creates a distorted vision of the history of an era. This is especially relevant for Kahlo and Izquierdo, who achieved similar professional status during their lives. That fact has been lost, especially outside of Mexico, by disproportionate attention on Kahlo. The problem of stardom is inextricably entwined with the excessive attention to the dramatic parts of artists' personal lives. Psychobiographical interpretations of art have removed the creators and their work from history, as Griselda Pollock has cogently argued.[21] The practice of equating the artist with his/her work, which is done with much greater frequency with female artists, banishes visual art to an ahistorical and apolitical realm. Margaret Lindauer observes that when a painting becomes synonymous with the painter "the artist is reduced to personal, psychological, and biological histories constructed parallel to, but separate from, social histories."[22] The related tendencies to focus on the superstars of the art world and to interpret art according to biography lead to a loss of social, political, and cultural history. This loss renders invisible the rich dynamics of the art world and the ways in which artists, writers, and other professionals exchange ideas and respond to each other on aesthetic and intellectual levels.

Izquierdo and Kahlo made conscious choices about the subjects, messages, and styles of their paintings. In addition to their thought-provoking oeuvres, they left verbal testimony of the importance of their minds. In 1950 Kahlo stated, "The most important part of the body is the brain."[23] That same year Izquierdo wrote, "You do not paint with your hands: the painting should be born in your soul, pass through your brain, and then your emotions must spill it onto a canvas, panel, or wall."[24]

Izquierdo and Kahlo probably had clearer ideas of the significance of their contributions to modern art than they publicly acknowledged. Rivera often said that Kahlo was a better painter than he was. Of course, he expected the listener to be amazed by such an outrageous claim and express disbelief, because his reputation overshadowed hers throughout their lifetimes. When he told the surrealist poet and painter Alice Rahon, who was a close friend of Kahlo, that his wife was the better painter, she replied, "Yes, she is." Later, when Rahon repeated the conversation to her friend, Kahlo laughed and said, "You must have hurt him terribly."[25] In the context of Izquierdo's radio presentation "La mujer y el arte mexicano," she asked, "Are not good women painters already arising everywhere, who even mark out new directions in art?"[26] Surely Izquierdo knew that she was among the contemporary women establishing new directions in art.

The bodies of work that Izquierdo and Kahlo created are integral and indispensable to modern Mexican art. Their work is as innovative and as fundamental to Mexican art as that of Orozco, Rivera, Siqueiros, and Tamayo. The nature of their innovations is different than those of Tamayo, who was primarily concerned with formal innovation,[27] and those of the muralists, whose concerns included monumentality, national identity, and political rhetoric. Izquierdo and Kahlo, in different ways, shared an interest in national identity but usually eschewed overt politics in favor of images that claimed interpretive power for themselves and other women. They responded to the challenges of their environment by creating images of women that were fundamentally different from the work of other artists. The two women achieved their place in Mexican art not by producing paintings that conformed to what was expected of women artists but by relentlessly challenging expectations with integrity, ingenuity, and wit.

NOTES

INTRODUCTION

1. The Mexican Revolution did not end abruptly at a precise date. Rebellions and uprising continued even after 1920.

2. Siqueiros and others, "Manifesto of the Technical Workers, Painters and Sculptors Union of Mexico," 461.

3. Siqueiros, *No hay más ruta que la nuestra*, 32, 33, 39, 40, 75, 94, 101, 110.

4. Ortner, "Is Female to Male as Nature Is to Culture?," 68–87.

5. Franco, *Plotting Women*, 102.

6. The avoidance of overt political messages in art is more typical of Izquierdo than of Kahlo. At the end of Kahlo's life, she painted *Marxismo dará salud a los enfermos* (Marxism Will Give Health to the Sick) of 1954 and an unfinished portrait of Joseph Stalin, both in the collection of the Museo Frida Kahlo. While Izquierdo usually eschewed politics, she belonged to LEAR (Liga de Escritores y Artistas Revolucionarios/League of Revolutionary Writers and Artists), which was founded in 1933.

7. Mulvey and Wollen, "Frida Kahlo and Tina Modotti," 13.

8. Barnitz, "Five Women Artists," 38.

9. For an excellent discussion of the representation of women in Mexico from the nineteenth century until the mid-twentieth century, see Zavala, *Becoming Modern, Becoming Tradition*.

10. Izquierdo and Villaseñor are the only women artists whose names are published in the catalogue to *Mexican Arts*, but they were probably not the only women whose work was included in the show. Hundreds of artisan objects were exhibited without their creators' names. Surely many of the anonymous artisans were women. *Mexican Arts*, 49, 52.

11. The biographical section of the catalogue includes short entries about Lola Álvarez Bravo, Rosa Rolando, and Isabel Villaseñor. The catalogue lists 155 works of art, but Charity Mewburn conservatively estimated that over one thousand objects were actually exhibited. Jacinto Quirarte believed that some three thousand works were shown. *Twenty Centuries of Mexican Art*, 160, 166, 184, and 189; Charity Mewburn, "Oil, Art, and Politics," 74; Jacinto Quirarte, "Mexican and Mexican American Artists in the United States," 69.

12. Manrique and del Conde, *Una mujer en el arte mexicano*, 111–112.

13. "Sí, señor Presidente, hay otro grupo que encabeza Carlos Ruano Llopis, pero no vale la pena y no se moleste usted en verlo."/"Y qué tal si los buenos resultan efectivamente los del grupo de Ruano Llopis?" Frida Kahlo, as cited in Manrique and del Conde, *Una mujer en el arte mexicano*, 113. Carlos Ruano Llopis (1878–1950) was a Spanish painter best known for his depictions of bullfights. After immigrating to Mexico ca. 1934, he also portrayed rodeos and *charros* (horsemen).

14. Ana Garduño, conversation with author, ca. 2010, Mexico City.

15. "Todos los gobiernos, y todos los presidentes de México, han estado interesados en el arte actual."/"Como instrumento de prestigio cultural y de orgullo presidencial." Inés Amor, as cited in Manrique and del Conde, *Una mujer en el arte mexicano*, 113.

16. Tibol, *Frida Kahlo*, 125.

17. José Clemente Orozco won the National Prize of Arts and Sciences. Additional prizes for painting were awarded to Kahlo, Dr. Atl (Gerardo Murillo), Julio Castellanos, and Francisco Goitia.

18. The cover of the small exhibition catalogue states: "You are invited to an exhibition of paintings by María Izquierdo, the first Mexican woman to show her work in this country." A copy of the exhibition catalogue is in the archives of the library of the Museum of Modern Art (MoMA), New York. I thank Sheelagh Bevan at the MoMA Library for sending me a scan of the catalogue.

19. Izquierdo was not the first Mexican woman to have a solo exhibition in Paris: that distinction goes to Rosario Cabrera, who exhibited at Chez M. M. Berheim-Jeune in Paris from December 14 to 24, 1925. Zurian, *Rosario Cabrera*, 57.

20. Prignitz-Poda, Grimberg, and Kettenmann, *Frida Kahlo.*

21. *María Izquierdo* (1988 exhibition catalogue).

22. Luis-Martín Lozano, conversation with author, June 15, 1996, Chicago.

23. Izquierdo, "Mi pintura," 25.

24. Cándido Posadas contributed to the support of Izquierdo and their children after Posadas and Izquierdo were divorced. Later, when the children were in their teens and twenties, Izquierdo married the Chilean painter Raúl Uribe. Little evidence remains of Uribe's painting career, which suggests that Izquierdo's work sold much better than his and was of far greater interest to critics.

25. Héctor Xavier, interview with author, July 11, 1986, Mexico City.

26. Izquierdo made her first published comment on Kahlo in 1942 after Rivera wrote an article in which he praised his wife's work and claimed that Izquierdo and Tamayo belonged to a group of painters that suffered from "Picassitis" and "Miroquiricosis," implying that their work was insufficiently Mexican and derivative of European modernism. Izquierdo refuted Rivera's accusation about her work after first expressing her admiration for Kahlo's work: "Diego's wife deserves [his] praise and much more. Her painting is very Mexican, her technique is perfect, and her style is very personal" (La esposa de Diego merece esos elogios y muchos más. Su pintura es muy mexicana, su técnica perfecta y su estilo personalísimo). María Izquierdo, cited in "Avansadilla."

In 1947 Izquierdo denounced Kahlo's teaching in her article "María Izquierdo vs. los tres grandes." She criticized the recent establishment of a three-member mural commission (Rivera, Orozco, and Siqueiros) that had the power to approve all mural commissions in Mexico. Izquierdo alleged that they would take all the best commissions for themselves. But if some insignificant little school or barrio market should be left over they would consider giving it to "some loyal disciple of that fraud named Frida Khalo [*sic*] . . . one of those students who, by having valiantly suffered her diet of drills and hopes, will have acquired the right to dream of being immortalized in some Freudian junk, and in some poor neighborhood's modest temple of knowledge" (algún discípulo fiel de ese fraude que se llama Frida Khalo [*sic*], uno de esos alumnos que, por haber sufrido valientemente su dieta de planillas y esperanzas, tendrá adquirido el derecho a soñar que se inmortaliza en algún mamarracho freudiano, y en algún modesto templo del saber de barriada). María Izquierdo, "María Izquierdo vs. los tres grandes."

In 1953 Izquierdo told Elena Poniatowska which Mexican painters she most admired: Orozco headed the list, followed by Tamayo and Soriano. She then asserted: "Of my female contemporaries, Frida Kahlo and Isabel Villaseñor are the only real Mexicans in their work" (De mis contemporáneas, Frida Kahlo e Isabel Villaseñor son las únicas verdaderamente mexicanas en su obra). Poniatowska, "Opina María Izquierdo."

27. Catha Paquette, personal communication, April 2013.

28. "La llamada escuela mexicana" and "lo que entonces se conocía de escuela mexicana de pintura." Ana Garduño, personal conversation, August 5, 2013, Mexico City.

29. Siqueiros and others, "Manifesto of the Technical Workers, Painters and Sculptors Union of Mexico," 461 (emphasis in the original).

30. Rochfort, *Mexican Muralists*, 33–50.

31. For an excellent history of the representations of indigenous peoples and Precolumbian culture in nineteenth-century Mexican art, see Widdifield, *The Embodiment of the National in Late Nineteenth-Century Mexican Painting.*

32. See Betty Ann Brown, "The Past Idealized: Diego Rivera's Use of Pre-Columbian Imagery," in *Diego Rivera: A Retrospective*, 139–155.

33. Siqueiros and others, "Manifesto of the Technical Workers, Painters and Sculptors Union of Mexico," 461.

34. In 1921 the painters Dr. Atl, Jorge Enciso, and Roberto Montenegro organized a landmark exhibition of Mexican folk art. Dr. Atl's book *Las artes populares en México* (Folk Art in Mexico) was published the following year.

35. One notable exception is José Clemente Orozco, who was extremely critical of folkloric elements.

36. Murals are collective because the principal painter employs assistants.

37. Rivera, *Arte y política*, 27.

38. Coffey, "Angels and Prostitutes," 207.

39. Zavala, *Becoming Modern, Becoming Tradition*, 199.

40. The *soldaderas* cooked, nursed, and did laundry for the soldiers, and some of them fought. In murals created during the postrevolutionary period the *soldaderas* are almost always represented as camp followers, not soldiers.

41. Franco, *Plotting Women*, 106.

42. Coffey, "Angeles and Prostitutes," 195–198.

43. One exception to the construction of national identity as masculine is José Clemente Orozco's *Alegoría de México* (Allegory of Mexico) of 1940 in the Gabino Ortiz Library in Jiquilpan, Michoacán. The central image of the mural is a woman riding a jaguar across a thicket of nopal cactuses. Above her a serpent coils around an eagle, strangling it in a vicelike grip. Orozco's image of a serpent strangling an eagle is a warning of mortal danger to the nation. (The image at the center of the Mexican flag is an eagle with a serpent in its talons.)

Desmond Rochfort writes that the mural, which was painted at the beginning of World War II, "seems to convey the idea of an independent Mexico constantly on guard against unspecified forces, that might threaten its integrity." One possible explanation for the presence of a female figure as the personification of Mexico is that Orozco wanted to emphasize the nation's vulnerability and thus chose not to use a male hero. Rochfort, *Mexican Muralists*, 162–164.

44. "Lo que quise expresar más intensa y *claramente*, fué que la razón por la que los gentes necesitan inventar o imaginarse *héroes* y *dioses* es el puro MIEDO. Miedo a la vida y miedo a la *muerte*" (emphasis in original)/"Como Moisés, ha habido y habrá gran cantidad de 'copetones,' transformadores de religiones y de sociedades humanas. Se puede decir que ellos son una especie de *mensajeros* entre la gente que manejan y los 'dioses' inventados por ellos, para poder manejarla" (emphasis in original). Kahlo, "Hablando de un cuadro mío," 71.

45. Unlike the rest of Kahlo's work, *Moisés* presents a panoramic vision of history; although it is modest in size (20 × 37 inches), the composition resembles that of a mural.

46. In 1931 Kahlo painted *Retrato de Luther Burbank* (Portrait of Luther Burbank), which employs the surrealist strategy of juxtaposing unexpected elements. Around 1933 she collaborated with Lucienne Bloch and Diego Rivera on exquisite corpse drawings, in the surrealist game in which each participant adds to a collective drawing without seeing the others' contributions.

47. In Kahlo's letters to Nickolas Muray she referred to the Parisian gallery as Pierre Colle, but the catalogue to the exhibition identifies it as Renou & Colle. *Mexique*, exhibition catalogue (Paris: Renou & Colle, 1939).

48. Frida Kahlo, letter to Nickolas Muray of February 16, 1939, in Kahlo, *Escrituras*, 171.

49. Ramírez summarizing the ideas of Charles Merewether, who is drawing on the work of Alejo Carpentier, in "Beyond 'the Fantastic,'" 236.

50. "Mexican Autobiography," 90.

51. Kahlo was away from Mexico City for several months in late 1938 and early 1939 while she was exhibiting her work at the Julien Levy Gallery in New York and in the *Mexique* exhibition at the Renou & Colle gallery in Paris.

52. Rivera and Breton (signed by Rivera and Breton but actually written by Trotsky), "Manifesto: Towards a Free Revolutionary Art." According to the chronology in *Diego Rivera*, Trotsky was the sole author. Scholars specializing in the work of André Breton give him credit as the co-writer. David Craven believed that all three men collaborated. *Diego Rivera*, 96; Craven, *Diego Rivera as Epic Modernist*, 148.

53. The language that Trotsky, Rivera, and Breton shared was French. There is no record of Kahlo's participation, but she must have been present during some of the conversations. Although Kahlo did not speak French, she no doubt would have learned about the ideas being discussed prior to the publication of the manifesto. Trotsky surely expressed his ideas about art during the year before Breton arrived in Mexico.

54. Karl Marx, as cited in Rivera and Breton, "Manifesto," 51.

55. Rivera and Breton, "Manifesto," 51.

56. Ibid., 53.

57. The shared studio on the rooftop was not a penthouse. Before Tamayo and Izquierdo used it as a studio, it was employed as servants' quarters. Aurora Posadas Izquierdo, author's interview, December 5, 1997.

58. Gabriel García Maroto, as cited in Zavala, *Becoming Modern, Becoming Tradition*, 208.

59. Zavala, *Becoming Modern, Becoming Tradition*, 208.

60. According to Guillermo Sheridan, 46 percent of the poetry published in *Contemporáneos* was written by members of the group and 75 percent was by Mexican authors. Sheridan, *Índices de "Contemporáneos,"* 10.

61. Robin Greeley alternately considers Samuel Ramos tangentially affiliated with the Contemporáneos and a full-fledged member, but this is an eccentric interpretation. Guillermo Sheridan and other scholars do not consider Ramos one of the Contemporáneos. Robin Adèle Greeley, "Nietzsche contra Marx in Mexico: The Contemporáneos, Muralism, and Debates over 'Revolutionary' Art in 1930s Mexico," in *Mexican Muralism*, ed. Anreus, Greeley, and Folgarait, 155, 166; Sheridan, *Los Contemporáneos ayer*.

62. Cordero Reiman, "Appropriation, Invention, and Irony," 173.

63. Rufino Tamayo, as cited in Zavala, *Becoming Modern, Becoming Tradition*, 208.

64. Oropesa, *The Contemporáneos Group*, xiii, 69–93.

65. Greeley, "Nietzsche contra Marx in Mexico," 148–173.

66. Studies on imagery in the poetry of the Contemporáneos and on Villaurrutia's drawings have been published. See essays by Elisa García Barragán, Vicente Quiarte, Miguel Ángel Flores, Enrique Franco Calvo, and Teresa del Conde in *Los Contemporáneos en el laberinto de la critica*, ed. Olea Franco and Stanton.

67. "Óleos de María Izquierdo."

68. For example, when Izquierdo held an exhibition titled *17 acuarelas* (17 Watercolors) in 1933, Jorge Cuesta and Celestino Gorostiza wrote essays for the catalogue. Celestino Gorostiza also gave a gallery talk about her work on the evening the exhibition closed, and his brother, José Gorostiza, spoke about her work at the opening. Salvador Novo, Bernardo Ortiz de Montellano, Rufino Tamayo, and Carlos Mérida attended the opening.

69. Zavala, "A Chronicle in Light and Shadow," 20.

70. This is a slightly modified version of a list that María González included in her dissertation. González, "The Art of María Izquierdo," 41.

71. After 1938 Izquierdo depicted nudes less frequently.

72. Izquierdo created almost as many (or more?) still lifes as circus scenes, but without a catalogue raisonné it is impossible to establish the exact number of each genre.

73. "Huyo de caer en temas anecdóticos, folklóricos y políticos porque dichos temas no tienen ni fuerza plástica ni poética." María Izquierdo, in *45 autorretratos de pintores mexicanos*, 90.

74. "Deseo lograr en [mi pintura], personalidad, calidad pictórica, mexicanismo (sin caer en el mexican curios), perfección técnica (sin descender al virtuosismo frío, preciso), unidad entre línea y el color, entre el dibujo y la materia colorística, pretendo también expresar en temas sencillos y sentidos, la humana y misteriosa poesía de mi país, ambicionó encontrar la luz y la sombra, el misterio de 'lo mexicano' en tono exacto que lo encontraron: Silvestre Revueltas en música; López Velarde en poesía; Guadalupe Posada en el grabado; los pintores de Bonampak en sus frescos, los arquitectos y escultores mayas, aztecas, totonacas, en sus obras imponderables y por ultimo mirar larga y rotundamente el rojo tezontle de la piedra mexicana, descubrir su misterio cromático, escuchar su mensaje, exprimir su color y en fin, esperar a que se produzca el milagro que algo de su esencia y de su rojo jugo se impregne en mis pinceles y como besos queden en mi cuadros." Izquierdo, "Mi pintura," 27–28.

75. Rufino Tamayo, "A Commentary by the Artist," in Tamayo and Lynch, *Tamayo*, 2.

76. Zavala, "María Izquierdo," 237.

77. The collection that Tamayo donated to the people of Mexico in 1981 represents modern and contemporary art from the United States with works by Willem de Kooning, Robert Motherwell, Louise Nevelson, Isamu Noguchi, Mark Rothko, and Andy Warhol. It contains modern and contemporary South American art by Carlos Cruz-Diez, Wifredo Lam, Julio Le Parc, Roberto Matta, and Fernando de Szyszlo. Mexican art is represented with works by Rufino Tamayo, Lilia Carrillo, José Luis Cuevas, Vicente Rojo, and Francisco Toledo. Rufino and Olga Tamayo donated additional pieces to the museum at a later date. *Maestros del arte contemporáneo en la colección del Museo Rufino Tamayo*.

78. Riding, "New Tamayo Museum."

79. Tamayo, as cited in ibid.

80. "El ridículo 'charro' y la insulsa 'china poblana.'" Orozco, as cited in *Facturas y manufacturas de la identidad*, unnumbered page. *China poblana* refers to the women of Puebla who wore a regional style of clothing. Countless legends surround the origin of the clothing.

81. Greeley, "Nietzsche contra Marx in Mexico," 149, 157.

82. "Yo era muy hipócrita, entonces yo pertenecía a todos los grupos. A veces no podía dormir de remordimientos. ¡Qué horror! Qué hipócrita soy, porque yo le decía una cosa a María Izquierdo y otra a Frida Kahlo." Juan Soriano, "Seminar with Juan Soriano," University of Texas at Austin, April 14, 1994.

83. Zavala, "A Chronicle in Light and Shadow," 20; *María Izquierdo* (1988 exhibition catalogue), 362, 363, 367.

84. Jaime Torres Bodet was the director of the Secretaría de Educación Pública from 1943 to 1946. At various times Celestino Gorostiza, José Gorostiza, and Carlos Pellicer were in charge of the Department of Fine Arts in the Secretaría de Educación Pública. Celestino Gorostiza served as the general director of the Instituto Nacional de Bellas Artes from 1958 to 1964. Ana Garduño, personal communication, November 5, 2012.

85. Ana Garduño, personal communication, December 18, 2013.

86. For an insightful discussion of the pivotal role of Inés Amor and the Galería de Arte Mexicano in Mexico and in the representation of Mexican art internationally, see Garduño, *Inés Amor*.

87. In one of the many contradictions that contribute to the complexity of modern Mexican art, María Izquierdo was a member of LEAR.

88. Rivera, "Antonio Ruiz," 251.

89. Hayden Herrera, "Frida Kahlo: Her Life, Her Art" (PhD diss., City University of New York, 1981).

90. Joan Borsa, "Frida Kahlo: Marginalization and the Critical Female Subject," 26.

91. Ibid., 26–27 (emphasis in the original).

92. Bergman-Carton, "Like an Artist," 36, 37.

93. Ibid., 36.

94. Ibid., 37.

95. Lindauer, *Devouring Frida*, 152.

96. Griselda Pollock, "Artists, Mythologies and Media," *Screen* 21 (1980): 96, cited in ibid., 151.

97. Lindauer, *Devouring Frida*, 151.

98. Judy Chicago, in Chicago with Borzello, *Frida Kahlo*, 11 (emphasis in the original), 15.

99. Kahlo, *The Diary of Frida Kahlo*.

100. Carlos Phillips, "Presentación," in *Frida Kahlo: Sus fotos*, edited by Pablo Ortiz Monasterio (Mexico City: Editorial RM, 2010), 7.

101. *Frida Kahlo: Sus fotos*, edited by Ortiz Monasterio.

102. Ortiz Monasterio, "Introduction," in *Frida Kahlo: Sus fotos*, 20. For an example of Ortiz Monasterio's assertion that many photographs in the Kahlo archives relate to her paintings, see the photograph of the Precolumbian ceramic figure of a dog (fig. 40) and the representation of the same ceramic figure in her *Still Life* of 1951 (fig. 39).

103. From the website of Princeton Architectural Press, http://www.papress.com/html/book.details.page.tpl?isbn=9781568988306; Barbara Levine and Stephen Jaycox, *Finding Frida Kahlo* (New York: Princeton Architectural Press, 2009).

104. The art historians who have expressed convictions that these objects were not created by Frida Kahlo include Teresa del Conde, Hayden Herrera, James Oles, and Raquel Tibol. The gallery directors include Mariana Pérez Amor and Alejandra Reygadas de Yturbe of the Galería de Arte Mexicano in Mexico City and Mary-Anne Martin of Mary-Anne Martin/Fine Arts in New York.

105. Mary-Anne Martin, as cited in Kaufman, "Forthcoming Frida Kahlo Book Denounced as Fake."

106. "Están escritas en un lenguaje prostibulario, soez y burdo, que no hay que confundir con el lenguaje popular y pícaro de Frida, un lenguaje con gracia y conveniencia." Raquel Tibol, as cited in García Palafox in "Las dos Fridas," 54 (translated by Debra Nagao).

107. Oles, "Finding Frida," 19.

108. This type of privately published book can sometimes be acquired through a specialized book dealer or very special bookstore such as the Libreria Madero in Mexico City. Two thousand copies of *María Izquierdo* were published by the Casa de Bolsa Cremi. According to the database WorldCat, only seven copies are found in libraries: two in Mexico and five in the United States.

109. The catalogue contains essays by Fernando Gamboa, José Pierre, Olivier Debroise, Sylvia Navarrete, and Lourdes Andrade. *María Izquierdo* (1988 exhibition catalogue).

110. The catalogue contains essays by Elizabeth Ferrer, Olivier Debroise, and Elena Poniatowska. Americas Society Art Gallery, *The True Poetry*.

111. Greeley, "Painting Mexican Identities," 57.

112. Lozano, *María Izquierdo*.

113. Aurora Posadas Izquierdo and Rosenda López Posadas, author's interview, March 20, 1995, Naucalpan.

114. Lozano's source of information is Izquierdo's younger daughter, Aurora Posadas Izquierdo. Lozano, *María Izquierdo*, 17. Not everyone in the Izquierdo family agrees on this topic. Izquierdo's elder daughter, Amparo Posadas de Carmona, claims that her mother's first husband was Cándido Posadas, who was a military man during the Mexican Revolution and a journalist after the war. Amparo Posadas de Carmona, author's interview, León, Guanajuato, December 28, 2003.

115. "Por razones nunca confesadas pero fáciles de comprender, María Izquierdo escapó de aquella relación para establecer vínculos sentimentales con un periodista, Cándido Posadas." Lozano, *María Izquierdo*, 17.

116. Adriana Zavala, "María Izquierdo," in Vaughan and Lewis, *The Eagle and the Virgin*, 72, 74.

117. Zavala, *Becoming Modern, Becoming Tradition*. Chapter 5, "*Desnudas, Amazonas*, and *Tehuanas*," discusses the art of Izquierdo and to a lesser extent her contemporaries Tamayo, Castellanos, and Kahlo in the 1930s.

118. For a critique of biographical interpretations of Izquierdo's work, see Viscoli, "The Revolution of María Izquierdo," 2–3.

119. Antonin Artaud, "Le Mexique et l'espirit primitif," *L'Amour de l'Art* 8 (October 1937), as cited in Tarver, "Issues of Otherness and Identity in the Works of Izquierdo, Kahlo, Artaud, and Breton," 4.

120. Antonin Artaud, "La peinture de María Izquierdo," *Revista de Revistas* (Mexico City), August 23, 1936, no pagination, as cited by Tarver in "Issues of Otherness and Identity in the Works of Izquierdo, Kahlo, Artaud, and Breton," 4, 24.

121. Tarver, "Issues of Otherness and Identity in the Works of Izquierdo, Kahlo, Artaud, and Breton," 8.

122. Rafael Solana, as cited in Zavala, *Becoming Modern, Becoming Tradition*, 205.

123. Viscoli, "The Revolution of María Izquierdo," 4.

124. Paz, "María Izquierdo," 264, 249.

125. Castells, *The Power of Identity*, 175–202.

126. Herrera, *Frida*, 19.

127. As an adolescent Kahlo watched Rivera paint *La Creación* (Creation) of 1922–1923 in the Anfiteatro Bolívar (Bolívar Amphitheater) of the Escuela Nacional Preparatoria. The stories about her teasing him at that time are an important component of the mythology surrounding "Frida" and "Diego."

128. Herrera, *Frida*, 87.

129. Ibid., 86–87.

130. Kahlo, as cited in ibid., 87. Herrara cites two sources for this passage: Bambi [Ana Cecilia Treviño], "Frida Kahlo es una mitád"; and Antonio Rodríguez, "Frida Kahlo, Expresionista de su Yo Interno," 68.

131. Rivera, as cited by Kahlo in Herrera, *Frida*, 87.

132. "Yo tenía una inquietud tremenda por pintar al fresco. Le mostré a Diego los trabajos que había hecho y me dijo: 'Su voluntad tiene que llevarla a su propia expresión.' Entonces empecé a pintar cosas que le gustaron. Desde entonces me admira, me quiere." Tibol, *Frida Kahlo*, 49.

133. Rivera with March, *Diego Rivera*, 170, 171.

134. Herrera, *Frida*, 95.

135. Frida Kahlo to Rafael Lozano, as cited in Herrera, *Frida*, 95.

136. Frida Kahlo to Mario Monteforte Toledo, as cited in Grimberg, *Frida Kahlo*, 20.

137. Rivera, "María Izquierdo."

138. In 1953, two years before her death, Izquierdo recounted to a secretary parts of her childhood, studies at the Escuela Nacional de Bellas Artes, and early career. Although the resulting unpublished manuscript has sometimes been referred to as an autobiography, it is written

in the third person, revealing that the secretary did not transcribe Izquierdo's exact words. The manuscript was in the María Izquierdo Archive when it belonged to Aurora Posadas Izquierdo. In July 2005 the archive was acquired by the Museo de Arte Moderno in Mexico City but arrived without this manuscript. I refer to it here as "María Izquierdo Memoirs." The page numbers begin again with each chapter, so the chapter number is included along with the page number in citations. "María Izquierdo Memoirs," chapter 3, pp. 3–4, and chapter 4, pp. 2–4. In 1918, when Rosario Cabrera was studying with notable success at the art school, she experienced a problem with hostility from male students. Francisco Días de León, Gabriel Fernández Ledesma, and Enrique A. Ugarte were suspended for eight days because they committed unspecified infractions against her. Zurian, *Rosario Cabrera*, 56.

139. *Diego Rivera*, 71.

140. "Creo que las recomendaciones que le habrá hecho Tamayo . . . fueron muy fructíferas para el arte de María Izquierdo. La relación de maestro-alumna en cuatro años de disciplinado trabajo . . . resultó muy positiva. Hay quien dice que fue al revés, que María enseñó e influyó en Tamayo, lo cual es absurdo, porque para entonces Tamayo era ya un pintor hecho y derecho." Fernando Gamboa, "María Izquierdo: Recuerdos," in *María Izquierdo* (1988 exhibition catalogue), 15.

141. "María Izquierdo, indígena absoluta, con el sentido del color innato de su raza . . . empezó a enseñar a Tamayo un lenguaje distinto, una manera de pintar distinto. El dibujo era sencillo, la composición, lo más simple posible, el color tomado al azar de las tierras ocres y sienas del paisaje mexicano, con los festivos verdes y azules de las pequeñas casas pueblerinas. La textura, ¡qué se puede decir de la textura! María pintaba con su sangre india en la punta del pincel y fue de allí de donde emergió Tamayo superando a todos sus compañeros y haciendo de cada etapa de su pintura la gloria del buen arte." Inés Amor, as cited in Manrique and del Conde, *Una mujer en el arte mexicano*, 66–67.

142. Manrique and del Conde, *Una mujer en el arte mexicano*, 45, 67.

143. Tamayo had a solo exhibition at the Art Center in New York from November 7 to 26, 1927, and knew the gallery director, Frances Flynn Paine. It seems virtually certain that he helped to arrange Izquierdo's exhibition.

PART ONE: THE PROBLEM OF THE HERO

1. Zavala, *Becoming Modern, Becoming Tradition*, 7.
2. Ibid., 12.
3. Franco, *Plotting Women*, 101.

CHAPTER 1: WOMEN ON THE WIRE

1. Franco, *Plotting Women*, xxi, 101, 102, 131, 133, 145.

2. Izquierdo's circus paintings range from about 26 × 21 cm (10 1/14 × 8 1/4 inches) to around 41 × 61 cm (16 1/8 × 24 inches). All of the smaller paintings are in watercolor or gouache, her usual media for this subject. She created her largest paintings of the circus in oil on canvas in 1945.

3. Walking a slack rope is more difficult than walking a tightrope. Rope walker and juggler Rafael Vázquez of the Circo Vázquez Hermanos en Tres Pistas (Vázquez Brothers Three-Ring Circus) observes, "It is much more difficult to walk on a wire when it is slack, because when you step the wire moves. . . . On the other hand, when the wire is tight, it is practically in the same place" (Es mucho más difícil caminar sobre la cuerda cuando está floja porque tu pisas y la cuerda se mueve. . . . En cambio, cuando la cuerda está dura está prácticamente casi en el mismo lugar). Rafael Vázquez, interview with Anitza Rodríguez and author, August 14, 2009, Tijuana.

4. Peta Tait has documented numerous examples of cross-dressing and gender bending in trapeze acts in Europe, the United States, and Australia. Tait, *Circus Bodies*, 66–89.

5. In addition to Izquierdo's depictions of circus scenes, she also incorporated images of clowns in a few still-life paintings and rural scenes, including *Mantel rojo* (Red Tablecloth) of 1940, *Trigo crecido* (Sprouted Wheat) of 1940, *Huachinango* (Red Snapper) of 1943, and *Alacena con paloma* (Cupboard with Dove) of 1954. In *Huachinango* a whiteface clown's mask with highly rouged cheeks lies horizontally on a table next to a red snapper; the mask and the fish each have one unseeing eye staring upward, creating a visual pun between the similarly colored mask and fish. In *Alacena con paloma* a small figure of a clown is one of two dozen artisan objects, knickknacks, and mementos that line the shelves of the cupboard. In her paintings of cupboards, Izquierdo depicted real objects that she owned; presumably each had personal associations. Several of the artisan objects that Izquierdo depicted in her cupboards and still-life paintings still belong to family members.

6. Olivier Debroise, "María Izquierdo," in *María Izquierdo* (1988 exhibition catalogue), 27–57, 41.

7. Zavala, "María Izquierdo," 237.

8. González and Gallegos, "María Izquierdo: Images of Women in the Circus," 140.

9. Ibid., 138, 144. González also collaborated with Jesse Sloan in an article titled "María Izquierdo: Images of the Circus," in which they provide information about the history of the circus in Mexico and discuss the first miracle of the Virgin of San Juan de los Lagos in relation to Izquierdo's paintings. González and Sloan develop the idea of the new role of women exemplified by the female circus performers and propose that these paintings represent an "otherworld" reserved for members of the closely knit circus families that is "denied to viewers." They claim that Izquierdo's circus paintings usually depict "the performers doing their acts in empty circus arenas" and ask if "María knew these actors well enough to attend and document rehearsals?" González and Sloan, "María Izquierdo," 238, 242.

I concur with the majority of assertions by González and her collaborators about Izquierdo's paintings of the circus, but on some issues I disagree. González and Sloan declare that Izquierdo's work represents performances in "empty circus arenas" and empty theaters, a claim that is not supported by the images. While Izquierdo only rarely portrayed the audience, her depictions of empty benches are equally unusual. The only paintings in which Izquierdo represented empty benches are *El circo* (The Circus) of 1939 and *Perritos* (Little Dogs) of 1939; in both cases the empty benches are at the periphery of the composition. She depicted an audience in *En el circo* (At the Circus) of 1939 and *El baile del oso* (The Dance of the Bear) of 1940. She produced over fifty circus paintings, so images that explicitly show an audience or the lack of an audience are highly unusual in her oeuvre.

Another point of disagreement is with González and Gallegos's assertion that female circus performers "were not dependent on any man" (140). In the same chapter they establish that Mexican circuses were family-run businesses. (This remains largely true.) Women circus performers were parts of teams; as such, they—as well as their male relatives and other colleagues—depended on the work, skill, and cooperation of everyone in the troupe.

I also disagree with González and Gallegos about the social standing of the *vedette* in Mexico. Citing the U.S. anthropologist Peter C. Haney, they claim that the *vedette*, a "Mexican singer-dancer stage idol," was both "respectable and sexually alluring." During Izquierdo's life, any paid work that a woman did outside the home was considered controversial by many Mexicans, and this was especially true of work related to the theater and entertainment. In 1992 the Mexican actress Clementina Otero recalled that she never could have become an actress if her father had not been traveling in Europe in 1928 when (at the age of seventeen) she joined the cast of the Teatro de Ulises, the vanguard theater directed by Salvador Novo and Xavier Villaurrutia. Otero unequivocally asserted: "At that time, no [respectable] young lady could be in the theater" (En esa época, ninguna señorita podía estar en el teatro). Clementina Otero, cited in "Los Contemporáneos en familia," in *Los Contemporáneos en el laberinto de la crítica*, ed. Olea Franco and Stanton, 270.

10. González and Gallegos, "María Izquierdo," 144.

11. "Hacía amistad con las bailarinas, con los payasos, con los malabaristas, con los malabaristas que hacen suertes también, hacía amistad con todos." Aurora Posadas Izquierdo, author's interview, January 6, 2004, Naucalpan.

12. "Le gustaba todo lo popular, lo mexicano directo: las carpas, las canciones, las ferias, los árboles, las frutas, las cantinas, los rincones de los pueblos, los circos que conforman su pintura, que es muy naif, y se nutre con los temas de la tierra. . . . El goce que María tenía de lo popular no era de espectadora, sino casi parecía estar dentro, como un elemento más de lo popular: no sólo le gustaban las carpas, sino que tenía un montón de amigos carperos y cancioneros." Álvarez Bravo, *Lola Álvarez Bravo*, 104.

13. "No es casual o folklórica, como en los casos de Seurat o de Degas, que visitaban circos o estudios de danza con las sola intención de pintarlos. María Izquierdo pinta cosas y seres que le son cercanos." Debroise, *Figuras en el trópico*, 156.

14. Debroise, "María Izquierdo," 40.

At the time Izquierdo began depicting the circus in 1932, or possibly 1931, El Circo Beas Modelo (Beas Modelo Circus) was continually working in and around Mexico City in an effort to rebuild the company after a catastrophic explosion and fire devastated what had once been a large traveling circus. On November 26, 1930, El Circo Beas Modelo suffered one of the worst accidents in the history of the Mexican circus. While the circus was traveling by train from Aguascalientes to Guadalajara, a derailed train car collided with a tank car filled with gasoline, which exploded and set fire to ten circus cars. Because the accident occurred twenty kilometers from the nearest town, little could be done to put out the raging fire. Twenty-eight members of the circus were killed, thirty members were injured, most of the animals died, and the tent and equipment were destroyed. The survivors stayed in the nearest town, Irapuato, for several months while the injured were cared for. From 1931 to 1933 El Circo Beas Modelo worked in and around Mexico City in order to avoid transportation costs while the circus rebuilt itself. In mid-1933 the circus participated in the Feria Nacionalista (Nationalist Fair) and set up a big show in a tent next to the Zócalo of Mexico City. In 1933 Izquierdo and her children lived on Santo Domingo Plaza, which put her within walking distance of the circus. Revolledo Cárdenas, *La fabulosa historia del circo en México*, 363–368; *María Izquierdo* (1988 exhibition catalogue), 302.

15. Debroise, *Figuras en el trópico*, 155–157; Gónzalez and Gallegos, "María Izquierdo: Images of Women in the Circus," 138–139.

16. "El bohemio y mágico mundo de los cirqueros en su más íntimo aspecto." María Izquierdo Memoirs, chapter 1, p. 1.

17. Aurora Posadas Izquierdo, author's interview, March 20, 1995, Naucalpan.

18. Raskob, "María Izquierdo," 288.

19. Rivera with March, *My Art, My Life*, 20–21.

20. "Michelagnolo [*sic*] was put out to nurse by [his father] Lodovico in that village with the wife of a stone-cutter: wherefore the same Michelagnolo, discoursing once with Vasari, said to him jestingly, 'Giorgio, if I have anything of the good in my brain, it has come from my being born in the pure air of your country of Arezzo, even as I also sucked in with my nurse's milk the chisels and hammer with which I make my figures.'" Vasari, *The Lives of the Most Excellent Painters, Sculptors, and Architects*, 341.

21. Santoscoy, *Historia de Nuestra Señora de San Juan de los Lagos*, 23–24.

22. The paintings are in the same horizontal format and of the same size (approximately 8 1/2 × 6 feet), but significant stylistic differences indicate that they were not painted by the same artist. The information about the dates of the paintings according to local tradition comes from Martín González Figueroa, the librarian at the Biblioteca Dr. Pedro de Alba in San Juan de los Lagos. Martín González Figueroa, conversation with author, San Juan de los Lagos, Jalisco, July 21, 2009.

23. Local descriptions of the painting sometimes refer to a swing, rather than a trapeze. The trapeze was invented in 1859. If a trapeze is represented, then, despite local tradition, the painting must have been created after 1859.

24. "En 1623 una familia de cirqueros paró en este lugar a trabajar, con tal mala suerte que la niña pequeña cayó en las dagas muriendo al momento" (notes from my visit to San Juan de los Lagos).

25. On December 29, 2003, Amparo Posadas de Carmona, Izquierdo's elder daughter, and I traveled from her home in León, Guanajuato, to San Juan de los Lagos, Jalisco. She showed me the place where Izquierdo's childhood home once stood. The Izquierdo family home has not survived, but a brass plaque on the small building that now stands there identifies the location as the place of María Izquierdo's birth. The Izquierdo family home was located on what is now the corner of Dr. Manuel Montero and Leonardo Zermeño streets. The Capilla del Primer Milagro and the chapel of the Pocito del Primer Milagro are on the corner of Primavera and Luis Moreno. Primavera and Dr. Manuel Montero are actually the same street, but the name changes somewhere between the chapels and the site where the Izquierdo home was located.

26. According to her memoirs, Izquierdo moved to Aguascalientes with her parents when she was six years old. María Izquierdo Memoirs, chapter 1, p. 8.

27. *Caballos engalanados* was originally reproduced in a newspaper article in *La Nación* that survives as an undated clipping in the María Izquierdo Archive. The dates of the three paintings reproduced in the article reveal that it was published in 1940 or later. A newspaper photograph of the *Caballos engalanados*, presumably the one published in *La Nación*, was included in the exhibition catalogue to Izquierdo's retrospective at the Centro Cultural, Arte Contemporáneo. Carlosleón, "María Izquierdo"; *María Izquierdo* (1988 exhibition catalogue), 321.

28. Fernando Gamboa (1909–1990) was a curator, museologist, and powerful cultural official. From the 1940s to the 1980s he was responsible for curating the most well-known international exhibitions of Mexican art that traveled to important cities in Europe and the United States. Izquierdo and Gamboa met in 1929 when she became a student at the Escuela Nacional de Bellas Artes and joined Germán Gedovius's painting class, in which Gamboa was already enrolled. In 1988 Gamboa claimed: "El circo por ejemplo es un motivo totalmente tamayesco." Fernando Gamboa, as cited by Sylvia Navarrete in "María Izquierdo," in *María Izquierdo* (1988 exhibition catalogue), 62.

29. Tamayo's paintings of the circus include *El circo* (The Circus) of 1932; *El circo* (The Circus), also known as *Carnaval* (Carnival) of 1936; and *El circo* (The Circus) of 1938.

30. The four prints that clearly depict circus subjects are *Juglar* (Juggler) of 1979, *Malabarista* (Juggler) of 1980, *La cirquera* (The Circus Performer) of 1984, and *Cruz de hierro* (Iron Cross) of 1988. Pereda, *Rufino Tamayo*, 206, 222, 254, 268.

31. Paz, "María Izquierdo," 263, 264.

32. "Sí, creo que hay una influencia extranjera en la pintura de México. Yo misma quiero mucho a pintores como Rousseau, Van Gogh, Picasso y Dalí." Poniatowska recounted a slightly different version of Izquierdo's words in a later publication: "I have also traveled and must recognize foreign influences in myself. I admire painters like Van Gogh, Picasso, Rousseau, Dalí. I met Dalí when he came to Mexico. The one I like best of all is Gauguin: his life and his work" (Yo también he viajado y debo reconocer en mí, influencias extranjeras. Admiro a pintores como Van Gogh, Picasso, Rosseau [*sic*], Dalí. Conocí a Salvador Dalí cuando vino a México. Al que más quiero de todos es a Gauguin; su vida y su obra). Elena Poniatowska, "Opina María Izquierdo"; Poniatowska, *Todo México*, 170.

33. The exact words of the article were:

> —¿Está usted de acuerda en que Diego la agrupe con los pintores que sufren todavía de "Picassitis" y "Miroquiricosia" aguda?
>
> —A Miró ni lo miro porque no me gusta. ¿"Picassitis"? (Sigue una risita que aún ignoramos si fue dirigida al espíritu de Diego, o a nosotros.) ¿Ha encontrado usted ahora que vio mis cuadros, algún arlequín flaco?

"Avanzadilla," *Ultimas Noticias de Excélsior* (Mexico City), March 26, 1942.

34. Manuel Manilla produced innovative graphics for circus posters and programs and designed the first issue of *El Clown Mexicano*. José Guadalupe Posada created illustrations for *El Clown Mexicano* and *El Moderno Payaso*. López Casillas, "Maravilla gráfica," 44–49.

35. The three members of ¡30–30! who were Izquierdo's classmates were Francisco Dosamantes, Erasto Cortés, and Benigno Rivas.

36. Izquierdo exhibited two paintings and Tamayo three paintings and four drawings in *Mexican Arts*. The titles of Izquierdo's works were *Still Life* and *A Woman*, while Tamayo's were *Athlete*, *Still Life*, and *Lovers*; his drawings were untitled. None of these works was reproduced in the catalogue. *Mexican Arts*, 49, 52.

37. The titles of the paintings that Izquierdo showed at the Art Center are *Flowers*, *Nudes*, *Two Heads*, *Still Life*, *Nude*, *Aviator*, *Woman Resting*, *Still Life*, *Children*, *Fruit*, *Church and Cows*, and *Church*. *Paintings by María Izquierdo*, no pagination.

38. "Durante un mes y días que permaneció en el puerto de Nueva York, ocupó todo su tiempo en visitar Museos, Salas de Exposiciones, de Concierto, teatros, rascacielos, el barrio negro de Harlem, los parques, jardines zoológicos, Nueva Jersey, el acuario y El Circo, Coney Island con su feria monumental, montañas rusas, juegos, y los famosos fenómenos humanos, por ejemplo la mujer gusano, los hombres más chicos, grandes, flacos, gordos, altos, etc. . . . Fue frenética su actividad en la ciudad más grande del mundo." María Izquierdo Memoirs, chapter 6, pp. 4–5.

39. "Los ojos y el alma pletóricos de nuevos elementos pictóricos y conocimientos humanos." Ibid., chapter 7, p. 1.

40. The survey of circus images shown in museums and galleries in New York during Izquierdo and Tamayo's 1930 visit to the city is based on articles published in *Art Digest*, *Art News*, and *Arts* during this period.

41. "A New Book on Picasso," *New York Times*, October 26, 1930; Elizabeth Luther Cart, "The Art of Picasso," *New York Times*, November 9, 1930; Maud Dale, *Picasso* (New York: Alfred A. Knopf, 1930).

42. The list of circus images mentioned or reproduced in magazines is based on issues of *Art Digest*, *Art News*, and *Arts* during the probable dates of Izquierdo and Tamayo's visit to New York.

43. "Exposiciones individuales de María Izquierdo," in *María Izquierdo: Monografía*, 19.

44. The list of individual exhibitions in *María Izquierdo: Monografía* states that the show took place on February 5, 1931, and boasts that it was "the first exhibition in America with themes exclusively of the circus." Several authors have repeated this assertion without adding additional information. The exception is Sylvia Navarrete, who quotes a passage from a 1931 article by Dr. Mauret praising Izquierdo's work. In the passage cited, however, Mauret makes general observations about Izquierdo's art without referring to paintings of the circus. In fact the article never mentions the circus, was published in June (over four months after the exhibition supposedly took place), and is illustrated with Izquierdo's painting of a girl holding a dog. Dr. Mauret, cited in Navarrete, "María Izquierdo," in *María Izquierdo* (1988 exhibition catalogue), 69; Doctor Mauret, "La pintura mexicana actual."

45. In 2006 I told María Izquierdo's younger daughter that I had not been able to locate any documentation of a signed and dated circus painting by her mother from before 1932 and asked if she knew how I could find a reproduction of a circus painting created before this date. She told me that she did not know how to locate these early works and would also like to find one or at least have a photograph of one of them. Aurora Posadas Izquierdo, author's interview, June 4, 2006, Naucalpan. Although there is no solid evidence of circus paintings before 1932, *Bailarina* (Dancer) of 1931 represents a dancer who may be in a *carpa* (music hall in a tent), which is a closely related subject. The painting is reproduced in the catalogue to Izquierdo's 1988 retrospective at the Centro Cultural, Arte Contemporáneo. *María Izquierdo* (1988 exhibition catalogue), 297.

46. The word "amazon," with the dual meaning of horsewoman and female warrior, appears in some circus literature in English. In the late nineteenth century an act called the Amazon March appeared in P. T. Barnum's circus. Rupert Croft-Cooke, *The Circus Book*, 120.

47. The work now in the collection of the Blanton Museum of Art at the University of Texas at Austin is reproduced in black and white in the exhibition catalogue to *17 acuarelas de María Izquierdo*. The painting is not identified by title, but the woman who balances on one foot atop a small pony is dressed in white; the image and title clearly correspond. *17 acuarelas de María Izquierdo*, 5; Adriana Zavala, "María Izquierdo," in *Blanton Museum of Art: Latin American Collection*, 237–239.

48. "Hoy se clausurara la exposición de la Srita. Izquierdo."

49. "La principal preocupación de María Izquierdo parece consistir en encontrar el punto de equilibrio perfecto entre lo trágico y lo cómico, del que nace una ironía mordiente, pero velada y sutil, que constituye la característica saliente de la personalidad mexicana." Celestino Gorostiza, "Una pintora mexicana," in *17 acuarelas de María Izquierdo*, 2.

50. "Hoy se clausurara la exposición de la Srita. Izquierdo."

51. According to the catalogue to Izquierdo's 1988 retrospective at the Centro Cultural, Arte Contemporáneo, she painted this self-portrait in 1933. Luis-Martín Lozano dates the painting 1936, but it was reproduced in the newspaper *El Nacional* in 1935. *María Izquierdo* (1988 exhibition catalogue), 302; Lozano, *María Izquierdo*, 16; "María Izquierdo," *El Nacional* (Mexico City), April 21, 1935.

52. The artistic dialogue that Izquierdo and Tamayo shared from 1929 to around 1934 is exemplified by the striking formal relationship between Izquierdo's *Autorretrato* (Self-Portrait) of 1933 and Tamayo's *Hombre y caballo* (Man and Horse) of 1934. Both works are dominated by the head of a single person, while a much smaller white horse in the

background leaps toward or away from the head in a way that creates an odd tangential relationship. In Tamayo's *Hombre y caballo*, the white horse appears to jump out of the man's head. In both paintings the juxtapositions are so bizarre that they suggest the artists were intentionally experimenting with disturbing compositions.

53. This painting is one of two self-portraits in which Izquierdo depicted herself with a small white horse. The other work is *Autorretrato* (Self-Portrait) of 1940, in which a figurine of a white horse appears on a pedestal next to the seated artist (fig. 7 and plate 5).

54. The majority of Izquierdo's circus paintings are in watercolor or gouache. However, in addition to the self-portrait of 1933, at least five works in the *El circo* exhibition of 1945 are in oil (four on canvas and one on Masonite).

55. Reff, "Harlequins, Saltimbanques, Clowns, and Fools," 32, 33.

56. Johnson, "Picasso's Parisian Family and the 'Saltimbanques,'" 90, 94.

57. Karen Cordero, "The Invention of 'Popular Art': A Strategy for the Construction of Modern Mexican Art," in *Facturas y manufacturas de la identidad*, 254.

58. Gómez-Peña, *Warrior for Gringostroika*, 49.

59. According to Aurora Posadas Izquierdo, the writer Álvaro Gálvez y Fuentes frequently invited her mother to participate in the round table discussions that he hosted for XEW radio. Posadas Izquierdo also recalls a period of approximately one year around 1945 or 1946 in which Izquierdo had a weekly radio show that delivered cultural news on the women's radio channel, XEX. Aurora Posadas Izquierdo, author's interview, August 17, 1998, Naucalpan.

60. "Era entonces un *delito nacer mujer*, y si la mujer tenía facultades artísticos, era mucho peor." María Izquierdo Memoirs, chapter 4, p. 3 (emphasis in the original).

61. "Exposición"; Roberto Guzmán Araujo, "Circo de nubes," in *Si entre yelos te nombro*, 56–59.

62. Guillaume Apollinaire, "Un fantôme de nuées," in *The Self-Dismembered Man*, 58–65.

63. "María Izquierdo toma ahora un tema también doloroso y, sorprendentemente, lo resuelve con unos dulces ojos de niña. Así, la atmósfera de miseria, de tristeza, de sordidez y de polvo que palpita en el circo que ven los mayores, no existe en estos cuadros llenos de dicha pueril y diáfana." Álvaro Gálvez y Fuentes, "Saeta a María Izquierdo," as cited in Navarrete, "María Izquierdo," 96.

64. After reviewing reproductions of the paintings that Izquierdo exhibited in *El circo*, Julio Revolledo Cárdenas wrote: "Los nombres no los puedo vincular a ningún artista de la época en que fueron pintados esos cuadros" (I cannot connect the names to any artist from the time those paintings were created). Julio Revolledo Cárdenas, personal correspondence, January 13, 2008.

65. "Que el chiste de esta alambrista era que, en lugar de hacen equilibrios sobre cualquier hilo telefónico, se ponía a caminar sobre los cables de la energía eléctrica con lo cual se ahorraba el pasaje del tranvía. A fuerza de hacer esas temeridades, un día se carbonizó." "Los circopetistas," no pagination.

66. Aurora Posadas Izquierdo, author's interview, July 31, 2010, Naucalpan. A reproduction of *La temeraria alambrista Bárbara Rodríguez* with its original title was published in Quiñones, "Mexicanos y españoles," 54. The same painting was published as *Equilibrista* (Tightrope Walker) in the catalogue to Izquierdo's 1988 retrospective. *María Izquierdo* (1988 exhibition catalogue), 230.

67. Raúl Uribe's *El mago* (The Magician) and *Payaso y ciclista* (Clown and Cyclist) are reproduced by Quiñones. Both works are identified as oil paintings but undated. Quiñones, "Mexicanos y españoles," 54–55.

CHAPTER 2: SAINTS AND GODDESSES

1. For example, Mexican women did not obtain the right to vote in presidential elections until 1953 and married women needed their husband's permission to work outside the home. See chapter 9 for a discussion of women's rights in Mexico during Kahlo's and Izquierdo's lives.

2. Helga Prignitz-Poda, "Die Legenden um Fridas Abstammung," in *Fridas Vater*, edited by Franger and Huhle, 45–47.

3. Franger and Huhle, *Fridas Vater*, 241.

4. I believe that the story of Guillermo Kahlo being a Jew was probably invented by Rivera. In Bertram Wolfe's first biography of Rivera, which was published in 1939, he identified Guillermo Kahlo as a "German-Jewish photographer." The date when the claim that Guillermo Kahlo was Jewish was first published tends to support the hypothesis that it was a reaction against Nazism. Wolfe titled his second version of the biography *The Fabulous Life of Diego Rivera*, because he had learned that Rivera's engaging stories did not always adhere strictly to facts. Wolfe, *Diego Rivera*, 275.

5. Herrera, *Frida*, 21.

6. "Llegó a la histeria por la religión."/"La emoción clara y precisa que yo guardaba de la Revolución mexicana fue la base para mi determinación. Hacia 1914 yo había oído en el tianguis de Coyoacán la propaganda en favor de Zapata." Kahlo, as cited in Tibol, *Frida Kahlo*, 26, 27.

7. Kahlo, *The Diary*, 243 (emphasis in the original).

8. Ibid., 248.

9. Ibid., 249.

10. Ibid., 249–250.

11. Ibid., 250.

12. Ibid., 251 (emphasis in the original).

13. Herrera, *Frida*, 326.

14. Freud used the name "Aton" rather than "Aten," and Kahlo employed his terminology. Freud, *Moses and Monotheism*.

15. Kahlo, "Frida Kahlo's 'The Birth of Moses,'" 4 (emphasis in the original). This is a bilingual edition of the essay that was first published as "Hablando de un cuadro mío."

16. "El toro alado Asirio, Amón, Zeus, Osiris, Horus, Jeová, Apolo, La Luna, La Virgen María, La Divina Providencia, La Santísima Trinidad, Venus y . . . el diablo." Kahlo, "Hablando de un cuadro mío," 71.

17. In her lecture Kahlo identified the Asian gods as "the Chinese god (dragon) and the Hindu Brahma." Kahlo, "Frida Kahlo's 'The Birth of Moses,'" 3.

In addition to a Chinese dragon, she depicted three Hindu gods. She represented Vishnu in human form sleeping on the coiled serpent Ananta (or Shesha) with Brahma arising from a lotus growing from his naval.

18. "El Relámpago, El Rayo y la Huella del Relámpago, es decir, Hurakán, Kukulkán y Gukamatz, Tlaloc, la magnífica Coatlicue, madre de todos los dioses, Quetzalcoatl, Tezcatlipoca, la Centeotl." There are discrepancies between Kahlo's words and images. While she uses Mayan names for three gods (Hurakán, Kukulkán, and Gukamatz), her images are based on central Mexican sculptures and Precolumbian codices from the area that is now the states of Puebla and Oaxaca. The gods she named and the gods she depicted also match imperfectly. For identification of Kahlo's visual sources of the Mesoamerican deities depicted in *Moisés*, see Deffebach, "Pre-Columbian Symbolism in the Art of Frida Kahlo," 54–55, 216–219; Kahlo, "Hablando de un cuadro mío," 71.

19. Kahlo's notes about which gods she intended to represent in *Moisés* survive in a notebook in the archives of the Museo Frida Kahlo.

Although Kahlo did not mention the Aztec cult deity Huitzilopochtli in her lecture, her notes reveal that she originally intended to include him. Huitzilopochtli is a solar deity and a war god. She intended to represent gods with a direct relation to the sun, so his absence from the painting is noteworthy. One possible interpretation of his omission is that Kahlo ultimately selected relatively benevolent Mesoamerican gods and eliminated the war god. Caja 2 (Box 2), Frida Kahlo Archive, Museo Frida Kahlo.

20. "Como Moisés, ha habido y habrá, gran cantidad de 'copetones,' transformadores de religiones y de sociedades humanas. Se puede decir, que ellos son una especie de *mensajeros* entre la gente que manejan y los '*dioses*' inventados por ellos, para poder manejarla." Kahlo, "Hablando de un cuadro mío," 71 (emphasis in the original).

21. *Posadas* are popular fiestas celebrated before Christmas. Mary and Joseph's search for shelter before the birth of Christ is reenacted with a series of neighborhood parties held in a different home each night from December 16 to 24.

22. Rivera and Colle, *Frida's Fiestas*, 100.

23. For a more extensive analysis of *Moisés*, see Deffebach, "Frida Kahlo," 185–189.

24. Kahlo expressed her interest in the dualism of Mesoamerica by repeatedly depicting a divided sky, half light and half dark, with the sun in the light side and the moon in the dark side. Kahlo was also interested in the Taoist concept of yin and yang, in which seemingly opposite forces are interdependent. She repeated the yin/yang symbol four times in the abstract drawing *Risa* (Laughter) of ca. 1945, drew a prominent yin/yang symbol in the lower left corner of *Ruina* (Ruin) of 1947, and subtly delineated it at the center of each floral design in the white lace ruffle of the Tehuana headdress surrounding her face in *Autorretrato* (Self-Portrait) of 1948. She also depicted the yin/yang symbol at least eight times in her diary. Rivera portrayed her holding the Taoist symbol in his portrait of her in *El sueño de un tarde dominical en la alameda central* (Dream of a Sunday Afternoon in the Alameda) in 1947.

25. Herrera, *Frida*, 284.

26. Ibid., 77.

27. Sarah Lowe and Eduardo Douglas were the first to note briefly Kahlo's connection to the Virgin of Sorrows; I have also written about this aspect of her work. Lowe mentions Kahlo's "identification with the Madonna of Sorrows (the image of the Virgin Mary who has lost her Son)." Douglas, in the context of an essay about Nahum B. Zenil, states that Kahlo equates herself with La Dolorosa (The Sorrowful One). Lowe, in Kahlo, *The Diary of Frida Kahlo*, 253; Douglas, "The Colonial Self," 20; Deffebach, "Images of Plants in the Art of María Izquierdo, Frida Kahlo, and Leonora Carrington," 104–105; Deffebach, "Frida Kahlo," 184.

28. Kahlo portrayed herself with tears flowing down her cheeks in *Henry Ford Hospital* of 1932, *Frida y el aborto* (Frida and the Miscarriage) of 1932, *Recuerdo* (Memory) of 1937, *La columna rota* (The Broken Column) of 1944, *Sin esperanza* (Without Hope) of 1945, *Diego y yo* (Diego and I) of 1949, and other works.

29. Kahlo painted *Mi nacimiento* after her mother died in 1932.

30. Herrera, *Frida*, 455 n. 74.

31. "Los esposos Guillermo Kahlo y Matilde C. de Kahlo dan las gracias a la Virgen de los Dolores por haber salvado a su niña Frida del accidente acaecido en 1925 en la esquina de Cuahutemozín y Calzada de Tlalpan."

32. Frida Kahlo, "Portrait of Diego," 95.

33. Zimmer, *Myths and Symbols in Indian Art and Civilization*, 211–212.

34. Nicholson, *Mexican and Central American Mythology*, 10.

35. Juan O'Gorman, author's interview, November 5, 1976, Mexico City (emphasis added).

36. "[Tamayo] vuelve a las raíces así del sentimiento de color y estética de los mexicanos antiguos, pero por arriba / los colores de la naturaleza mexicana que fueron empleados en la antigüedad y formaron un gusto por el color." Fernando Gamboa, author's interview, August 20, 1984, Mexico City.

37. Although isolated examples of Precolumbian symbolism appear in Kahlo's work before 1937, most follow her creation of *Mi nana y yo*. Examples of Precolumbian elements in Kahlo's early work include the Precolumbian necklace that she wears in *Autorretrato* (Self-Portrait) of 1929 and the pyramid and artifacts represented in *Autorretrato en la frontera entre México y los Estados Unidos* (Self-Portrait on the Border between Mexico and the United States) of 1932.

38. Deffebach, "Pre-Columbian Symbolism in the Art of Frida Kahlo," 46.

39. Kahlo signed a letter to her lover Nickolas Muray as Xochitl (February 16, 1939) and referred to herself as Xochitl in another letter to him (February 27, 1939). Kahlo may have only used this nickname with Muray. Kahlo, *Escrituras*, 90, 170–172, 176, 347.

40. Arturo Estrada, cited by Herrera in *Frida*, 334, 483.

41. Caso, *Thirteen Masterpieces of Mexican Archaeology*, 41.

42. Joyce, *Mexican Archaeology*, 61.

43. Eduard Seler, "Collected Works," vol. 1, 103. Unpublished English translation of *Gesammelte Abhandlungen zur Amerikanischen Sprach- und Alterthumskunde*, made under the supervision of Charles P. Bowditch, in the collection of Newberry Library, Chicago.

44. Linda Schele, conversation with author, spring 1991, Austin, Texas.

45. Isolda Kahlo, author's interview, July 21, 1984, Mexico City.

46. Fr. Bernardino de Sahagún, *Historia de la cosas de Nueva España*, plate 35.

47. "México Coyoacán.—Para el Señor Sigmund Firestone y sus hijas Alberta y Natalia pinté éste autorretrato con todo cariño, en Febrero de 1940—Frida Kahlo."

48. Kahlo, *Diary*, 211.

49. Fr. Bernardino de Sahagún, *Códices matritenses de la Historia general de las cosas de Nueva España*, plate 23; Bernardino de Sahagún, *Historia de las cosas de Nueva España: Códices Matritenses*, vol. 6, 77.

50. Miller, *The Art of Mesoamerica*, 49.

51. Miller and Taube, *The Gods and Symbols of Ancient Mexico and the Maya*, 48.

52. Miller, *The Art of Mesoamerica*, 49–50; Miller and Taube, *The Gods and Symbols*, 48–49.

53. Miller and Taube, *The Gods and Symbols*, 49.

54. Durán, *Book of the Gods and Rites and The Ancient Calendar*, 403.

55. I do not know Kahlo's day sign according to the Aztec calendar but think it probable that Kahlo did (or thought she did). Without knowing which system she used and whether she was using her real birth date (July 6, 1907) or the one she claimed (July 7, 1910), it is not possible to reconstruct what she thought her day sign was.

56. Miller and Taube, *The Gods and Symbols*, 70.

57. Caso, *The Aztecs*, 15.

58. Isolda Kahlo, author's interview, July 21, 1984, Mexico City.

59. Bergman-Carton, "Like an Artist," 37.

60. Carlos Monsiváis, "Of All the Possible Fridas (A Minimal Selection)," translated by Richard Moszka, in Monsiváis, *Frida Kahlo*, 102.

PART TWO: LEGITIMATING TRADITIONS

1. Zavala, *Becoming Modern, Becoming Tradition.*

CHAPTER 3: REVITALIZING THE PAST

An earlier version of this chapter was published as "Frida Kahlo y el Occidente de México," in *Apropiarse del arte: Impulsos y pasiones: XXXII Coloquio Internacional de Historia del Arte*, ed. Olga Sáenz (Mexico City: Universidad Nacional Autónoma de México, 2012), 157–176.

1. The paintings that represent a Precolumbian artifact from West Mexico are *Autorretrato en la frontera entre México y los Estados Unidos* (Self-Portrait on the Border between Mexico and the United States) of 1932, *El superviviente* (The Survivor) of 1938, *The Square Is Theirs*, also known as *Cuatro habitantes de la Ciudad de México* (Four Inhabitants of Mexico) of 1938, *La mesa herida* (The Wounded Table) of 1940, *Autorretrato con changuito* (Self-Portrait with Small Monkey) of 1945, and *Naturaleza muerta* (Still Life) of 1951.

2. For a discussion of how belief in authenticity has been used to limit and distort the presentation and exhibition of Mexican art outside of Mexico, see Ramírez, "Beyond 'the Fantastic,'" 236–237.

3. "Que cuesta mucho ser auténtica, señora. Y en estas cosas no hay que ser rácana. Porque una es más auténtica cuanto más se parezca a lo que se ha soñado de sí misma." Pedro Almodovar, *Todo sobre mi madre* (1999).

4. "Allí en ese lugar, se despertó mi interés por la arqueología, por eso desde los seis años me dediqué a coleccionar caritas y figuras que los indígenas de cuando en cuando traían a vender a mi ciudad." Diego Rivera, cited in Zendejas, "Diego, el millonario guardador de tesoros."

5. "Estaban muy enterados de toda la cultura de Occidente. Ya en casa de mi abuela había piezas muy bellas de Occidente, y mi padre las vio y se empezó a interesar por ir a los estados que están en el Occidente." Guadalupe Rivera Marín, author's interview, June 9, 2006, Mexico City.

6. Judy Sund writes that Rivera began to acquire artifacts from West Mexico in the 1930s. Barbara Braun asserts that Rivera's "serious collection only began around 1930." Mexican archaeologist Felipe Solís Olguín suggests that Rivera promoted many myths surrounding his collection by telling several writers about acquiring Precolumbian art while he was still a boy. Solís notes that the earliest hard evidence of Rivera's collecting is a letter dated 1932 to his wife, Guadalupe Marín, instructing her to pay 400 dollars for six "idols." Sund, "Beyond the Grave," 744; Braun, *Pre-Columbian Art and the Post-Columbian World*, 235; Solís Olguín, "Testimonios de una gran pasión," 151.

7. Médioni and Pinto, *Art in Ancient Mexico.*

8. The Formative culture of Tlatilco was another great focus of Rivera's collection. The ancient cemetery of Tlatilco was discovered beneath a brickyard on the outskirts of Mexico City in 1936. Rivera and Miguel Covarrubias frequently visited Tlatilco to collect figurines, vessels, masks, and other objects. Covarrubias directed the first scholarly excavation of Tlatilco in 1942 and later published articles about the site. Eventually artifacts from Tlatilco became an important part of Rivera's collection, but, oddly, objects from Tlatilco are not represented in *Art in Ancient Mexico.*

9. Toscano, Kirchhoff, and Rubín de la Borbolla, *Arte precolombino del Occidente de México.*

10. The other artists who lent Precolumbian artifacts to the exhibition were Manuel Álvarez Bravo, Roberto Montenegro, Carlos Orozco Romero, Jesús Reyes Ferreira, and Juan Soriano.

11. One of the artifacts is reproduced in both *Art in Ancient Mexico* and *Arte precolombino del Occidente de México.*

12. Rivera with March, *My Art, My Life*, 250.

13. Ibid., 251.

14. "Anahuacalli," 34.

15. Braun, *Pre-Columbian Art and the Post-Columbian World*, 235.

16. Solís Olguín, "Testimonios de una gran pasión," 150–151.

17. Ibid.

18. An exception to this statement is that artifacts from Tlatilco are well represented at Anahuacalli but were not represented in *Art in Ancient Mexico.*

19. Barbara Braun, "Western Mexican Art and Modern Artists," in *Ancient West Mexico*, ed. Richard Townsend, 268; Braun, *Pre-Columbian Art and the Post-Columbian World*, 240–241.

20. Braun, *Pre-Columbian Art and the Post-Columbian World*, 241.

21. Furst has been advocating shamanistic interpretations of Mesoamerican art since at least 1978. Furst, *The Ninth Level*, 26–27, 42–43.

22. Sund claims that it is the "burlesque aspects of Nayarit, Jalisco, and Colima effigies" that caused Rivera to avoid frequent references to them in his murals. While I think that this part of Sund's argument is colored by her discussion of Kahlúa advertisements—which really do present the West Mexican figures as comic—her point about the relative rarity of references to West Mexican artifacts in Rivera's murals is accurate and insightful. Sund, "Beyond the Grave," 744.

23. Ibid.

24. Rivera, as cited in ibid.

25. "La belleza de movimiento." Arturo Estrada, author's interview, June 13, 2006, Mexico City.

26. "Diego Rivera, coleccionista, era como un niño alucinado por la belleza de las formas de las esculturas occidentes."/"contenido de la forma"/"la forma en movimiento." Guillermo Monroy, author's interview, June 7, 2006, Cuernavaca.

27. "Le gustaban mucho las figuras del Occidente por la libertad de la forma."/"El arte occidental es eventualmente el arte más libre de todas las expresiones de diversas culturas. Abarca un panorama muy largo, de muchos siglos. Es un arte funerario. No es un arte de divinidades. Es un arte que representa personas—a veces sanas, a veces atléticas, a veces enfermas, a veces grotescas—pero es un arte doméstico. No hay un solo dios allí." Fernando Gamboa, author's interview, August 20, 1984, Mexico City.

28. Kahlo, "Retrato de Diego," 5.

29. Peter T. Furst, "Shamanic Symbolism, Transformation, and Deities in West Mexican Funerary Art," and Mark Miller Graham, "The Iconography of Rulership in Ancient West Mexico," in *Ancient West Mexico*, ed. Townsend, 169–189 and 191–203.

30. Karen Cordero, "The Invention of 'Popular Art': A Strategy for the Construction of Modern Mexican Art," in *Facturas y manufacturas de la identidad*, 253.

31. Ana Garduño, "The Elitism of Folk Art," in *Facturas y manufacturas de la identidad*, 233.

32. Nancy Deffebach, "Frida Kahlo and Surrealism: An Uneasy Alliance," paper presented at the College Art Association conference in Chicago, February 1992.

33. Herrera, *Frida*, 153.

34. Betty Ann Brown, "The Past Idealized: Diego Rivera's Use of Pre-Columbian Imagery," in *Diego Rivera*, 142–143.

35. Quirarte, "Mexican and Mexican American Artists in the United States," 53.

36. Malinalco was excavated under the direction of José García Payón from 1936 to 1939. García Payón, *Los monumentos arqueológicos de Malinalco*, 5 and fig. 15.

37. While the skull artifact is too generic to identify a specific source, it is represented with a tenon below the skull, which suggests that the skull may once have been inserted into a wall. Fausto Ramírez, conversation with author, December 3, 2008, Lima, Peru.

38. By 1946, if not before, Rivera's collection included a nearly identical but undamaged figure of a woman suckling an infant and holding a bowl of food. It is worth noting that Kahlo chose to represent the damaged figure in *Autorretrato en la frontera entre México y los Estados Unidos*. The undamaged artifact, which is from Colima, is reproduced in Toscano, Kirchhoff, and Rubín de la Borbolla, *Arte Precolombino del Occidente de México*, fig. 51, no pagination. Kahlo's miscarriage occurred on July 4, 1932. She began painting *Autorretrato en la frontera entre México y los Estados Unidos* on August, 31, 1932. Herrera, *Frida*, 141, 152.

39. Médioni and Pinto, *Art in Ancient Mexico*, fig. 208.

40. Lekson, "Dating Casas Grandes."

41. Lucienne Bloch, letter to author, April 26, 1990 (emphasis in the original).

42. "Guerrero jugador de pelota (según Diego Rivera), procede de Las Animas, Colima, Cultura colimense, Colección Diego Rivera." Toscano, Kirchhoff, and Rubín de la Borbolla, *Arte precolombino del Occidente de México*, fig. 62, no pagination.

43. Jane Stevenson Day, "The West Mexican Ballgame," in *Ancient West Mexico*, ed. Townsend, 151–152.

44. Ibid., 152; Miller, *The Art of Mesoamerica*, 120.

45. Day, "The West Mexican Ballgame," 153.

46. Miller, *The Art of Mesoamerica*, 121.

47. Toscano, Kirchhoff, and Rubín de la Borbolla, *Arte precolombino del Occidente de México*, fig. 62, no pagination.

48. Examples of male figures from West Mexico with this type of attire are reproduced in Townsend, ed., *Ancient West Mexico*, 43, fig. 12 and 112, fig. 5; Toscano, Kirchhoff, and Rubín de la Borbolla, *Arte precolombino del Occidente de México*, figs. 61, 62, no pagination; Médioni and Pinto, *Art in Ancient Mexico*, figs. 63, 67, no pagination.

49. "Ribbon around Bomb," 19.

50. Krauze, *Mexico*, 475.

51. Pach, "Frida Rivera," 15.

52. Frida Kahlo, as recorded by Parker Lesley during a conversation on May 27, 1939, cited by Hayden Herrera in "Frida Kahlo's Art," 26.

53. Médioni and Pinto, *Art in Ancient Mexico*, fig. 60.

54. Kahlo, cited by Herrera in *Frida*, 334.

55. "Pareja en actitud amorosa." Toscano, Kirchhoff, and Rubín de la Borbolla, *Arte precolombino del Occidente de México*, fig. 7, no pagination.

56. A photograph of the marriage pair on top of the display stand is included in Deffebach, "Pre-Columbian Symbolism in the Art of Frida Kahlo," 213.

57. A café and gift shop were added and numerous changes were made to the Museo Frida Kahlo to accommodate the dramatic increase in the number of visitors due to Kahlo's increased fame since the early 1980s. The changes also reflect a shift toward neoliberal economic policies in the Mexican art world and the greater role internationally of marketing in museums.

58. *Frida Kahlo: Portraits of an Icon*, fig. 43; Grimberg, *I Will Never Forget You*, fig. 45.

59. In the catalogue to *Arte precolombino del Occidente de México*, the sculpture from Nayarit is shown with another piece that is also in a pensive attitude. The one that Kahlo depicted is on the left side of the reproduction. The figures are identified as a couple from the state of Nayarit in the collection of Diego Rivera. Toscano, Kirchhoff, and Rubín de la Borbolla, *Arte precolombino del Occidente de México*, fig. 2, no pagination.

A black-and-white photograph of the same two artifacts was among the documents found in 2004 at the Museo Frida Kahlo. The newly discovered photograph is not identical to the one reproduced in the 1946 catalogue, but it was shot from a similar angle.

60. *Museo Dolores Olmedo*, 89; Miller and Taube, *The Gods and Symbols of Ancient Mexico and the Maya*, 80.

61. "Furioso, Rivera recorrió la casa persiguiéndolo con una machete de gran tamaño, decidido matarlo."/"Señor Xólotl, emperador de Xibalba, señor de las tinieblas, es usted el mejor crítico de arte." Tibol, *Frida Kahlo*, 106; Rivera, cited in ibid.

62. Sund interprets *Autorretrato con changuito* in relation to "primitivism." She believes that Kahlo expressed her equivocal relation to the primitive with the figure from Nayarit in the painting. The Precolumbian effigy, the monkey, and the dog are "markers of indigenous Mexicanness, here possessed, domesticated, and artfully displayed." Sund asserts that "Kahlo holds herself aloof from and superior (in position and scale) to her pets and her primitive, yet at the same time she portrays herself literally tied to the periphery they occupy, a space at the boundary of nature and culture." For Sund, the yellow ribbon connects Kahlo to "the place of the primitive" and "indicates the artist's unruly entanglement with it." Sund, "Beyond the Grave," 734.

I acknowledge the relationship of Mexican modernism to the early twentieth-century European interest in "primitivism," but my interpretation of this painting is almost the opposite of Sund's. For me, the pensive Precolumbian figure embodies profound thought. Kahlo's rendering of the ceramic figure mimics the formal qualities of Auguste Rodin's *The Thinker* in order to emphasize the meditative quality of the Precolumbian figure and insist that it *thinks* as profoundly as Rodin's figure.

63. "Soy de Samuel Fastlicht. Me pintó con todo cariño, Frida Kahlo, en 1951. ~ Coyoacán ~."

64. I am indebted to Fausto Ramírez for drawing my attention to references to life and death in more than just *Autorretrato con changuito*. Ramírez, conversation with author, December 3, 2008, Lima.

65. Graciela Téllez Trevilla, personal communication, August 30, 2013.

66. "Se pueden llamar definitivamente mexicanos, porque se engastan magníficamente en la tradición que viene desde los remotos y extraordinarios tarascos de Colima y Nayarit." Rivera, "Antonio Ruiz," 251.

CHAPTER 4: BEYOND THE PERSONAL

An earlier version of this chapter was published as "Beyond the Personal: Frida Kahlo's *La niña, la luna y el sol*" in *Original—Copia . . . Original?* (Buenos Aires: Centro Argentino de Investigadores de Arte, 2005), 147–157.

1. "La 'nana' nutridora . . . [con] máscara india de piedra dura." / "Frida, sola en el espacio maquinizado, tendida sobre un catre, desde donde ve llorando que la vida-feto es flor-máquina, caracol lento, maniqui y armadura óseas en su apariencia." / "Tras la puerta del cielo, abierta de par en par, sólo había el espacio implacable y maravilloso, desde donde el sol y la luna están al mismo tiempo sobre las pirámides, portentosas de grandeza en su microscópico tamaño en relación al astro

y al planeta, e inmensas en sus sistemas de proporciones que son los del universo entero. La niña sentada en el centro del mundo, poseía el avión juguete que iguala en velocidad, mucho mayor que la de la luz, a la de la imaginación-razón." Rivera, "Frida Kahlo y el arte mexicano," 99, 101.

2. In the one-page catalogue to Kahlo's exhibition, *Mujer de sarape* from the collection of Frederick Davis appears as number eight in the list of works exhibited. The catalogue was not illustrated, but the newspaper *El Nacional* reproduced five pieces from the exhibition, including this painting with the title *Mujer de sarape.* "Obras de Frida Kahlo," *El Nacional* (Mexico City), April 23, 1953.

3. Zamora, *Frida*, 223.

4. I have not seen the verso of the painting, but I have studied a photograph of the inscription. The phrase "la tehuacana Lucha María" is followed by "Frida Kahlo 1942," implying that the artist has signed and dated the statement. The words are casually written in brown oil paint with a slightly dry brush; the first line ("la tehuacana") is blurred and almost illegible. The message does not resemble the carefully composed, relatively small signatures in oil on the front of Kahlo's paintings. The style of writing on the back of the painting is also distinct from her handwriting in her diary and letters. The disparity might be explained by the difference in media. Kahlo wrote her diary and letters in pen and ink, a fluid medium that probably predisposes most writers to link letters and add occasional loops, qualities that occur with less frequency in the lettering on the back of the painting than in Kahlo's diary and correspondence. While I am less skeptical of the authorship of the inscription than before studying the photograph, I cannot confirm that it is in the artist's handwriting. I believe that the painting should be examined by a handwriting expert who specializes in artists' signatures. I am indebted to Susan Webster for sharing her thoughts about the difficulties of comparing an artist's signatures when they have been written in different media. Susan Webster, conversation with author, August 2013.

5. Tehuacán is located in the state of Puebla. The Peñafiel company has a bottling plant there and markets the brand of mineral water named Tehuacán. A number of archaeological sites are located in the Tehuacán Valley, but the site depicted in the painting is not one of them.

6. Arturo Estrada, author's interview, December 13, 1985, Mexico City.

7. Rivera and Colle, *Frida's Fiestas*, 147.

8. Miller, *The Art of Mesoamerica*, 80, 103.

9. *Teotihuacán*, 3.

10. "Lo que los indígenas habían logrado en esa bella arquitectura que era impulsada . . . por los dioses. O *para* los dioses. Esto era una parte en la que Frida insistía. Es decir la gran fuerza religiosa en el indígena para llegar a hacer obras de la magnitud que son las dos pirámides." Héctor Xavier, author's interview, July 11, 1986, Mexico City (emphasis in the original).

11. Sahagún, *Florentine Codex*, book 7, 4–8.

12. The site depicted in *La niña, la luna y el sol* is irrefutably Teotihuacan, but Kahlo made one alteration worth noting. At Teotihuacan the Pyramid of the Moon is at the north end of the Way of the Dead and the Pyramid of the Sun is on the east side. Kahlo depicted the pyramids as if the fronts of both could be seen straight-on from the same vantage point simultaneously, but that is not possible at the site.

13. Sahagún, *Historia de las cosas de Nueva España*, 5, plate 43.

14. Dolores Olmedo, author's interview, August 10, 1984, Mexico City.

15. Tablada, *Historia del arte en México*, 28, 30.

16. Eder, "Frida Kahlo," 156.

17. Alejandro Gómez Arias, author's interview, August 21, 1986, Mexico City.

18. Rodríguez Prampolini, *Juan O'Gorman*, 54–55.

19. Rivera with March, *My Art, My Life*, 177.

20. "La niña del aeroplano es México, el sol y la luna . . . el día y la noche; México, con su afán de las pirámides de Teotihuacan; en el fondo el mundo antiguo, y la niña teniendo en sus manos la era moderna." Guillermo Monroy, author's interview, May 22, 1986, Mexico City.

21. "En el fondo se ve las pirámides de Teotihuacan y en sus manos lleva un avioncito como para mostrar el mundo moderno así en las manos del mexicano." Arturo García Bustos, author's interview, August 14, 1984, Mexico City.

22. Deffebach, "Beyond the Personal," 150; Eduardo Matos Moctezuma, "La tehuacana, niña Lucha María," 214; Eder, "Frida Kahlo," 156.

23. The work, which was lot number 13, is not listed in Sotheby's sales results. According to Sotheby's an omitted lot number indicates that the item was "withdrawn, passed, or unsold."

24. Kahlo's oeuvre was declared a *monumento nacional* by the Mexican government in 1984. This designation means that her work is recognized as part of the national patrimony of Mexico and is subject to laws that control its ownership, exhibition, and reproduction. Paintings by artists whose works have been declared *monumentos nacionales* cannot legally be sold to collectors outside of Mexico.

CHAPTER 5: MOTHER OF THE MAIZE

1. Franco, *Plotting Women*, xxi, 101, 102, 131.

2. When I first consulted the botanist and ethnobotanist Miguel Ángel Martínez Alfaro about these paintings, I perceived them as landscapes. But Martínez Alfaro, who as an ethnobotanist spends considerable time in rural Mexico, referred to them as gardens or orchards. I now believe this to be an important distinction. Miguel Ángel Martínez Alfaro, conversation with author, June 15, 1995, Mexico City. Stephanie Ross writes about the difficulty in defining a garden and the impossibility of creating a definition that would list all the necessary and sufficient conditions: a set of properties possessed by all and only by all gardens. Ross, *What Gardens Mean*, 1–10.

3. An image of the unpublished work survives in the María Izquierdo Archive.

4. At least one of these works was made when a collector wanted a painting that already belonged to someone else and insisted that Izquierdo make another just like it. According to Aurora Posadas Izquierdo, her mother would sometimes agree to make an identical painting for a potential client, but it would never turn out exactly the same because she would change things. Nevertheless, *Los gallos* of 1944 is a near duplicate of *Los gallos* of ca. 1942 and is surely the result of such a petition. Others in the series may have fulfilled similar requests in a less literal manner. Aurora Posadas Izquierdo, author's interview, November 2, 1996, Naucalpan.

5. "Gran olla de barro, cesto de mimbre o troje de madera para almacenar el maíz en mazorca." Cabrera, *Diccionario de aztequismos*, s.v. *coscomate* and *cozcomate.*

6. Many of Izquierdo's works are known by titles other than those under which she originally exhibited them. It is not clear whether the title *Coscomates* was used by Izquierdo herself or was given to this work after it left her possession.

7. I am indebted to geographer Barbara Fredrich for sharing her research about the geographical distribution of this type of *coscomate.*

8. Aurora Posadas Izquierdo, author's interview, November 2, 1996, Naucalpan.

9. Penrose, *Max Ernst's Celebes*, 14–15.

10. Kim Grant, personal communication, June 2012.

11. Max Ernst exhibited five works in the *Exposición internacional del surrealismo* (International Exhibition of Surrealism) at the Galeria de Arte Mexicano in 1940. The works are listed in the catalogue with the titles translated into Spanish: *Pareja zoomorfa* (1933), *El huevo* (1930), *Combate de mantas religiosas* (1935), *Bosque y sol* (no date), and *Bosque* (no date). *Exposición internacional del surrealismo*, no pagination.

Leonora Carrington, who was Ernst's significant other from 1937 to 1940, immigrated to Mexico in 1943, but Izquierdo and Carrington did not know each other. Deffebach, "Images of Plants in the Art of María Izquierdo, Frida Kahlo, and Leonora Carrington," 10.

12. Other artists who depicted the type of *coscomate* typical of Morelos include Miguel de la Sotarriva and Erasto Cortés Juárez. Around 1946 Francisco Goitia depicted another type of granary in *Santa Mónica, Zacatecas, by Moonlight*.

13. Rivera created this drawing for Chase's *Mexico: A Study of Two Americas*, 175.

14. To my knowledge, Zalce and Méndez created all of the images of the type of *coscomates* typical of Morelos after Izquierdo began her series of rural scenes with *coscomates*. Méndez had created one earlier image of a different type of corn crib, a woodcut titled *Las trojes* (The Granaries) of 1930 that shows the conical silos typical of Zacatecas. Méndez's *Las trojes* was published in *Mexican Folkways* in 1932. Zalce's and Méndez's depictions of the type of *coscomate* typical of Morelos appear to follow Izquierdo's lead. *Mexican Folkways* no. 4 (October–December 1932): 211.

15. The Taller de Gráfica Popular was founded in the late 1930s by a group of artists dedicated to working collectively and using prints to stimulate progress and democratic interests. It dealt with topics and issues of regional and national importance and offered its services to labor organizations and progressive movements. The group was staunchly antifascist. The artists who participated in the TGP created a large number of images of *coscomates*, but the images seem to be the personal work of the artists, not a group project.

16. "Una forma muy extraña y muy campesina, muy indígena, porque es una construcción rarísima. Parece una cosa más bien de adorno, una copa." Alfredo Zalce, author's interview, December 8, 1997, Morelia, Michoacán, Mexico.

17. "El gusto indígena tan bonito."/"Unos son más anchos, otros son más delgadas, unas muy altas, depende." Ibid.

18. "Los campesinos lo hacen como una cosa personal, con un gusto, porque es para ellos, no es para otro." Ibid.

19. Mariana Yampolsky, author's interview, December 3, 1997, Mexico City. In 1980 Mariana Yampolsky collaborated with Elena Poniatowska to create the book *La casa en la tierra* (The House on Earth). In addition to its primary subject of homes in rural Mexico, the book contains photographs of granaries in Morelos, Guerrero, and the Estado de México. Below an elegant photograph of a cylindrical Nahua granary in Tepalcingo, Morelos, is the message: "The only treasure is the grain, and for it the round, triangular, solid coscomate" (El único tesoro es el grano y para él el coscomate redondo, triangular, macizo). Yampolsky and Poniatowska, *La casa en la tierra*, 46–47, 70.

20. Yampolsky, author's interview, December 3, 1997, Mexico City. In addition to the *coscomates* in Morelos, Yampolsky also especially liked the ones in the Estado de México, which are made of slats of wood and are constructed in series. She explained that when there is a good harvest another section is added; as the corn is used, the structure is taken down.

21. Ibid.

22. Ibid.

23. The revolutionary *corrido* titled "Del agrarista" includes the lines "Fué el grito de rebelión: / ¡Libertad, Trabajo y Tierra!" (The shout of rebellion was: / Liberty, Work, and Land!). Mendoza, *El corrido mexicano*, 87.

24. Brenner did not cite the source of this quotation. To me it seems highly improbable that a member of the Mexican nobility, which was supported by tribute payments, would have claimed that the land belonged to agricultural laborers. A possible explanation is that this citation was posthumously attributed to Netzahualcoyotl (also Nezahualcoyotl) by a twentieth-century Mexican who wished to have this highly respected source appear as a precursor of the goals of the Mexican Revolution and the purported values of postrevolutionary Mexico. Brenner, *Idols behind Altars*, 108.

25. Méndez's *Cuando nace un hombre* is reproduced in several books. Virtually the only scholar who has written about it, however, is Deborah Caplow, who claims that it was created as a New Year's card. According to Caplow, Mariana Yampolsky remembered seeing the artist make the print and recalled that "the idea of the image was that the human birth depicted in it symbolized the birth of the new year." Caplow points out the disturbing elements in the image that I have described and notes that the caption at the bottom of the print bears the date 1945 even though the print was made in 1949. She concludes that "the print is ambiguous." In late 1964 Méndez made a separate print depicting the room with the birth and used this as a New Year's card for the incoming year (a calendar with the date 1965 hangs on the wall of the room). The scene takes place in a campesino home and is based on the detail of the room in *Cuando nace un hombre*. Although the New Year's card repeats a small section of the earlier print, the mood is optimistic: the midwife hands the newborn to the mother, who reaches for her baby with open arms. This card does not contain any of the disturbing characters that inhabit *Cuando nace un hombre*. I do not believe that *Cuando nace un hombre* was ever used as a New Year's card. Rather, the card that Yampolsky remembered was really the 1964 print. Caplow, *Leopoldo Méndez*, 188–190; *Leopoldo Méndez*, fig. 117.

26. Zalce recalled: "Cuautla, in the state of Morelos, . . . is where I have seen the most *coscomates*. Perhaps there are other places nearby, but where I have seen the most is in the state of Morelos" (Cuautla, del estado de Morelos, . . . es donde más he visto coscomates. Tal vez hay otros lugares cercanos, pero donde los he visto más es en el estado de Morelos). Zalce, author's interview, December 8, 1997, Morelia. For people who knew rural Mexico well in the 1940s, the shape of these *coscomates* would have placed them in Morelos. For viewers who were unfamiliar with rural Mexico, this information is provided in some of the titles; for example, Izquierdo's painting *Paisaje de Cuautla* and Zalce's print *Paisaje de Cuautla*. Méndez even specifies the town's name in the legend at the bottom of *Cuando nace un hombre*.

27. The rise of civilization in Mesoamerica is inextricably bound to the domestication of maize, which is the staff of life in Mexico and has been for millennia. According to the creation myths of the ancient Maya recorded in the *Popol Vuh*, the gods successfully made humans from maize dough, after previous attempts had failed to create people from mud and wood. The Aztec pantheon included the maize god Centeotl, the maize goddess Chicomecoatl, and the rain god Tlaloc. The Aztecs called white maize "our flesh and bones" and handled all forms of corn with honor and respect. Before an Aztec woman put maize into the cooking pot, she breathed on it so that it would not fear the fire. If an Aztec woman accidentally scattered kernels of corn on the floor, she picked them up so they would not complain to their lord and cause

her to starve. Sophie Coe notes that when the Spaniards arrived in the sixteenth century they "instantly identified maize as the equivalent to their own principal carbohydrate staple, wheat, and classified it as *pan*, or bread, with all the religious and social connotations that that word implied." Coe, *America's First Cuisines*, 9.

Today maize in numerous forms still represents approximately half the total volume of food consumed in Mexico each year and provides about half of the calories. This percentage is higher for low-income groups, especially campesinos. Guillermo Bonfil Batalla writes: "Maize, society, culture, and history are inseparable. Our past and our present have their basis in maize. Our life is based on maize. We are the people of maize" (Maíz, sociedad, cultura e historia son inseparables. Nuestro pasado y nuestro presente tienen su fundamento en el maíz. Nuestra vida está basada en el maíz. Somos gente de maíz). *El maíz, fundamento de la cultura popular mexicana*, 7.

28. As the historian John McNeely has observed, the Plan de Ayala "lists all the four remedies ever suggested for agrarian reform: *ejidal* grants (communal lands), agricultural colonies, town sites, and small private holdings (*la pequeña propiedad*)." McNeely, "Origins of the Zapata Revolt in Morelos," 166.

29. Krauze, *Mexico*, 288.

30. During the Mexican Revolution the provincial city of Cuautla played an even more crucial role than Cuernavaca, the capital of Morelos. By May 1911 Porfirio Díaz's government retained only two strongholds in the state of Morelos: Cuernavaca and Cuautla. When Zapata occupied Cuautla on May 19, Díaz heard the news with alarm. A few days later, on May 25, he resigned and went into forced exile. Later he recalled: "I was calm until the South rose." Porfirio Díaz, as cited by Krauze, *Mexico*, 285.

31. *Exposición de María Izquierdo*.

32. Tiziano, "La exposición de María Izquierdo."

33. I would like to thank Marsha Weidner, art historian and equestrian, for pointing out that the body language of the horses in *Tumba de Zapata* indicates fear.

34. Krauze, *Mexico*, 279 (quotation), 283, 297, 302–303.

35. Ibid., 299.

36. "La troje, como madre del maíz que guarda en su seno." López Austin, "Términos de nahuallatolli," 23. López Austin's study was based on words used in Hernando Ruiz de Alarcón's *Tratado de las supersticiones de los naturales de esta Nueva España* (1629). Ruiz de Alarcón, a parish priest at Atenango, collected information from the area that now includes Morelos and parts of Guerrero and Puebla. I am using J. Richard Andrews and Ross Hassig's translation of López Austin's definition of *monantzin*, which was published in Ruiz de Alarcón, *Treatise on the Heathen Superstitions*, 350, n. 6.

37. Most of the major Precolumbian deities associated with the earth are female. They include Coatlicue (Serpent Skirt), Cihuacoatl (Woman Serpent), and Teteo Inan (Mother of the Gods), who is also called Tlalli Yollo (Heart of the Earth). Another earth deity, Tlaltecuhtli, can be either male or female. Tlaltecuhtli's name literally means "earth lord." Despite the male gender of the name, Miller and Taube observe that most Aztec representations clearly depict Tlaltecuhtli as female. In 2006 a monumental sculpture of Tlaltecuhtli was discovered on the north side of the Templo Mayor (Great Temple), the archaeological site located in the historic center of Mexico City. The rectangular monolith, believed to weigh approximately thirteen tons, was found face upward. It portrays the deity in a birth-giving squat with an iconograph that communicates her life-giving and life-consuming roles. Elsewhere in Aztec art Tlaltecuhtli's image is sometime carved on the bottom of sculptures, where her/his/its image makes direct contact with the earth. Heyden, *Mitología y simbolismo de la flora en el México prehispánico*, 115–117; Miller and Taube, *The Gods and Symbols of Ancient Mexico and the Maya*, 167; and didactic information at the archaeological zone of the Templo Mayor.

38. A Zapatista is a follower of Zapata, as cited by Krauze in *Mexico*, 297.

PART THREE: THE WALL OF RESISTANCE

1. Luis-Martín Lozano, "Regarding Modern Mexican Painting, María Izquierdo (1902–1955)," in *María Izquierdo (1902–1955)* (Chicago: Mexican Fine Arts Center Museum, 1996), 47; unidentified article ca. 1942 in the María Izquierdo Archives.

CHAPTER 6: WHAT SEX IS THE CITY?

I presented an earlier version of this research under the title "La revocación del contrato mural de María Izquierdo en 1945: Cuestiones de género, poder e identidad nacional" at the annual colloquium of the Instituto de Investigaciones Estéticas, which was held in Mexico City in 2010. The current text has been revised and expanded based on new information and suggestions from Ana Garduño, who read the text; Fausto Ramírez and Gloria Hernández, who attended the conference and made valuable observations; a subsequent interview with Fernando Serrano Migallón; and correspondence with Walther Boelsterly.

1. "La primera mujer que logra en América romper la tradición pictórica que requería que únicamente pintores se encargaran de obras murales monumentales."/"Diego Rivera y David Alfaro Siqueiros, entre los de más renombre, habían hasta hoy acaparado este trabajo rudo de pintura." Denegri, "María Izquierdo."

2. Conflicting dates for the contract have been published. On February 14, 1945, Denegri wrote about the commission as if the contract had been signed. The following year, however, in a letter to Mexican president Manuel Ávila Camacho, Izquierdo stated that the contract was signed on February 19, 1945. María Izquierdo, letter to President Manuel Ávila Camacho, February 21, 1946, Archivo General de la Nación, Fondo Presidentes, Manuel Ávila Camacho, caja 534, expediente 505.1.

3. The information about the contract comes from Izquierdo's letter of February 21, 1946, to Ávila Camacho. Archivo General de la Nación, Fondo Presidentes, Manuel Avila Camacho, caja 534, expediente 505.1.

4. Carlos Monsiváis, "María Izquierdo: La idolatría de lo visible," in *María Izquierdo*, 15.

5. "María Izquierdo no estaba dotada para la pintura 'de mensaje' y por ello no debemos lamentar demasiado que su proyectos murales para la escalera y plafones del edificio del Departamento Central no se llevaran a cabo." Conde, "La pintura de María Izquierdo."

6. "Sin embargo, yo preferiría hacer mi primer mural en México." María Izquierdo, as cited in Torriente, "Murales que desataron pasiones."

7. "A usted le dirán que nosotros tenemos prejuicios reaccionarios para la obra de esa pintura [*sic*]. Respondemos secillamente [*sic*] que no son prejuicios reaccionarios el exigir un mínimo de dibujo, de modelado, de sabiduría en el manejo de óleo a un pintor. ¿Cree usted que quien ni siquiera ha sido capaz de resolver los escasos problemas que tiene el fondo de un retrato, va a saber encontrar la respuesta para los inmensos problemas de una decoración monumental? ¿Cree usted que

quien no tiene siquiera una mediana fama de retratista, tenga el magisterio que se requiere para afrontar los problemas superiores de un muro?" Letter from Islas Garcia to Lic. Javier Rojo Gómez, as cited in Rodríguez, "Escándalo artístico."

8. Islas García, "Nuestros jóvenes pintores," 7, 13.

9. When Rivera assumed the directorship of the Escuela Nacional de Bellas Artes in 1929, an exhibition of student work was organized so that he could see what was being done at the academy. Izquierdo had three canvases in the show. Rivera declared them "lo único que allí valía" (the only work there that was worthwhile). María Izquierdo Memoirs, chapter 3, p. 3.

10. Rivera, "María Izquierdo" (October 1929).

11. María Izquierdo Memoirs, chapter 4, pp. 2–3.

12. "No tenía la menor confianza en el futuro artístico de ella." Islas García, "Nuestros jóvenes pintores," 7.

13. "Puede ser considerada mejor pintora que cualquier alumno de pintura de San Carlos." Islas García referred to the art school by a shortened version of its former name, Academia de San Carlos, rather than its name at the time the events occurred, Escuela Nacional de Bellas Artes. Ibid., 13.

14. As a young man Luis Islas García had been part of the political left and a founding member of the vanguard art group ¡30–30! formed in 1928. Later he did a political and artistic about-face. He became an archconservative Catholic, who wrote primarily about religious art. Personal correspondence from Ana Garduño and Diana Briuolo, September 16, 2011.

15. "Yo estaba convencida de que el edificio no sufriría tales cambios pero tampoco podía aceptar la idea de que se tramara una intriga que obstaculizara mi labor." María Izquierdo, as cited in Torriente, "Murales que desataron pasiones."

16. "Comencé a comprender que se me estaba saboteando." Ibid.

17. Torriente, "Murales que desataron pasiones."

18. "María Izquierdo demandará al Gobierno del D. Federal."

19. Torriente, "Murales que desataron pasiones."

20. "Apenas vieron Siqueiros y Rivera que la obra iba en serio, empezaron a criticar el tema y a poner miles de obstáculos: en una palabra a luchar por todos los medios contra la ejecución del mural que se me había encargado." Izquierdo, as cited in "María Izquierdo, víctima del monopolio muralista," 6.

21. "Ellos tuvieron dos actitudes: una pública, oficial digamos, en la que sostenían que ese edificio por ser colonial no se debía pintar al fresco pues "se echaba a perder la cantera" (ellos por primera vez tenían ese escrúpulo, Diego pintó el Palacio de Cortés en Cuernavaca que no puede ser más colonial y Siqueiros, otros edificios por el estilo). Junto con eso argumentaban que yo no había pintado al fresco antes y que al hacerlo por primera vez echaría a perder todo (siempre existe una primera vez, creo que el mismo Rivera y Siqueiros algún mural harían primero que el otro, y nadie se los impidió entonces). Aparte de esta actitud y argumentos públicos había algo más de fondo, Siqueiros y Rivera querían dictaminar sobre el tema, querían obligarme a darle un fondo y contenido político, cosa que yo nunca acepté, por dos razones: yo jamás he pertenecido a ningún partido político y nunca he querido que mi pintura sea cartel o proclama social." Ibid., 7.

22. "Darle a mi pueblo, que amo sinceramente lo mejor de mi sensibilidad artística, color, forma, poesía, y arte mexicano, entregarle parte de mi ser en forma de cuadros, para que tenga un deleite estético auténtico, nunca le daré una mentira artística, un camuflage [*sic*], mezcla de colorida demagogia y de bandera partidista."/"Esto lo sabían y lo saben muy bien Siqueiros y Rivera por eso lucharon contra mí y temporalmente triunfaron." Ibid.

23. "Yo por orgullo artístico y sobre todo porque no quería que el monopolio muralista hiciera y deshiciera a su arbitrio, no acepté pintar en otro edificio." Ibid.

24. "En nombre del prestigio artístico de María Izquierdo, de su valiosa obra nacional y del alto concepto que en las otras naciones ha ganado ella para honor de México, se digne disponer la reposición del contrato que el gobierno del Distrito Federal firmó." Rodríguez, "Escándalo artístico."

25. "Gestiones en pro de María Izquierdo ante el gobernador del Distrito Federal."

26. Izquierdo told an anonymous journalist: "Hice estos muros para demostrar que soy capaz de pintar al fresco y con proporciones monumentales, y que se me trató injustamente al rescindir mi contrato" (I made these murals to demonstrate that I am capable of painting in fresco and with monumental proportions and that I was treated unjustly when my contract was rescinded). "Murales al fresco."

27. Aurora Posadas Izquierdo, author's interview, August 17, 1998, Naucalpan.

28. Michelena, "Exposiciones de los murales de María Izquierdo."

29. "No puede decirse que el trabajo realizado—y que ella exhibe sólo como una parte—tenga la fuerza que exige la pintura mural. Algo le falta, algo que es genialidad, destello de lo grandioso, epopeya y armonía universal." Torriente, "Murales que desataron pasiones."

30. "El pez con gafas," 46.

31. Rivera painted his first mural, *La creación* (Creation), in encaustic in 1922–1923 at the Escuela Nacional Preparatoria (today the Colegio de San Ildefonso); he began painting frescos for the first time at the Secretaría de Educación Pública in 1923. This is presumably an error in the transcription of the conversation: it is unlikely that Rivera forgot where he painted his first mural or when he used fresco for the first time.

"Es justo que se le ofrezca una oportunidad . . . cuando yo pinté la Secretaría de Educación Pública intentaba la pintura mural por primera vez [*sic*], ¡y al fin que no salió tan mal!" (the suspension points are in the original). Rivera, cited in Torriente, "Murales que desataron pasiones."

32. "Creo que es inútil. Ya Rojo tiene una opinión formada y nadie se la cambiará: es un hombre muy firme." Ibid.

33. "Creo que María se ha subido en la higuera." Ibid.

34. "[A]ctitud magnífica"/"Cuando Rojo me llamó, yo le pedí los bocetos de María: no había bocetos . . . Después yo no podía juzgar por lo que había en las paredes: en ellas no había nada . . . Sin embargo opiné que había que dejarla trabajar y ver lo que hacía." Ibid.

35. "Problema professional." "Alfaro Siqueiros aclara el incidente con María Izquierdo."

36. Ibid.

37. Salazar Mallen, "¡Esta metrópoli . . . !"

38. *Diego Rivera*, 92.

39. Wolfe, *The Fabulous Life of Diego Rivera*, 341–349.

40. *Diego Rivera*, 107.

41. Wolfe, *The Fabulous Life of Diego Rivera*, 348.

42. Museo Nacional de Arte, *Portrait of a Decade*, 218; Pablo Neruda, *Confieso que he vivido*, cited in the prologue to Raquel Tibol, *Palabras de Siqueiros*, 15.

43. Charlot, *The Mexican Mural Renaissance*, 257–258.

44. Rivera, cited in ibid., 277, 278.

45. Charlot, *The Mexican Mural Renaissance*, 271–279.

46. Ibid., 257–258, 271–279.

47. Leonora Carrington, author's interview, August 20, 1998, Mexico City.

48. The ideology of the muralists was the dominant artistic

discourse in Mexico from the early 1920s through the 1950s, but it was never uncontested. Visual artists (including Tamayo and Izquierdo) who associated with the literary group called the Contemporáneos did not advocate monumentality, political art, or didactic art.

49. Siqueiros and others, "Manifesto of the Technical Workers, Painters and Sculptors Union of Mexico," 461.

50. Cresswell, *In Place/Out of Place*, 11.

51. "Bien, pero no para confiarle la salud del Presidente de la República." Alfonso Corona del Rosal, cited in Michelena, "Gestapo en la pintura," 21.

52. Cresswell, *In Place/Out of Place*, 13.

53. The image of the man standing and rowing a flat-bottomed boat probably comes from the Codex Mendoza or the Tira de la peregrinación. Izquierdo represented the kneeling warrior in a smaller scale than the standing *tlatoani*, thus using hierarchical scale to indicate relative status; but the kneeling figure also wears the *xiuhuitzolli*. The contradictory messages conveyed through scale and dress suggest that Izquierdo did not realize the degree to which the turquoise diadem was associated with rulership.

54. In *El canto y la música* and other murals, Tamayo demonstrated his skill at working in monumental scale while maintaining his recognizable style and avoiding political art.

55. The central image of an indigenous woman painting a portrait seems to be an allusion to Izquierdo herself. Izquierdo was mestiza, with pronounced indigenous features. This move from allegory to something bordering on portraiture (or self-portraiture) and the inclusion of one man to some extent destabilizes the meaning of the nine images, slightly shifting the ensemble away from a cluster of allegorical figures toward a group of active artists who are predominantly female.

Art historian Miranda Viscoli points out that Izquierdo's allegorical female figures are intently engaged in creating the art forms they represent. Viscoli contrasts Izquierdo's active monumental figures with Rivera's passive allegorical figures of the arts in his *La creación* mural of 1922–1923 at the Escuela Nacional Preparatoria. Viscoli, "The Revolution of Maria Izquierdo," 106.

56. "Notas de Arte."

57. "No se conoce que tenga la documentación histórica necesaria para concebir una obra pictórica que refleje, como es de fuerza, los dramas extraordinarios, la epopeya que vivió esta ciudad—precisamente en la Plaza de Armas—de que aquel edificio es verdaderamente la sede." Rodríguez, "Escándalo artístico."

58. Alegría de la Colina and Hernández Monroy, *El Centro Histórico*, 10.

59. "Notas de Arte."

60. Aurora Posadas Izquierdo, author's interview, November 2, 1996, Naucalpan.

61. An *olotera* is a tool made of "corncobs stacked together and bound on end with wire or an iron strip." Madsen, *The Virgin's Children*, 44.

62. Rivera, "María Izquierdo" (December 1929), 33.

63. Olcott, *Revolutionary Women in Postrevolutionary Mexico*, 22.

64. "María Izquierdo, víctima del monopolio muralista."

65. Blair Paltridge first called my attention to this issue.

66. Franco, *Plotting Women*, 102.

67. "[La pintura monumental] cesó de emplear como héroes centrales de ella a los dioses, los reyes, jefes de Estado, generales heroicos, etcétera; por la primera vez en la historia del arte, repito, la pintura mural mexicana hizo héroe del arte monumental a la masa, es decir, al hombre del campo, de las fábricas, de las ciudades, al pueblo. Cuando entre éste aparece el héroe, es como parte de él y su resultado claro y directo." Rivera cited by Raquel Tibol in the prologue of Rivera, *Arte y política*, 27.

68. Allegorical figures of women in Mexican murals include Siqueiros's dynamic portrayal of his wife, Angélica Arenal, as an allegorical figure of democracy in *Nueva democracia* of 1944–1945 and Orozco's representation of two lewd prostitutes as allegories of corruption in *Katharsis* of 1934.

69. Oropesa, *The Contemporáneos Group*, 26.

70. "Ocurre la decepción máxima, el gran encuentro con el machismo que es discriminación moral y artística." Monsiváis, "María Izquierdo: La idolatría de lo visible," 15.

71. Untitled document from the Archivo Fernando Gamboa (Fernando Gamboa Archive), from the file labeled "Informes del Departamento de Artes Plásticas del INBA 1947" (Reports from the Department of Visual Artes of INBA 1947). I am indebted to Ana Garduño for telling me about this document and providing a transcript.

72. "Si en el Renacimiento se hubiera nombrado árbitro de la producción artistica a un genio, actualmente indiscutible, como Miguel Angel, con ser quien era, habria hecho fracasar el Renacimiento, puesto que ni a Leonardo le reconocía talento. Es sabida igualmente la opinión deprimente que, a su vez, el Greco tenía de Miguel Angel y que un escritor de su época nos transmite. Teotocópulos al ser interrogado sobre si conocia a Miguel Angel durante su estancia en Roma, dice "Si, lo conocí. Era un buen hombre, pero el pobre no sabía pintar."

Todas estas cosas las cito para demostrar que ni los verdaderos genios, ni nadie, pueden ser árbitros del arte y en el caso preciso de los Tres Grandes, menos que nadie." Fernando Leal, cited by Rodriguez, "La pintura mural no puede sujetarse a ningún control."

73. O'Gorman, *Autobiografía*, 180. I wish to thank Ana Garduño for sending me this important information.

74. Goldman, *Contemporary Mexican Painting in a Time of Change*, 15.

75. "La Jefatura del monopolio de la pintura mural"/"Retratos que es lo mejor que hace." "María Izquierdo, víctima del monopolio muralista."

76. "Es un verdadero crimen." María Izquierdo, as cited in Bambi [Ana Cecilia Treviño], "Habla María Izquierdo."

77. Sylvia Navarrete, "María Izquierdo," in *María Izquierdo* (1988 exhibition catalogue), 94.

78. *María Izquierdo* (1988 exhibition catalogue), 348.

79. Two diagrams of the panels, which were created at the time of the evaluation of their state of conservation, survive in the archives of the Centro Nacional de Conservación y Registro del Patrimonio Artístico Mueble (National Conservation Center and Register of Moveable Artistic Patrimony). One of the diagrams is dated 1976. I am grateful to Walther Boelsterly for sending me these diagrams and other documents via email on June 1, 2012.

80. Walther Boelsterly, email, June 1, 2012.

81. Eliseo Mijangos, document dated May 22, 2012, emailed to author by Walther Boelsterly, June 1, 2012.

82. Fernando Serrano Migallón, author's interview, August 19, 2011, Mexico City. Dr. Serrano Migallón is now the cultural and artistic minister of the Consejo Nacional para la Cultura y las Artes (CONACULTA: National Council for Culture and the Arts). I am indebted to Gloria Hernández for telling me that the fresco panels had been restored and were now at the Facultad de Derecho at the Universidad Nacional Autónoma de México. Gloria Hernández, personal conversation, October 28, 2010, Mexico City.

83. I wish to thank Gerardo Hierro Molina for arranging for me to see the murals when I visited the Facultad de Derecho on August 15, 2011.

84. Fernando Serrano Migallón, author's interview, August 19, 2011, Mexico City.

85. According to the *New York Times*, since 2005 the Universidad Nacional Autónoma de México "has been ranked as the best university in Latin America, Spain, and Portugal." Hollander, "A Campus Serves as a Needed Oasis in a Crowded City."

PART FOUR: STILL-LIFE PAINTINGS

1. David Alfaro Siqueiros's still-life paintings include *Tres calabazas* (Three Squashes) of 1946, *Naturaleza muerta con pescados* (Still Life with Fish) of 1949, and *Calabaza* (Squash) of 1953. He probably painted additional still lifes, but the lack of a catalogue raisonné impedes determining how many. Regardless of the exact number, still-life painting represents a minuscule percentage of Siqueiros's oeuvre.

I know of only four still-life paintings by Orozco: *Broken Glass* of 1929, *Naturaleza muerta* (Still Life) of 1944, *La vela* (The Candle) of 1948, and a work from 1944 that has been published as *Laureles* and *Naturaleza muerta* in Mexico and as *Cabbages* abroad.

CHAPTER 7: *PICANTES PERO SABROSAS*

I presented an earlier version of this research at the biennial art history conference of the Centro Argentino de Investigadores de Arte (CAIA) in Buenos Aires in 2007. Nancy Deffebach, "Picantes pero sabrosas: Las Naturalezas Muertas de Frida Kahlo," in *Imágenes perdidas: Censura, olvido, descuido* (Buenos Aires: Centro Argentino de Investigadores de Arte, 2007), 271–283.

1. Bryson, *Looking at the Overlooked*, 9.

2. "[D]reht er sich in einem makabren Reigen der Zerstückelung gleichsam um sich selbst. Für Kahlo ist in dieser Welt kein Platz mehr." Helga Prignitz-Poda, "Wissenschaft und Pflanzen, Liebe, Tod und Teufel," in Prignitz-Poda, Grimberg, and Kettenmann, *Frida Kahlo*, 48.

3. Grimberg, "Frida Kahlo's Still Lifes," 25–26.

4. Grimberg, *Frida Kahlo*, 21. *Still Life with Roses* strongly resembles Guillermo Kahlo's paintings of flowers. For an example of his flower paintings, see Agustín Arteaga, *Frida Kahlo y sus mundos* (Puerto Rico: Museo de Arte de Ponce, 2005), 78. Neither *Still Life with Roses* nor *Still Life with Piggy Bank and Black Horses* was published during Kahlo's life; information about provenance and attribution is needed.

5. "Estas cosas que son preciosas, hay que darles un acomodo bonito. Entonces, yo lo voy a acomodar así. ¿Qué les parece, muchachos?" Frida Kahlo, as cited by Guillermo Monroy, author's interview, May 22, 1986, Mexico City.

6. "Pues se ve muy bonito, maestra. Les daban ganas de comerlo rápidamente." Guillermo Monroy, author's interview, May 22, 1986, Mexico City.

7. "Muy bien. Ahora tú. Te lo voy a desbaratar. Ahora acomódalo tú. A ver qué acomodo le das. . . . Las frutas son muy bellas. Y no te va a costar trabajo, porque en tu casa de seguro que tu mamá acomoda muy bonito las cosas cuando llega del mercado." Kahlo, as cited in ibid.

8. "Era una verdad lo que estaba diciendo. Desde luego en proporción, porque, pues, yo era de una familia bastante pobre." Guillermo Monroy, author's interview, May 22, 1986, Mexico City.

9. Ibid.

10. Brenner, "A Critic's View," 131.

11. Wyndham and King, *Trotsky*, 154.

12. Rivera and Colle, *Frida's Fiestas*, 16.

13. Guadalupe Rivera Marín, author's interview, July 31, 2013, Cuernavaca, Morelos.

14. "Mientras más populares, más le gustaban." Ibid.

15. Ibid.

16. Martha Zamora dates *Tunas* 1937, while Hayden Herrera dates it 1938. Zamora, *Frida*, 290; Herrera, *Frida*, 218–219.

17. Nicholson, *Firefly in the Night*, 154.

18. Brundage, *The Fifth Sun*, 209.

19. "Azteca tlapalli. Vieja sangre de tuna. El más vivo y antiguo." Kahlo, *The Diary*, unnumbered page.

20. The mushrooms are *Ramaria*, *Pleurotus*, and *Lentinus*.

21. Squash was probably first cultivated for the protein- and oil-rich seeds or the hard shells that could be used as containers. In Precolumbian Mesoamerica the flowers, fruit, and seeds of squash were eaten. Squash still forms an important part of the modern Mexican diet.

22. Guadalupe Rivera Marín, cited in Grimberg, *Frida Kahlo*, 82.

23. Héctor Xavier, author's interview, July 11, 1986, Mexico City.

24. While intentionally provoking a collector may seem illogical, Kahlo had already created *Suicide of Dorothy Hale* (1939), which was commissioned by Clare Boothe Luce with the understanding that it would be given to Dorothy Hale's mother. Although Kahlo created a spectacular painting, it would not have provided comfort to a bereaved mother. When Luce received the work, her first impulse was to destroy it in front of a witness. The person she chose to witness the destruction was an artist, who convinced her to return it to Kahlo after he removed the statement, in Spanish, that it had been created at the request of Clare Boothe Luce. Herrera, *Frida*, 292–293.

25. Franco, *Plotting Women*, xxi, 101, 102, 131.

26. Joyce, *Mexican Archaeology*, 40.

27. Durán, *Book of the Gods and Rites and The Ancient Calendar*, 404.

28. Kahlo, *Escrituras*, 170–177.

29. Herrera, *Frida*, 318. In the Spanish translation of Herrera's biography, the original title of the painting is given as *La flor de la llama* (Flame Flower). Hayden Herrera, *Frida: Una biografía de Frida Kahlo* (Mexico City: Editorial Diana, 1985), 267.

30. "¡Caramba, hazme el favor de felicitar a Diego!" Fernando Gamboa, author's interview, July 27, 1984, Mexico City.

31. Herrera, *Frida*, 318.

32. Fernando Gamboa, author's interview, July 27, 1984, Mexico City.

33. "Es una estupidez que esto no lo vea la gente. ¡Esto es la vida! Esto aparte de que está envuelto simbólicamente en una forma vegetal, como es el hongo, pero es el pene masculino. ¡Mira qué distintas formas! ¡Qué extraordinarias interpretaciones!" Kahlo, as cited in ibid.

34. The three paintings are *Naturaleza muerta con "Viva la vida"* (Still Life with "Long Live Life") of ca. 1951–1954, *Naturaleza viva* (Living Nature) of 1952, and *Fruta de la vida* (Fruit of Life) of 1953. Each painting contains a white dove.

35. The pitahaya (*Hylocereus undatus*) grows wild in tropical areas of Mexico.

36. Kahlo based her image of a rabbit in the moon on a sixteenth-century illustration in the *Florentine Codex*. Sahagún, *Florentine Codex*, book 7, 3–7, illustration 7.

37. This wordplay is used in the titles of four still-life landscapes by Izquierdo: *Naturaleza viva con huachinango* (Living Nature with Red Snapper) of 1946, two works titled *Naturaleza viva* (Living Nature) of 1946, and *Naturaleza viva* (Living Nature) of 1947. It is not clear when these paintings were given the titles by which they are now known. Art critic Margarita Nelken used the phrase *naturaleza viva* to describe

Izquierdo's still-life paintings in a 1951 article. The title *Naturaleza viva* does not show up in Izquierdo's exhibition catalogues until her posthumous show at the Galería Arte Moderno in 1956. Nelken, "La 'naturaleza viva' de María Izquierdo."

38. Frida Kahlo, as cited by Grimberg, "Frida Kahlo's Still Lifes," 25.

39. Herrera, *Frida*, 440.

CHAPTER 8: GRAIN OF MEMORY

An earlier version of this chapter was published as "Grain of Memory: María Izquierdo's Images of Altars for *Viernes de Dolores*," in *La imagen sagrada y sacralizada: XXVIII Coloquio Internacional de Historia del Arte*, edited by Peter Krieger (Mexico City: Universidad Nacional Autónoma de México, 2011), 201–215.

1. In recent decades several museums in the Federal District have erected temporary altars for Viernes de Dolores, including Museo de El Carmen, Museo Nacional de Culturas Populares, and Museo Dolores Olmedo. A number of churches in the Federal District also erect temporary altars for Viernes de Dolores.

2. Jaime Cuadriello, author's interview, March 30, 1996, Mexico City.

3. Images of the Virgin of Sorrows occasionally appeared in supporting roles in Mexico in the sixteenth century, but her cult took on greater importance in the seventeenth century. In colonial Mexico the cult of Dolores was promoted by the Franciscans (especially the Third Order), the Jesuits, and confraternities dedicated to this aspect of the Passion. According to Francisco de Icaza Dufour, the custom of erecting domestic altars for the Virgin of Sorrows on Viernes de Dolores probably began in the eighteenth century in the town of Santa Anita, near Xochimilco, and was probably promoted by the Jesuits. Arturo Camacho, a researcher at the Colegio de Jalisco in Zapopan, insists that the custom began in Jalisco. Sebastián Verti attributes the spread of the custom to viceroy Bernardo de Gálvez, who during his short tenure had to deal with the famine of 1785. The viceroy donated 12,000 pesos of his own money to alleviate the suffering and erected an altar to the Dolorosa, in the style of the Santa Anita altars, in an effort to obtain divine favors. Nineteenth-century Mexican chronicles and memoirs are sprinkled with references to the altars and customs associated with them. Icaza Dufour, *El altar de Dolores*, 64, 86; Arturo Camacho, personal communication, October 26, 2004, Campeche; Sebastián Verti, *Tradiciones mexicanas*, 82.

4. Jaime Cuadriello, author's interview, March 30, 1996, Mexico City.

5. Frances Calderón de la Barca was the wife of the first Spanish diplomat sent to Mexico after it won independence from Spain. Her account of the two years they lived in Mexico was originally published in 1843. Madame Calderón de la Barca, *Life in Mexico*.

6. Jaime Cuadriello, author's interview, March 30, 1996, Mexico City.

7. The six paintings in the series are *La Dolorosa* (The Dolorosa) of 1943, *Ofrenda del Viernes de Dolores* (Offering for the Friday of Sorrows or Offering for the Friday of the Virgin of Sorrows) of 1943, *Altar de Dolores* (Altar [for the Virgin] of Sorrows) of 1943, *Altar de Dolores* (Altar [for the Virgin] of Sorrows) of 1944, *Altar de Dolores* (Altar [for the Virgin] of Sorrows) of 1946, and *Dolorosa con trigo* (Dolorosa with Wheat) of 1948.

8. According to the catalogue of Izquierdo's 1956 exhibition at Galería Arte Moderna, Marte R. Gómez owned *Trigo crecido*. At the time it was painted, Gómez was the secretary of agriculture. *Exposición homenaje a María Izquierdo*.

9. According to Aurora Posadas Izquierdo and María Rosenda López Posadas, the image represents the Virgin of Guadalupe. Aurora Posadas Izquierdo and María Rosenda López Posadas, author's interview, March 20, 1995, Naucalpan.

10. I wish to thank Judith Sobré for this insight.

11. Two scholars have independently told me that the images of the Virgin represented in Izquierdo's Viernes de Dolores altars are chromolithographs; both scholars identified the source as an Italian Baroque artist, but they named different artists: Carlo Dolci and Guido Reni. I have not found an exact match for any of the images of the Virgin that are depicted on Izquierdo's altars, but both Dolci and Reni created works that resemble them.

12. *La Dolorosa* of 1943 and *Ofrenda de Viernes de Dolores* of 1943 appear to include the same picture of the Virgin.

13. Aurora Posadas Izquierdo, author's interview, November 2, 1996, Naucalpan.

14. In addition to the more obvious religious allusions within secular subjects, there are many subtle religious references such as the repeated use of trinities. The farmer, worker, and soldier appear together as a powerful triad in many murals. Orozco also used the trinity of the worker, artist, and scientist. Cuauhtémoc Medina, personal communication, October 2004, Campeche; Ramírez, "Artistas e iniciados en la obra mural de Orozco," 61–62.

15. These works include *La manda* (The Promise) of 1933, *Mujer y cruz* (Woman and Cross) of 1933, *Calvario* (Calvary) of 1933, *Ex-Voto* of 1939, *El calvario* (The Calvary) of 1940, *La creación* (Creation) of 1940, *Madona* (Madonna) of 1943, *Madona roja* (Red Madonna) of 1944, *Los peregrinos* (The Pilgrims) of 1945, *Hacia el paraíso* (Toward Paradise) of 1954, three versions of Adam and Eve, and several types of domestic altars. Some of Izquierdo's images of individual mestizas and indigenous women make them look like the Virgin Mary, and some of her depictions of a Mexican mother with a baby recall the Madonna and Christ Child. Thus paintings with secular titles like *Maternidad* (Maternity) of 1943 and *La primavera* (Spring) of 1943 function as religious icons and elevate ordinary Mexican women to heroic roles.

16. María Izquierdo Memoirs, chapter 1, pp. 3–5.

17. "Era bastante creyente sin ser fanática. La educación que tuvo de pequeña . . . y desde chiquita yo creo que fue muy espiritual, le gustaba mucho quizá soñar y estar cerca a un algo. Y ya de grande siguió una filosofía que nos arrancó totalmente de la religión, pero . . . le gustaba y respetaba la religión." Aurora Posadas Izquierdo, author's interview, May 1, 1995, Naucalpan.

18. Aurora Posadas Izquierdo believed that her mother read about Buddhism; María Rosenda López thought that she read about Buddhism or Islam. Aurora Posadas Izquierdo and María Rosenda López Posadas, author's interview, May 1, 1995, Naucalpan.

19. Aurora Posadas Izquierdo, personal communication, December 26, 2004.

20. "Me siento atraída frecuentemente por ALGO que, sin poderlo determinar con nombre propio, inspira mi ingenio y me hace actuar sin temores ni vacilaciones por lo que piensen los demás; confiadamente me entrego a mi pintura, y me siento más satisfecha cuando estoy segura de que no estoy imitando a nadie, sino obedeciendo a la intuición propia mía. 'Yo creo que en el "Más Allá" existe una comunidad de seres incorpóreos, de átomos de un alma universal que mueven las almas de los individuos terrestres; que aquellos seres, en extremo sutiles, se agrupan en familias afines con los sectores humanos que, a la vez, se hallan en planos bien determinados de una escala selectiva. Y creo, por último, que uno de aquellos grupos o células del alma universal es el de

quienes fueron mis antepasados, los de la era precolonial de mi país, y que son ellos quienes me inspiran.'" María Izquierdo, as cited in "El 'Más Allá' de María Izquierdo" (emphasis in the original).

21. According to Linda Dalrymple Henderson, this passage suggests a "general belief in the higher dimensional consciousness as preached by people like Edward Carpenter and P. D. Ouspensky." Linda Dalrymple Henderson, personal communication, January 13, 2005.

22. González Mello, *La máquina de pintar*, 15, 48–51, 73, 81–83, 85, 101, 104.

23. Amparo Posadas de Carmona, author's interview, December 28, 2003, León.

24. Izquierdo's first images of a mother and child are from 1943, when she began a series of paintings depicting a mother and infant that she named after the seasons: *La Primavera* (Spring), *Verano* (Summer), and two versions of *Invierno* (Winter), all from 1943. She painted the series while her daughter was ill, working on an easel by her daughter's bedside.

25. Jaime Cuadriello, author's interview, October 27, 2004, Edzná, Campeche, Mexico.

26. Kassner, *Chucho Reyes*, 41–43.

27. I asked Aurora Posadas Izquierdo whether she thought that María Izquierdo's paintings with religious themes were related to the church or if they were reflections on the beliefs of the people. She responded: "Pues yo creo que es una cosa de las costumbres del pueblo . . . La tradición" (Well, I believe it is something related to the customs of the people . . . tradition). Amparo Posadas de Carmona believes that the altars express her mother's interest in popular art, explaining that the altars are rendered with great attention to detail. Aurora Posadas Izquierdo, author's interview, May 1, 1995, Naucalpan; Amparo Posadas de Carmona, author's interview, December 28, 2003, León.

28. Jaime Cuadriello, author's interview, October 27, 2004, Edzná.

29. Izquierdo represented candles on most of the altars, but they are never lit. This could be explained by her aesthetic preferences. While she is renowned for her use of color, she never emphasized the effects of light and shadow or rendered directional light, which she presumably considered academic and old-fashioned. These tools would be necessary to capture the effects of flickering light on an altar.

30. "Se los sabía en verdad de memoria, desde siempre. Y los hacía volver a la vida." Margarita Michelena, "Pintar a María," in *María Izquierdo: Monografía*, 9. While Michelena recalls that Izquierdo did not use a model for still-life paintings, the artist's younger daughter remembers that her mother sometimes painted from memory and at other times used a model. As an example of how rapidly her mother worked, she recalls that her mother would go shopping in the morning, buy a fresh fish, paint it, and cook it for dinner. Aurora Posadas Izquierdo, author's interview, June 19, 1995, Naucalpan.

31. Izquierdo's two daughters have independently stated this. Aurora Posadas Izquierdo, author's interview, March 20, 1995, Naucalpan; Amparo Posadas de Carmona, author's interview, December 28, 2003, León.

32. "¿Qué tanto sabes de los Altares de Dolores?" http://www.jalisco.gobmx/cultura.nsf/Cuestionario2?openform.

33. In 1943, the year in which Izquierdo began this series, she had a major exhibition at the Palacio de Bellas Artes, a significant achievement by any standards but a phenomenal accomplishment for a woman artist in the 1940s. Aurora Posadas Izquierdo, author's interview, November 2, 1996, Naucalpan.

34. "Es mi primer cuadro desde que he vuelto a la vida. Lo pinté todavía con mucho esfuerzo, ayudando a mi mano derecha con la izquierda. Es el cuadro más 'izquierdo' que tengo." María Izquierdo, as cited in "La pintora recobra su salud."

35. "Es un remanso de tranquilidad o de esperanza." María Rosenda López Posadas, author's interview, March 20, 1995, Naucalpan.

36. Aurora Posadas Izquierdo, personal communication, September 25, 2004.

37. Ferrer, "María Izquierdo," 120.

38. I am indebted to Kim Grant for significant contributions to the conclusion of this text.

PART FIVE: WOMEN'S RIGHTS IN MODERN MEXICO

1. Luis-Martín Lozano, "María Izquierdo: Regarding Modern Mexican Painting," in Mexican Fine Arts Center Museum, *María Izquierdo, 1902–1955*, 45–46.

2. Cano, "Feminismo," 243.

3. Olcott, *Revolutionary Women in Postrevolutionary Mexico*, 16, 17, 46.

CHAPTER 9: BEYOND THE CANVAS

1. For thorough discussions of the history of Mexican women's struggle for equality see Macías, *Against All Odds*; and Soto, *Emergence of the Modern Mexican Woman*.

2. Macías, *Against All Odds*, xiii, 37.

3. In "Hombres necios" Sor Juana criticized men for seducing women then condemning them for lacking chastity. Literary critic Emilie Bergmann interprets the poem as mocking men's condemnation of prostitution as immoral, when they perpetuate it. To demonstrate her point Bergmann cites the verse:

¿O cuál es más de culpar,
aunque cualquiera mal haga:
la que peca por la paga
o el que paga por pecar?
When each is guilty of sin,
Which is the most to blame:
She who sins for payment,
Or he who pays for the sin?

The citation of this passage succinctly demonstrates Bergmann's point, but I interpret the poem in its entirety as a broader critique of male/female relations. The translation of the first stanza of "Hombres necios" above is by Bergmann, "Sor Juana Inés de la Cruz," 158.

4. Macías, *Against All Odds*, xiii.

5. According to Gabriela Cano, in 1903 the influential politician and intellectual Justo Sierra used the term "feminism" to refute then current ideas about the intellectual inferiority of women. Cano, "Feminismo," 242.

In 1907 José Guadalupe Posada published an etching with the caption "El feminismo se impone" (feminism demands it), which showed six men in drag working at household chores around a gigantic number "41." The number refers to the forty-one homosexuals who were arrested on November 20, 1901, in a police raid of a formal ball at La Paz street in San Angel. Half of the men wore white tie and tails; the other half wore evening gowns. The scandal was well publicized by Posada's prints and a *corrido* titled "Los 41 maricones" (The 41 Queers). Tyler, *Posada's Mexico*, 133; Tinker, *Corridos and Calaveras*, 8.

6. Macías, *Against All Odds*, 70–71, 104.

7. Ibid., 36, 119, 121.

8. Gamio, *Forjando patria*, 128.

9. Macías, *Against All Odds*, xv.

10. Ibid., xiv.

11. Soto, *Emergence of the Modern Mexican Woman*, 126–127.

12. Carr scarcely mentions feminism in Mexico before the 1970s, noting that Carlos Monsiváis was "one of the first figures on the literary left to engage with the politics of the personal and in particular with sexual politics (feminism, gay liberation)." In this regard "Monsiváis played a vanguard role, since the Mexican left was notoriously hostile to counter-cultural and superstructural concerns, whether they had to do with the women's movement, the environment, or nuclear power." Carr, *Marxism and Communism in Twentieth-Century Mexico*, 240, 288.

13. Macias, *Against All Odds*, 144.

14. Adelina Zendejas met Frida Kahlo when they both attended the Escuela Nacional Preparatoria. Zendejas was a journalist, author, and activist.

15. "Hacía muchas declaraciones. Apoyaba toda las acciones que nosotros hacíamos."/"Participaban los dos en todas las luchas populares." Adelina Zendejas, author's interview, October 23, 1984, Mexico City.

16. Soto, *Emergence of the Modern Mexican Woman*, 126. Mexican historian Julia Tuñón Pablos also states that Kahlo was a member of Frente Único. Tuñón Pablos, *Women in Mexico*, 101–102.

17. In July 2010 I tried to find documentation of Kahlo's membership in Frente Único or any feminist activity in the newly opened archives at the Museo Frida Kahlo and Anahuacalli. I found nothing. But access was limited to the part of the archives that was pertinent to my search. I did not see everything in the archives, so I cannot be positive that documentation does not exist.

18. Kahlo joined the Young Communist League in 1927, then enrolled in the Communist Party in the first half of 1928. Kahlo, *The Diary*, 289; Herrera, *Frida*, 79–80.

19. Zamora, *The Brush of Anguish*, 93.

20. "La mujer debe ante todo unificarse y luchar, fuertemente unida, por mejorar su condición. La mujer debe dejar de ser ya un objeto de lujo y transformarse en un factor dentro de la lucha de clases; debe evolucionar socialmente y participar en forma directa en la lucha revolucionaria." María Izquierdo, cited in Ramos Malzarraga, "La mujer, factor decisivo en la lucha de clases." The article reports on the exhibition of revolutionary posters by women painters that opened in Guadalajara in 1935.

21. Aurora Posadas Izquierdo, author's interview, August 17, 1998, Naucalpan; Joy Elizabeth Hayes, "National Imaginings on the Air: Radio in Mexico, 1920–1950," in *The Eagle and the Virgin*, edited by Vaughan and Lewis, 254.

22. Deffebach, "Images of Plants in the Art of María Izquierdo, Frida Kahlo, and Leonora Carrington," 36.

23. Lozano, "María Izquierdo," 46; Zavala, *Becoming Modern, Becoming Tradition*, 237.

24. While the date of "La mujer y el arte mexicano" is uncertain, it was clearly written before February 1945, because Izquierdo did not mention her mural commission or the problems that resulted from it.

25. "Las feministas no han conquistado nada para la humanidad ni para ellas, y que en vez de ayudar al engrandecimiento de la mujer (por tantos siglos esclava de todo), entorpecen su emancipación." Izquierdo, "La mujer y el arte mexicano," 1.

26. Ibid., 2–3.

27. Gamio, *Forjando patria*, 119–132; Zavala, *Becoming Modern, Becoming Tradition*, 237.

28. "Inquietudes y ambiciones, en la lucha por incorporar a la mujer a la civilización definitivamente." Izquierdo, "La mujer y el arte mexicano," 3.

29. "*Opino que para que la mujer llegue a triunfar, no debe estar amarrada, ni a las religiones, ni a los prejuicios, ni a los partidos políticos*, debe tener un amplio espíritu de autocrítica, espíritu de lucha, y jamás perder su feminidad, sentirse mujer siempre física y espiritualmente, sentirse con fuerza para crear, y jamás sentirse inferior ni superior al hombre, sentirlo siempre su compañero en igualdad de condiciones. Todo esto es difícil obtenerlo, pero si una mujer logra tener conciencia, ambición, encausar [*sic*] sus fuerzas, saber qué quiere conquistar, en qué terreno y qué cosa, entonces sí estoy segura que triunfará, siempre que pase por sobre todos los obstáculos que se le presenten." Ibid. (emphasis added).

30. "Es difícil hablar sobre una expresión artística, quien nace de la emoción y la sensibilidad, y esta destinada a estimular el espíritu y las sensaciones más finas de los individuos." Ibid., 4.

31. "Muchas veces he oído decir que la mujer nunca llegará a igualar a los grandes maestros de la pintura, es cierto que hasta ahora no ha surgido una mujer con la fuerza creadora de un Miguel Ángel (además no se necesita en nuestra época) pero hay razones muy explicables; ¿no es acaso una razón el hecho que la mujer primitiva, de la edad media, o del renacimiento, estuviera completamente desplazada de los trabajos artísticos e intelectuales? Todos sabemos que sólo en nuestro siglo a la mujer se le empieza a dar oportunidad para que estudie y trabaje en lo que le guste, antes a la mujer no se le permitía hacer otra cosa que no fuera, cocinar, bordar y atender a su esposo, ¿han olvidado en la condición que estaba la mujer en la edad media? Solamente ahora se le empieza a dar oportunidad a la mujer para que desarrolle su talento, por eso no me extraña que no haya igualado todavía a los maestros inmortales de la pintura. Pero creo, que si la mujer sigue conquistando más y más libertad de expresión, llegará tan alto en las artes plásticas ¿por qué no? [¿]No comienzan ya a surgir en todo el mundo pintoras muy buenas que hasta marcan nuevos rumbos al arte[?]." Ibid., 4–5.

32. Nochlin, "Why Have There Been No Great Women Artists?," 22–39, 67–71. This essay also appeared in *Woman in Sexist Society: Studies in Power and Powerlessness*, ed. Vivian Gornick and Barbara K. Moran (New York: Basic Books, 1971), 344–366.

33. González, "The Art of María Izquierdo," 1; Deffebach, "Images of Plants in the Art of María Izquierdo, Frida Kahlo, and Leonora Carrington," 39.

34. "Yo pinto porque siento necesidad de hacerlo, la emoción que me produce el hecho mismo de pintar me hace feliz, mi único maestro es mi propia sensibilidad, no pertenezco a ninguna escuela pictórica, ni me interesa definir mi estilo, pero no pinto por el placer egoísta de gozar con mis propias pinturas, me gusta que los demás gocen y sientan también emoción agradable o de otra índole. No copio la naturaleza tal como es, porque no tendría con ello la sensación de crear. No imito a otros pintores, porque creo que todos los artistas debemos expresar personalmente lo que nos emociona y sugerir nuestra manera de ver y sentir la belleza de lo que nos rodea, aportando algo nuevo al mundo del arte. No puedo explicar a Uds. cuanto me emociona el color, pero todo mi esfuerzo es hacerlo sentir a los demás en mis cuadros. . . . Nada me emociona más en las artes plásticas que el color, lo siento maravilloso, mágico ¡indescriptible!" Izquierdo, "La mujer y el arte mexicano," 5.

35. "Muchas personas dicen que actualmente es México el primer país del mundo en pintura, comparando el movimiento moderno de

Europa con el de México, indudablemente que aquí se está haciendo algo más interesante. . . . me atrevo a decir que ya está en decadencia el movimiento que inició Picasso, en cambio México está abriendo nuevos rumbos a la pintura actual."/ "La opinión casi universal, de que México es un país de pintores, y que es grandiosa toda la cantidad y calidad de los pintores de mi país."/ "No todos los mexicanos son pintores, ni todos los pintores mexicanos son buenos."/ "Hay mexicanos que calculan que existen aquí doscientos buenos pintores, estoy en absoluto desacuerdo con este cálculo. ¡Francamente creo que no lleguen a diez!" Ibid., 5–6.

36. "Agradezco sinceramente la atención dispensada a mis palabras, Buenas Noches, María Izquierdo de Uribe." Ibid., 6.

37. The name on María Izquierdo's birth certificate is María Cenobia Izquierdo Gutiérrez. (Gutiérrez is her mother's maiden name. Both the father's and mother's surnames are included in Spanish. The paternal surname precedes the maternal surname.) Izquierdo began using the shorter "María Izquierdo" during her first year at the Escuela Nacional de Bellas Artes. This shortening of her name appears to be one of the ways in which she established her artistic identity. María Izquierdo Memoirs, chapter 3, p. 2.

38. Ramona Pérez, personal communication, ca. 2011.

39. Ramona Pérez, personal communication, November 7, 2012.

40. Hayes, "National Imaginings on the Air," 246, 248.

41. Ibid., 247.

42. Aurora Posadas Izquierdo, author's interview, August 17, 1998, Naucalpan.

43. María Izquierdo, "La pintora chilena Mireya Lafuente"; Izquierdo, "Ann Medalie," 54; Izquierdo, "Tina Modotti," 58.

44. Izquierdo, "Dos exposiciones," 63, 82; María Izquierdo, "La mujer mexicana, su pensamiento y su acción."

45. "El primer obstáculo que tiene que vencer la mujer pintora es la vieja creencia de que la mujer sirve sólo para el hogar y sus obligaciones derivadas; cuando logra convencer a la sociedad que ella también puede crear, se encuentra con una gran muralla de incomprensión formada por la envidia o complejo de superioridad de sus colegas; después vienen los eternos improvisados críticos de arte que al juzgar la obra de una pintora casi siempre exclaman: ¡para ser pintura femenina . . . no está mal!, como si el color, la línea, los volúmenes, el paisaje o la geografía tuvieran sexo. Casi nunca los pintores ven en la mujer que pinta una colega más, que se dedica con la misma seriedad que ellos al mismo trabajo creador, no, por el contrario, ven en ella a una competidora estorbosa e inferior que atacan venenosamente." Izquierdo, "La pintora chilena Mireya Lafuente," 52.

46. "Duro, ¡terriblemente duro!, es el sendero que tiene que recorrer la mujer que pinta; por eso cuando una mujer logra consagrarse como gran pintora o conquista un nombre en el universo artístico, me mueve a fervoroso respeto y admiración su personalidad.

Una vez me dijo un talentoso crítico de arte centroamericano: ¡desengáñese usted, amiga, a la mujer que pinta la comprenden y estiman solamente los hombres y las mujeres inteligentes . . . y son tan pocos!" Ibid., 52.

47. Izquierdo, "El copihue chileno."

48. "Cuando se case no se convertirá en una esclava, porque al saber ganarse la vida no sentirá complejos de inferioridad ante el marido. Estos complejos los siente la mujer anticuada o de mentalidad provinciana que se agota esperando a que le caiga, del cielo o de la ciudad próxima, el hombre que la hará su esposa: a este hombre obedecerá y seguirá ciegamente porque ella sabe o intuye que si él la abandona, la convierte en un ser inútil, incapaz de sostenerse a sí misma y mucho menos a sus hijos, si los tiene." Izquierdo, "Carta a las mujeres de México."

49. "Yo no soy feminista tipo clásico." Ibid.

50. Asunción Lavrín, "Some Final Considerations on Trends and Issues in Latin American Women's History," in *Latin American Women*, edited by Lavrín, 316.

51. "Creo que ya a nadie se le hará en la actualidad una injusticia como la que yo sufro. Parece ser que ya no será un delito nacer mujer." María Izquierdo, as cited in "María Izquierdo, víctima del monopolio muralista."

52. "Era entonces un *delito nacer mujer*, y si la mujer tenía facultades artísticas, era mucho peor." María Izquierdo Memoirs, chapter 4, p. 3 (emphasis in the original).

53. Castells, *The Power of Identity*, 175, 176, 193.

54. Ibid., 200.

CONCLUSION

1. De Lauretis, *Technologies of Gender*, 9 (emphasis in the original).

2. The catalogue to the retrospective at the Centro Cultural, Arte Contemporáneo includes reproductions of nineteen or twenty self-portraits by Izquierdo (one drawing and eighteen or nineteen paintings).

3. Barnitz, "Five Women Artists," 38.

4. Rivera, as cited in Tibol, *Frida Kahlo*, 49.

5. O'Gorman, speaking in the documentary *The Life and Death of Frida Kahlo*, directed by Karen Crommie and David Crommie, 1966.

6. Herrera, *Frida*, 320.

7. Kahlo, "Hablando de un cuadro mío," 71.

8. "María Izquierdo, víctima del monopolio muralista." The caption to the reproduction declares that the oil painting is the "only mural" by Izquierdo, but the same article also claims that *Trigo crecido* (the title was not used) is a Day of the Dead altar, which is not true.

9. Antonin Artaud, as cited in Tarver, "Issues of Otherness and Identity in the Works of Izquierdo, Kahlo, Artaud, and Breton," 4; Izquierdo, "Mi pintura," 26.

10. Kahlo, letter to Eduardo Morillo Safa, October 11, 1946, in Kahlo, *Escrituras*, 272.

11. Kahlo, as cited in "Ribbon around Bomb," 19.

12. Salomon Grimberg, in *Christie's New York Latin American Sale, Wednesday, May 26, and Thursday, May 27, 2010*, 56. Rivera asked Kahlo for a divorce in 1939, the year after she painted *El superviviente*.

13. I do not mean to imply that the painting is not by Kahlo. *El superviviente* remained in Walter Pach's family from the time he purchased it in 1938 until it was offered to Christie's in 2010, a provenance that contributes strongly to its acceptance as an authentic Kahlo. The painting is beautiful, enigmatic, and highly original. No visual documentation of the work exists prior to 2010, which means that the paper trail for this work is less than ideal. Thus the sale of *El superviviente* for $1,178,000 is all the more remarkable.

14. Olivier Debroise, "The Shared Studio: María Izquierdo and Rufino Tamayo," in Americas Society Art Gallery, *The True Poetry*, 49–63; González, "The Art of María Izquierdo."

15. The *Archivo María Izquierdo del Museo de Arte Moderno* was published after I delivered the manuscript for this book to the University of Texas Press. Consequently I have cited the original sources of María Izquierdo's writings rather than this publication.

16. Izquierdo suffered serious strokes in February 1948 and September 1952. The first stroke left her paralyzed on the right side and unable to speak. Through tremendous force of will, Izquierdo relearned to speak and recuperated the use of her right hand, but she never achieved

the level of manual dexterity that she had before her first stroke. According to Aurora Posadas Izquierdo, her mother had a total of five strokes. The first occurred in 1948 and the last one caused her death on December 2, 1955. Aurora Posadas Izquierdo, author's interview, August 21, 1995, Naucalpan; *María Izquierdo* (1988 exhibition catalogue), 359, 363, 369.

17. Aurora Posadas Izquierdo, author's interview, August 21, 1995, Naucalpan. According to the chronology in the catalogue to the Izquierdo retrospective at the Centro Cultural, Arte Contemporáneo, during the presidency of Ruiz Cortines the secretary of the cabinet, Adolfo López Mateos (the next president of Mexico), provided a secretary so that Izquierdo could record her autobiography. The chronology of the catalogue to the retrospective dates this event to 1954; however, the manuscript states that it was written in 1953. *María Izquierdo* (1988 exhibition catalogue), 366; María Izquierdo Memoirs, chapter 1, p. 4, and chapter 2, p. 8.

18. Based on her conversations with Izquierdo's children and friends about the memoirs, María González believes that "although the accounts of Izquierdo's life seem to be elaborated in some parts," the document is largely factual. González, "The Art of María Izquierdo," 30. The problem is that no one seems to have asked which parts of the manuscript are factual and which are not.

19. Aurora Posadas Izquierdo, as cited in ibid., 30.

20. Aurora Posadas Izquierdo, author's interview, August 21, 1995, Naucalpan.

21. Pollock cited in Lindauer, *Devouring Frida*, 151.

22. Lindauer, *Devouring Frida*, 151.

23. Frida Kahlo, from an interview conducted by Olga Campos in 1950, in Grimberg [and Campos], *Frida Kahlo*, 87.

24. Izquierdo, "Mi pintura," 25.

25. Alice Rahon, conversation with author, November 3, 1980, Mexico City.

26. Izquierdo, "La mujer y el arte mexicano," 5.

27. The exception to my claim about the differences in the innovations between Izquierdo's and Kahlo's work and those of the male artists is Tamayo and Izquierdo's shared approach to color. In addition to its tantalizing sensual appeal, it establishes their approach to expressing Mexican identity through color. Despite the similarity between Tamayo's and Izquierdo's paintings during the years when the two artists shared a studio, there are also differences. For Izquierdo the messages conveyed via art seem to be of greater importance than they were for Tamayo. Tamayo usually prioritized formal beauty over content, with some exceptions.

BIBLIOGRAPHY

ARCHIVES

Archivo Diego Rivera, Anahuacalli, Mexico City.

Archivo Fernando Gamboa, Mexico City.

Archivo Frida Kahlo, Museo Frida Kahlo, Mexico City.

Archivo General de la Nación, Mexico City.

Archivo María Izquierdo, Museo de Arte Moderno, Mexico City. Until July 2005 the María Izquierdo Archive was in the collection of Aurora Posadas Izquierdo.

PERSONAL INTERVIEWS

Leonora Carrington, August 20, 1998, Mexico City.

Jaime Cuadriello, March 30, 1996, Mexico City, and October 27, 2004, Edzná, Campeche, Mexico.

Arturo Estrada, December 13, 1985, and June 13, 2006, Mexico City.

Fernando Gamboa, July 27, 1984, and August 20, 1984, Mexico City.

Arturo García Bustos, August 14, 1984, Mexico City.

Alejandro Gómez Arias, August 21, 1986, Mexico City.

Isolda Kahlo, July 21, 1984, Mexico City.

María Rosenda López Posadas, March 20, 1995, and May 1, 1995, Naucalpan, Estado de México.

Guillermo Monroy, May 22, 1986, Mexico City, and June 7, 2006, Cuernavaca, Morelos.

Juan O'Gorman, November 5, 1976, Mexico City.

Dolores Olmedo, August 10, 1984, Mexico City.

Amparo Posadas de Carmona, December 28, 2003, León, Guanajuato.

Aurora Posadas Izquierdo, March 20, 1995; May 1, 1995; June 19, 1995; August 21, 1995; November 2, 1996; December 5, 1997; August 17, 1998; January 6, 2004; and June 4, 2006, Naucalpan, Estado de México.

Guadalupe Rivera Marín, June 9, 2006, Mexico City, and July 31, 2013, Cuernavaca, Morelos.

Fernando Serrano Migallón, August 19, 2011, Mexico City.

Rafael Vázquez of the Circo Vázquez Hermanos en Tres Pistas, interviewed by Anitza Rodríguez and author, August 14, 2009, Tijuana.

Héctor Xavier, July 11, 1986, Mexico City.

Mariana Yampolsky, December 3, 1997, Mexico City.

Alfredo Zalce, December 8, 1997, Morelia, Michoacán.

Adelina Zendejas, October 23, 1984, Mexico City.

PRIMARY SOURCES

Abreu Gómez, Ermilo. *Pirrimplin en la luna.* Illustrated by María Izquierdo. Mexico City: Ediciones Mensaje, 1942.

"Alfaro Siqueiros aclara el incidente con María Izquierdo." *Excélsior* (Mexico City), July 25, 1946.

"Avansadilla." *Últimas Noticias de Excélsior* (Mexico City), March 26, 1942.

Bambi [Ana Cecilia Treviño]. "Habla María Izquierdo." *Excélsior*, September 12, 1953.

Brenner, Anita. *Idols behind Altars.* New York: Payson and Clarke, 1929.

Carlosleón. "María Izquierdo: La pintura hípica y circense." *La Nación*, undated clipping in the María Izquierdo Archive.

Caso, Alfonso. *Thirteen Masterpieces of Mexican Archaeology.* Translated by Edith Makie and Jorge R. Acosta. Mexico City: Editoriales Cultura y Polis, 1938.

Chase, Stuart. *Mexico: A Study of Two Americas.* New York: Macmillan, 1931.

"Los circopetistas." *Don Timorato*, June 22, 1945.

45 autorretratos de pintores mexicanos. Mexico City: Museo Nacional de Artes Plásticas, 1947.

Denegri, Carlos. "María Izquierdo, encargada de pintar los frescos del ex Palacio Municipal." *Excélsior*, February 14, 1945.

17 acuarelas de María Izquierdo. Exhibition catalogue. Mexico City: Estudio de Frances Toor, 1933.

"Exposición." *Esto* (Mexico City), June 28, 1945.

"La exposición de 'El Circo.'" *México al Día*, July 15, 1945.

Exposición de María Izquierdo. Exhibition catalogue. Lima: Sala de Exposiciones del Instituto Peruano Americano, 1944.

Exposición homenaje a María Izquierdo. Exhibition catalogue. Mexico City: Galería Arte Moderno, 1956.

Exposición internacional del surrealismo. Exhibition catalogue. Mexico City: Galeria de Arte Mexicano, 1940.

Freud, Sigmund. *Moses and Monotheism.* Trans. Katherine Jones. London: Hogarth Press/Institute of Psycho-analysis, 1939.

Frida Kahlo. Exhibition catalogue. New York: Julien Levy Gallery, 1938.

Gamio, Manuel. *Forjando patria* (1916). 2nd ed. Mexico City: Librería de Porrúa, 1960.

"Gestiones en pro de María Izquierdo ante el gobernador del Distrito Federal." *Esto* (Mexico City), January 9, 1946.

Guzmán Araujo, Roberto. *Si entre yelos te nombro: Poesía.* Mexico City: Ediciones de la Revista "America," 1945.

"Hoy se clausurara la exposición de la Srita. Izquierdo." *Excélsior* (Mexico City), February 15, 1933.

Islas García, Luis. "Nuestros jóvenes pintores." *Gráfico* (Mexico City), October 13, 1929.

Izquierdo, María. "Ann Medalie." *Hoy* (Mexico City) 318 (March 27, 1943): 54.

———. "Carta a las mujeres de México." *Zócalo* (Mexico City), October 24, 1950, María Izquierdo Archive.

———. "El copihue chileno." *Excélsior* (Mexico City), November 28, 1944.

———. "Dos exposiciones." *Hoy* (Mexico City) 305 (December 26, 1942): 63, 82.

———. "María Izquierdo vs. los tres grandes." *El Nacional* (Mexico City), October 2, 1947.

———. "La pintora chilena Mireya Lafuente." *Hoy* 296 (October 24, 1942): 52–53.

———. "Mi pintura." *Verdisela: Una Revista para la Mujer Continental* (June 1950): 25–28.

———. "La mujer mexicana, su pensamiento y su acción: La galería de Arte Mexicano de Inés Amor." *Novedades* (Mexico City), March 5, 1942, second section, 5.

———. "La mujer y el arte mexicano." Manuscript of radio presentation. María Izquierdo Archive.

———. "Tina Modotti." *Hoy* (Mexico City) 268 (April 11, 1942): 58.

Kahlo, Frida. *The Diary of Frida Kahlo: An Intimate Self-Portrait.* New York: Harry N. Abrams/La Vaca Independiente, 1995.

———. *Escrituras.* Selected and annotated by Raquel Tibol. Mexico City: Universidad Nacional Autónoma de México, CONACULTA, 2001.

———. *Frida Kahlo: Diario.* Mexico City: La Vaca Independiente, 1994.

———. "Frida Kahlo's 'The Birth of Moses.'" *Tin-Tan* 1 (Summer–Fall 1975): 2–6.

———. "Hablando de un cuadro mío." *Así* (August 18, 1945): 70–71.

———. "Portrait of Diego." Trans. Nancy Deffebach [Breslow] and Amy Weiss Narea. *Calyx* 5 (October 1980): 92–108.

———. "Retrato de Diego." *Novedades* (Mexico City), Supplement, "México en la Cultura," July 17, 1955, 5.

"María Izquierdo demandará al Gobierno del D. Federal." *El Popular* (Mexico City), December 27, 1945.

"María Izquierdo, víctima del monopolio muralista," *D.F.* (Mexico City), December 7, 1952.

"El 'Más Allá' de María Izquierdo." *Estampa* (Mexico City), May 20, 1941.

Mauret, Doctor. "La pintura mexicana actual." *El Universal* (Mexico City), June 21, 1931.

Médioni, Gilbert, and Marie-Thérèse Pinto. *Art in Ancient Mexico: Selected and Photographed from the Collection of Diego Rivera.* New York: Oxford University Press, 1941.

Mexican Arts. Exhibition catalogue. New York: American Federation of Arts, 1930.

"Mexican Autobiography." *Time*, April 27, 1953, 90.

Mexique. Exhibition catalogue. Paris: Renou et Colle, 1939.

Michelena, Margarita. "Exposiciones de los murales de María Izquierdo." *América* (June 1946): 73–76.

———. "Gestapo en la pintura." *Tiras de los Colores* 51 (February 1946): 19–22.

"Murales al fresco." *El Tiempo* (Mexico City), May 31, 1946.

Nelken, Margarita. "La 'naturaleza viva' de María Izquierdo." *Excélsior* (Mexico City), October 20, 1951.

"Notas de Arte." *Esto* (Mexico City), May 20, 1945.

"Obras de Frida Kahlo." *El Nacional* (Mexico City), April 23, 1953.

O'Gorman, Juan. *Autobiografía.* Mexico City: Universidad Nacional Autónoma de México, 2007.

"Óleos de María Izquierdo." *Contemporáneos* 5, no. 16 (1929): 103–106.

Pach, Walter. "Frida Rivera: Gifted Canvases by an Unselfconscious Surrealist." *Art News*, November 12, 1938: 15.

Paintings by María Izquierdo. Exhibition catalogue. New York: Art Center, 1930.

"El pez con gafas." *Futuro* (July 1946), 44–46.

"La pintora recobra su salud." By M. T. P. *Excélsior* (Mexico City), March 1949, María Izquierdo Archive.

Poniatowska, Elena. "Opina María Izquierdo." *Novedades* (Mexico City), July 18, 1953.

Quiñones, Horacio. "Mexicanos y españoles." *Hoy* (Mexico City), July 28, 1945, 54–55.

Ramos Malzarraga, Javier. "La mujer, factor decisivo en la lucha de clases." Unidentified newspaper clipping (ca. 1935) in the María Izquierdo Archive.

Raskob, Joseph. "María Izquierdo: From Easel Painting to Frescoes." *School Arts* 41, no. 8 (April 1942): 278–279, 288.

"Ribbon around Bomb." *New Yorker*, November 12, 1938, 19.

Riding, Alan. "New Tamayo Museum: A Monument to Himself?" *New York Times*, June 6, 1981.

Rivera, Diego. "Antonio Ruiz." In *Diego Rivera: Textos de arte*, collected by Xavier Moyssén, 240–254. Mexico City: Universidad Nacional Autónoma de México, 1986.

———. *Arte y política*. Mexico City: Grijalbo, 1979.

———. "Frida Kahlo y el arte mexicano." *Boletín del Seminario de Cultura Mexicana* 2 (Mexico City: Secretaría de Educación Pública, October 1943): 89–101.

———. "María Izquierdo." *El Universal* (Mexico City), October 6, 1929.

———. "María Izquierdo." *Mexican Life* (December 1929): 33.

Rivera, Diego, and André Breton (signed by Rivera and Breton but written by Leon Trotsky). "Manifesto: Towards a Free Revolutionary Art." *Partisan Review* 6, no. 1 (Fall 1938): 49–53.

Rivera, Diego, with Gladys March. *My Art, My Life: An Autobiography*. New York: Citadel Press, 1960.

Rodríguez, Antonio. "Escándalo artístico." Unidentified and undated clipping in the María Izquierdo Archive.

———. "La pintura mural no puede sujetarse a ningún control." *El Nacional* (Mexico City), August 24, 1947.

Salazar Mallen, Rubén. "¡Esta metrópoli . . . !" *Ultimas Noticias de Excélsior* (Mexico City), July 26, 1946.

Siqueiros, David Alfaro. *No hay más ruta que la nuestra: Importancia nacional e internacional de la pintura mexicana moderna*. Mexico City: n.p., 1945.

Siqueiros, David Alfaro, and others. "Manifesto of the Technical Workers, Painters and Sculptors Union of Mexico." In *Inverted Utopias: Avant-Garde in Latin America*, edited by Mari Carmen Ramírez and Héctor Olea, 461. New Haven: Yale University Press/Museum of Fine Arts Houston, 2004.

Tablada, José Juan. *Historia del arte en México*. Mexico City: Compañía Nacional Editora, 1927.

Tiziano. "La Exposición de María Izquierdo." *La Crónica* (Lima), August 28, 1944.

Torriente, Loló de la. "Murales que desataron pasiones." *¡Ya!* (Mexico City), June 5, 1946.

Toscano, Salvador, Paul Kirchhoff, and Daniel F. Rubín de la Borbolla. *Arte precolombino del Occidente de México*. Mexico City: Secretaria de Educación Pública, 1946.

Twenty Centuries of Mexican Art. Exhibition catalogue. New York: Museum of Modern Art, 1940.

SECONDARY SOURCES

Alegría de la Colina, Margarita, and Rosaura Hernández Monroy. *El Centro Histórico: Cuatro recorridos para forasteros*. Mexico City: Universidad Autónoma Metropolitana, Azcapotzalco, 1991.

Álvarez Bravo, Lola. *Lola Álvarez Bravo: Recuento fotográfico*. Mexico City: Editorial Penélope, 1982.

Americas Society Art Gallery. *The True Poetry: The Art of María Izquierdo*. Exhibition catalogue. New York: Americas Society Art Gallery, 1997.

"Anahuacalli: Museo Diego Rivera." Special issue of *Artes de México* 64/65, year 12 (1965).

Anreus, Alejandro, Robin Adèle Greeley, and Leonard Folgarait, eds. *Mexican Muralism: A Critical History*. Berkeley: University of California Press, 2012.

Apollinaire, Guillaume. *The Self-Dismembered Man: Selected Later Poems of Guillaume Apollinaire*. Translated by Donald Revell. Middletown, CT: Wesleyan University Press, 2004.

Barnitz, Jacqueline. "Five Women Artists." *Review: Latin American Literature and Arts* 75 (Spring 1975): 38.

Bergman-Carton, Janice. "Like an Artist." *Art in America* 81 (January 1993): 35–38.

Bergmann, Emilie. "Sor Juana Inés de la Cruz: Dreaming in a Double Voice." In *Women, Culture and Politics in Latin America: Seminar on Feminism and Culture in Latin America*, 151–172. Berkeley: University of California Press, 1990.

Borsa, Joan. "Frida Kahlo: Marginalization and the Critical Female Subject." *Third Text* 12 (Autumn 1990): 21–40.

Braun, Barbara. *Pre-Columbian Art and the Post-Columbian World*. New York: Harry N. Abrams, 1993.

Brenner, Anita. "A Critic's View." *Atlantic Monthly* 213, no. 3 (March 1964): 131.

Brundage, Burr Cartwright. *The Fifth Sun: Aztec Gods, Aztec World*. Austin: University of Texas Press, 1979.

Bryson, Norman. *Looking at the Overlooked: Four Essays on Still Life Painting*. Cambridge, MA: Harvard University Press, 1990.

Cabrera, Luis. *Diccionario de aztequismos*. Mexico City: Oasis, 1980.

Calderón de la Barca, Madame. *Life in Mexico*. Garden City, NY: Doubleday, 1966.

Cano, Gabriela. "Feminismo." In *Léxico de la política*, 242–247. Mexico City: Facultad Latinoamericano de Ciencias Sociales, 2000.

Caplow, Deborah. *Leopoldo Méndez: Revolutionary Art and the Mexican Print*. Austin: University of Texas Press, 2007.

Carpenter, Elizabeth, ed. *Frida Kahlo*. Exhibition catalogue. Minneapolis: Walker Art Center, ca. 2007.

Carr, Barry. *Marxism and Communism in Twentieth-Century Mexico*. Lincoln: University of Nebraska Press, 1992.

Caso, Alfonso. *The Aztecs: People of the Sun*. Norman: University of Oklahoma Press, 1958.

Castells, Manuel. *The Power of Identity*. Malden, MA: Blackwell, 1997.

Charlot, Jean. *The Mexican Mural Renaissance, 1920–1925*. New Haven: Yale University Press, 1963.

Chicago, Judy, with Frances Borzello. *Frida Kahlo: Face to Face*. Munich: Prestel, 2010.

Christie's New York Latin American Sale, Wednesday, May 26, and Thursday, May 27, 2010. New York: Christie's, 2010.

Coe, Sophie D. *America's First Cuisines*. Austin: University of Texas Press, 1994.

Coffey, Mary K. "Angels and Prostitutes: José Clemente Orozco's *Catharsis* and the Politics of Female Allegory in 1930s Mexico." *CR: The New Centennial Review* 4, no. 2 (Fall 2004): 185–217.

Conde, Teresa del. "La pintura de María Izquierdo." Unidentified and undated catalogue in the María Izquierdo Archive.

Cordero Reiman, Karen. "Appropriation, Invention, and Irony: Tamayo's Early Period, 1920–1937." In *Tamayo: A Modern Icon Reinterpreted*, edited by Diana C. Du Pont, 165–187. Santa Barbara: Santa Barbara Museum of Art, 2007.

Craven, David. *Diego Rivera as Epic Modernist*. New York: G. K. Hall, 1997.

Cresswell, Tim. *In Place/Out of Place: Geography, Ideology, and Transgression*. Minneapolis: University of Minnesota Press, 1996.

Croft-Cooke, Rupert. *The Circus Book*. London: S. Low, Marston, 1948.

Debroise, Olivier. *Figuras en el trópico: Plástica mexicana 1920–1940*. Mexico City: Océano, 1984.

Deffebach, Nancy. "Beyond the Personal: Frida Kahlo's *La niña, la luna y el sol.*" In *Original—Copia . . . Original?,* 147–157. Buenos Aires: Centro Argentino de Investigadores de Arte (CAIA), 2005.

———. "Frida Kahlo: Heroism of Private Life." In *Heroes and Hero Cults in Latin America*, edited by Samuel Brunk and Ben Fallow, 171–201. Austin: University of Texas Press, 2006.

———. "Frida Kahlo y el Occidente de México." In *Apropiarse del arte: Impulsos y pasiones: XXXII Coloquio Internacional de Historia del Arte*, edited by Olga Sáenz, 157–176. Mexico City: Universidad Nacional Autónoma de México, 2012.

———. "Grain of Memory: María Izquierdo's Images of Altars for *Viernes de Dolores.*" In *La imagen sagrada y sacralizada: XXVIII Coloquio Internacional de Historia del Arte*, edited by Peter Krieger, 201–215. Mexico City: Universidad Nacional Autónoma de México, 2011.

———. "Images of Plants in the Art of María Izquierdo, Frida Kahlo, and Leonora Carrington: Gender, Identity, and Spirituality in the Context of Modern Mexico." PhD diss., University of Texas at Austin, 2000.

———. "Picantes pero sabrosas: Las Naturalezas Muertas de Frida Kahlo." In *Imágenes perdidas: Censura, olvido, descuido*, 271–283. Buenos Aires: Centro Argentino de Investigadores de Arte (CAIA), 2007.

———. "Pre-Columbian Symbolism in the Art of Frida Kahlo." Master's thesis, University of Texas at Austin, 1991.

Diego Rivera: A Retrospective. New York: Founders Society of Detroit Institute of Arts/W. W. Norton, 1986.

Douglas, Eduardo de Jesús. "The Colonial Self: Homosexuality and Mestizaje in the Art of Nahum B. Zenil." *Art Journal* 57, no. 3 (Fall 1998): 14–21.

Durán, Diego. *Book of the Gods and Rites and The Ancient Calendar.* Translated by Doris Heyden and Fernando Horcasitas. Norman: University of Oklahoma Press, 1971.

Eder, Rita. "Frida Kahlo." In *Iconos mexicanos*, 150–175, 272. Mexico City: Smurfit Kappa, 2012.

Facturas y manufacturas de la identidad: Las artes populares en la modernidad mexicana. Exhibition catalogue. Mexico City: Museo de Arte Moderno, 2010.

Ferrer, Elizabeth. "María Izquierdo." In *Latin American Artists of the Twentieth Century*, 116–121. Exhibition catalogue. New York: Museum of Modern Art, 1993.

Fort, Ilene Susan, and Tere Arcq with Terri Geis, eds. *In Wonderland: The Surrealist Adventures of Women Artists in Mexico and the United States.* Munich: Los Angeles County Museum of Art/Museo de Arte Moderno, 2012.

Franco, Jean. *Plotting Women: Gender and Representation in Mexico.* New York: Columbia University Press, 1989.

Franger, Gaby, and Rainer Huhle, eds. *Fridas Vater: Der Fotograf Guillermo Kahlo; von Pforzheim bis Mexico.* Munich: Schirmer Mosel, 2005.

Frida Kahlo: Portraits of an Icon. Madrid: Turner/Throckmorton Fine Arts, 2002.

Furst, Peter T. *The Ninth Level: Funerary Art from Ancient Mesoamerica: Selections from the Gerald and Hope Solomons Collection.* Exhibition catalogue. Iowa City: University of Iowa Museum of Art, 1978.

García Palafox, Galia. "Las dos Fridas." *Gatopardo* 107 (December 2009): 48–57, 112–113.

García Payón, José. *Los monumentos arqueológicos de Malinalco.* Mexico City: Biblioteca Enciclopédica del Estado de México, 1974.

Garduño, Ana. "El elitismo de arte popular." In *Facturas y manufacturas de la identidad: Las artes populares en la modernidad mexicana*, 3–39. Exhibition catalogue. Mexico City: Museo de Arte Moderno, 2010.

———. *Inés Amor: "La galería soy yo"—Abrevian ensayos.* Mexico City: Centro Nacional de Investigación, Documentación e Información de Artes Plásticas/Instituto Nacional de Bellas Artes/CONACULTA, 2013.

Goldman, Shifra. *Contemporary Mexican Painting in a Time of Change.* Austin: University of Texas Press, 1981.

Gómez-Peña, Guillermo. *Warrior for Gringostroika: Essays, Performance Texts, and Poetry.* Saint Paul, MN: Graywolf Press, 1993.

González, María de Jesus. "The Art of María Izquierdo: Formative Years 1929 to 1934." PhD diss., University of Texas at Austin, 1998.

González, María de Jesus, and Lucelley Gallegos. "María Izquierdo: Images of Women in the Circus." In *The Many Worlds of Circus*, edited by Robert Sugarman, 137–145. Newcastle, UK: Cambridge Scholars Publishing, 2007.

González, María de Jesus, and Jesse Sloan. "María Izquierdo: Images of the Circus." *Journal of Popular Culture* 40, no. 2 (April 2007): 238–248.

González Mello, Renato. *La máquina de pintar: Rivera, Orozco y la invención de un lenguaje emblemas, trofeos y cadáveres.* Mexico City: Universidad Nacional Autónoma de México/Instituto de Investigaciones Estéticas, 2008.

Greeley, Robin Adèle. "Painting Mexican Identities: Nationalism and Gender in the Work of María Izquierdo." *Oxford Art Journal* 23, no. 1 (2000): 51–72.

Grimberg, Salomon. "Frida Kahlo's Still Lifes." *Woman's Art Journal* 25, no. 2 (Fall 2004/Winter 2005): 25–30.

. *Frida Kahlo: The Still Lifes.* London: Merrell, 2008.

———, ed. *I Will Never Forget You: Frida Kahlo and Nickolas Muray, Unpublished Photographs and Letters.* San Francisco: Chronicle Books, 2006.

Grimberg, Salomon [and Olga Campos]. *Frida Kahlo: Song of Herself.* London and New York: Merrel, 2008.

Herrera, Hayden. *Frida: A Biography of Frida Kahlo.* New York: Harper and Row, 1983.

———. "Frida Kahlo's Art." *artscanada* 230–231 (October-November 1979): 25–28.

———. *Frida Kahlo: The Paintings.* New York: HarperCollins, 1991.

Heyden, Doris. *Mitología y simbolismo de la flora en el México prehispánico.* Mexico City: Universidad Nacional Autónoma de México, 1985.

Hollander, Kurt. "A Campus Serves as a Needed Oasis in a Crowded City." *New York Times*, January 27, 2008.

Icaza Dufour, Francisco de. *El altar de Dolores: Una tradición mexicana.* Mexico City: Miguel Ángel Porrúa, 1998.

Johnson, Ronald. "Picasso's Parisian Family and the 'Saltimbanques.'" *Arts* 51, no. 5 (January 1977): 90–95.

Joyce, Thomas A. *Mexican Archaeology.* New York: G. P. Putnam's Sons, 1914.

Kassner, Lily. *Chucho Reyes.* Mexico City: Editorial RM, 2002.

Kaufman, Jason Edward. "Forthcoming Frida Kahlo Book Denounced as Fake." *Art Newspaper* (August 20, 2009): http://www.theartnewspaper.com/articles/Forthcoming-Frida-Kahlo-book-denounced-as-fake/18682.

Krauze, Enrique. *Mexico: A Biography of Power.* New York: Harper Collins, 1997.

Latin American Art: New York, November 16 & 17, 2004. New York: Sotheby's, 2004.

Lauretis, Teresa de. *Technologies of Gender*. Bloomington: Indiana University Press, 1987.

Lavrín, Asunción, ed. *Latin American Women: Historical Perspectives*. Westport, CT: Greenwood Press, 1978.

Lekson, Stephen H. "Dating Casas Grandes." *Kiva* 50, no. 1 (1984): 55–60.

Leopoldo Méndez: Dibujos, grabados, pinturas. Mexico City: Fondo Editorial de la Plástica Mexicana, 1984.

Lindauer, Margaret A. *Devouring Frida: The Art History and Popular Celebrity of Frida Kahlo*. Hanover, NH: Wesleyan University Press, 1999.

López Austin, Alfredo. "Términos de nahuallatolli." *Historia mexicana* 17, no. 1 (1967): 1–36.

López Casillas, Mercurio. "Maravilla gráfica: El clown mexicano." *Artes de México* 84 (2007), special issue *Circo II: Leyenda y color*.

Lozano, Luis-Martín. *María Izquierdo: Una verdadera pasión por el color*. Mexico City: Landucci, 2002.

Macías, Anna. *Against All Odds: The Feminist Movement in Mexico to 1940*. Westport, CT: Greenwood Press, 1982.

Madsen, William. *The Virgin's Children: Life in an Aztec Village*. Austin: University of Texas Press, 1960.

Maestros del arte contemporáneo en la colección del Museo Rufino Tamayo. Mexico City: Américo Arte Editores/Fundación Olga y Rufino Tamayo, 1997.

El maíz, fundamento de la cultura popular mexicana. Exhibition catalogue. Mexico City: Museo Nacional de Culturas Populares, 1982.

Manrique, Jorge Alberto, and Teresa del Conde. *Una mujer en el arte mexicano: Memorias de Inés Amor*. Mexico City: Universidad Nacional Autónoma de México, 1987.

María Izquierdo. Introduction by Carlos Monsiváis and bibliographic research by Luis Mario Schneider. Mexico City: Casa de Bolsa Cremi, 1986.

María Izquierdo. Exhibition catalogue. Mexico City: Centro Cultural, Arte Contemporáneo, 1988.

María Izquierdo: Monografía. Guadalajara: Departamento de Bellas Artes, Gobierno de Jalisco, 1985.

Matos Moctezuma, Eduardo. "La tehuacana, niña Lucha María." In *Frida Kahlo: 1907–2007*. Mexico City: Instituto Nacional de Bellas Artes, 2007.

McNeely, John H. "Origins of the Zapata Revolt in Morelos." *Hispanic American Historical Review* 46 (1966): 153–169.

Mendoza, Vicente T. *El corrido mexicano*. Mexico City: Fondo de Cultura Económica, 1954.

Mewburn, Charity, "Oil, Art, and Politics: The Feminization of Mexico." *Anales del Instituto de Investigaciones Estéticas* 20, no. 72 (spring 1998): 73–133.

Mexican Fine Arts Center Museum. *María Izquierdo, 1902–1955*. Exhibition catalogue. Chicago: Mexican Fine Arts Center Museum, 1996.

Miller, Mary Ellen. *The Art of Mesoamerica: From Olmec to Aztec*. New York: Thames and Hudson, 2012.

Miller, Mary, and Karl Taube. *The Gods and Symbols of Ancient Mexico and the Maya: An Illustrated Dictionary of Mesoamerican Religion*. London: Thames and Hudson, 1993.

Monsiváis, Carlos. *Frida Kahlo: Un homenaje*. Mexico City: Artes de México and Museo Dolores Olmedo Patiño, 2004.

Mulvey, Laura, and Peter Wollen. "Frida Kahlo and Tina Modotti." In *Frida Kahlo and Tina Modotti*, 7–27. London: Whitechapel Gallery, 1982.

Museo Dolores Olmedo. Mexico City: Museo Dolores Olmedo, 2007.

Museo Nacional de Arte. *Portrait of a Decade: David Alfaro Siqueiros, 1930–1940*. Mexico City: Museo Nacional de Arte, 1996.

Nicholson, Irene. *Firefly in the Night: A Study of Ancient Mexican Poetry and Symbolism*. London: Faber and Faber, 1959.

———. *Mexican and Central American Mythology*. London: Paul Hamlyn, 1967.

Nochlin, Linda. "Why Have There Been No Great Women Artists?" *ARTnews* 69 (January 1971): 22–39, 67–71.

Olcott, Jocelyn. *Revolutionary Women in Postrevolutionary Mexico*. Durham, NC: Duke University Press, 2005.

Olea Franco, Rafael, and Anthony Stanton, eds. *Los Contemporáneos en el laberinto de la crítica*. Mexico City: El Colegio de México, 1994.

Oles, James. "Finding Frida." *Association for Latin American Art Newsletter* 21, no. 2 (October 2009): 19.

Oropesa, Salvador. *The Contemporáneos Group: Rewriting Mexico in the Thirties and Forties*. Austin: University of Texas Press, 2003.

Ortiz Monasterio, Pablo, ed. *Frida Kahlo: Sus fotos*. Mexico City: Editorial RM, 2010.

Ortner, Sherry B. "Is Female to Male as Nature Is to Culture?" In *Woman, Culture and Society*, edited by Michelle Zimbalist Rosaldo and Louise Lamphere, 68–87. Stanford: Stanford University Press, 1974.

Paz, Octavio. "María Izquierdo, Seen in Her Surroundings and Set in Her Proper Place." In *Essays on Mexican Art*, 246–265. New York: Harcourt Brace Jovanovich, 1993.

Penrose, Roland. *Max Ernst's Celebes*. Newcastle upon Tyne, England: University of Newcastle upon Tyne, 1972.

Pereda, Juan Carlos. *Rufino Tamayo: Catalogue Raisonné: Gráfica/Prints 1925–1991*. Mexico City: Fundación Olga y Rufino Tamayo/CONACULTA–INBA, 2004.

Poniatowska, Elena. *Todo México*. Vol. 2. Mexico City: Editorial Diana, 1993.

Prignitz-Poda, Helga, Salomón Grimberg, and Andrea Kettenmann. *Frida Kahlo: Das Gesamtwerk*. Frankfurt: Verlag Neue Kritik, 1988.

"¿Qué tanto sabes de los Altares de Dolores?" http://www.jalisco.gobmx/cultura.nsf/Cuestionario2?openform.

Quirarte, Jacinto. "Mexican and Mexican American Artists in the United States: 1920–1970." In *The Latin American Spirit: Art and Artists in the United States, 1920–1970*, 14–71. New York: Bronx Museum of the Arts/Harry N. Abrams, 1988.

Ramírez, Fausto. "Artistas e iniciados en la obra mural de Orozco." In *Orozco: Una relectura*, 61–102. Mexico City: Universidad Nacional Autónoma de México, 1983.

Ramírez, Mari Carmen. "Beyond 'the Fantastic': Framing Identity in U.S. Exhibitions of Latin American Art." In *Beyond the Fantastic: Contemporary Art Criticism from Latin America*, edited by Gerardo Mosquera, 229–246. Cambridge, MA: Institute of International Visual Arts/MIT Press, 1996.

Reff, Theodore. "Harlequins, Saltimbanques, Clowns, and Fools." *Artforum* 10, no. 2 (October 1971): 30–43.

Revolledo Cárdenas, Julio. *La fabulosa historia del circo en México*. Mexico City: CONACULTA, 2004.

Rivera, Guadalupe, and Marie-Pierre Colle. *Frida's Fiestas: Recipes and Reminiscences of Life with Frida Kahlo*. New York: Clarkson Potter, 1994.

Rochfort, Desmond. *Mexican Muralists: Orozco, Rivera, Siqueiros*. San Francisco: Chronicle Books, 1998.

Rodríguez Prampolini, Ida. *Juan O'Gorman: Arquitecto y pintor*. Mexico City: Universidad Nacional Autónoma de México, 1982.

Ross, Stephanie. *What Gardens Mean.* Chicago: University of Chicago Press, 1998.

Ruiz de Alarcón, Hernando. *Treatise on the Heathen Superstitions That Today Live among the Indians Native to This New Spain, 1629.* Translated and edited by J. Richard Andrews and Ross Hassig. Norman: University of Oklahoma Press, 1984.

Sahagún, Fr. Bernardino de. *Códices matritenses de la Historia general de las cosas de Nueva España.* Madrid: Ediciones José Porrua Turanzas, 1964.

———. *Florentine Codex: General History of the Things of New Spain, Book 7—The Sun, Moon, and Stars, and the Binding of the Years.* Trans. Arthur J. O. Anderson and Charles E. Dibble. Santa Fe, N.Mex.: School of American Research, 1953.

———. *Historia de la cosas de Nueva España.* Facsimile edition by Francisco del Paso y Troncoso. Book 4. Madrid: Secretaría de Instrucción Pública y Bellas Artes de México, 1905–1907.

———. *Historia de las cosas de Nueva España: Códices Matritenses*, vol. 6, facsimile edition published by Francisco del Paso y Troncoso. Mexico City: Departamento Universitario and Bellas Artes, 1906–1907.

Santoscoy, Alberto. *Historia de Nuestra Señora de San Juan de los Lagos y del culto de esta milagrosa imagen.* Edición Conmemorativo del V Centenario de la Evangelización, undated reprint of a book originally published in 1903. N.p., n.d.

Self Portrait in a Velvet Dress: Frida's Wardrobe. Edited by Denise Rosenzweig and Magdalena Rosenzweig. San Francisco: Chronicle Books, 2008.

Sheridan, Guillermo. *Los Contemporáneos ayer.* Mexico City: Fondo de Cultura Económica, 1985.

———. *Indices de "Contemporáneos" (Revista Mexicana de Cultura, 1928–1931).* Mexico City: Universidad Nacional Autónoma de México, 1988.

Solís Olguín, Felipe. "Testimonios de una gran pasión: La colección arqueológica de Diego Rivera." In *El Anahuacalli de Diego*, 146–215. Mexico City: Banco de México, 2008.

Soto, Shirlene. *Emergence of the Modern Mexican Woman: Her Participation in Revolution and Struggle for Equality, 1910–1940.* Denver: Arden Press, 1990.

Sund, Judy. "Beyond the Grave: The Twentieth-Century Afterlife of West Mexican Burial Effigies." *Art Bulletin* 82, no. 4 (December 2000): 734–767.

Tait, Peta. *Circus Bodies: Cultural Identity in Aerial Performance.* London: Routledge, 2005.

Tamayo, Rufino, and James B. Lynch. *Tamayo: A Commentary.* Exhibition catalogue. Phoenix: Phoenix Art Museum, 1968.

Tarver, Gina McDaniel. "Issues of Otherness and Identity in the Works of Izquierdo, Kahlo, Artaud, and Breton." Research Paper Series No. 27. Latin American Institute, University of New Mexico (1996).

Teotihuacán: Official Guide of the Instituto Nacional de Antropología e Historia. Mexico City: Instituto Nacional de Antropología e Historia, n.d.

Tibol, Raquel. *Frida Kahlo: Crónica, testimonios y aproximaciones.* Mexico City: Ediciones de Cultura Popular, 1977.

———. *Palabras de Siqueiros.* Mexico City: Fondo de Cultura Económica, 1996.

Tinker, Edward Larocque. *Corridos and Calaveras.* Austin: University of Texas Press, 1961.

Townsend, Richard, ed. *Ancient West Mexico: Art and Archaeology of the Unknown Past.* New York: Thames and Hudson/Art Institute of Chicago, 1998.

Tuñón Pablos, Julia. *Women in Mexico: A Past Unveiled.* Austin: University of Texas Press, 1999.

Tyler, Ron, ed. *Posada's Mexico.* Exhibition catalogue. Washington, D.C.: Library of Congress, 1979.

Vasari, Giorgio. *The Lives of the Most Excellent Painters, Sculptors, and Architects.* Translated by Gaston du C. de Vere. New York: Modern Library, 2006 (this translation was first published in 1896 by Scribner's).

Vaughan, Mary Kay, and Stephen E. Lewis, ed. *The Eagle and the Virgin: National and Cultural Revolution in Mexico, 1920–1940.* Durham, NC: Duke University Press, 2006.

Verti, Sebastián. *Tradiciones mexicanas.* 8th ed. Mexico City: Diana, 1997.

Viscoli, Miranda. "The Revolution of María Izquierdo: Constructs of Gender and Nation in the Artist's Female Figures." Master's thesis, California State University, Long Beach, 2009.

Widdifield, Stacie G. *The Embodiment of the National in Late Nineteenth-Century Mexican Painting.* Tucson: University of Arizona Press, 1996.

Wolfe, Bertram D. *Diego Rivera: His Life and Times.* New York: Alfred A. Knopf, 1939.

———. *The Fabulous Life of Diego Rivera.* New York: Stein and Day, 1963.

Wyndham, Francis, and David King. *Trotsky: A Documentary.* Harmondsworth, Middlesex, England: Penguin, 1972.

Yampolsky, Mariana, and Elena Poniatowska. *La casa en la tierra.* Mexico City: n.p., 1980.

Zamora, Martha. *The Brush of Anguish.* San Francisco: Chronicle Books, 1990.

———. *Frida: El pincel de la angustia.* La Herradura, Estado de México: n.p., 1987.

Zavala, Adriana. *Becoming Modern, Becoming Tradition: Women, Gender, and Representation in Mexican Art.* University Park: Pennsylvania University Press, 2011.

———. "A Chronicle in Light and Shadow: The Photography of Lola Álvarez Bravo." In *Lola Álvarez Bravo and the Photography of an Era*, 17–25. Mexico City: Consejo Nacional para la Cultura y las Artes/Instituto Nacional de Bellas Artes/Museo Casa Estudio Diego Rivera and Frida Kahlo, 2012.

———. "María Izquierdo." In *Blanton Museum of Art, Latin American Collection*, edited by Gabriel Pérez-Barreiro, 237–239. Austin: Blanton Museum of Art/University of Texas Press, 2006.

Zendejas, Adelina. "Diego, el millonario guardador de tesoros." *El Gallo Illustrado.* Sunday supplement of *El Día* (Mexico City), September 20, 1964.

Zimmer, Heinrich. *Myths and Symbols in Indian Art and Civilization.* New York: Harper Torchbooks, 1962.

Zurian, Tomás. *Rosario Cabrera: Creation between the Time of Restlessness and Forgetting.* Mexico City: Instituto Nacional de Bellas Artes, 1998.

FILMOGRAPHY

All About My Mother. Directed by Pedro Almodóvar. Spain, 1999.

The Life and Death of Frida Kahlo. Directed by Karen Crommie and David Crommie. USA, 1966.

INDEX

Note: Italic page numbers refer to figures.